Botcherby
A Garden
Village

Patricia M. Hitchon

P3 Publications

P3 Publications

ISBN-13: 978-0-9931835-2-2

I would like to thank Hunter Davies and the Cumbria Community Foundation for awarding me a Bursary of £1000 towards production costs of this book. In addition I have received generous sponsorship from CROWN Bevcan and the Botcherby Forever Community Group, which is much appreciated.

Typeset in Calibri

First published in Great Britain in May 2017 by:

P3 Publications

13 Beaver Road

Carlisle

Cumbria

CA2 7PS

Printed and bound in Wales by:

Gomer Press

Llandysul Enterprise Park

Ceredigion

SA44 4JL

www.p3publications.com

This book is dedicated to:

My godmother Alicia Grice who was its first inspiration.

Members of the Botcherby Forever Community Group who have supported the project throughout.

Jackie Stubbs, Botcherby's own local historian, who has given me unlimited access to his archives and memories with gracious generosity and practical support.

The people of Botcherby, past and present, without whom this story could not have been written.

Contents

Author's note

It's worth commenting on the approach I have adopted in writing the book. Rather than simply follow a strict chronology, I felt that it would be more readable to group the story around some broad themes, interweaving the history and recollections side by side. Consequently, some of the information is repeated briefly, to help set the context for a particular theme. And I'm not suggesting that the coverage is comprehensive - most of the memories are from the 1930s through to the 1960s, so there is plenty of scope to record more recent memories in the future, as well as to collect more photographs!

Foreword

Like many people, I have waited many years for a book on Botcherby and I am so glad that at last it is a reality thanks to the skill and expertise of Pat Hitchon. But it is also tinged with sadness that my good friend and neighbour, Mrs Elsie Baty, is not here to share the book launch with us.

Because Elsie, like myself, loved living in Botcherby and she also typified the community spirit that I found in abundance when I came to live here in 1950.

It was like living in the country then, being surrounded by green fields. It was a natural adventure playground for people growing up here. Not so many people had televisions so we had to make our own enjoyment, but there were so many things to do we were never bored.

Many of my friends were from large families and wore hand-me-down clothes from older brothers and sisters, and some slept head-to-toe in their beds. Their parents were good hard-working people who taught their children right from wrong.

The community spirit built up during the austere war years was still strong: door keys could be hung on a string behind the letter box, or under a brick or stone in the garden.

The members of the Evergreen Club and Carnival Committees helped maintain the spirit, as did Botcherby School and the youth club, as well as the local churches. The Magpie Inn also played a vital part as a social meeting place for the people to relax and unwind, playing bowls, darts and dominoes.

Botcherby has also had its fair share of characters over the years as many of you will know.

I have no regrets at all in coming to live in Botcherby. I am proud of the fact that my wife Barbara was born here, and together we brought up our family here, in dear old Botcherby.

I would just like to say thank you to Pat's brother, Gil, for his painstaking work on editing the text and illustrations, and to the many, many people who gave stories and loaned photographs and other information, or helped in any way that allowed Pat to create this book.

J Stubbs

Jack Stubbs

♦♦♦

Introduction

Do you remember Belinda Carlisle's song *Heaven is a Place on Earth*? It topped the charts in the late 1980s. I have been reminded of that catchy tune while researching this book about Botcherby. The sheer warmth and enthusiasm I have received from people when I have been out and about, meeting and mixing, has overwhelmed me.

But perhaps, even more surprising to me, is the depth of affection that so many former and current residents hold for Botcherby itself. They have dug out old photo albums, given me poetry, maps, street directories, rung up old friends on my behalf, given me notes and writings they had done, recalled old memories, taken photographs for me, and generally enveloped me in the 'feel-good' factor. Yes, it is people who make heaven on earth.

So many memories - 9am on a freezing cold March morning - the snow pelting down and I visit the Hamilton brothers. They have wonderful photos of Kevin Beattie and Botcherby Football Club, and give me a warm welcome. Or I visit Bramerton Lodge where Derek Nash unfolds the amazing story of the barn that was a chapel and how Botcherby people campaigned to save it. I go to the Botcherby Forever Community Group where enthusiasm is high and people come to share their memories. At the Community Centre I find Elsie Baty, Mary Jones, Mary McCabe and Kathleen Dixon at the bingo and, in the tea break, everyone crowds around to tell me of memories and contacts, and David Geddis's aunt lends me her scrapbooks.

Some people were more elusive, such as Jackie Stubbs, a Botcherby historian - until the day when he turned up with Alex Proudfoot at the group meeting and shared his work and told us of the ghosts! Theo Grice hosted a get-together where the memories poured out. I was given a contact with Barbara Millican in Australia and she sent me wonderful information about the Durranhill Railway Cottage and the Prisoner of War Camp. From Scotland, June M. Dunn sent me her fascinating memoir of her mother 'Lady Isobel' and life in Botcherby in the 1930s, and Stan Sullivan gave me memories of evacuees and Botcherby Hall. Sister Rosemary Clerkin came from Chigwell to tell us the history of Durranhill Convent. And this is only a tiny fraction of the great support I have received. In fact, the project turned out much larger than I expected because of the amount of stories people brought me - this has slowed down the production of the book but it seemed important to capture as much as possible of such a vibrant community.

All this generosity is the lifeblood of the book – it is what makes it the story of a special place and its people. It is testament to the hard work, laughter, camaraderie, long friendships and neighbourliness that have characterised Botcherby throughout its history. There may have been problems when the headlines did not make good reading, but have you seen the good headlines, such as the ladies who have given 50 years each to voluntary service at the Community Centre? People like this are truly the salt of the earth.

My interest in writing about Botcherby stems from my earliest memories. As a tiny child I was taken every Monday to stay with my great-aunt Annie Grice for the day. She would take me to Croft Nurseries to see Charlie and David and Bobby the horse, then to Mr Kitchin's in Wood Street for ice cream and, sometimes, we went to tea at Aunt Mary McIntyre's at 7 Botcherby Avenue, where we sat in the parlour and the lace tablecloth and best china came out. Then my Uncle Harry would take me home across the Path on Melbourne Park. Later, when I lived in Borland Avenue, I came to appreciate the good people who lived all around, and I met some of the people who I love most in the world.

I hope I have done the story justice and I hope you enjoy reading it.

Patricia M. Hitchon

Pat Hitchon, Carlisle, February 2017

◆◆◆

In the mists of time...

Long before it was called Botcherby, people were living here. In this chapter we look at those early years, through the turbulent Middle Ages and up to the invasion of Bonnie Prince Charlie...

Early settlement

At the moment, the earliest record we have of people living in the Botcherby area dates from around 4,000 years ago, during the Late Neolithic/Early Bronze Ages.

In 1998 an excavation revealed pottery at Scotby Road in a site overlooking the point where Durranhill Beck meets the River Eden. This included Grooved Ware and Beaker pottery associated with that period. Archaeologist Kate Hirst reported that two palisaded enclosures were found and pits and post-holes. One pit contained a large quantity of re-deposited burnt material including burnt bone and pre-historic pottery. Near the base lay 10 unburnt clay blocks and underneath more burnt material - one possible explanation is that it had some ritual role involving the cremation of animals or humans. Their locations - on well-drained sands and gravels - suggest the sites were originally chosen deliberately, because of the lie of the land and its fertility.

Further down Durranhill Beck, near what became the Garlands Hospital, similar findings open up the possibility that this was an extended or inter-connected community. At the very least, Durranhill Beck seems to have played a central role in these early communities.

Roman remains

Botcherby Nurseries, on the right of the hill leading up Victoria Road to Mount Florida, also proved an attractive site for Botcherby's early residents. The first hint of this came to light in Victorian times, when John Hamilton had the nurseries. On 2 May 1879 a rather grisly discovery was reported in the *Carlisle Patriot*:

> **'Discovery of Human Remains at Botcherby**
>
> 'Last Friday a lead coffin was unearthed in the grounds of Mr John Hamilton and Son, nurserymen,

Botcherby. For some time workmen have been engaged removing a large quantity of sand in the garden adjoining Botcherby Road, and Mr John Douglas uncovered a coffin which lay about seven feet from the surface. It is about 5 feet 4 inches long, and about 16 inches in width at the head, but tapers at the other end to about twelve inches. It has no lid, and from the vestiges of wood found underneath, there is no doubt but it had been placed in a coffin of wood. Inside the coffin were found some pieces of bones... The coffin is plain, and of the usual thickness of lead; weighing about 14 or 15 cwt. It lay with the head to N.W. and the feet S.E. The joining of the lead is by overlaps, showing that soldering had not been in practice at the time it was made. From various marks about the place, it is conjectured that the spot where the coffin lay is in the centre of a piece of ground which has been trenched round, like some of the Roman camps.'

A day or so later a second coffin was found, and a further two were later dug up nearby.

On Saturday, 17 August 1996, the *News & Star* asked *'Could Roman remains lurk beneath this wild rhubarb patch?'* The plan was to sell off part of the old Botcherby Nursery site, once owned by Mr Willie Feddon, to Impact Housing for some new homes: before anything was finalised, however, archaeologists were to carry out exploratory excavations.

Two years later, archaeologist Richard Barkle reported on the outcome of the dig: this had revealed a number of prehistoric postholes and post-pits plus a ditch thought to be of Roman origin, but there was also pottery thought to be from the Bronze Age. He concluded that *'the function of this site is clearly open to speculation, but the possibility that the main feature represents a timber ring of "ritual" significance is worth further consideration.'*

From Roman times until the Norman Conquest, we know little about what happened specifically in Botcherby - still just a clearing in Inglewood Forest. In fact, when the *Domesday Book* was completed in 1086, Cumbria, for the most part, was not included: the Normans had yet to conquer it.

That all changed from 1087 when William Rufus ascended the throne. In 1092, when the red-haired, 32-year-old monarch came to Carlisle with a great army, restoring the city and building a castle, his purpose was to establish a new border between England and Scotland and to bring the border counties of Cumberland and Westmorland under English rule. To do this William brought in many foreign craftsmen to reconstruct the city, as well as peasant families with their cattle to cultivate the land.

 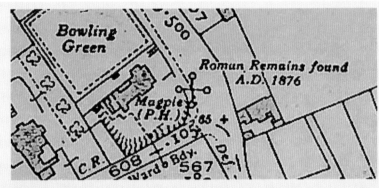

Evidence of the first settlers in the area

Left: excavations at Scotby Road showing evidence of Late Neolithic/Early Bronze Age settlement - two palisade slots, a ditch (left) and pits. Right: the location of the Roman burials found beside where the Magpie now stands. Newspaper reports have the date of the finds as 1879, not 1876 as shown on this later map.

Botcherby gets its name

One of these workers is said to have been a Flemish stonemason named Burgheard or, in the Normanised version, Bochard, who made the settlement in what we now know as Botcherby. He must have been a mason of some standing, as he also gave his name to Carlisle's major thoroughfare to the south, Botchergate; to English Street (Vicus Bochardi) and English Gate (Porta Bochardi). Apart from the name, these had no particular link with Botcherby, a royal demesne, as Botchergate was held by the priors of Carlisle.

Many of the Lordships around Carlisle were named after their earliest foreign lords. Most of the prominent families lived within the safety of Carlisle's city walls, but owned land, hamlets and farms in the surrounding countryside.

It was from farming here that they supplied food for their households and for visitors. Botcherby is one of many places, such as Rickerby, Aglionby, Upperby, Denton Holme, whose names are derived from these early foreign landowners.

In the Pipe Roll of 1191, the place-name is shown as Botchardebi, and appears to be the first official mention in a document although, in other 12th- and 13th-century documents, a number of other ancient variations are used.

When Bochard the stonemason quit Carlisle for Anglesey, along with the other Flemings, he left the farm to his daughter Isold and her husband, Guy the Hunter. According to William Hutchinson, *'King Henry I confirmed Bochardby, to hold the same by cornage, paying yearly 6s. 2d. cornage silver to the king.'* (Cornage was a form of tax based on the number of horned cattle farmed.) Then the land passed to his son, Ralph and on to Odo, before reaching William, Odo's son, during King John's reign. He adopted the surname 'de Bochardby' as did his successors.

The *Testa de Nevill* (today known as *The Book of Fees*) is a collection of documents showing the fees paid by manorial lands to the King's Exchequer. Under Henry III and Edward I, the manor of Botcherby was still held at a cornage rent of 6s 2d a year - the de Bochardby family had managed to hold the place at the same rent for over a hundred years!

After William's day, it was passed on to another William and Adam of Bochardby. In the late 1220s, this William's son, Radulph, took over and left it to his sisters, Alice, Pavy and Agnes.

Another of the de Botchardby family, Walter, made an important grant of lands to Wetheral Priory in 1233. From reading the Charter it appears that he was concerned with the salvation of the souls of his family and sought to do good deeds for the Church.

The Charter is interesting reading as it mentions a number of sites in Botcherby and Walter says that he grants:

> *'all that land in the demesne of Wetheral which is called Eldewric flat with the meadow adjoining that land which... lies between the boundary of Scotby and the stream of the well of St Helena, so that the monks shall have... land and meadow in free, pure and perpetual alms with all rights and easements of the vill of Botcherby belonging to such lands.'*

The monks were also given permission to enclose some of the land, erect buildings and given *'a portion of my land containing 12 feet in length and breadth from the public way of Botcherby to Eldewric for making free passage to and from the land without any impediment from myself or my heirs.'*

An additional charter by Walter's brother, Adam, gives the monks a right of way across his croft adjoining the stream of St Helen's Well. So here we see from earliest days the links between church and state.

The line of de Bochardby came to an end in the last quarter of the 13th century. Alice, one of the heiresses, had a son Thomas Snowball, who inherited the manor. Other holders of land at Botcherby about this time included Ralph de Dacre, William, son of Ivo of Carlisle, Alan de Pennington and Christina, widow of Robert de Brus.

Edward Longshanks

King Edward I, known as 'Longshanks' because of his imposing height, came to the throne in 1272 at the age of 33. Much of his reign was spent in reforming the law and strengthening Parliament. In 1284, at the end of the Welsh wars, he brought the Principality of Wales under English rule. His 17-year-old son Edward was invested as the first Prince of Wales in 1301.

After the death of King Alexander III in a riding accident in 1286, the question of the Scottish succession caused Edward to become embroiled in more disputes. His granddaughter Margaret was heir, but was only three years old and lived in Norway with her father King Eric II. Known as the 'Maid of Norway' she was seven when she sailed for Scotland in the autumn of 1290 to be crowned Queen. Sadly, the young Queen took ill and died on the journey, in Orkney, without ever setting foot in Scotland. This was the beginning of the succession crisis.

The two main contestants for the crown were John Balliol and Robert de Brus, and King Edward was invited to arbitrate. John Balliol was crowned but proved incapable and Edward forced him to abdicate in 1296, and then attempted to annex Scotland into the Kingdom of England. The next 10 years saw Scotland without a monarch and constant warfare and skirmishes on both sides of the border, as William Wallace (Braveheart) and Robert the Bruce fought battles against the English. In 1306 Robert the Bruce (grandson of the earlier contender) was crowned King of Scots at Scone.

Edward 1 in the Borders

Clockwise from above: statue of Edward 1 at Burgh by Sands, commemorating his final journey attempting to quash the rebellion in Scotland; Wetheral Priory played host to Edward, Prince of Wales, in 1307 - and his unruly followers and pets, including a lion; pageant outside Carlisle Castle in 1977, celebrating the anniversary of the stay of Edward 1 in 1307; the memorial to Edward 1 on Burgh by Sands Marsh, marking the place where he died - within clear sight of Scotland, across the Solway Firth.

This was the background to King Edward's decision to make a prolonged stay in Carlisle in 1307. He had planned to come earlier, writing on 10 August 1306 that he was *'coming immediately to remain at the Priory of Carlisle,'* but was taken ill at Lanercost on 29 September and forced to remain there for several months.

The visit of the King, accompanied by his young second wife, Queen Margaret, and his son Edward, together with his large retinue had a huge impact on Carlisle and the surrounding villages. The Queen and her attendants stayed in the royal apartments at the castle where a bath was especially installed for her and a temporary suite of rooms was built for the King in the Priory complex at the Cathedral. A vast depot for his stores was made at the castle and supplies of food, drink and clothing were regularly taken out to Lanercost to support the entourage of soldiers, cooks, messengers, musicians, doctors and as many as 200 people that made up the King's court. The King's decision to call a Parliament at Carlisle in 1307 would stretch the city's accommodation and resources to bursting point, as up to 400 lords, churchmen and commons, together with their attendants, made their way to Carlisle and are likely to have doubled the city's population of 2,000.

The 23-year-old Edward, Prince of Wales, stayed at Wetheral Priory and was noted for the mayhem that he and his boisterous companions caused on their journeys through the countryside. It was no different at Botcherby and it is recorded that at the end of March he had to pay 10s to Joan of Botcherby:

> *'in recompense of the damage she sustained from the journeys made by the prince and his household between Wetheral and Carlisle going through her garden and croft in the time of the Parliament.'*

As his retinue comprised not just the usual dogs and hawks but a lion as well, the local residents were probably thankful to see the back of him when, in April, Prince Edward left Wetheral, heading South! He was followed in May by Queen Margaret.

King Edward's health was still poor but, partly to offset rumours of his death, he decided to march on Scotland to suppress the rebellion of Robert the Bruce. He left Carlisle on horseback on 26 June but was soon forced to pitch camp on Burgh marsh where he died on 5 July 1307.

What followed was devastating for Carlisle and the surrounding area during the next decade. With Edward II pre-occupied with problems elsewhere in his kingdom, Robert the Bruce took the opportunity to wreak havoc in the North of England. In 1315, Botcherby was one of the townships outside Carlisle laid waste by the Scottish monarch.

For the rest of the 14th century, Cumbria remained a troubled area with 'peace' and war producing many varieties of violence and upheaval. Gradually, however, some leading landowning families emerged, including the Parvings, lords of Botcherby, who had holdings in the city of Carlisle itself.

On the basis of the earliest Ordnance Survey map and a tithe award map, the archaeologist Mike McCarthy has suggested that, in the Middle Ages, the layout of Wood Street may have been mirrored in the area now occupied by the first houses in Botcherby Avenue (2 to 60), although there is no hard evidence for houses. He believes that *'the medieval village may have extended westwards across the present Durranhill Road... In this context, Banks Lane would have been a back lane providing access to the rear of properties, the site of which is currently occupied by St Cuthbert's RC School and its playing fields.'*

He also suggests that, at this time, access to Botcherby may have been via Tilbury Road up Wood Street and then leading on to Durranhill Road and Harraby, rather than via Victoria Road, which was then no more than a lane.

In the 15th century, against a persisting backdrop of lawlessness and destruction, land disputes over property in Botcherby seem to focus around a small group of families - including the Dacres, Stapletons and Bethoms: these families did not necessarily live in Botcherby, but farmed the land there.

By the 16th century, the boundaries between Carlisle and villages like Botcherby were increasingly blurred by migration from one to the other and the economies of both became more interdependent.

The Civil War: a state of siege

War and rumours of war were also features of 17th-century Carlisle, and Botcherby did not escape unscathed, especially during the Civil War. Carlisle Castle, a Royalist stronghold was besieged by General David Leslie, leading the Parliamentary forces in 1644. Most of what we know about that time comes from the work of an eyewitness, Isaac Tullie, in *A Narrative of the Siege of Carlisle, in 1644 and 1645*. The Roundheads set up a series of siege works around Carlisle, including one at Botcherby. Tullie recalls two incidents relating to it. The first refers to Captain Forester, a Cavalier who was killed earlier in a skirmish with Roundhead troops:

> *'About this time [February 1645] there was a common report that Captain Forester's ghost appeared nightly at the Roundhead's worke at Botcherby; fiercely demanding of y^m if they were not yet converted to the King; when they replied "no" he was wont to call on Cap. Philipson to fall upon them with horse and foot. Instantly to their Imaginations, horse and foot fired upon them, and they answered wth shott from the worke, wch being heard at Stanwix some horse were sent to assist them, two of which were*

drowned in crossing the ford at Rickerby. Major Barwis being asked by Philipson in a parley of the truth hereof, protested he could bring 500 souldiers eye witnesses of it.'

Captain Philipson was to feature in many stirring tales of the siege and Botcherby was the scene of one of his most daring escapades. According to Tullie, on 28 February, 1645:

The Civil War

A silver coin minted in Carlisle in 1645 when the city was under siege, during the English Civil War.

Two similar coins sold at auction in 2015 for more than £75,000!

(Courtesy of Tullie House Museum & Art Gallery)

'Philipson and Major Wiltshire rid out wth 16 horses towards [blank space] only, to take the aire; the Roundheads marched towards them with 60 horses and foot, but durst not engage. From thence they raked towards Botcherby, along ye riverside where was drawn out a troupe of horse, and about 40 or 50 foot. By this time, ten Cavaleres came to Philipson who charging through the foot, killed eight, took 6 and pursued the rest to their works. Their releif was newly come up, which made the Roundheads horse 180; but seeing the Cavaleres on the backs of their fellows, durst not releive them. The Cavaleres at their pursuit, but were so galliantly kept in play by three and no more, Knaggs, Corporall Vere and Ja^s Evins, y^t their 60 horse could not advance 20 yards in a Quarter of an hour; yet these three being above a Quarter of a mile from Philipson, put them all to the Chase, in which Vere being close at their backs was unfortunately shot in the breast, and some 4 days after died.'

(The erratic spelling and grammar are typical of the time.)

The Cavalier garrison at the castle held out until June that year, when King Charles lost the Battle of Naseby and the Cavalier cause seemed lost. Within two weeks the garrison was replaced with Scottish troops, supporters of the Roundheads.

Wi' a hundred pipers, an' a', an' a'

Carlisle suffered its last siege in 1745 when Bonnie Prince Charlie came to town with his army. As with the Roundheads a hundred years before, he set up siege works in the villages around the city, controlling access along the main roads in and out. Botcherby was one of these. The would-be king stationed himself in a house in Brampton.

All was not well within the ranks, however, as one of his commanders, Lord George Murray, had been against the invasion of England from the outset and now felt undermined by his leader. In a letter to his brother the Marquis of Tullibardine, written from Harraby, he clearly shows the dissension that had already arisen among the officers of the besieging army. He thus expresses his disapproval of Botcherby as a place for a fort:

'I posted the men in the villages, so as to stop the communication to and from Carlisle, according to the note I gave to his Royal Highness, but I believe there must be some alteration this day, for I think of calling Shian from Butcherby [Botcherby] where there is no occasion for a party, to reinforce this post [Harraby] and that commanded by Lord Nairn [Blackhall], as both will be pretty much exposed if the enemy should attempt to sally, as they will be some miles distant from one another, so that no succour could go in from the one post to the other, and quite at a distance from the rest of the army.'

He goes on to propose that, in order properly to serve the battery which had been set up against Carlisle not far from the site of the Post Office, *'fifty men be drafted out of each of the battalions that are at Brampton with proper officers, and at least two majors out of the six battalions, and be sent to quarter of Butcherby, which I believe is within a mile of the battery; and as I suppose 150 men will mount guard at the battery, these six battalions will furnish two guards; your men will furnish one; General Gordon and Lord Ogilvie's one; which in whole makes four guards or reliefs; and I think by that time the town will be either taken or the blockade removed.'*

The proposal was rejected and Murray resigned his commission but was soon re-instated, due to pressure from the ranks.

Murray evidently thought he would have to storm Carlisle Castle as he had not reckoned on the peaceful surrender of the garrison. Once it became clear to the militia defending it that the hoped-for reinforcements from Newcastle would not arrive, they gave up the fight. The next day the Mayor of Carlisle surrendered the keys of the city to the Jacobites in Brampton. Bonnie Prince Charlie is then said to have entered Carlisle on a white horse with a hundred pipers accompanying him. While in Carlisle he stayed at Highmore House, on the site now occupied by Marks and Spencer.

Spurred on by the ease of taking Carlisle, the Jacobites marched South but after a series of disastrous battles and skirmishes with the English army, were soon back in Carlisle where the castle was once again under siege - this time from the English army! It was an uneven contest and the disheartened Jacobites surrendered on 30 December 1745. The last siege of Carlisle was over.

The '45 Rebellion

Clockwise from above: Charles Edward Stuart, or Bonnie Prince Charlie, painted in 1745 by Allan Ramsay; the house in High Cross Street, Brampton where Bonnie Prince Charlie made his HQ before his march on Carlisle; Highmore House, English Street, Carlisle, which housed Bonnie Prince Charlie after he captured the city (Tullie House Museum & Art Gallery); plaque on the outer wall of Marks & Spencer, commemorating the location of Highmore House; plaque commemorating the stay of Bonnie Prince Charlie in Brampton.

♦♦♦

The developing village...

In the 18th century, Botcherby was little more than a handful of houses in Wood Street and a couple more at the top of Mount Florida. But at the beginning of the 19th century it started to take the shape we know today...

Wood Street and its listed buildings

By the 1820s, Botcherby was developing: Wood Street had more houses and farms on both sides, leading down to Tilbury Road where Botcherby Farm stood on the left-hand side.

The properties on the north and south sides of Wood Street form two rectangular blocks of land or rows with common rear-garden boundaries. Beyond the rear-garden boundaries were long, strip tofts, known as crofts, possibly formerly attached to the properties on the street frontage – and possibly a remainder of the site of the crofts of medieval times.

The entrance to Botcherby village from Carlisle in these years may have been along Warwick Road, turning right onto Tilbury Road and then leading to Wood Street. Access to the south to Durranhill and Harraby would have been by Durranhill Road.

A map dating from 1823 depicts a time before Warwick Road extended as far as Botcherby Bridge and

The village in the late-18th and early-19th centuries

Left: in 1774 the village mostly comprised a handful of houses in Wood Street and a few at the top of Mount Florida. Right: by the 1820s, more houses had appeared in Wood Street and at the top of Mount Florida. Carleton House can be seen opposite Banks Lane. The Brick and Tile Works are also shown, as well as Durranhill House.

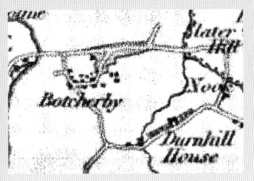

Grade II listed buildings in Wood Street...

31 Wood Street (Orchard House) - mid- or late-18th C.

29 Wood Street (Church Farmhouse) - now a private house with adjoining barn. Mid-18th C. The barn is probably a late-18th C. replacement.

19 Wood Street (The Beeches) - originally a farmhouse, now a private house with adjoining former barn or stable. Dated over entrance 1767.

15 Wood Street (Laburnum Cottage) - originally a farmhouse, now a private house with adjoining former stable. Probably 18th C. with extensive mid-20th C. alterations.

11 Wood Street (Norman House) and 13 Wood Street (Norman Nook) - 11 is dated and initialled in raised brick on right gable. The bolection surround to the front doorway is under the roofline of the adjoining house, 9 Wood Street. One of a pair with 13 Wood Street, divided into two at rear.

9 Wood Street (Botcherby House) - forms part of a pair with 11. Early-18th C.

7 Wood Street (Holme Farmhouse) - now a private house. Early-18th C. with later alterations. Was Mr Clark's farm.

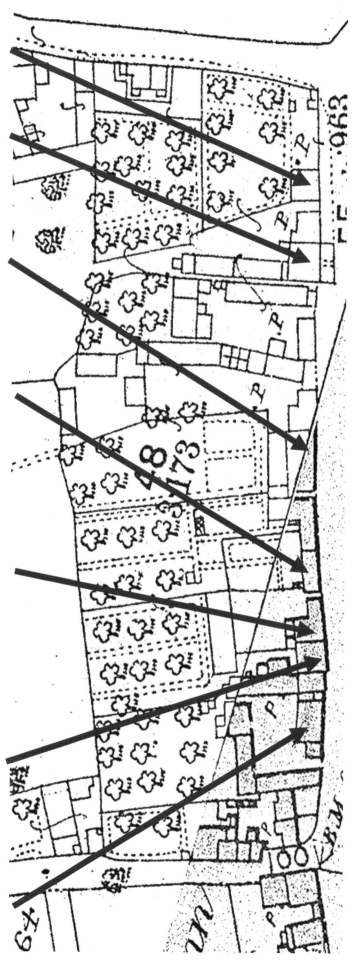

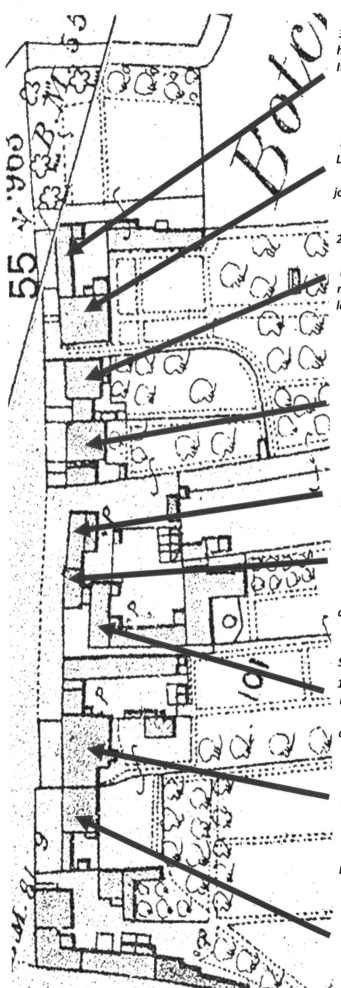

34 and 32 Wood Street - two houses in a row. Early 19th C. It has been suggested that 32 was probably originally the stable range for 34.

30 Wood Street (Bramerton Lodge) - private house. Early-19th C. This was formerly joined with 28 Wood Street as one house.

28 Wood Street (Bramerton) - private house. Probably late-18th C. with extensive mid-19th C. alterations. The left recessed bay was added to link with Bramerton Lodge, when they were made into one house.

26 and 24 Wood Street (Ashleigh House and garage) - early-19th C. 24 was a cottage but now forms the garage to 26.

22 Wood Street - single storey house - mid- or late-18th C.

20 Wood Street (The Jovial Hatter) - mid-17th C. The name came about through an inn sign being painted on the wrong house - it was meant for a pub in Wood Street, Newtown Road area.

18 Wood Street - farmhouse, now a private house - early-18th C. with later alterations. Partly hidden by 20 Wood Street which stands directly in front.

16, 14 and 12 Wood Street (Stable Croft, Grange Garth and The Grange) - with former stable converted to house and adjoining barn. Early-19th C. (the barn could be earlier).

10 Wood Street (Mayfield House) - at end of row. Early- or mid- 19th C.

Greystone Road was still the main route from Carlisle to the village. Botcherby Mill, beside the Petteril, is clearly visible, as is 'Durnhill House' (later Durranhill Convent), built around 1811. Most of the houses were in Wood Street, with a few dotted down Victoria Road, and a largish house at the head of Wood Street where Park House stands today, its history still an enigma.

The map pre-dates the building of the houses in Wellington Place, but the building opposite Banks Lane is probably Carleton House. The brickworks at Low Durranhill are also shown.

There are two theories about how Wood Street got its name. The first is the simplest - Inglewood Forest stretched to near Bramerton Orchard, at the bottom of the hill: the name could be a contraction of this. Denis Perriam has suggested a more interesting possibility: perhaps it was named after William Wood, an early entrepreneur of cotton spinning in Carlisle, who died at Botcherby in 1830, aged 76. He was described by the *Journal* as *'formerly an extensive cotton twist manufacturer in this city.'* His factory was on Backhouse Walk, West Walls, and he employed over 200 people in 1791 - a lot of workers for a single enterprise at that time. He married Sarah Cliffe in 1795, daughter of Major Cliffe of Carlisle. He retired in 1807 and by 1818 the building was converted to a hat factory.

His widow Martha, who must have been his second wife, died two years later in 1832 and it is possible that such an influential family gave their name to Wood Street.

Whatever the origins of its name, Wood Street has an amazing number of buildings of historic interest.

Bramerton Lodge, a case history

Derek Nash and his family have lived at Bramerton Lodge - 30 Wood Street - since 1984 and his assiduous research into its history has added greatly to our knowledge of Wood Street since the 18th century.

The date of Bramerton Lodge's construction remains unknown but James Fairbairn, a widower, coachmaker and owner of the Bush Hotel in English Street, Carlisle, was living there in 1805. Upon his death in 1807, the estate passed to his son James - also a coachmaker - and his wife Mary. Their story is told later in the section on the Fairbairn family, in the chapter on Botcherby's nursery gardens. After her husband's death in 1835, Mary Fairbairn continued to live there but had sold the house long before she died in 1882.

In 1865 it was bought by John Augustus Cory, surveyor and architect for Cumberland, who had worked on the building of the Garlands Hospital and whose work places him in the mainstream of the Victorian Gothic Revival. He also carried out significant reconstruction to the interior and exterior of the property.

His origins were in Norfolk, where the family name was associated with 'Bramerton Hall' from the 1400s - so we can be fairly sure that he first gave the name 'Bramerton Lodge' to 30 Wood Street. A man of strong religious convictions, he converted the barn in his garden into a mission chapel in 1867 for St John's parish, Upperby, as the carving of his initials alongside his wife Emily's above the church door testifies. The final demise of the barn-chapel in the 1980s became something of a local *cause célèbre*: its story is told later in

Bramerton Cottages

Left: Bramerton Cottages (34 and 32 Wood Street) had fallen into disrepair when this picture was taken in 1987, prior to the development of Bramerton Orchard. Right: today, Bramerton Cottages present a very different picture.

this book in the chapter on faith communities.

At some point, Cory took in a tenant, John Wood, a civil engineer with a background in the railways, who was still living there at the time of Cory's death in 1887. We don't know the precise relationship between the two men but it was clearly a good one as Cory, in his will dated 1884, had made provision for Wood to continue living at Bramerton Lodge for the rest of his life should Cory predecease him. In the event, Wood bought the

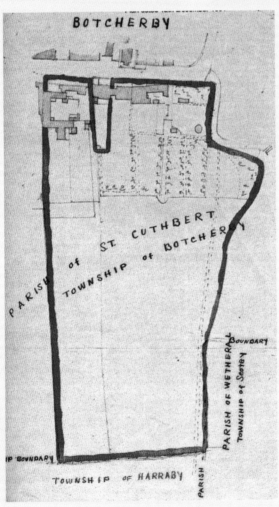

Bramerton Lodge

Clockwise from top left: Bramerton Lodge today; garden party at Bramerton Lodge after the wedding of the Simpsons at St Aidan's Church; Golden Wedding of the Simpsons, 1940; the back garden of Bramerton Lodge in the 1940s; the back view of Bramerton Lodge in the 1980s; Bramerton Lodge estate map, December 1891, showing the extensive land owned by the estate at that time.

property when it was finally placed on the market in 1891 and was living there with his wife, three children, a nurse and two servants at the time of the Census. At one time 30 and 28 Wood Street were a single property (Bramerton), so it seems likely they were divided after Cory's death.

When Wood died in 1916, the estate he left comprised 34, 32, 30, 28 and 26 Wood Street. The latter was variously known as Ashleigh, Ashleigh House or Ashlea. It was sold separately to the 'Misses Bell', and Joseph Simpson, a saddler and poultry farmer, bought the rest of the estate in 1917. A year later he sold the 'west wing' of Bramerton Lodge (presumably what we now know as Bramerton) to the 'Misses Irving': the old estate was gradually being dismantled.

Simpson was a keen sportsman, interested in otter hunting, shooting, athletics, rugby and football, and was a director of Carlisle United in 1909 when it moved to Brunton Park. He continued to live at Bramerton Lodge with his family until 1940 when he sold it, along with 34 and 32 Wood Street, to Evelyn Jean Baxter, a teacher and daughter of the Rev. William Baxter. Her father resided there with her in his retirement and resumed church services in the old barn. He died in 1954, aged 88, and Evelyn died in 1966, leaving the house to Dorothy Joan Scott, who had lived there since 1950.

Dorothy shared the property with Elsie May Jones, who had been at Bramerton Lodge since the early 1960s. Both were teachers at Margaret Sewell School and, when Dorothy died in 1982 after a long illness, Elsie inherited the house but only lived there a few more years before selling it to Derek Nash in 1984. Sadly, Elsie was killed in a traffic accident in 1989, when she was 75.

Since 1984, Bramerton Lodge has echoed to the sounds of the Nash family, who have steadily expanded and improved the property while retaining its central role in the development of Botcherby village.

The Grange, a chequered past

The Grange - 12 Wood Street - and its associated buildings - Stable Croft and Grange Garth, became listed buildings in 1972: a large attractive property, a house with the former stable converted into an adjoining house together with a barn. It was built in the early-19th century, although the barn could be earlier with 20th-century alterations.

From the 1880s it was the home of Thomas and Martha Barton (a Bowman from Newcastle). The wealthy Barton family were well known in Carlisle as they had a horse-harness and coach-building company started in 1820 by Thomas Barton's father, William, who originated from Oulton Hall in Wigton. By 1831 he went into partnership with Thomas Tweeddale and their premises were at Albert Square, off Blackfriars Street, where Tesco's supermarket stands today. They built quality London-style carriages and in 1836 produced their first omnibus for the Bush Hotel owned by the Fairbairn family. The firm also supplied horses for mail coaches during the 1830s-40s.

William Barton lived at 1 The Crescent and in 1840 the firm moved to a yard behind the house: as they expanded further, their premises extended as far as Cecil Street. Barton's Lane, locally known as 'the Post Office back lane' was laid over their land, and today the name Barton's Yard is remembered as part of the Halston aparthotel and bistro, on the site of the former Warwick Road General Post Office, which was built in 1916 on Barton's premises.

William Barton died in 1846 leaving his wife Mary and two young sons, 17-year-old Robert and 13-year-old Thomas, to run the business, as Thomas Tweeddale retired and would die in 1853. By 1881 the brothers still lived at 1 The Crescent, with their mother and employed 25 men in the coachbuilding works.

Things soon changed for 48-year-old Thomas as he met 30-year-old Martha Bowman and, by 1884, they were married with two sons and living at The Grange in Botcherby. When his mother Mary died in 1890, she left the business to Thomas but he died in 1892 and Robert, now a farmer with little interest in the business, leased it to Boag and Sons.

Thomas's two young sons, Harry and Bertie Bowman, attended Carlisle Grammar School and Bertie went on to become a barrister. He was a Lance Corporal with the 10th King's Royal Rifle Corps in WW1 and lost his life at the Battle of Cambrai on 30 November 1917 at the age of 33.

Probably the next residents at The Grange were James and Annie Little, with their six young sons. James was a businessman operating from property he owned at 32 Bridge Street, Caldewgate, where he advertised himself as a joiner contractor and undertaker. The premises were destroyed as part of the development of the Sainsbury supermarket.

The Little family boys had their lives touched significantly by WW1. First the eldest, Isaac, went missing in October 1917, presumed killed in action in France - it took a year for this to be confirmed for the family. Another son, William was invalided out of service due to war wounds, and - on 13 October 1918 - the youngest, Thomas, was killed in an air crash at Upavon, Wiltshire. He had enlisted in the Royal Engineers and was transferred to the Royal Flying Corps where - only six months earlier - he had received his certificate as pilot first-class. This left a distraught James and Annie with two other sons still serving - they, thankfully, survived the war.

James finally sold his business in 1920 and he and Annie were later living at 310 Warwick Road (later the home of Michael Casey). He died in 1931 and Annie survived him until 1943.

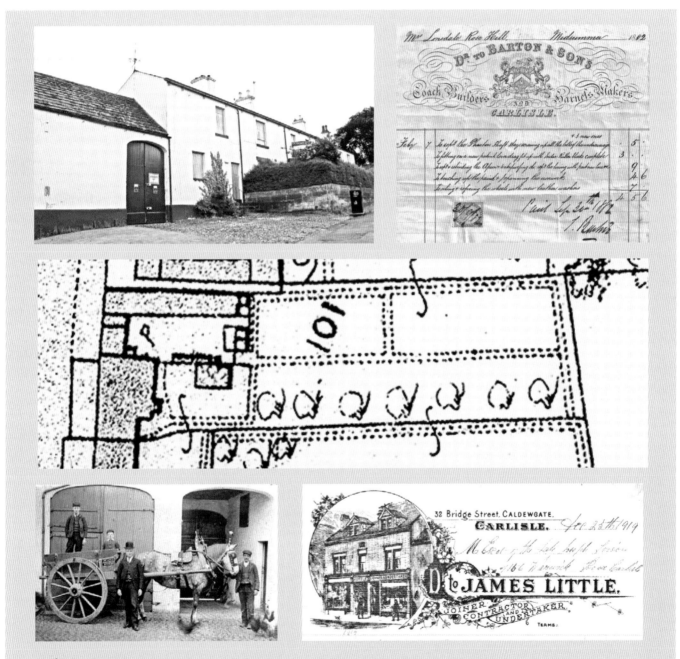

The Grange

Clockwise from top left: Stable Croft, Grange Garth and The Grange House; 1882 invoice from Barton and Sons for repair work done to a phaeton carriage; 1864 map of The Grange, showing the extensive land to the rear of the house; letter heading for James Little, undertaker, whose shop was in Bridge Street and lived at The Grange in the late 19th/early 20th century; James Little, staff and some of his family in the yard of The Grange.

Later in the 20th century, the house had another notable character in residence: William Henry Lakeman, Chief Constable of Carlisle. He took up his post in September 1938 and would remain until his retirement on 15 November 1961. He became a well-known figure in Botcherby as, in July 1940, the Watch Committee purchased The Grange for £1,450 from Mr E. J. Williams, and it became the home of the Chief Constable.

Chief Lakeman arrived at a difficult time, just twelve months before war broke out, and he would see Carlisle through many innovative developments. Juvenile delinquency was a problem in the city, but in April 1939, launching a new initiative, he said: *'Boys are not born criminals... My slogan is "Get the parents on the side of the police".'*

It was the beginning of a scheme, commonplace today, where first-time juvenile offenders are cautioned by a senior police officer in the presence of their parents. Mr Lakeman himself took on this role.

The street pillar system was also introduced in 1941, where every area in the city was linked in communication with the Police Station. Patrolling Constables on the beat were required to make contact with headquarters every hour, and the general public had direct access to the emergency services. The pillar standing on Durranhill Road opposite Merith Avenue, with its flashing orange light was a familiar sight.

There were many other developments under Chief Lakeman's watch: the 999 emergency telephone system came in, and an Information(Control) Room was established at Police Headquarters.

The Grange, was eventually used as a residential care home for young people by Cumbria County Council for many years, until its closure in 2012. This came after a damning report by Ofsted inspectors who uncovered a catalogue of failings, when the home failed to meet with minimum standards. In spite of this assessment several former residents who had lived there spoke up in defence of staff, saying that they had made a positive and lasting difference to their lives.

The Grange stood empty and boarded up for the next two years until Cumbria County Council issued a consultation document in January 2014 as part of a review of care services for young people. Local residents, supported by Councillor Robert Betton, expressed fears that, if it was again used as a residential home, they would again return to problems of vandalism and abuse. In July 2014 the Council decided that the six-bedroom property was no longer needed and would be put up for sale.

By Spring 2016 The Grange had been sold privately and let to a second party, who were sub-contracted to run a service providing seven units for the care of vulnerable adults. At the time of writing, work had started on its renovation.

Left: William Henry Lakeman, Chief Constable of Carlisle (1938-1961) lived at The Grange until his retirement. Right: a street pillar similar to this was situated opposite Merith Avenue. It enabled the patrolling bobby to keep in contact with HQ.

Margery Jackson: a famous resident

Had she lived in another age, Margery Jackson might have been a top businesswoman but, back in the 18th century, women had no such prospects. Today she creates great interest in Carlisle, even to the extent of having a musical show based on her life, and in the street-names that bear her name, Margery Street and Jackson Street.

She was born in January 1722 at her father's home and drapers shop at 77 Scotch Street in Carlisle's city centre. Joseph Jackson was a man of some wealth, owning a corn mill (Botcherby Mill on Greystone Road) as well as farms and houses and, in the year she was born, he was Mayor of Carlisle.

Left: Margery Jackson at Carlisle Cross, painted around 1810, attributed to William Brown. Right: Court Mantua dress from about 1750 which is said to have belonged to the Jackson family - evidence of their wealth, although Margery probably never wore it. (Both Tullie House Museum & Art Gallery.)

Margery's mother, Isabell Nicholson, was connected to the Aglionby family who were prominent in the city and had produced Mayors and Members of Parliament. She was a woman of fashion and had little to do but supervise the care of her four children and her household.

As a child, Margery was taught reading and writing at home, as well as social skills such as dancing, the only prospect in view being to marry a suitable husband. Her life was to change dramatically when her father died in January 1732, and her eldest brother William, not yet 21, left Queen's College, Oxford, to return home to take over his father's estate.

He found his mother buying more properties, but with her declining health she travelled to London to seek better medical care. It was to no avail and she died in February 1733, leaving the three younger children in William's care.

Margery, as an orphaned 11-year-old girl, was put in the care of her cousin Elizabeth James, who treated her with great strictness. The James family also interfered in the running of the Jackson estates and soon had the young William under their thumb, exploiting their position. Thomas James was a self-appointed lawyer and that year was Mayor of Carlisle. Margery's father died a wealthy man and left no debts, but many local people were indebted to him, often owing large amounts of money.

Thomas James used his advantageous position to start debt collecting on the Jackson estate and had soon collected £500, which he kept for his own use. William Jackson could do little about it as he relied on the James family to look after young Margery. Soon William consolidated his financial security and also fulfilled his ambitions to enter Holy Orders by becoming a licensed curate for the parish of Bromfield - he was now the Reverend Mr Jackson and a man of property.

Left: Wood Street won the Quality Street Award in 1991. Right: Hunter Davies presents the residents of Wood Street with the award.

His religious office did not prevent him from taking financial advantage of his younger siblings, however. Under the terms of his father's will he was left all estates and two hundred pounds. His siblings, Joseph, Jerome and Margery, were left legacies of one thousand pounds each, held in trust until they reached 21 years of age. In the meantime, the interest was to be used to pay for their maintenance and education. In addition their mother had left her sons £500 each and Margery £200 to be paid within a year.

William considered that Margery was well looked after with her *'hooped petticoats, scarlet stockings, ribbons and fans'* and her dancing lessons, and Joseph's school fees were paid, so he decided that he would hold on to the other children's money. The effects of this decision were to dominate Margery's life until her death many years later and turn her bright intelligent mind towards her obsession with seeking justice and hoarding money.

Joseph had a commission in the Army and died aged 25 in 1746 and Jerome, at Oxford, died aged 23 in 1751. Both were unmarried, leaving Margery to inherit part of their fortune. There was little brotherly love towards Margery from William and he refused to pay any of the money due to her. Despite angry scenes he was adamant, and Margery responded by filing a Bill of Chancery against him, compelling him to account for the property inherited from their parents and to pay her the legacies given by their wills. In 1776, with the Chancery suit still pending, William made his will and died. He only left Margery an annuity and, as he had no children, the rest of his estate was left to a distant cousin Thomas Hodgson. Margery, by now aged 54, was incensed and nearly destitute, but her fighting spirit and thirst for justice spurred her on.

She put her case in the hands of Joseph Bowman, a Quaker who lived at Botcherby, and instructed her solicitor Mr Robert Mounsey, the London agent for Mounseys of Carlisle, and went to London to pursue the case against Thomas Hodgson for the legacies which were rightly hers. Thomas died unmarried in 1788 and added further complications to the case by leaving his property to be sold and shared among 15 of his cousins. The cousins came to a compromise and in 1791 Margery paid them £100 each and they signed over to her all of the property previously held by her brother.

Now aged 69, Margery returned to Carlisle in some style, travelling in her father's carriage. The long years of fighting for justice from her own family had embittered Margery, and sharpened her sense of self-sufficiency. Living in the family mansion on Scotch Street she became a lonely old woman, behaving like a miser and hoarding the gold sovereigns that she collected from rents on her property.

Joseph Bowman had long been a good friend to Margery, who had often locked up her house in Scotch Street to escape the noise and dirt of the city centre and gone to stay at the Bowman's house in Wood Street. Joseph, along with her solicitor, helped her manage her extensive estates. As well as owning Botcherby Mill and property within the city, she owned farms, including Ambrose Holme in Botcherby township, and in Westmorland.

By 1809, at the age of 87, the old lady decided to leave her house in the centre of Carlisle and remove to the countryside and the rural delights of Botcherby for good. She travelled there by horse and cart, and beneath the straw lay her iron chest containing nine thousand guineas in gold. She went to live with Joseph Bowman and his family in Wood Street where he had a large house and a productive orchard. Information on the property is hard to find today. Author Gerald Findler in his 1969 book *Ghosts of the Lake Counties* writes:

'Before Carlisle Corporation built its rows and rows of council houses Botcherby was a pretty old-world village. My late father-in-law, with his wife and family of young children, lived in a large farm cottage at the top of the hill which has since been demolished and replaced by a grocery store. The cottage, I was often told, was haunted by a miserly old woman, whose name was Margery Jackson and who died in February 1812.'

In her 1991 book on Margery Jackson's life, H. R. Hallaway noted that the house still stood in Wood Street although most of the orchard had been built upon.

When Margery died on 10 February 1812 at Wood Street she left £50,000 (around £3 million in today's money) and her property to her friend Joseph Bowman. Her will stated that the Bowman family had to take on the name Nicholson, but instead Joseph Bowman left all the inheritance to his friend John Norman, a solicitor, who changed the family name to Norman Bowman prior to Joseph's death and this family subsequently inherited Margery Jackson's wealth. Some of the Bowman family lived in Newcastle and later generations bequeathed Margery Jackson's gowns to Tullie House.

Wood Street's farms and dairies

Three families were associated with Botcherby's farms and dairies for many years: the Clarks at 7 Wood Street, the Robinsons at 29 Wood Street and the Caseys at Botcherby Farm in Tilbury Road.

Holme Farm (Clark's Farm)

Tom Clark had Holme Farm at the top of Wood Street, and owned a butcher's shop that stood at the entrance to his cobbled farmyard and adjoining dairy. During the food rationing period of WW2, customers had to register with the local shops to receive their supplies. June M. Dunn describes the butchers shop in her memoirs:

'Tom had two daughters, Elsie and Mary. Mary was married with a family but Elsie remained a spinster

Clark's Farm

Clockwise from top left: 5 and 7 Wood Street, known as Holme Farm or Clark's Farm - these recent photos show the house in a bad state of repair; Rogation Day procession in 1953 through Clark's Farm; the inner yard of Clark's Farm in the 1980s.

and served in her father's shop. Elsie was very thin, she had short black curly hair and wore clogs. They had metal corkers on the soles and clattered on the concrete floor of the small shop and when she crossed the yard to the dairy for fresh milk she balanced on the uneven cobblestones, walking quickly, slightly bent forward with her arms held up and out like a tightrope walker. She wore a white overall with a blue and white striped butcher's apron over that and in winter a pair of woollen mittens covered her hands. She had a cheerful manner and a ready smile.'

Elsie was kind to the customers, often slipping marrow bones, small ham shanks and the odd egg into baskets when times were hard.

'As a farmer/butcher, Tom Clark was allowed to slaughter only a certain number of animals for sale to the customers registered in his shop. Rationing of meat was strictly controlled, but he had a supply of meat, slightly higher in price and off ration to his regular customers. It went onto the scales when the shop was quiet... the illegally slaughtered meat was of prime quality, never a big joint, but stewing steak, chops, pork fillets... and the inevitable mince with a lump of suet to make dumplings.'

Tom Clark's daughter Elsie married John Richardson who was known as 'Captain John' of the original *Queen Mary* liner. John was an enthusiastic beekeeper. They lived at 11 Wood Street.

Church Farm (Robinson's Farm)

Next door to St Andrew's Church stands Church Farm at 29 Wood Street – it is remarkable for the initialled plaque set into the front wall which says:

H

I   A

1798

It was a dairy with a milking parlour later made into the kitchen.

Better known as Robinson's Farm, it was from here that the famous Miss Sarah Hodgson, locally known as 'Sally', would deliver the milk around the estate. She was out in the early morning with her faithful trolley full of glass bottles doing her milk round in Botcherby. She made the same deliveries for 37 years, including during the big freezes of 1947 and 1963, and never had a day off work with colds or flu. With her rosy complexion and ready smile she was a picture of health. Her recommendations for keeping healthy were *'an outdoor life and plenty of activity.'*

Robinson's Farm

Left: Church Farm and St Andrew's Church. Right: the familiar figure of Sally (Sarah Hodgson) doing her milk delivery round.

Botcherby Farm (Casey's Farm)

Botcherby Farm stands just around the corner from the end of Wood Street on what was Tilbury Road and dates from 1763. It has had a long and varied history and may even have been an early chapel in Botcherby: when Annie Casey and her friend, Mary Horseman of Botcherby Avenue, were redecorating a bedroom just after WW2, stripping off the wallpaper revealed a large painting of the Crucifixion. Possibly an interesting piece of social history? No, but with sick children and work to do, they simply painted over it! The farm had, in fact, been bought by Martin Casey in the early 1900s. The Caseys originally came from Clonmel in County Tipperary and, by the end of the 19th century, Martin Casey lived on Corporation Road and had married Ann Milbourne at the old St Bede's Church on Wigton Road.

While living on Newtown Road, two sons were born, Michael and John, and by 1904 the family moved to the farm. Martin's business was mainly cattle dealing and he was a well-known landowner in the area.

Tragedy struck the family in 1933 when their son Gerard was killed in an accident and, in 1936, Martin and Ann moved the family back to Ireland with the exception of two sons, Michael and John, who stayed to run the farm at Botcherby. Michael lived in Eldred Street and at 310 Warwick Road, and became well known as the organist at Our Lady and St Joseph's Church on Warwick Road.

Casey's Farm

Clockwise from top left: Botcherby Farm; one of the old outbuildings; John and Annie Casey; map of Botcherby Farm, showing its location in Tilbury Road (now part of Wood Street); John and Michael Casey as small boys; Eileen Casey with her two brothers, John and Martin, plus family pet Larry the Lamb; Michael and John Casey on the boat to Ireland; Botcherby Farm around 1900 showing the wide dispersion of its fields.

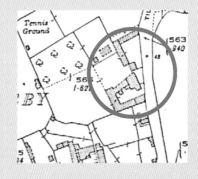

Casey Brothers was a partnership but it was John Casey whose name would become known in the Botcherby community. He married Annie Leslie, of the long-established Nursery Gardens on Durdar Road, and they had three children, Martin, John and Eileen. Eileen has many happy memories of growing up on the farm with her two brothers. A working farm has few animals who are pets, but Eileen recalls her pet lamb, aptly named Larry the Lamb, with affection. He liked to follow her about, but sometimes was too enthusiastic about this!

Irish cattle had long been favoured by farmers due to their easy fattening qualities, and John and Michael Casey made regular trips to Dublin to buy the cattle at the Irish auctions and bring them to the farmlands at Botcherby. Passengers and cattle would sail from Dublin via the Isle of Man to Silloth on the *Yarrow*, a steam ship especially built for the route in 1893. By the late 1920s the ship was re-named the *Assaroe* and would provide good service until she was broken up in the mid-1950s. Bringing the cattle over was no small task, as special farm workers had to prepare the pens and bedding in the hold and ensure that the cattle were evenly distributed, so that the weight would not disturb the steering of the ship.

By the time they reached Silloth, the cattle were gradually led up the ramp to be watered and put in stalls in the lairage. There they awaited transportation. A hundred years ago there were cattle drovers, who drove or walked the cattle down country roads to their destination. The coming of the railways meant that the cattle were moved more quickly, and eventually road haulage took over.

Bell's Farm – 18 Wood Street

Bells of Wood Street were one of the first companies to introduce road haulage for transporting cattle and were used by Caseys.

Bell's Farm

Left: 18 Wood Street is a former farmhouse with an extensive yard at the rear; right: Bell's Yard, behind the house, photographed during the 1980s.

Other Wood Street buildings

Prominent omissions from the listed buildings in Wood Street are the two properties you first see at the top of the street: numbers 1 - the Post Office - and 3. They simply haven't been around long enough to be listed!

Over the years, the properties in Wood Street have been put to a variety of uses and new developments added - these are addressed in the chapters on shops, businesses, and new housing developments, later in this book.

Victoria Road

Carleton House, Linden House, Wellington Place, all Grade 11 listed buildings

The oldest properties in Victoria Road, these houses are all Grade II listed buildings (since 1972) and formed part of the Victoria Road Conservation Area in 1968. Mostly built in the 1830s or 1840s, they mark the

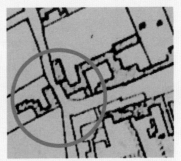

Left to right: 1 Wood Street (Botcherby's Post Office) and 3 Wood Street - neither of these properties had been built in the 1860s as the blue circle on the map on the left shows. By the 1920s (map with red circle) both of these properties had been erected and Park House on Mount Florida had been completely rebuilt.

beginnings of Botcherby's 19th-century expansion - as the table below shows, it was slow but fairly steady.

Year	1801	1811	1821	1831	1841	1851
Population	94	118	125	144	125	155

Carleton House was built in the 1770s and features on some of the earliest maps. Today it marks the entrance to Eden Park estate, but historically it held a dominant position at the top of Mount Florida.

Village life in Botcherby in the 19th century revolved around the local businesses, the market gardens, the farms, the brickworks, and the local inns. The population was sparse and had few amenities. There was not even a letter box to post your Christmas cards, as this letter of complaint from an unknown resident shows. It was published in the *Carlisle Journal* on 17 December 1869:

'LETTER BOX WANTED FOR BOTCHERBY

'We are very much in need of a letter box for the above village. The postman on passing here sounds a horn, which you may or may not hear, and never being sure of when he will arrive we are continually on the lookout. Warwick has a wall box and we are undoubtedly entitled to one also.

A Resident.'

The first post box in the UK was erected in Botchergate, Carlisle in 1853, so perhaps 'A Resident' had a point!

Wellington Place

Early maps show that Wellington Place did not extend as far down Botcherby Lane as Warwick Road - it was set back from the road and consisted of a terrace of five houses. It was still the official name of that part of the road until the 1880s, and it retained this name up to the 1931 electoral register, when the estate had been built with a large expansion in Botcherby's population. The minutes of the City Council of 1929-30 report that the re-numbering of houses in Victoria Road had been agreed, changing 1 to 5 Wellington Place into 35 to 43 Victoria Road.

Storm in a post box!

Residents of Botcherby were among the first to demand a post box. The first UK post box had been erected in Botchergate in 1853, as the commemorative plaque (left) shows. But do you remember this old box (right)? It was at the tradesman's entrance to Botcherby Home, down Banks Lane.

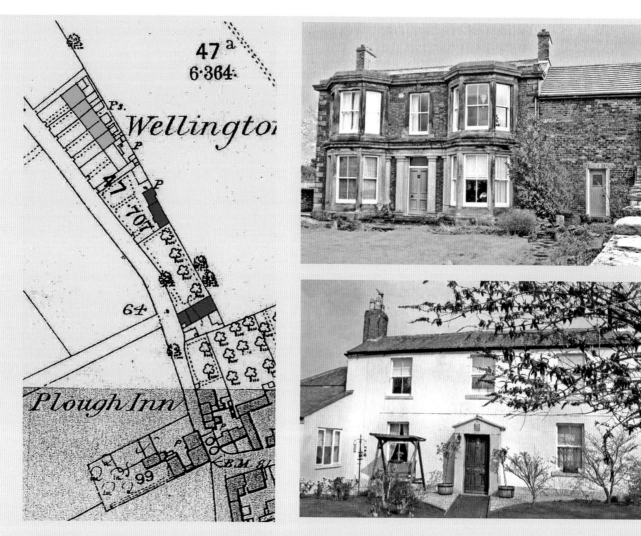

Linden House and Carleton House

Linden House and Carleton House are marked in red on this 1864 map, which also shows Wellington Place (in green); top - Carleton House dates from the 1770s; below - Linden House. Carleton House and Nos 35 to 43 Victoria Road form part of a conservation area, designated in 1968.

Carleton Terrace

This row of eight houses was built some time after Wellington Place but features on many of the older photographs of Victoria Road before it was widened. It used to have a name plaque attached to the terrace but this has disappeared over successive refurbishments.

Botcherby Hall

Botcherby Hall became a well-known landmark, sitting at the top of the hill, with its lodge standing on the long driveway leading to Warwick Road. The building is a castle-like structure with stained glass windows.

It was built in 1882 by Mr Wilson and advertised for sale or let in the *Carlisle Journal* on 7 September 1883:

> '*The Mansion has been recently built by the present owner and occupier, and is replete with all modern appliances and accessories. With the House may be had any quantity of fertile Garden Land adjoining, and a handsome Stone Lodge, at the approach from the Warwick Road, may be had or not, at the discretion of the tenant of the Mansion.*
>
> *C. P. HARDY, General Agent, 47 Lowther Street, Carlisle. August 16th, 1883.*'

Yet again on 23 September 1887 the *Carlisle Patriot* published the following advert:

> '*BOTCHERBY HALL to LET or SOLD. Early possession may be obtained. The above is pleasantly situated, has a charming view, spacious apartments with every convenience, including Stable, Coach house, &c. – Offers to S. HARRIS, House Agent, 36, Cecil Street.*'

Wellington Place and Victoria Road

Clockwise from top left: vignette of Wellington Place; 35 to 43 Victoria Road - formerly Wellington Place - five houses forming part of a terrace built in the 1830s or 1840s - 41 and 43 Victoria Road are of higher roof line, Grade II listed in 1994; looking up Botcherby Lane before the road was widened - it is still little more than a country lane but many of the houses we know today have already been built - the school is on the right, setting the date of the photo after 1900; Carleton Terrace, built after Wellington Place; later houses leading to the original schoolmaster's house for Botcherby School; 41 and 43 Victoria Road.

The property seems to have had a chequered history regarding ownership, as on 31 May 1889 the *Carlisle Journal* reported on the auction for its sale at the County Hotel, Carlisle. Among those bidding were Rev. Father James Thompson (Our Lady and St Joseph's Church), Mr T. Johnson, Mr Doughall, Mr Reay, Mr Briggs (Harraby), Mr Yates (Workington), and Mr Matthews. Bidding was brisk with Fr Thompson bidding up to £1,050 before dropping out, leaving Mr Doughall and Mr Yates as the final bidders. Mr Yates made the last bid of £1,250 but, as this did not reach the reserve of £1,500, the property was withdrawn from sale.

The Musgrave family lived in the hall by the turn of the century and it is under their ownership that it was to become a hub in the community's social events. Henry Musgrave was known as the 'Botcherby Squire' and, by June 1914, Mrs Musgrave was holding a garden party to raise funds for the East Window at St Aidan's Church. The weather was delightful and there was tennis, clock golf, sack races and cake stalls.

Other garden parties and events took place, some of which were attended by Lord Lonsdale and, in 1916, the Red Cross Garden Party was held there. After the end of the war Mrs Musgrave held a garden party in June 1920 to raise funds for the Botcherby War Memorial.

Botcherby Hall

Above: the map (centre) shows its 'strategic' position between Botcherby Home and the Magpie Inn. During WWI, Botcherby Hall was a favourite venue for fundraising events and garden parties. Clockwise from below left: school children and families; Lord Lonsdale with a small white pony; a Red Cross garden party, 1915; a Red Cross garden party, July 1916.

In 1928 the hall, lodge and grounds were up for sale with the agents being Waugh and Musgrave, solicitors of Cockermouth.

The City Treasurer reported to the Finance (Sub) Estates Committee on 31 December 1931 that Dr Philip de Mello had offered to purchase Botcherby Hall, together with the garden and a portion of the drive, comprising in all 2.096 acres, for the sum of £1,175.

> 'Resolved: That, subject to the approval of the Ministry of Health, the offer be accepted, in lieu of the proposal to sell the material in the building to the Carlisle and District State Management Scheme ... for £500.'

The sale went through and it was said locally that the doctor had bought the property to prevent a public house being built too close to St Joseph's Home. The Magpie, of course, was built in front of the hall on Victoria Road by 1933.

Dr de Mello was a 56-year-old Indian doctor who had qualified at Edinburgh and Oxford and had a medical practice at 30 Spencer Street in 1921 and, by 1928, at 2 Cecil Street. In that year also he went on a seven week trip to Bombay, departing Liverpool on the Anchor Line's SS *California.* He was well known locally as a kind and caring doctor who helped patients regardless of whether they could pay the fees. My grandparents were friends of his and recalled his philanthropic ideas long before there was a National Health Service. He is still remembered by Botcherby-born people today – some of whom were delivered by him!

In 1931 the Finance Committee of the City Council had negotiated with him to: *'Throw part of his land into the highway for the widening and improving of the Warwick Road/Victoria Road area.'* He must have felt under threat as the SMS indicated that it was prepared to purchase approximately 4,278 square yards of land fronting Victoria Road at an actual purchase price of £2000. It was also prepared to purchase and remove the hall buildings and pay the Corporation on that account.

In January 1932 Botcherby Hall and its grounds were under discussion again regarding the widening of Victoria Road. On 5 January, the Town Clerk reported to the Finance Committee that the Carlisle South End Cooperative Society had withdrawn its offer to purchase a piece of land, part of the Hall estate and fronting Victoria Road. They would eventually buy land near Croft Nurseries to build the shop in 1933.

At one point it looked as though the property might be requisitioned by the Army - after WW2 they tried to acquire it under defence regulations. Once it became apparent that it had already been leased to two families with a third lease in the offing, the bid was dropped.

St Joseph's Home and Botcherby Hall both had driveways that wended their way down to Warwick Road, and both had lodges halfway down the drive. On 6 April 1948 the Council Finance Committee considered reports by the Surveyor and Chief Sanitary Inspector regarding the condition of Botcherby Hall Lodge. Through the war years it had fallen into disrepair, and the Surveyor reported that: *'there is no immediate prospect of any re-building of the premises being possible.'* Authorisation was given to demolish the building and Mr R. Liddle was paid £5 to do the work.

Today, with the demolition of St Joseph's Home, Botcherby Hall with all its memories still stands proudly like a turreted castle overlooking the Magpie Inn. Surrounded by housing developments, it is now turned into apartments.

Charlotte Terrace

Charlotte Terrace is the pretty row of 12 cottages off Warwick Road, standing around the corner from the old Star Inn and back-to-back with Victoria Road. They first appear in the Carlisle Directory in 1890 and, if bricks could speak, no doubt the cottages could tell some tales!

Charlotte Terrace

Clockwise from top left: the midden man clearing out night waste in Charlotte Terrace; a 19th-C. drainage ditch collecting the waste from houses adjacent to Warwick Road. It passed under the houses and joined the sewer which discharged in front of the Star Inn; the old grain store at the end of Charlotte Terrace; today's replacement - a bed centre; the houses in Charlotte Terrace today.

Tilbury Road

Before Eastern Way was built, Tilbury Road used to stretch from Warwick Road to the bottom of Wood Street. In those days, it was home to Bill Bradley and his sister. He worked on the dustcarts and acquired a considerable collection of unwanted china ornaments which he proudly displayed on his garden wall. No doubt, some of his Staffordshire dogs would merit a place on the *Antiques Roadshow* today! Also on the original part of Tilbury Road lived Brian Dixon and his family - his father worked for the Caseys at Botcherby Farm. Today a much reduced Tilbury Road simply comprises 14 terraced houses in front of Rosehill Industrial Estate.

Tilbury Road

Left: Tilbury Road in the early-20th C.
Below right: Tilbury Road today.
Below left: map showing Tilbury Road before the building of Eastern Way - in those days it was a continuation of Wood Street. The brick and tile works can be seen behind the terraced houses.
For more information on Tilbury Road, see the later section on WW1 and the Anderson family.

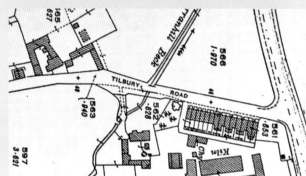

Ambrose Holme, last house in the township

Jackie Stubbs and Alex Proudfoot, along with other Botcherby men, have memories of a childhood place which stirred their imagination. They played there often in the 1950s – there were two brick walls standing which could have held a window or a fireplace, a few trees from a long-gone orchard where apple trees were turning back to crabs, the remains of gooseberry bushes, all encircled by a raised mound which offered little protection from the rain and floods which would often cover the area.

To get there you had to go over Warwick Road at Wheelbarrow Hall, beyond Johnny Bulldog's Lonning (shown below in Alan Cleaver's picture) and across towards Linstock, within sight of the river Eden. There were memories from the 1920s of coffins being carried high onto flat-bed trucks and taken down the lane to the church. But there was a magic and mystery about the place. It was not until this book was being researched that this strange place found its name.

It had been the last house in the township of Botcherby and named Ambrose Holme, standing a few hundred yards from the Eden, and within a loop of the river. All that now remains are a few bricks lying among the grass and undergrowth. But it had an interesting past and links with the renowned Carlisle miser: a schedule of Margery Jackson's property compiled in 1791 shows that she owned the estate and collected an annual rent of £10. At this time she also owned Botcherby Mill and many other local properties.

Home to the Hudsons

Ambrose Holme estate was a unique property, not only in its location but in its size. The deeds in 1807 record

that there was a farmhouse, barn, stable, cowhouse, garden, orchard and 50 acres, and a nearby well. In addition, there were four seats in pew 107 in St Cuthbert's Church in Carlisle.

The puzzle is why would anyone build such a property so close to the river and on a well-known flood plain? James Robinson has often asked himself this question, as he has traced his family history back to the days when his ancestors, the Hudson family, farmed Ambrose Holme.

The 1841 census shows that Thomas Hudson, a husbandry labourer, aged 55, and his wife Jane, aged 50 and born at Lanercost, along with their three children, Elizabeth 10, John 7 and Thomas 5 all lived at Ambrose Holme. On 29 September 1847 tragedy struck the family as Thomas senior died of chronic bronchitis, and Jane was left to carry on the work on the farm.

Four years later in 1851 the house was quite full, as Jane was housekeeper, helped by Thomas junior, by now 14, working as well as studying at school. She also had Isabella Sill, a 16-year-old servant girl from Hayton to help. Her nephew, seven-year-old John Modlin from Newcastle was staying there and Margaret Bell, a 30 year-old widow from Wetheral, was visiting along with her eight-month-old twins, Elinor and Margaret.

The tragedy of James Edward Bell

A sad event occurred in December 1854 when a young man lost his life at Ambrose Holme. He was James Edward Bell, an apprentice to a millwright in Cockermouth whose parents lived in Wigton. He had been spending Christmas at the Tait Street home of his sister and brother-in-law Daniel Johnstone in Carlisle. A few days after Christmas he left the house at 9.30am in good spirits, intending to spend a sporting day shooting small birds and saying he would be back for dinner. He did not return and the next afternoon his body was discovered in Ambrose Holme, by the side of the Eden, about a mile east of Botcherby Lane-end (now Victoria Road) and opposite the village of Linstock.

The coroner's inquest was held at Botcherby on Saturday, 30 December, in the Dixon's Arms Inn (later called the Star Inn) and was reported in the *Carlisle Journal* on 5 January 1855. It appears that James Bell was a victim of a freak accident and died of a gunshot wound. He had been trying to cross a place where there were two rails as part of a thorn fence, over a mound allowing flood water to pass from one field to another. With his feet on one rail and holding the other with his hands while still holding the gun, he had fallen as he leapt off the rail and his gun had gone off causing wounds to his lungs and a major artery. The place where the accident occurred was directly under Rose Hill Lodge and a quarter of a mile from any dwelling.

Mr Carrick, the coroner summed up the evidence saying that the trigger could have caught on thorns from the fence causing it to go off. A verdict of 'accidental death' was recorded.

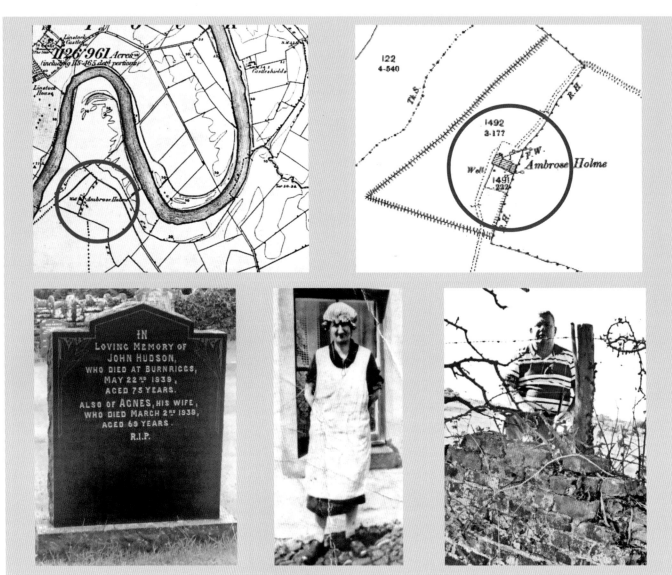

Clockwise from the top left: two old maps showing the location and layout of Ambrose Holme; James M. Robinson, whose research into his Hudson ancestors unearthed the fascinating story of Ambrose Holme; Lizzie Hudson (1896-1931), grandmother to James M. Robinson; the grave of John Hudson at St Leonard's Church, Warwick-on-Eden.

Fighting back the floods

Floods must have been a way of life for the Hudson family and their neighbours. On Friday, 19 December 1856, the *Carlisle Journal* headlined *'THE LATE FLOOD'* giving a vivid description of the deluge the previous Sunday and Monday:

> *'From Corby the river rushes with immense force past Warwick Bridge and Warwick Hall - after which its course becomes more level, and the banks being lower it has more room to spread... it was impossible to look at the immense volume of water sweeping along with resistless force over hedges, banks, and everything which had previously been considered a barrier against the inroad of even the highest flood, and not be sensible of the devastation it was committing in its course.'*

It seems that Ambrose Holme and other local farmsteads relied on high earth embankments to protect their livestock and property. Mr Hall of Warwick Holme and Mr Wannop of Castle Shields *'toiled for hours in a fruitless attempt to keep out the water in that direction.'* It was a dramatic night: each time they rescued sheep they would turn to find broken banks and water making its way into the farmyards and fold yard. Mrs Hall waded through the water without light to set the cattle loose, where they made their way to the embankment that surrounded the buildings and stack-yard, but many were drowned as the waters rose above the bank. The horses in the stables were reached by getting through the hay lofts from boats.

> *'Four horses belonging to Mr Robson, of Linstock Castle, stood upon the top of a narrow embankment, a few inches above water, a great part of Sunday, but were got to swim behind a boat to Ambrose*

Holme... Mrs Hudson, of Ambrose Holme, saved her fat pig, about 13 or 14 stones weight, notwithstanding the proverbial obstinacy of those animals, by getting it upstairs.

'The damage done is very great, holes being made that will take thousands of yards of soil to fill up, all along through Warwick holme and Linstock holme.'

By the time of the 1861 census Jane, by now 70 years old, is shown as the only occupant along with her unmarried daughter, 29-year-old Elizabeth Jane. Thomas is not recorded on the census, but on Friday, 1 April 1864 this notice appeared in the *Carlisle Journal*:

'Lost, about the 13th of February, from WETHERAL ABBEY, a GREY CUR DOG, with White on fore legs, breast and face, and long shaggy hair, answers to the name "HEMP". Whoever has found the same on returning it to Mr. THOMAS HUDSON, Ambrose Holme, Carlisle, will be rewarded for their trouble. Anyone detaining it after this notice will be prosecuted.

March 30 1864'

We haven't heard if Hemp was found!

In 1871 Jane was still there now aged 80, along with Elizabeth and a visitor Mary Dixon. A few years later, after more than 40 years of struggling with difficult conditions, Jane left Ambrose Holme and went to live at nearby Aglionby with her son Thomas. He had married Elizabeth Fletcher from Langholm and had three daughters, Margaret 13, Elizabeth 10, Mary Ellen 4. The couple also had a son, John, who was born in 1863. Jane at 90 years old is noted on the census as a 'lodger boarder' and would live there until her death on 19 February 1884 at the age of 93. What stories she might have told of her life on the edge of Botcherby township.

By 26 November 1897, Cartmell and Burnett, solicitors at 27 Lowther Street, Carlisle were advertising in the *Carlisle Journal* that Ambrose Holme grazing land was to let.

'To be let, with entry at Candlemas next, for a term of years, or as may be agreed upon, all that Grazing land, situate at and called Ambrose Holme, in the Township of Botcherby, Carlisle and containing 57 Acres, or thereabouts, together with the Shepherd's Cottage, Garden and Outhouses occupied therewith.'

A suicide by the river

Another tragedy struck at Ambrose Holme and was reported in the *Carlisle Express and Examiner* on 5 June 1898. This time the report was of a suicide when 25-year-old Herbert Lees, a draughtsman at Cowans Sheldon & Co. Engineering Works on London Road was found dead at the edge of the river Eden opposite Rickerby Rocks. He was the son of Mr Herbert Lees, the much-respected master at Carlisle School of Art. Two walkers discovered his body and ran to the County Police Station in Earl Street to raise the alarm. A silver-plated revolver was found beside the body. The coroner's inquest took place at the Star Inn and the foreman of the jury was Mr Richard Graham of Botcherby. Dr Barnes of Portland Square told the inquest that he had known Herbert all his life and that he was a strong healthy man until three months ago when he suffered a seizure while at the theatre and was unconscious for four hours. He diagnosed him as suffering from organic brain disease which caused suicidal tendencies, and had no doubt that he was temporarily insane when he shot himself.

This was confirmed as the verdict and much sympathy was extended to Mr Lees and his family.

By 1901 a 60-year-old couple, Charles Lambert and his wife Mary, lived at the farmstead where Charles worked as a cattle stockman. He was born in London and Mary was from Stockdalewath. Their son George was a railway engine fitter and daughter Mary was a domestic servant.

The Hudson family would continue to live at Aglionby through the next generations, as John married Agnes Bradley and had a daughter Lizzie, born in 1896. Lizzie married James Robinson and was grandmother to James M. Robinson.

The resting place of generations of Hudsons is at St Leonard's Church, Warwick-on-Eden.

We still do not know what life at Ambrose Holme was really like. How they coped with the constant floods as the Eden burst its banks and they lived amid a sea of water. The difficulties are unimaginable. Eventually it seems that Ambrose Holme farmhouse was left derelict, at the mercy of the elements, until it disintegrated into the few bricks that it is today.

The area remains today dwarfed by the M6 motorway. On 31 December 2009 the *Cumberland News* reported that the village of Linstock was to get a £250,000 noise barrier to protect it from the sound of the M6 motorway:

'The improvements, funded by the Department of Transport, will take place at the Ambrose Holme, Johnny Bulldog's Lonning and Rosehill flood relief bridges, all on the M6 north east of Carlisle. Work will be carried out to renew waterproofing, joints and parapets... the bridges, between junctions 43 and 44 of the M6 carry a one mile section of the motorway, just south of the River Eden.'

Jane Hudson would never have believed it.

The view from Ambrose Holme today - with the M6 motorway in the background, bricks and rubble are all that remain of the old house.

Nothing besides remains...

On a brilliantly sunny day in July 2014, James, Alex Proudfoot and I went to see Ambrose Holme and reminisce on what it must have been like to live there. The farmer was helpful and gave permission for us to go through the gates and down the tracks by the barley fields that brought us within a short distance of the lovely meandering river Eden. After braving the final gate and a herd of inquisitive cows there it was, the land of Ambrose Holme. It was very flat, with a mound visible where the boundary of the farm had been, and small fragments of brick walls. We captured the pictures and marvelled at how anyone survived extensive floods here: in the distance was the hum of the motorway, a modern reminder of a different way of life. Next we paid a visit to the graveyard at St Leonard's Church where John Hudson is buried, and then on to the Antiques Fair and tea at Warwick Hall. A perfect summer's day.

Rose Hill House and Wheelbarrow Hall

Although, strictly speaking, both Rose Hill House and Wheelbarrow Hall were just outside the boundaries of the old Botcherby township, their histories are so intertwined with the village's life, that they merit inclusion here.

Rose Hill House, Scotby was built on the site of the original farmhouse by the Bond family who had land in the area since the 17th century. They owned an estate near Aglionby of 70 acres, including Wheelbarrow Hall (in the area known as Holme Park) and Rose Hill. In April 1788 the estate was advertised for sale in the *Newcastle Courant* but members of the family still lived in the area and still owned land at Scotby. In the late 18th century Wheelbarrow Hall was used as the Parish Workhouse. John Smith Bond (1779-1835) married Elizabeth Powe (1793-1855), who was a granddaughter of Isaac Bond, and they returned to live at Rose Hill where they built the mansion in 1835. It must have been a beautiful sight when, in 1848, Joshua Major and Son, landscape gardeners of Knosthorpe, Leeds, were commissioned to design and lay out the grounds. Elizabeth Bond also bought back the adjacent Wheelbarrow Hall.

Wheelbarrow Hall and Rose Hill House

Clockwise from top left: old map showing the proximity of Wheelbarrow Hall and Rose Hill House; Wheelbarrow Hall today; detail from Ogilby's map from 1675, showing Wheelbarrow Hall and the road to 'Botcherbie'; Rose Hill House and Lodge, photographed in the 1980s.

John Smith Bond was a doctor and his only surviving child Eliza Indiana married another doctor Henry Lonsdale (1816-1876) on 26 May 1851. They had three sons and three daughters. Eliza died in June 1905 aged 81. Carlisle-born Henry Lonsdale was a gifted man having studied medicine in Edinburgh and Paris and was a Member of the Royal College of Surgeons. In 1846 he returned to Carlisle and was a physician at the Cumberland Infirmary for the next 22 years. He wrote several learned books.

His descendants continued to live at Rose Hill House until Amelia Lonsdale left the property in memory of her husband, another Henry Lonsdale 'for the benefit of Cumbria's gentlefolk'. Amelia died in 1975 and by 1981 the Henry Lonsdale Trust opened it as a residential care home for 40 residents.

Mr Joseph Fell bought the historic Wheelbarrow Hall in 1979 after his father and uncle had tenanted the land since 1911 and farmed the 500 acres until his untimely death in October 2002. Seventy-five-year-old Mr Fell collapsed with a stroke the day after hundreds of sheep on the farm were culled following a foot and mouth disease outbreak on a neighbouring farm. He left an estate of more than £1 million. On one memorable occasion in 1998 flash floods in one of his fields left him stranded on the roof of his tractor. Drivers on the M6 motorway fortunately saw him and he was rescued by fire fighters using an inflatable walkway: the river Eden once again causing danger to those farming this area leading to Ambrose Holme. Mr Fell's son Neil became the fourth generation of the family at Wheelbarrow Hall. Today Wheelbarrow Hall is used as a nursery school housed in two converted farm buildings.

The city beckons

Throughout the 19th century Botcherby township had developed slowly but surely - and with a strong sense of independence from its larger neighbour, Carlisle. With the dawn of the 20th century all this was about to change.

On 22 December 1903, just a few days before Christmas, the *Carlisle Journal* reported on a meeting held in Botcherby School. The subject was one of great contention and a good number of the local ratepayers attended to give their views. Carlisle Corporation was proposing to extend the city limits to include Botcherby, Harraby and part of Wetheral and therefore receive the rates from these areas. The reason was not to the benefit of the areas, but rather, to gain more money for the city's coffers and was fiercely resisted. The area came under the Rural District Council at this time.

It was a very lively meeting as the report shows:

'THE CITY EXTENSION SCHEME. OPPOSITION AT BOTCHERBY

'Mr. Butler, Durran Hill House presided and amongst those present were Mr. Wood, Bramerton Lodge; Mr. Nutsford, Carleton House; Miss Norman, Messrs. J. R. Matthews, R. Graham, W. Graham, R. Robinson, George Fairbairn, J. Holme, Arthur Bell, Bristowe, Cartner, Simpson, McBride, Thompson, R. Davidson, Grice, and Chapman, Botcherby; Mr. Baty, the Brickworks; Hodgkinson, Harraby Green; and Wilson, Harraby.

'The Chairman said... The question was whether or not they would accept with open arms the Corporation of Carlisle, who wished to take them into their bosom, although he did not know what they intended doing when they got them there. (Laughter.) Carlisle appeared to want to shove something down their throats and to educate them when they had got a little past the age. Botcherby had done very well in the past and could do equally well in the future. Of course, the city had grown and wanted to extend its boundaries, whether on account of its past maladministration or the prospects of better administration in the future he could not say.

'If the Carlisle rates had got to a certain point – and he believed they were pretty oppressive in the city – why should they be included in the city to pay for things on which their views had never been asked? He could not see what they were to get by being included. Householders might get a little, but the people who held land would get nothing. The Carlisle scheme was to increase the credit of the city and enable it to borrow more money in the future (Hear, hear.) The scheme touched their pockets, which were the sorest points about a man. (Laughter.) He believed that Mr. Baty and he were the only ratepayers of Wetheral who were to be included in the city and he would be delighted to join with Botcherby to do anything that could be done to protest in some proper and legal way against the scheme. (Cheers.)'

A committee was appointed to consider what steps should be taken to oppose the Carlisle Corporation Bill and its effects. The report continues:

'In Botcherby the rates were 3s. 2d. in the £, as compared with 6s. 5d. in the city, to say nothing of what they would be when the Geltsdale and sewage schemes were carried out... there were scores of acres of land within the present city boundary still unbuilt on, and there was no need for the city to cross the Petteril.'

It seems that the Botcherby ratepayers won the day as Botcherby did not come within the city boundaries at that time. But it was only a fate deferred until 1912, when the city redrew the boundaries to absorb Botcherby. The days of the Botcherby township were finally over.

1912 – the end of Botcherby township

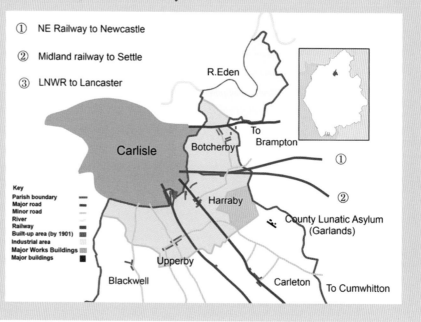

Above: a boundary stone on London Road showing the newly extended boundaries of the city of Carlisle in 1912 - a process that saw Botcherby finally lose its township status (Martin & Jean Norgate/Portsmouth University). Right: detail of map showing 1912 boundary changes marked in green (Eric Apperley/ Cumbria County History Trust).

① NE Railway to Newcastle

② Midland railway to Settle

③ LNWR to Lancaster

Key
Parish boundary
Major road
Minor road
River
Railway
Built-up area (by 1901)
Industrial area
Major Works Buildings
Major buildings

◆◆◆

Early trade and transport

The 19th century and early 20th century saw a gradual increase in trade in Botcherby township and a significant development in road, rail and – briefly – air links. Here we look at some of the key changes and events over that time...

Botcherby Mill

Botcherby Mill marks the outer limits of the old township bordering on Carlisle's city boundary. The picture above, by W. Hodgson, shows it in its heyday, during Victorian times. It was located in Greystone Road and was serviced by its own mill race feeding into the river Petteril, grinding corn from at least 1644. It appears on G. Smith's 1746 map of Carlisle commemorating the Jacobite siege but subsequently *'with some cattle, was quite swept away'* in the great flood of 1771.

In 1790 Margery Jackson rebuilt the old family asset and marked the fact with a tablet above the front door bearing the inscription:

> *'Miss Margery Jackson, sister of W. N. Jackson Esq., rebuilt this mill 1790'*

During the 19th century it trad a number of owners but still functioned as a mill. In 1822 it was owned by a Mr Waugh, who lost three pigs in the floods (floods are a recurring theme in this area of Botcherby); in 1829 the miller was Richard Irving but, in 1834, the name is given as Irwin; by 1847, W. Robinson is shown as

Botcherby Mill and after

Clockwise from above left: Botcherby Mill in the 1970s when it was home to a tyre company; the site of the old Botcherby Mill - now part of the Riverside Way development; this 19th C. map clearly shows the mill race feeding into the river Petteril at Botcherby Bridge; advert for the Cumberland Tyre Co.; part of the new Riverside Way development; the back of old Botcherby Mill; evidence of the old mill waterwheel in the worn away stones of the mill wall.

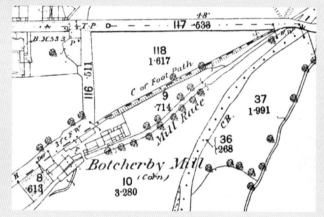

manager, and in the 1861 census, Elizabeth Rayson is resident, with a 'corn miller' as a servant and two apprentices. In 1863 it was being advertised to let with Mr Robinson given as the present tenant.

By the 20th century it was no longer milling corn and had become a dairy farm, run by Thomas Johnston. He and his wife, Jane Ann, were still resident there, but by then they had paid a high price for their family's contribution to the war effort, having lost two sons - Rowland, aged 26 in 1915, and Thomas Henry, aged just 19 in 1918. For further information about Botcherby's war dead, see the next chapter.

In 1934, it was housing an engineering company and in the 1950s the Cumberland Tyre Company had located there. After that it stood empty for some years before the, now derelict, buildings burned down in 1995. Nowadays, the site is part of the Riverside Way development.

.

The Brick and Tile Works

When Paul Marshall was working on a chimney stack at John Hartley's house at Aglionby, he found that the bricks were from Botcherby Brickworks, dating from the 1880s. It made a fascinating connection on two counts: the origin of the bricks, and the fact that the Hartley family were well-known residents of Botcherby in the 1950s and 1960s.

Bricks had been made at Botcherby since the 18th century - as described in an early surviving document, a building contractor's account for bricks and plastering of the Town Hall during alterations to the inner hall of the gallery in 1733. It notes that *'1500 bricks from Botcherby, 500 from Gosling Sike and 100 from Town Dike Gate were used.'* There is even earlier evidence of brick usage, dating to 1400, with the infill between the timber frame on the Guildhall and also in the tile tower in Carlisle Castle, built in 1483.

Today it is still possible to see the date 1700 in raised bricks on the right gable end of one of the earliest

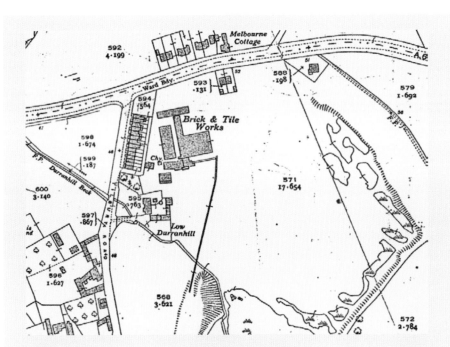

The Brick and Tile Works

Clockwise from top left: map showing the Brick and Tile Works in the 1920s, with extensive clay pits that provided the raw material for over two centuries; Norman House, Wood Street with the date '1700' marked out in Botcherby brick on the gable end; a Botcherby brick; site of the brick works with the outbuildings of Low Durranhill House in the centre and Tilbury Road to the right; Low Durranhill house, once home of the brick works manager, off Tilbury Road.

houses in Wood Street, Norman House. These bricks would have been made at the Botcherby brickfields. The brick works stood at Low Durranhill on an extensive area to the eastern side of Tilbury Road which today is part of Rosehill Industrial Estate, off Warwick Road. There are few surviving photos of the brickworks, but the illustrations from 1922 give an idea of the clay pits which, together with the firing kilns and rail tracks, made up the extensive operation.

The bricks were made in the local area to avoid transporting them, and Botcherby bricks were used in building houses at Aglionby and surrounding areas.

Botcherby Brickworks seem to have been very successful and by 11 March 1826, John Holme was advertising in the *Carlisle Journal* that large quantities of bricks were for sale. An interesting letter appeared in the *Citizen* on 1 September 1828 when George Dobinson wrote *'I cast clay for a brick kiln, the Botcherby people led it away to the bank of the Eden...'*

Adverts for the sale of bricks often appeared in the local press, as in the *Carlisle Journal* on 2 June 1832 when T. Robson & Co. of Botcherby Brickfields had bricks 'constantly on sale' from their premises at 27 West Walls. By 1869 the company was owned by Allan's and adverts in the local papers announced an inexhaustible supply of clay and water for making bricks and tiles, with four kilns of bricks for sale in Allan's Close, where three acres of water and clay were available.

The company changed hands between 1874 and 1894 and was sometimes called Durranhill Brickworks. The white house built for the manager still stands today.

In 1876 Thomas Mounsey was the proprietor and by 1884 Robert Metcalf was the manager.

Botcherby brick works in 1922, cutting the clay. Left: looking south-west, showing the method of cutting laminated clay;. Right: looking north-east, showing laminated clay with overlying sand and the method of cutting clay (National Environment Research Council).

In the *Carlisle Journal* on 27 July 1886 an advert stated that *'a working foreman brickmaker was wanted at once to live at the works. Free house and coals. Apply 84 London Road.'*

A letter in the *Carlisle Journal* on 10 April 1894 complained of an 'offensive smell' on the road between the Star Inn and the beck that comes out of the brickfield's stagnant ditch. *'Warwick Road is the most fashionable promenade of the citizens of Carlisle and it is desirable that it should be kept free from dangers of health.'*

James Baty & Sons owned the brickworks by the 1890s and business was brisk by 1907, when the *Carlisle Journal* reported that the building of new schools had increased the demand for bricks. James Baty died on 12 December 1909 and his will shows that he left £7,929 18s 2d gross to his sons, Christopher and William.

The start of WW1 brought problems to the brickworks, with a shortage of workers and a shortage of bricks, as staff were drafted into the armed forces. Such was the extent of the problem that Messrs Baty appealed to a Tribunal to gain the release of a key worker. The report in the *Carlisle Journal* on 29 February 1916 details the appeal: George Graham was the foreman brick setter at the kilns at Botcherby - his employers stated that he was indispensible and if the firm lost his services they would have to close down the works. William Baty informed the Tribunal that Graham had to set his bricks to be baked and it was technical work for which he had only trained four men in 24 years. He was given an exemption until 31 May!

But the problem persisted and by 23 May 1919 the *Carlisle Journal* again reported that Baty's wanted the release of Joseph Carr and George Graham from the Army:

> 'The firm of Messrs J. Baty & Sons, Botcherby Brickworks, who are the employers of these men are unable to supply bricks owing to the retention of these men in the army.'

The Editor commenting on the brick industry said the greatest difficulty was the shortage of bricks: *'at one time nearly every builder had his own brickfield.'*

In 1925 Forster Ridley & Sons were listed as owners. By 1936 coal was being supplied by Chapel Burn colliery, over in Durham, and described as of a good class and being well-suited to brick works. It was supplied to brickworks at Botcherby and Kingmoor. Brian Dixon recalls that: *'the clay ponds had a narrow gauge railway and a pony pulled the bogey, the pony was guided.'*

Botcherby Brick & Tile Co. has long gone, but there are still many 'young' Botcherby boys who recall their childhood escapades from years ago. The clay pits were a place of danger and stern warnings were issued by many mothers: it did not deter the intrepid explorers and many a tale can be told.

A memory of this time is recalled by James Ord:

> 'There were two ponds at the clay pits 30 to 40 feet deep, and there were swans and bulrushes there... the boys would build a raft with empty barrels and straddle the barrels, gradually their legs got further apart and they fell in the water. They went home and told their mothers that they had fallen in the beck, as they were forbidden to go to the clay pits... one boy, Joe, fell in the pond in winter and got pneumonia – he was given the last rites, but he recovered. The ponds froze in winter, in 1942 and '47 there was a slope down and the boys wore clogs - the ice was cracking – loads of boys went.'

John Myers recalls that, in the 1940s, the knights of the road would come over the footpath to Botcherby Avenue, where his mother would give them sandwiches and tea. They would journey on to the brickworks for heat – and end up covered in red dye. After the clay pits were filled in, it was discovered that breeze blocks could be made of the ash left over from the brick-making process and Ginger Liddle, later of Mountelm Ltd, used the ash out of the clay pits to supply the market. They were later re-filled by the Corporation.

It seems that the brickworks did not survive long after the end of WW2 as the *Cumberland News* reported on 6 September 1947 that the landmark at Botcherby *'and familiar to those travelling to and from Wetheral has disappeared... so long a feature seen by the golfers at Durranhill.'*

William Baty, the long-time owner of the brickworks, died in March 1949 and the *Cumberland News* gave interesting information in his obituary. He died at his home at Blackwell Vale and was survived by one son and six daughters and grandchildren. He had married Elizabeth Grigg whose parents had the Black Bull at Upperby. The second son of Mrs James Baty of Currock Terrace, he started his career in his father's business. One of his early jobs was the laying of the first and last stones of the museum and art gallery at Tullie House. He was connected with the Botcherby Brickworks until his retirement.

For years after this, the future of the land that once housed the brickworks was undecided. In 1955-56 the Carlisle City Minutes reveal that the Department of Education reported that the owner of the land wanted to know the future use of the land earmarked for educational use. It was agreed that no action be taken. Again in 1957 the City Council was reviewing the situation regarding playing fields and educational use. The situation was finally resolved with the building of Rosehill Industrial Estate.

Carlisle Steam Laundry

Carlisle Steam Laundry on Warwick Road started business around 1890 in the old Raven Nook Woollen Mill which was built in 1850 off Greystone Road, and traded under the name of Raven Nook Steam Laundry. Due to its success it was decided to remove to a site of almost two acres on Warwick Road on the banks of the river Petteril and, by April 1892, tenders were invited to design the new building.

Designed by T. Taylor Scott, architect of Carlisle, and built by James Beaty of Kingstown Brickworks, it opened in 1893 with further additions being made to the building in 1902 and 1905. As well as the laundry building, a row of twelve houses known as Petteril Bridge Terrace was also erected in 1895. The original promoters were Mr J. T. Graham and Mr James Pearson, with directors Mr William Graves and the late Mayor, Mr Matthew Johnstone.

Carlisle Steam Laundry

Clockwise from top left: postcard of the original laundry; the same view today; 1893 elevation of the proposed steam laundry; 1893 plan of the steam laundry; 1927 map showing the steam laundry before the building of Warwick Terrace.

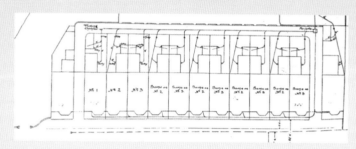

The new laundry was considered the largest and most complete modern laundry in the North of England and over the years would employ many Botcherby people. Renamed the Carlisle Steam Laundry and Carpet Beating Company, it provided a service second to none. On 3 March 1893 the *Carlisle Journal* gave a detailed report on the state-of-the-art building whose smart horse-driven vans became a familiar sight on Warwick Road, trotting along beside the tram lines:

> 'The vans, after collecting the goods, enter a large vestibule, from which the articles are taken into a large sorting room fitted up with benches and bins. After all the articles have been carefully arranged and entered in their proper sections, they are transferred to the large washhouse, equipped with all the most modern machinery. This building is parallel with the machinery and ironing room, covering an area of about 4,000 superficial feet, and is divided from it by glass screens, and the busy line of workers, all smartly attired with white blouses, presents an interesting sight to the visitor.'

The laundering techniques were surprisingly modern: wringing the clothes was a thing of the past, as the water was extracted from them by means of compressed air. The drying was unique, with a powerful fan drawing a current of air through a tube from the outside of the building, which passed over a series of steam-heated pipes, delivering it into the chamber where the clothes were hung. Curtains, flannels and fancy-coloured fabrics were washed in distilled water and dried in a special chamber with a mild and even temperature.

> 'The large ironing machines are marvels of simplicity. The collar machines turn out their work at a rapid rate, many thousands of this one article alone being done every week... the old-fashioned flat irons have been consigned to the scrap heap and their place taken by internally-heated gas irons kept at one uniform heat. A new feature is the glass screen airing room heated to a high temperature, into which all goods pass on leaving the hands of the workers, and afterwards into the large heated packing room, where they are arranged in trellis bins, packed, and sent home.'

A separate building held the carpet-beating department where, in addition to the normal beating, the carpets were brushed by machinery. Other buildings held powerful engines and the boiler, together with van sheds, stabling for the horses and the store house.

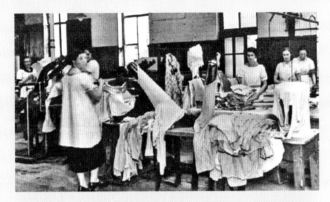

Clockwise from top left: working as part of the war effort, 1942 (Carlisle Library); advert for the steam laundry during Carlisle Pageant celebrations 1951; Carlisle Steam Laundry stand at an exhibition in Carlisle Drill Hall; van drivers around 1950: left to right - Jack Kyle, Wilson Johnstone, Dick Routledge, William Brown, Dave Birrell, Bobby Potts, Tommy Thompson, Willie Young, the manager William Batsen, Tommy Day, Alf Taylor, John McGuiggan, Len Houston and Fred Whalley; one of the fleet of electric delivery vans; laundry staff taking a break in the 1950s - Alice Grice is at the front, kneeling; letter heading 1934; an early delivery van.

Twenty years later, in a special feature on Carlisle industries, the *Carlisle Journal* reported on 18 November 1913 on the continued success of the laundry:

> *'Today the laundry is a household word, and eight vans travel in Carlisle and within a radius of 12 or 14 miles of the city... but not all of the goods arrive by van... In practically every town in the North of*

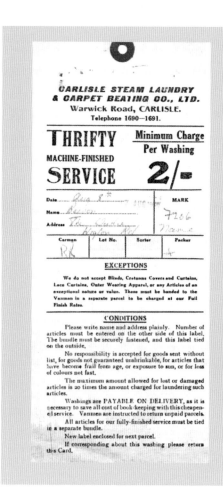

Carlisle Steam Laundry bill

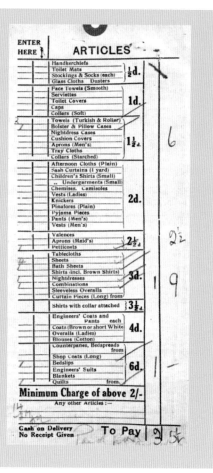

The price of keeping clothes clean: minimum 2/- a wash!

This particular wash came to 3s 51/2d, comprising:

3 towels

1 bolster/pillow case

4 sheets

1 bath sheet

1 nightdress

1 combinations

1 bedslip

1 quilt

England and over the Border agents gather articles to be cleaned, and despatch them weekly by rail, some immense packages being received in this way, either for washing, dyeing, beating, or what is termed "dry cleaning" or as it is called in the laundry "French" cleaning.'

Mr John Stewardson was manager by this time and his son, Edgar Marsden Stewardson, assisted his father at the laundry before moving to Messrs Spiers & Pond's Laundry in London. He enlisted with the Rifle Brigade in 1915 and was killed in action at the Battle of the Somme on 16 September 1916 at the age of 25. He is remembered on the Thiepval Memorial in France.

Stan Sullivan of Dumfries has memories of the Steam Laundry in 1939 when he had an 'unofficial' Saturday job there. Stan was born at Botcherby Avenue in August 1930 and lived there until he married in 1952. His father was from Waterford in Southern Ireland and came over to Carlisle at the same time as the Casey, Dias and Fitzgerald families. Stan recalls:

'I went to Brook Street School before passing the Merit exam. I took a job (unofficial) with the Carlisle Steam Laundry on Warwick Road. I went with a van driver, Norman Pascoe who had a club foot and I collected the laundry and delivered the cleaned laundry. Our route on Saturday was from Burgh Road, Carlisle to Port Carlisle and surrounding villages. I was nine years old and Norman showed me how to drive the van, which was electric and only had two pedals. After two miles outside the Carlisle boundary I usually drove the van. I stayed in the job (Saturdays only) for a year then worked at Ridley's the Chemist at the top of English Street.'

Botcherby Bridge

A wintry Botcherby Bridge in 1929 showing the steam laundry on the left and the Star Inn in the distance. As the volume of traffic continued to grow, it became apparent that neither the bridge nor the road were up to the future demands on them. Something had to happen!

Petteril Bridge Terrace

As part of the steam laundry development on Warwick Road a dozen new houses were built in front of it - this became Petteril Bridge Terrace, completed in 1895. The plan shows the design for the manager's house, drawn to cater for the awkwardly shaped entry to the steam laundry - dictated by the course of the river.

The van only travelled at five or six miles an hour and Stan vividly remembers the day at Drumburgh when he hit a cow: happily it survived!

The laundry provided regular employment for many people from Botcherby. Ann Ditchburn, for example, recalls that her mother, Mrs Olive Wilson, worked there from 1949 to 1973 and was presented with a wrist-watch on her retirement. Ann's uncle, Jack Quigley, also worked there before becoming a barman at the Magpie.

Turnpike Trusts and tolls

In the days before the establishment of the County Councils and County Borough Councils in 1888, Botcherby came under the control of the civil parish, and had township status. The road east out of Carlisle to Brampton was very often in a poor state of repair, and the increase in wheeled carts and heavy wagons travelling in the late 17th and early 18th centuries meant that maintenance of the roads was inadequate. Between 1555-1835 road maintenance was the responsibility of unpaid parish surveyors and statute labour and only adequate for the roads that the parishioners used themselves. It was unsatisfactory for principal highways used by long-distance travellers as the parish rates were insufficient to pay for the wear and tear on the roads.

Parliament decided to introduce a system of turnpike roads whereby local trusts would be set up with Trustees responsible for collecting the tolls and maintaining the highways. The Trustees were not paid but were often local businessmen who benefited from the improved flow of trade between towns. The Trusts erected turnpike gates on the sections of road affected and there would be a cottage for the toll-keeper. By the 1750s they were responsible for erecting milestones between main towns. A fixed toll was charged and, eventually, the Trusts were allowed to auction a lease to collect tolls to local business people.

The Turnpike Trust Act of 1773 had seen many major roads taken over by the Trusts, and in Carlisle turnpikes with toll gates were established on major roads radiating from the city. Such was the rutted state of the old road that General Wade was unable to move his artillery from Newcastle to fight Bonnie Prince Charlie in 1745 and the 'military' road from Carlisle to Newcastle was set up as a turnpike because of this in 1753.

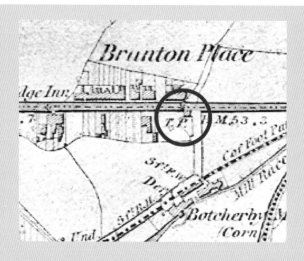

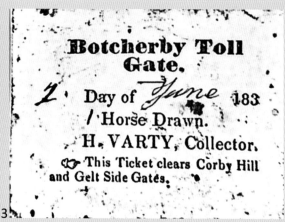

This Ticket clears Corby Hill and Gelt Side Gates.

Botcherby Toll Gate.

Day of June 183

Horse Drawn.

H. VARTY, Collector.

Botcherby's Toll Gate

Clockwise from top left: site of Botcherby toll bar, on the corner of Greystone Road and Warwick Road, opposite Brunton Park; old map showing location of turnpike (T P); Botcherby Gate turnpike toll rates; notice of turnpike tolls being let by auction, 1834; new tolls for new times - charges for powered vehicles; ticket for Botcherby Toll Gate, 1830s.

TOLLS to be taken for LOCOMOTIVES

For every Locomotive propelled by any Power containing within itself the Machinery for its own propulsion for every Two Tons or fractional part thereof that such Locomotive shall weigh the sum of ___ 3

For every Waggon, Wain, Cart or Carriage drawn or propelled by any Locomotive for each Wheel the sum of ___ ___ ___ 3

JOHN NORMAN
Clerk to the Trustees.

25th September, 1833.

TURNPIKE TOLLS.

NOTICE IS HEREBY GIVEN, that the TOLLS arising at the Toll-Gates upon the Turnpike Road leading from the City of CARLISLE to BRAMPTON, by Warwick Bridge, and called BOTCHERBY GATE, CORBY HILL GATE, and GELTSIDE GATE, will be LET, by AUCTION, to the best Bidders, at the Court-House, in the City of CARLISLE aforesaid, on the 22nd Day of FEBRUARY next, between the Hours of Twelve and Two, in the manner directed by Acts passed in the Third and Fourth Years of the Reign of his late Majesty King George the Fourth, "For regulating Turnpike Roads;" which Tolls were Let last Year at the several Rates following, by the Year, viz.:

BOTCHERBY GATE............£245
CORBY HILL GATE............182
GELTSIDE GATE................62

And will be put up at those Sums.

Whoever happen to be the best Bidders must, at the same time, pay One Month in advance of the Rents at which such Tolls may be Let; and give Security, with sufficient Sureties, to the satisfaction of the Trustees, for payment of the rest of the Rents, at such times as they shall direct.

ROBERT NORMAN,

January 23, 1834.   Clerk to the Trustees.

BOTCHERBY TOLL GATE

A Table of tolls authorised to be demanded and taken at this Gate by virtue of an act passed in the fifth year of the reign of his present Majesty GEORGE the Fourth intiteled an act for making and maintaining a Turnpike Road from the City of Carlisle in the County of Cumberland by way of Warwick Bridge to the Market town of Brampton in the said County

For every Horse or other Beast drawing any Coach, Landau, Chariot, Curricle, Berlin, Phaeton Calash, Hearse, Diligence, Van, Caravan, Chaise, Chair, Gig or other such like Carriage, the Sum of __	4½
For every Horse or other Beast, drawing any Stage Coach, the Sum of __	4½
For every Horse or other Beast, drawing any Waggon Wain, or other such like Carriage, not laden with Lime or Coal, the Sum of __	6
For every Horse or other Beast, drawing any Waggon, Wain, or other such like Carriage, laden with Coal or Lime, the Sum of __	6
For every Horse or other Beast drawing any Waggon, Wain, Cart, or other such Carriage, having the Fellies of the breath of four and a half inches, and less than six inches at the Bottom one sixth less than the above tolls	
And for every Horse or other Beast, drawing any such Carriage, having the Fellies of the breadth of six inches or upwards, one third less than the above tolls __	
For every Horse, Mule, or Ass, laden or unladen and not drawing the Sum of __	4½
For every Drove of Oxen, Cows, or other neat Cattle the Sum of eight pence per Score and so in Proportion for any less number __	8
And for every Drove of Calves, Sheep, Lambs Hogs or Swine, the Sum of four pence per Score, and so in proportion for any less number __	4

A Ticket from this Gate clears the Corby Hill and Gelt-Side Gates

JOHN NORMAN, Clerk

50

In 1785 the first mail coach came through Carlisle and the *Carlisle Pacquet* reported on the arrival and despatch of mails on 7 December that year. It became big business and a number of coachbuilding companies set up in Carlisle, now a centre for the coach trade. The City Archives hold records of a Memorandum of Agreement on 10 October 1808 between the Mayor and citizens of Carlisle and Henry Fairbairn and Thomas Wilson of Carlisle, coach masters *'to take tolls due to the Corporation on parcels & packages carried by coaches into, out of or through the City for a term of six years at an annual rent of £70.'*

By 1821 the newspaper was reporting that the mail coach would leave Carlisle at 11am and reach Newcastle by 7.30 in the evening. It was around this time also that John Loudon McAdam was revolutionising ideas about road construction, leading to the new technology of 'macadamised' roads, and did pioneering work with the Turnpike Trusts.

There were toll gates at Crosby, Kingstown, Harraby, Cummersdale, and Botcherby. In 1828 a group of Carlisle businessmen and landowners met at the Bush Inn to establish the Carlisle to Brampton Turnpike Trust led by Peter Dixon of Langthwaite cotton mill at Warwick Bridge. The Minute book gives this information: *'That the Road from Lowther Street to the bend at Ledgett Hill be 60 feet wide with a footpath on each side from thence to Botcherby Bridge be 36 feet including a footpath 6 feet on the North side of the same.'*

By 1835, with the city becoming a Municipal Borough, the repair responsibility was handed to the newly created Highway Boards, who replaced the parish surveyor, and roads were gradually de-turnpiked.

On 25 November 1854, reflecting other improvements in local amenities, a further Minute of the Carlisle to Brampton Turnpike Trust notes that: *'The Botcherby Tollgate and House be lighted with Gas, a lamp to be put up on the outside of the House.'*

Some of the toll cottages have survived, but not the one for Botcherby. The turnpike for the Carlisle to Brampton road stood at the junction of Greystone Road and Warwick Road and covered the stretch along to the next toll gate cottage at Corby Hill, and then onwards to Gelt Side toll cottage.

The advent of the railways saw an end to this older way of life and the last mail coach ran from Carlisle to Hawick on 31 August 1862. By 1876 the toll cottages were sold off, the one at Corby Hill being sold to P. H. Howard for £85 and, by the end of December 1876, the Trust was wound up. It was not until 1949 that toll collecting was finally suspended in Carlisle.

The toll gate cottage at Corby Hill. Left to right: the cottage as it looked in 1829-30; the plaque on the cottage wall; a much re-modelled cottage as it looks today.

Botcherby Bridge is falling down

Botcherby Bridge, crossing the river Petteril at the east end of Warwick Road, has a long and eventful history, and at times it appears to have been falling down more than it was standing up! It was prone to the severe flooding which periodically plagued the area, where the river Eden burst its banks and the river Petteril followed suit.

The bridge's existence was noted in a Will going back to 1380. In 1687, on a visit by the Judges to the city, the bridge and road were washed away by floods and a petition was made to the Cumberland Quarter Sessions by Mr James Nicholson of Carlisle for a further rate to pay for the whole cost of re-building it in 1691.

This was agreed with a sum of £70 being approved, in addition to the £103 11s 7d already paid. A new road replaced the one washed away and the bridge was built of stone. By 1715 the Surveyor's report on the County Bridges showed that Botcherby Bridge needed paving to the cost of five shillings and again in 1736 it needed further repair.

The following year saw the Surveyor reporting that Botcherby Bridge: *'Needs repair at foot,'* adding *'Rubish*

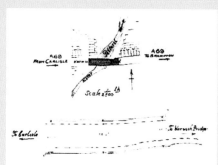

Botcherby Bridge

Clockwise from top left: the cause of all the trouble - the river Petteril, barring the route from Carlisle to Botcherby; today's solution - the current bridge (David Rogers/Creative Commons); sketch of the bridge from a report on the condition of the bridge in 1930; widening the bridge in 1931; commemorative plaque on Botcherby Bridge, celebrating the completion of its reconstruction in June 1932.

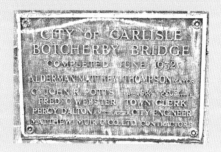

of Old Buildings, is carried out of Carlisle, and laid in the Middle of the River Eden, and on the Banks thereof, which may Prove A Damage to Eden Bridge.'

On 13 January 1816, the *Carlisle Journal* headlined 'the collapse of Petteril Bridge at Botcherby', relating how Peter Dixon with two ladies had just passed over to view the extension works at Warwick Bridge when it collapsed in a mass of ruins.

By 9 February 1822, the *Carlisle Patriot* reported that floods had so damaged the bridge that it would have to be rebuilt. This was bad news for the builders as they had a bond to maintain it for seven years which did not expire until 1824, it having only been erected in 1817!

On 24 August, 1822 the *Carlisle Journal* reported that a new bridge was built but that, on removing the wooden centre, the newly erected structure gave way 'as it is now lying a heap of ruins.' However, persistence prevailed and by 7 October 1822 the *Cumberland Paquet* noted that the work 'goes on with great spirit: it will be passable in a short time.'

Such optimism may have been misplaced, as in 1826 there were again plans to rebuild to a design by Christopher Hodgson. It appears to have been rebuilt in 1836.

.

Condemned as a death trap

On 23 August 1887 an inquest was held at Botcherby on the death of seven-year-old Joseph Metcalfe who had fallen from the bridge. The jury made the following addendum to the Coroner's verdict:

> 'The jury are unanimously of opinion that Petteril Bridge, between Botcherby and Carlisle, is dangerous, both for pedestrians and carriage traffic, and they request that a strong recommendation be made by the coroner to the County Authority to reconstruct the bridge, and to substitute a V coping for the present stone coping.'

The County Bridgemaster, G. J. Bell, noted that if this recommendation was carried out it would set a precedent for all similar bridges and:

> 'the ratepayers must be prepared for a vastly increased county rate, and respectfully request that some members of your committee will view the bridge, before adopting the sweeping recommendation of the jury.'

It was noted that other bridges were being carefully attended to and under existing contracts nothing further could be done at that time.

Botcherby was still outside the city boundaries and came under the authority of the newly formed County Council. The city authorities and many local people wanted the County to build a new bridge but, as the County had a great many other bridges and main roads to deal with, it was decided that the existing Botcherby Bridge could be made safe simply by lighting it with gas lamps and making some alterations to its shape.

The shape of the old Bridge was described in the *Cumberland News* on 23 February 1968:

> 'From all accounts it must have been rather an odd structure. One who lived near it said that it was not set at right angles to the river, that it had a very bad skew at each end and also had a very high crown, so that conveyances pulled across each other's course before they could see each other.'

Farmers, nursery gardeners and others who used the bridge to bring their produce to Carlisle Market had long complained that it was dangerous. Finally, the inevitable happened when near the end of 1890 there was a fatal accident there and a man was thrown off his cart and killed.

Botcherby Brig – the Devil's work!

Such was the infamy of the bridge that a poem written about it by *'Spectator'* and published in the *Cumberland News* ascribed the bridge's oddities to the work of the Devil.

> When folks were building Botcherby Brig,
> The Devil came by in a mason's rig,
> The stones and the mortar were hardly set,
> So he switched his tail at the parapet,
> And said he, "Some day some unfortunate wight,
> Will be driving home on a Saturday night,
> I will tickle his horse or give it a fright,
> And then if ahead he sharp don't look,
> I expect his wheel will catch at the crook,
> And over will go his cart and all,
> And he'll get an uncommonly mighty fall."
> For a hundred years the people went
> Over Botcherby Brig unharmed and content,
> For the Carlisle marketer's mostly see
> Straight, even when they are out on a spree;
> And artists come from far to look
> And to sketch the brig with the Devil's crook.
> For what if a farmer's cart should swerve?
> There's use and beauty in every curve.
> But at last one pitch dark Saturday night,
> The Devil he gave the horse a fright
> And the horse which was full of brewer's grains,
> Cared little or nothing for curb or reins,
> So smack at the crook in the parapet ran,
> And threw the cart over and killed the man.
> And the Devil he laughed and danced a jig.
> On the parapet curve of Botcherby Brig.   **Spectator**

Warwick Terrace and Warwick Road

Clockwise from top left: an early photo of Warwick Road south, before the north side was built - note the tram making its way into Carlisle - the turreted house to the left later became home to the Casey family; a view of the south side of Warwick Road some years later; the builders of Warwick Terrace pause for a photo opportunity; the corner of Warwick Terrace today, looking towards Petteril Bridge Terrace; the six houses that were Warwick Terrace.

It was obviously time to do something to improve the safety of the bridge. Alterations were made in 1892 when it was widened on both sides – no doubt in response to the jury's addendum at the inquest above. Tenders were to be submitted to G. J. Bell, Bridgemaster!

Proposals for the building and construction of Henry Street (later re-named Warwick Road) were the catalyst for plans being drawn up by John Studholme for a new road and footways to Botcherby Bridge, and the development of the area.

A brave new era dawns

The years 1924-25 saw the start of a time of great activity in the city as a programme of road widening and bridge improvement went ahead. This was important for Botcherby, where developments in the community and easy access to the city were paramount. By October 1930 the Highways and Streets Committee were committed to the project:

> **'Widening and improvement of Warwick Road.**
>
> 'The Committee conferred with the owners of property in Petteril Bridge Terrace and Warwick Terrace regarding the scheme for the widening of Warwick Road from Thirlwell Avenue to the city boundary, the raising of the road above flood level and the reconstruction of the bridge over the River Petteril in view of the receipt of a petition from certain of the owners of property in Warwick Terrace objecting to the raising of the road and the Surveyor submitted full details of the proposals.
>
> 'After discussion , the owners present approved the scheme as suggested by the corporation.'

By 23 October 1930 the Committee was also considering plans and estimates for the widening of Warwick Road and Victoria Road:

'and Victoria Road (from Warwick Road to the lane adjoining Botcherby school House) at a total estimated cost of £34,000. Resolved: approved subject to grants being available. Town Clerk to apply to Ministry of Health to borrow £5,272, additionally to the sum of £28,728 authorised by the Highways and Streets Committee.'

The Highways Department today holds two very large cloth drawings prepared by Percy Dalton, the City Engineer and Surveyor, dated 10 January 1931. It is clear from them that today's bridge is considerably wider than its 95-year-old predecessor, as Dalton's architectural drawings show this as being 60 feet between the parapets whereas the old bridge had two arches, one for the river at 40 feet and the other for the mill stream at 5 feet 6 inches. The drawings also show the entrance to the laundry which remains today.

The elusive Warwick Terrace

The minute from the Highways and Streets Committee in October 1930 (mentioned above) refers to 'Warwick Terrace'. This is something of a puzzle, as you won't find it anywhere on contemporary maps of the area.

We knew the names of people who lived there, such as Joseph Iveson, a grocer recorded as living at 6 Warwick Terrace, Botcherby, but not its exact location. Eventually after a great deal of searching archives, directories and maps it was located. It was in fact an extension of six houses to those previously built at Petteril Bridge Terrace.

The northern side of Warwick Road was built at a later date than the southern side but, with the road-widening scheme going ahead in 1931 and completed in 1932, the road was re-numbered at some time after 1934 but before 1940. It was then that Petteril Bridge Terrace and Warwick Terrace lost their identities and became part of Warwick Road.

Today Petteril Bridge Terrace still has a plaque high in the wall showing its original name, but there is no visible remembrance of Warwick Terrace.

Carriages, trams and motor buses

The Carlisle Carriage Company began their horse-drawn bus service on 29 April 1896 with two routes in the city, from Harraby Green to Stanwix and from Boundary Road via English Street to the Infirmary. A third route was planned, just beyond Botcherby, from Petteril Bridge to Warwick Road through Denton Holme to Holme Head. The *Carlisle Journal* reported that the service would run from 8am to 8pm and that the horses would be changed each day at noon, with a fresh driver and conductor taking over at that time.

The buses were brightly painted in red and yellow with seats for 12 persons inside and 14 outside, reached by a spiral staircase. They became immensely popular with children and on the opening day over 1,400 people used them. Fares were two pence from one terminus to another and a penny to go to the Citadel Station. There was one bus per hour on each route, which soon proved inadequate due to their popularity.

When competition was announced from the Carlisle Bus Company to run seven routes with one penny fares, the Carriage Company doubled their service to Stanwix and the Infirmary, and put a bus with sofa seats, instead of garden seats, to suit the bridge on the route between Botcherby and Holme Head. They also began a half-hourly service and made all fares a penny. Initially the buses were three-horse but it was reported that a second two-horse bus for the Warwick Road and Denton Holme route was being built at Boag's Crescent Carriage works to start running in August. It is likely that this is the bus illustrated in this chapter which shows a Botcherby name-plate. The competition did not take off but, as the buses were run to suit public convenience rather than profit making, they were priced off the road by trams after only four years.

At the turn of the 20th century Carlisle's population had risen to 50,000 and there was a growing need for improved transport systems. In 1880 an early proposal for a horse-worked tramway system had been suggested, but did not go forward for Parliamentary powers to construct a tramway. By 1898 under the Carlisle Tramways Order, a Birmingham consortium obtained powers to build and operate electrical tramways within the city. The main promoter was the Manchester Traction Company, formed in 1897 with a capital of £100,000 and based at 13 Spring Gardens, Manchester.

The promoters were authorised to construct 5½ miles of 3½-foot gauge tramway with a track mileage of 7¾ miles. Carlisle Corporation gave their consent on condition that all electric current was taken from the municipal power station, with a guaranteed minimum consumption per annum.

Construction work went ahead, as the Carlisle Tramways Order of 1898 authorised 28 routes to operate throughout the city. There were interconnecting junctions between routes, and Botcherby was served by Tramway No. 9, which commenced on Warwick Road at a junction with No. 8 from Botchergate and No. 19 from English Street. It continued along Warwick Road, terminating at a point 10 chains east of the intersection of the centre lines of Botcherby Old Road and Warwick Road, just before Petteril Bridge. Here there was a junction where No. 10 travelled eastwards and terminated at a junction between Carleton Terrace and Warwick Road.

The tramway replaced the horse omnibuses and opened for public service on 30 June 1900 with fares costing one penny. The Botcherby route was single line with loops at Howard Place, St Aidan's and the terminus at Petteril Bridge, where serious flooding sometimes covered the lines.

Over the years motor buses began to supplement the tramway routes and, by 1926, Botcherby was served by Huntington's of Warwick Road, whose route covered Carlisle to Botcherby via Grey Street and also served

Public transport to Botcherby in the late-19th and early-20th centuries

Clockwise from top left: the horse-drawn carriage to Botcherby run by the Carlisle Carriage Company with driver Jack Temple on board; a tram heading towards the town after crossing Botcherby Bridge; the view from the other side of Warwick Road; floods at the bottom of Victoria Road but the Grey Street-to-Botcherby bus soldiers on (note the old lodge to Botcherby Hall in the background); the No. 40 Botcherby bus negotiates the new road level in Warwick Road.

Durranhill and Blackwell. Simpson & Thompson of 1 Victoria Road ran a service between Botcherby and Carlisle with a bus to Talkin Tarn on Sundays.

By 1930, with transport provision in the city in a chaotic condition caused by development of the city outskirts which left some areas without transport, a new solution was sought. Months of negotiation followed and the final outcome was that Ribble Motor Services of Preston, having submitted a scheme for the scrapping of the tramways and the co-ordination of local transport services to the Northern Traffic Commissioners, were granted a licence.

It was the end of the line for the trams and the tramways ended on Saturday 21 November 1931.

The railways come to town

Everyone of a certain age will remember the excitement of standing on Carlisle Station waiting for the train for Silloth to arrive – puffing and steaming and promising a day of delight among the sand dunes. It soon filled up with excited children anxious to be on their way.

Carlisle started its long history as a railway city in 1838 when the first line to Newcastle was opened by the Newcastle & Carlisle Railway amid much junketing and celebrations. The following years saw further development, with other companies building lines to Maryport, Dumfries and, by 1862, to Edinburgh.

The Citadel Station was built as a joint station in 1847 and enlarged in 1862 as more companies used it instead of the original smaller stations as the network developed. Between 1875 and 1922 there were seven companies, all with different locomotives and livery using the station, making a vibrant and colourful scene. After 1923 they grouped into four major companies with standardised livery and locomotives.

The Midland Railway had become a national operator with its lines extending north as far as Lancaster and Ingleton in Yorkshire. It had long set its sights on extending to Carlisle. It met with opposition from other railway companies but, by 1870, it started building the difficult 72-mile line from Settle to Carlisle. Goods services opened in 1875, with the passenger service opening on 1 May 1876, costing a total of £3.8 million. It became one of the most scenic routes in northern England.

The Newcastle and Settle lines now ran parallel at Durranhill. Here the Midland railway shed was located to the south of the Midland line, about half a mile east of Petteril Bridge Junction, and opened in 1875 for the operation of goods services. The building consisted of a single roundhouse, where there was a turntable, with the later addition of two straight roads on the north side. Until 1926, there were also two fitting sheds behind, which undertook heavy general repairs. By 1923 the Midland became part of the larger London, Midland & Scottish Railway Company (LMS). Before amalgamation, over 70 locomotives were allocated to Durranhill but, by September 1933, there were just 49 locomotives there (including the *Sir Gilbert Claughton*) and, by 15 February 1936, LMS rationalisation brought closure to the sheds. The remaining 27 locomotives and work duties were split between the Upperby and Kingmoor sheds.

It was not quite the end for the Durranhill sheds as they were used for a time during the war and, when the railways were nationalised under British Rail in 1948, they continued to be used as an engine store and service point until 1959. By 1965 the buildings were demolished and the site cleared.

The railway companies built houses – the row of terraced cottages at Durranhill View on Durranhill Road were available to railway employees.

Many Botcherby men worked on the railways and some were members of the Catholic Railwaymens' Guild which was organised by Fr Michael O'Connor at Our Lady & St Joseph's Church in Warwick Square.

In the 1940s and 1950s the railway became a magical thing: grandfathers took their grandchildren for walks

The railways at Botcherby

Clockwise from top left: the Midland Railway Bridge, looking across Botcherby; the North Eastern Railway Bridge, Durranhill Industrial Estate in the background; Durranhill Junction; the view across Botcherby in 1954 to the open fields where the Metal Box would be built; the road across Durranhill Bridge to Harraby; Durranhill View street sign, still just legible today; the terrace of cottages in Durranhill View, built in the 19th C. for railway workers; Midland's shed at Durranhill shortly before its closure in 1936.

around Durranhill and to the old iron railway bridge on the road going over to London Road and Harraby. The excitement of steam billowing over the parapets as the Newcastle train thundered below was breathtaking.

Old railwaymen who lived at the bottom end of Borland Avenue tell of sitting in the outside loo and leaving the door open to watch the trains making their way in and out of Carlisle Station. Children would lie in bed at night listening to the shunting at Durranhill, and weaving stories of the adventures they would find in travelling the railways. Courting couples would wend their way from Holywell Crescent to the bridge and on towards Harraby, where the delights of the Argyll Cinema and, later, the Cosmo awaited.

Later the Metal Box Company would use the line that ran along the back of their factory to transport cans to Carnation Milk in Dumfries.

The Durranhill crossing murder

On Friday 22nd November 1861 the people of Carlisle awoke to the news of one of the city's most infamous crimes. The horrific murder had taken place the previous night at the Durranhill level crossing on the Newcastle & Carlisle Railway. The victim was 72-year-old widow Jane Emmerson who, after her husband Anthony's death six years earlier, had continued to take on the duties of crossing keeper. It was her task every night, after the last train had passed at 10.30pm, to close the gate across the line, and take into the house two lamps. She hung one lamp on a signal post on the Botcherby side of the line, and the other in a small wooden cabin on the Harraby side. She then had nothing further to do until re-opening the crossing at 4am the next morning.

The pretty rose- and honeysuckle-covered cottage was in an isolated position. Instead of the network of railway lines and sidings which came later there were just two lines of the north-eastern railway extending westwards for three-quarters of a mile to Carlisle. There was no bridge or elevated roadway from which the railway could be observed, and the road from Botcherby to Harraby, which led over the level crossing was like a quiet country lane with high hedges. Hamilton's Nurseries grew cabbages in the fields leading from Botcherby to the cottage. Jane was alone that week as her married daughter and two children had gone to Liverpool on a visit.

Jane's badly beaten body was found at 6.30am on the Friday morning, lying near the line and her cottage porch, by a passing railway worker, William Blaylock. He lived at Botcherby and was on his way to work at the railway station in Carlisle. The flooded meadows near the river Petteril meant he could not take his usual shortcut and he had gone by the crossing.

The police were called and found a blood-stained hedge slasher and a pick-axe nearby. The cottage door had been broken down and bedroom drawers ransacked. When Jane's daughter was brought to the scene, she confirmed that silver spoons, linen sheets and £6 or £7 in cash had been taken. A man's footprints were traced from behind the post of the south gate, on the Harraby side, along the line, and across to the window.

At the scene of the murder the police carried out some excellent detective work. They found that the footprints had a very distinct stud pattern and called in Joseph Pickering, a Carlisle sculptor, who made plaster casts for use as evidence. They also deduced that the murderer knew Jane and her movements; knew how to open a very complicated lock system to gain access to the garden; and also knew that her daughter was away. The police surgeon estimated the time of death as after the last train had gone through the crossing.

The following day an inquest was opened at the Plough Inn, Botcherby, under the County Coroner, Mr William Carrick. The jury was sworn in and Mr John Norman appointed foreman. Others on the jury included Mr Thomas Hamilton, Mr John Robinson, Mr Isaac Kitchen and Mr Joseph Bulman. There was little progress for some weeks while the police continued to accumulate evidence. The Directors of the Railway and the Home Office offered a reward of £150 for the discovery of the culprit.

The police found a suspect in William Charlton, train driver, aged 35, married with three children and a fourth on the way. He knew Jane well and had a motive for robbery, having run up debts including to the landlord of a public house on London Road. A strong case was built up against Charlton without him being aware of it. After 30 days the police arrested him and held him while they searched his house – they found the shoes with the distinctive studs removed. When questioned as to why he removed these studs Charlton tried to blame his brother-in-law, Thomas Robinson, whom he said had borrowed the shoes on the night of the murder and must have taken out the studs to destroy evidence of the crime. Further searching resulted in these items being found hidden in a wall cavity.

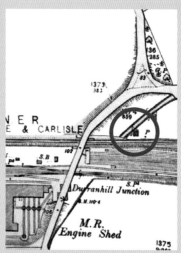

Durranhill Railway Cottage – sad and happy memories

Above, clockwise from top left: Durranhill Cottage and crossing, engraved by H. Scott; the plaque on the old Court Houses, commemorating the execution of William Charlton for the murder; map showing Durranhill railway bridge in 1877 and the position of the cottage; the cottage in the 1960s, with the Army Camp houses in the background.

Below, from left to right: Bill and Mary Millican with their little cousin Grace Sewell outside Durranhill Cottage in the 1950s; Barbara Millican as a young girl; Mary Millican, who lived in the cottage in the 1950s, was a gifted singer who took lessons from Ena Mitchell in Carlisle. The internationally famous singer Charlie Kunz on hearing her sing offered to pay for singing lessons and accommodation in London. However, as she was only 17 years old, her father would not allow her to go.

Thomas Robinson had a cast iron alibi for the night in question, having been at Ivegill, nine miles from Carlisle, at a wedding celebration since the previous Saturday. He had been with friends playing cards and drinking on the night of Thursday 21 November, and shared a bed with them. Next morning he had helped secure a stallion that had broken loose and did not return to Carlisle until Friday afternoon. He had many upright witnesses to these events and the charges of being an accomplice were discharged.

Other incriminating evidence against Charlton included the fact that someone had gone back to the crossing to open the gates for the first train to Newcastle at four o'clock in the morning. Charlton was spotted walking up the line from the crossing to the engine sheds just before four o'clock by a signalman going to the early shift on the Durranhill signal box. He himself was driving the 4.30am train to Newcastle that day, and, when passing the crossing, diverted the fireman's attention by pointing out the cabbage plants in Hamilton's gardens.

The Assize trial took place in the Crown Court in Carlisle on Monday, 24 February 1862 before Mr Justice Willes when William Charlton was indicted for the wilful murder of Jane Emmerson. The evidence put before the jury was overwhelming and he was found guilty. The death sentence was passed and William Charlton was hanged in Carlisle jail on Saturday, 15 March 1862. At this time the public spectacle of hanging was distasteful to the authorities so, as a diversion, cheap fares on the train to Silloth were organised for the day, but to no avail. A crowd of over 6,000 people watched from across the road on English Street as the condemned man took one long last look down Botchergate towards his home where his wife and children were. In moments it was all over. An old lady had lost her life and a family had lost their father. He was buried in the jail grounds. This was the last public execution in Carlisle.

Today if you walk beside the old jail walls near the former Woolworth's building and look up you will see a round Civic Trust plaque which includes the statement: 'Here was the last public execution in Carlisle 15th March 1862.' This is the site where William Charlton, a railway-engine driver from Harraby Street was hanged.

Many years after the murder the cottage was occupied by the Millican family and Barbara who now lives in Australia has given me her unique description of life then:

> 'I not only lived in Durranhill Cottage, I was born there 3 August 1933. My family was father, William Millican, mother Barbara (née MacDonald), sister Mary born 1922, brother Bill, born 1926 and my cousin Grace Sewell, born 1926. Grace joined our family about the same time as I did.

> 'The cottage was small, two rooms downstairs and one large room upstairs. We had electricity for lights, but no gas so my mother cooked all meals over an open fire and baked in the oven at the side of the fire. There was no water in the cottage but a few steps away was a "wash house" with cold water and a coal fired "tub" for heating water and boiling clothes on wash day. We had a large tin bath in there which was brought into the cottage and placed in front of the fire for the weekly bath. No indoor toilet of course, just a dry lavatory at the bottom of the garden.

> 'There was a path, known as "the Lonnen" from the cottage to Durranhill Road. My Dad had the garden on one side of the lonnen and grew vegetables for us and sold some at Carlisle market on Saturdays. Billy Feddon, a market gardener grew vegetables in the large garden on the other side of the lonnen.

> 'It must have been a bit crowded for two adults and four children but in those days I think having two or three in a bed was commonplace. My mother told me that the family who had lived in the cottage before us had 13 children. There were large ceiling beams in the upstairs room with lots of large hooks and my mother maintained that the parents must have kissed each child goodnight then hung him or her from a hook! I lived there until I was six then we moved to 57 Borland Avenue.'

The cottage finally disappeared with the building of Eastern Way.

Robert James Jardine, railway hero

If the coming of the railways changed the lives of Carlisle citizens, it also saw the development of a large group of skilled railway workers with loyalty to their companies and camaraderie with their fellow workers: even leading to acts of great heroism. Robert James Jardine was one such hero.

Robert Jardine lived in a parlour house at 22 Durranhill Road and had served in the Army in WW1, fighting in Passchendaele and at the Battle of the Somme, having been awarded the Somme Star as well as other medals. But it was not until his grandson, Chris Jardine, was clearing out the house after his grandmother's death in 2011, that further evidence of his heroism came to light, for Chris Jardine found a civilian award for the Order of Industrial Heroism.

Chris said, 'You get pieces of the story off family members. It's part of our folklore, but we don't have the exact story.' With a little more research, however, the full facts came to light. The Order of Industrial Heroism was awarded to people by the *Daily Herald* newspaper – now *The Sun* – to honour heroic acts in ordinary life.

Robert James Jardine – railwayman hero

Top left: Jardine during the First World War in the Westmorland and Cumberland Yeomanry.
Top right: Jardine and his train team.
Left: letter from the Mayor of Carlisle recommending Jardine for the Order of Industrial Heroism Award.
Below: the award medal, dated 8 April 1934; right - the obverse of the medal, designed by Eric Gill.
Bottom: left - Jardine on holiday with his wife; centre - Jardine in his railwayman's uniform; right - at home in his garden at 22 Durranhill Road.

There were only 440 of the medals awarded between 1923 and 1964 and Robert Jardine was the 96th of those, awarded it on 8 April 1934.

Working as a guard for the London, Midland & Scottish Railway, Robert Jardine was the only survivor of a terrible accident between Newsholme and Hellifield stations on the Blackburn-Hellifield line in the early hours of 19 December 1933, which resulted in the train driver and the fireman being killed and Robert Jardine being badly injured.

The official report on 2 February 1934 by Lieut Colonel E. P. Anderson for the Ministry of Transport into the accident sets the scene:

> *'During shunting operations at Hellifield South Junction signal box a 20-ton goods brake van ran away on the down goods loop, and out on to the down main line through the facing connection at Hellifield Goods Yard Signal box. It ran in the facing (up) direction for about 1½ miles down a steep gradient (of about 1 in 103) and collided head on with the 11.15 p.m. down freight train, Ancoats (Manchester) to Carlisle, which was running under clear signals in the proper direction on the same line.*

> *'I regret to report that the driver, J. Farrell and the fireman, W. Murphy, of the goods train were fatally injured and the guard suffered from cuts, concussion and shock.'*

It was a foggy morning with poor visibility, and errors in the marshalling of the goods brake van had tragic consequences, as it seemed that nothing could be done to stop it once it was on its path to the main line. Robert Jardine as the only survivor had to walk, badly injured, five miles to the nearest station to get help.

By 30 January 1934 the Mayor of Carlisle, E. Gray, was writing to the Editor of the *Daily Herald* requesting that Robert be put forward for the medal - Robert was still seriously ill as result of the accident. His case was also taken up by the local Labour councillor for Botcherby, Mr W. Goody, and Mr M. Clifford, Secretary to Carlisle Trades Council, who wrote:

> *'I am sure nobody deserves an honour of that description more than Mr. Jardine especially in view of the fact of the cool and heroic way in which he performed his duties after going through such a terrible ordeal.'*

The Award was quickly approved and arrangements went ahead for the presentation ceremony, to take place at 3pm on Sunday 8 April 1934 in the Co-operative Hall, Botchergate. This was the first time that the Hall had been let on a Sunday and it was given free of charge. Posters and handbills were printed advertising the event and, amid a large attendance, the presentation was made by Mr P. J. Dollan of the *Daily Herald*'s Scottish Office in Glasgow.

So Robert Jardine became Botcherby's hero, but he still preferred the quiet life and tending his roses in his garden on Durranhill Road.

Botcherby Airfield

After WW1 there were many men who had been trained in aviation. These were ex-members of the Royal Naval Air Service, the Royal Flying Corps and the Royal Air Force. At the same time there was a boom in civil aviation in the 1920s and these flyers were keen to be involved. Two local men, Percy Ingham of Carlton Gardens, Stanwix, and Bob Little of Penrith formed the Border Aviation Company, with a registered office at Saul and Lightfoot (Solicitors) in Castle Street. Lionel Lightfoot had been a fighter pilot in the war, achieving wing commander rank, and had a keen interest in the new company.

Percy Ingham had flown with the Royal Naval Air Service (RNAS) at Windermere in 1915, where seaplanes had been developed since 1911. He was to be the pilot in the new company, assisted by other local men including Mr Roberts (who would later co-found the well-known motor company, Graham & Roberts Ltd in Botchergate) and Bob Liddle who helped to finance the purchase of one Avro 504K two-seater aircraft.

They needed a flat, open space for the airfield and a 25-acre site at Walkmill Fields Botcherby was leased, from local cattle dealer Martin Casey of Botcherby Farm, on an initial six-month lease. It was located on land between St Joseph's Home (now demolished) and the bottom of what is now Botcherby Avenue. On 10 May 1920 this became the first officially recognised civil aerodrome in the region licensed by the Air Ministry.

The first flight into the airfield of the newly purchased aeroplane was from Alexandra Park, Manchester via Blackpool (for fuel) on 14 May 1920. It must have been quite a sight when flying for the public started on Thursday, 20 May. It was half-day closing in Carlisle and a large crowd attended, at an entrance fee of eight pence, to watch a flying display given by Captain Hudson who delivered the aircraft. The plane made continuous loops above Botcherby and the stunt flying had everyone holding their breath. Captain John Oliver

Botcherby takes to the air

Clockwise from top left: an Avro 504K of the type flown from Botcherby (TSRL/Creative Commons); the view from the back of Botcherby Home, once Botcherby airfield; resting between flights - left to right: Mrs F. J. Liddle, Capt J. Oliver, P. H. Ingham, R. F. Little and F. J Liddle with Botcherby Home in the background; Border Aviation staff: back from left to right: P. H. Ingham, Capt J. Oliver, J. Little; front from left to right: F. J. Liddle, W. Clayton, W. Gower; the wreck of G-EANQ, burnt out on Burgh sands; old map showing the location of the airfield, behind Botcherby Home.

AFC, was left under contract for the public flying and afterwards the public were given short flights charged at one guinea (£1.05). The first hire was from a Mr Smith who engaged Captain Oliver to fly him over his farm at Lazonby.

Later in the summer the aircraft, while based at Oliver's Mount in Scarborough for joy flights for holidaymakers, suffered engine failure in flight. It struck a hayrick on landing in the Scarborough area damaging the aircraft. Fortunately no one was hurt and in October it returned to Botcherby for winter storage.

By now the firm's finances were in a poor state, not helped by Mr Ingham's habit of throwing unpaid bills on the fire! The mechanics returning by car from the Scarborough base had a lucky escape, when a front tyre blow-out at High Hesket caused them to crash into the bay window of the toll cottage, ejecting the car occupants through the windscreen into the front room!

The company went into liquidation but in June 1921 the firm, under a new name, Ingham & Little Aviation Co. Ltd, started operations again at Botcherby with a new pilot (ex-RNAS Windermere in WW1) and an additional aircraft was purchased, to be based on Heysham foreshore for Morecambe holidaymakers. Flying from a field near Cockermouth also commenced with reduced prices, due to increasing competition. The cost was half a guinea for a 7-8 mile flight rising up to 1,000 feet and a guinea for a flight over Bassenthwaite Lake. Stunt flying was on offer for three guineas.

It had been a brave and exciting venture, but the Botcherby-based aircraft came to a sad end later in the summer. After suffering engine failure, the pilot landed on Burgh marshes and a watching resident rushed out to save the two crew, including Percy Ingham. Soon after, the aircraft caught fire and burnt out. With no insurance this meant the end of the company and of flying from Botcherby.

◆◆◆

Murmurations and rumours of murmurations...

Over recent years, Botcherby has become something of a 'go-to' place if you want to see huge flocks of starlings twisting and wheeling through complex flight patterns in the early evening sky before they settle down to roost for the night. The spectacular murmurations have been attracting people from far and wide. This picture, taken in March 2016, shows an impressive performance at the top of Wood Street (*CN - The Cumberland News*).

The Great War hits hard

The Great War may have ended with the signing of the Armistice on 11 November 1918, but it was not until 1920 that all the troops returned home. The street parties went ahead, as communities celebrated peace and families were re-united. It was those who did not return who were in the hearts and minds of the many Botcherby families touched by the loss of loved ones. Something had to be done to mark their sacrifice...

The War Memorial

In Carlisle, the Citizen's League had surplus funds at the end of the war and, in September 1920, it was agreed to buy Rickerby Park at a cost of £11,500 in memory of those who had lost their lives in war. Plans went ahead and the Cenotaph was built and unveiled by Lord Lonsdale on 25 May 1922, and the Memorial Bridge over the river Eden was also erected.

Villages and towns throughout the country were all building memorials remembering their war heroes and Botcherby was no exception. The *Cumberland News* carried a detailed report on 26 June 1920 of a garden fête and sale of work held in the grounds of Botcherby Hall:

> *'A movement is on foot for the provision of a war memorial for Botcherby. Several young men from the village fell in the war, and it is felt that their sacrifice ought to be commemorated in some suitable way. The exact character of the memorial has not yet been decided upon, and will greatly depend on the amount of money raised. The local Committee to which Mrs. Barnfather of Botcherby acts as secretary, and Mrs. Musgrave of Botcherby Hall as treasurer have £3 in hand as the proceeds of a Christmas dance... to augment this fund a garden fête was held... the afternoon was fine and the grounds which were decorated with flags and festoons of bunting presented a pretty picture... the stalls were arranged upon the tennis court.'*

In memory and honour of the men of Botcherby who fell in
the Great War.

2nd Lt. Tom Story

2nd Lt. Thomas H. Little

Cpl. H. Miller Crook

Pte. Harry Armstrong

"   Joseph Armstrong

"   Robert Cartner

"   Robert W. Caddle

"   Thomas W. Hall

"   George H. Hall

"   Roland Johnston

"   Thomas H. Johnston

"   Richard J. Kirk

"   Joseph Routledge

"   Stanley Winthorpe

Spr. J. H. Skelton

"TO OUR GLORIOUS DEAD"   1914 - 1918

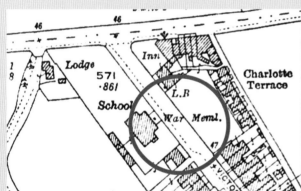

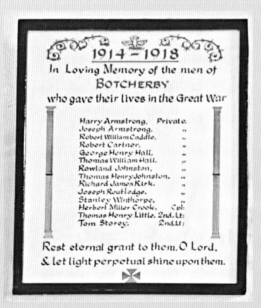

Remembering Botcherby's sacrifice in WW1

Clockwise from top left: the memorial today; the names of the men who died, as they appear on the memorial; advert for Beattie & Co. showing a stonemason at work on the memorial; the memorial roll of honour from St Andrew's Church; the original location of the memorial in front of Botcherby School, before the widening of Victoria Road.

The phrase *'several young men'* is something of an understatement: for such a small place, Botcherby paid a high price for the part it played in World War One (WW1).

The names of the ladies who took charge of the stalls are worth recording as many of them still resonate with Botcherby people today:

> *'Work stalls: Mrs. Barnfather, Mrs. Ferguson, Mrs. Clay, Mrs. Thompson, Mrs. Parker, Mrs. H. Robinson, Mrs. Jones, Mrs. Francis, Mrs. Haddow, and Miss Alice Baty. Cake Stall: Mrs. Shaw, Mrs. Story, Miss M. Little, Miss M. Feddon, Mrs. G . Simpson and Miss Noble. "White Elephant" stall: Miss Clark, Miss Iris Ferguson, Miss E. Baty, Miss Rene Baty and Miss Wilson.*

> *'There was also a stall of fruit and flowers given by Mrs Musgrave and an ice-cream stall given by Miss Musgrave.'*

Mrs T. Ridley, the Mayoress, opened the fête and Mr H. K. Campbell, presiding at the opening ceremony, thanked Mr and Mrs Musgrave who were always ready to advance any good cause affecting Botcherby. The Mayoress said she was delighted to have the opportunity to open the Sale of Work on behalf of the memorial fund for the brave men who sacrificed their lives for their country. Everyone thoroughly enjoyed the afternoon and the amount of £60 was raised.

The fundraising carried on apace and by 23 October 1920 a further report appeared in the *Cumberland News*:

> **'BOTCHERBY WAR MEMORIAL**

> *'The house-to-house collection on behalf of the Botcherby war memorial, organised by the secretary (Mrs. Barnfather) and the treasurer (Miss E. L. Musgrave), has so far realised over £45. Other subscriptions have been promised, and it is expected that the sum realised by the collection will altogether reach £50.*

> *'A beautiful grey rustic granite cross has been chosen as the memorial for the twelve Botcherby young men who fell in the war, and it is expected that it will be ready early in the New Year.'*

There are in fact 15 names on the war memorial.

Great enthusiasm for the project had been generated and a photograph of the craftsman carving the memorial was published in an advert for Beattie & Co., the stonemasons who were making it. At last, on Sunday 28 March 1921, the great day dawned. An advance announcement appeared in the *Cumberland News* on 26 March 1921:

> **'BOTCHERBY WAR MEMORIAL**

> *'Botcherby War Memorial, which will be unveiled on Sunday first, consists of a rustic cross of grey Scottish granite over eight feet high. On the front side of the rough boulder on which the cross rests there is a sheathed sword and laurel wreath carved in relief. There is also a portion dressed, on which is engraved the inscription and the names of the fallen. On the face of the cross there is some simple interlacing work in a sunk panel. The cross was designed and executed by Messrs Beattie and Co. of Murrell Hill.'*

The war memorial was originally built on land outside Botcherby School but, with the road-widening, was later moved to its current site within the Community Centre grounds. The 100-year commemorations of the Great War in 2014 saw the cleaning and restoration of the memorial.

At the unveiling Major Sandeman spoke of the spirit of the trenches and that 48 men went off to war and the 15 named were killed.

Remembering Private Joseph Routledge

Today, Remembrance Sunday 2014, I am looking at the life of a young man who gave his life in the Great War. His name appears on the Botcherby War Memorial along with his fellow soldiers. He is Private Joseph Routledge who lived at 8 Charlotte Terrace and worked for the Midland Railway. He was born in Bewcastle in 1891 and his family later moved to Botcherby. In 1911 the family lived at Botcherby Hall Lodge where his father, 55-year-old Thomas Routledge, worked as a gardener for the Musgrave family of Botcherby Hall. His mother, 44-year-old Annie, was from Glasgow and he had two brothers, 18-year-old Richard who also worked as a gardener, and 16-year-old Alec. Joseph, aged 20, was working as a porter on the railway at this time. The family later moved to 8 Charlotte Terrace.

In memoriam...

Private Joseph Routledge

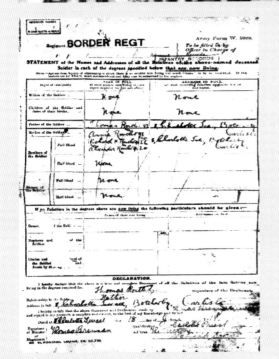

Clockwise from top left: Joseph Routledge's name on the war memorial at Our Lady & St Joseph's church; the signed receipt for his medals and the application made by the family for the medals.

I hereby acknowledge the receipt of the British War Medal Victory Medal *granted in respect of the service of* BORDER REGT
Date 25/11/21 Signature Anne Routledge
POST WITHOUT FASTENING.

Below, left to right: 8 Charlotte Terrace, home of the Routledge family; commemorative scroll from the Thiepval Memorial, Picardy (Commonwealth War Graves Commission); war memorial at Our Lady & St Joseph's, Warwick Road.

In Memory of
Private
Joseph Routledge

13694, 11th Bn., Border Regiment who died on 01 July 1916

Remembered with Honour
Thiepval Memorial

Commemorated in perpetuity by
the Commonwealth War Graves Commission

At the outbreak of war in 1914, 23-year-old Joseph joined B Company, the 11th Service Battalion of the Border Regiment, the famous 'Lonsdales' raised by Lord Lonsdale on 17 September 1914. After initial training at Carlisle Racecourse, the regiment eventually proceeded to France and landed at Boulogne on 23 November 1915. They saw action at the Battle of the Somme where so many lost their lives on 1 July 1916. Joseph Routledge was among those killed in action that day: he had been in France for 175 days.

When the news of his loss came through to Charlotte Terrace, the sorrow of his parents and brothers can only be imagined. Their pain must have been compounded when the Army forms had to be filled in, and a declaration had to be completed on the members of the family still living. The declaration was witnessed on 18 June 1919 by Fr Thomas Brennan of Our Lady and St Joseph's Church in Warwick Square, where Private Joseph Routledge is also remembered on the War Memorial. He was posthumously awarded the Victory Medal and the British War Medal.

The Thiepval Memorial, Picardy, in northern France, commemorates those who died with no known grave

 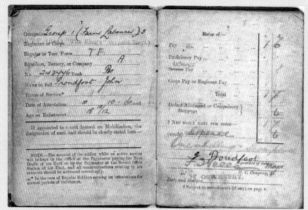 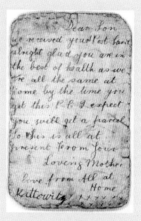

John Proudfoot's war

Above left to right : John with his brother and father; .John Proudfoot's army papers showing that he joined up in 1916; a heartfelt postcard from his mother at home.

Below, clockwise from left:- the story unravels in cold newsprint telling nothing of the agonies that the Proudfoot family - and so many others - had to endure. In this case there was a happy ending, with John Proudfoot being repatriated in 1919 ; prisoners of war at the Kattowitz camp, where John was interned; the Victory Medal and the British War Medal.

The following Carlisle men are missing, and their friends would welcome intelligence respecting them:—Private H. Glaister, Grenadier Guards, Kendal Street; Private A. Mitchell, Border Regiment, Trafalgar Street; Sergeant T. Dunn, Border Regiment, grandson of Mrs. McLean, Thomas's Place, Milbourne Street; Private W. Daly, Border Regiment, Duke Street; and Private John Proudfoot, King's Liverpool Regiment, West Walls.

Private A. G. McNaughton, Esther Street,

Missing.

Private W. Daly, Border Regiment, Warwick Street, Carlisle, has been missing since April 16th and 18th.

Mr. and Mrs. Proudfoot, 37, West Walls, have received official notice that their son, Private John Proudfoot, King's Liverpool Regiment, is reported missing since the 21st March. Any information will be gladly received.

and Joseph Routledge is remembered there too. This is the largest British battle memorial in the world. The Lonsdale Cemetery is a short distance from the Liepzig Redoubt, an area of fierce fighting, and in view of the Thiepval Memorial.

The importance of the war memorials, medals and scrolls to families of lost soldiers cannot be overestimated and, on 10 September 1919, Thomas Routledge wrote the poignant letter (on the next page) to the authorities from 8 Charlotte Terrace:

'Dear Sir

'I should like to draw your attention to the fact that acting under your instructions many months ago we filled in a form and returned same regarding the scroll which we were entitled to in respect of our deceased soldier son, the late Pte. Joseph Routledge, No. 13694 Border Reg't, who was killed in action July 1st 1916 and we have not yet received any reply.

'Therefore I shall be glad if you will let me have the scroll per return as I cannot understand what is causing the delay.

Yours truly

Thomas Routledge.'

Today, the Commonwealth War Graves Commission issues scrolls for those commemorated on the Thiepval Memorial, and I am proud to include Joseph Routledge's in this book.

It is a sad fact that Botcherby, at this time a small village, should lose so many of its young men to war and affect the lives of so many families.

... and Private John Proudfoot

There was a happier outcome for the family of John Proudfoot, although there were months of worry and heartache before they knew this. John was 18 years old when he enlisted on 10 October 1916 and joined the King's Liverpool Regiment. He received training at Park Hall, an impressive Tudor building in Oswestry, Shropshire, which was taken over by the Army in 1915 to use as a training camp. From there he was sent to France.

The local newspapers at this time printed lists of those killed, missing or wounded and they make poignant reading. These were unofficial reports and one can only imagine how terrible it must have been for the families and friends perusing these sad columns for news.

On 7 September 1917 the *Carlisle Journal* listed the names of men from regiments other than the Border Regiment. It shows eight men had been killed in battle and two died of their wounds, and among the 34 men listed wounded was Private John Proudfoot.

By Tuesday, 28 May 1918 the *Journal* reported lists of missing soldiers and among them this notice:

> *'Mr and Mrs. Proudfoot, 37 West Walls, have received official notice that their son, Private John Proudfoot, Kings Liverpool Regiment, is reported missing since the 21st March. Any information will be gladly received.'*

A week later on 4 June the paper in its unofficial report again said: *'The following Carlisle men are missing and their friends would welcome intelligence respecting them.'* Among them again is John Proudfoot.

News was sparse and it is from a postcard sent by John's mother that we learn what had happened to him: he was in a prisoner-of-war camp in Kattowitz. We can only guess what she must have gone through before sending these everyday words, masking a million feelings:

> *'Dear Son*
>
> *'We received your Post Card alright. glad you are in the best of health as we are all the same at home. By the time you get this PC I expect you will get a parcel. so this is all at present.*
>
> *From your*
>
> *Loving Mother*
>
> *Love from All at home*
>
> *xxxxxxx*
>
> *xxxxxx'*

Kattowitz was in Upper Silesia, part of Germany, although today it is part of Poland and known as Katowice. It was a thriving industrial town and centre of the coal industry. The camp was mainly for Russian and Romanian prisoners but British prisoners were sent there in April 1918.

Receiving mail from home was vital for prisoners and they were allowed to write two letters every month and four postcards, although this right was often denied by the German authorities. They relied on parcels from their families to supplement the meagre diet of the camp - hence Mrs Proudfoot's comment about the parcel.

The Great War ended and slowly soldiers and prisoners returned home. For the Proudfoot family the *Carlisle Journal* on Friday, 7 February 1919 made the best reading with its report headlined:

'THE RETURN OF PRISONERS.

'*Further List of Repatriated Men... We have received from the Carlisle Citizen's League the following list of N.C.O.'s and men of the Border Regiment who have been repatriated to date.*'

There among the list of 'Other Regiments' was the name Pte J. Proudfoot, Liverpool Regt. (Carlisle).

Keeping in touch with the folks back home...

Letters and postcards home were an important way for families to keep in touch during WW1 and space was always at a premium.
My grandfather, Gig Hitchon, served with the Loyal North Lancashire Regiment and fought at Ypres. As the war ended, while travelling through Belgium and France, he sent the pencil-written postcard (left) home to his mother-in-law in Carlisle.

Shown below, clockwise from the left; Gig Hitchon in his army uniform; a postcard from the front; the ruins of Ypres where so many lost their lives; three examples of the skill and sentiments that went into producing the greetings cards.

Campagne de 1914. — Ruines d'YPRES
11 Incendie des Halles et rue de Lille (22 novembre 1914).

It was a happy homecoming for the Proudfoot family and in a few years they would move from West Walls to the newly built houses on Botcherby Avenue where they lived for many years.

My grandfather, Gig Hitchon, served with the Loyal North Lancashire Regiment and fought at Ypres. As the war ended he sent a pencil-written postcard home to his mother-in-law in Carlisle describing his journey back through Belgium and France:

> '21 October 1918
>
> *We are still on the move. The country where we are now has not been damaged much by Fritz. We had a grand reception in one town I've stayed in... the people gave us flags, coffee and all. The streets were decorated with flags and they nearly pulled our arms out with wanting to shake hands. They've been under German rule for four years which treated them badly. Well, Ma, what price a trip to the Palace tonight, it won't be long till we do go... kisses for Frank and Fanny. Your loving son, Gig.'*

After the horrors these men had seen in the trenches, the war was finally over; Belgium and France were liberated; and a trip to the Palace Theatre in Carlisle seemed like something good to look forward to.

For more details about the price Botcherby paid in the Great War see *Botcherby Heroes Remembered - 1914-1918* by James M. Robinson, Alex Proudfoot, and Derek Nash (P3 Publications, 2016) - it gives a biography of each of the servicemen commemorated on the War Memorial and powerfully records their sacrifice in the context of the times in which they lived and died.

Women at war... the Anderson sisters

On the home front, women played a major role in the war effort, particularly in the munitions factories. In 1915 the war was progressing on the Western Front with the policy of using heavy guns to control the battlefield. This meant a vast increase in the number of artillery shells needed and stocks were soon depleted as manufacturers struggled to keep up production. The shortage became a political scandal and, from this, a

Women at war – the Anderson sisters of Tilbury Road – Munitionettes

Clockwise from the far left: Annie and Jeanie Anderson; Jeanie with her husband, Harry Mills; the Munitionettes football team, East Cumberland Shell Factory; at work in the factory in the Drill Hall, Strand Road, Carlisle.

new coalition government was formed, with David Lloyd George being appointed Minister of Munitions.

The UK's largest munitions factory was built at Gretna, adjacent to the Solway Firth – known as HM Factory, Gretna – and stretched 12 miles from Mossband near Longtown in the east to Dornock-Eastriggs in the west, straddling the English-Scottish border. Munitions production began in April 1916 and by 1917 women were the largest portion of the workforce, known as Munitionettes. It was dangerous, working with hazardous chemicals, but the women were a major part of the war effort and worked cheerfully producing cordite, known locally as 'Devil's Porridge'.

Two such women were Jeanie and Annie Anderson of 3 Tilbury Road, Botcherby. The two sisters decided not to stay in the wooden hostels which had been built at Gretna and Eastriggs to house the workers, but chose to live at home, making the daily train journey between Carlisle and Gretna. It was on these daily travels that Jeanie found romance, when she met a tall good-looking young man, Harry Mills, whose poor eyesight had prevented him from being called to active service. He had been sent to work at Gretna from his hometown of Stoke where he worked in the pottery industry, and he lodged in Adelaide Street in Carlisle. Jeanie had been promoted to chargehand and Harry was part of the team that she managed. It was a happy day for the Anderson family when Jeanie and Harry were married on Christmas Eve 1917 at St Aidan's Church by the Reverend Frederick Millard. The happy couple made their home with Jeanie's parents at 3 Tilbury Road.

Annie meanwhile played football for the Munitionettes football team - sports were encouraged at the factory to keep morale high. It was quite a novelty to see the ladies playing football and always drew a good crowd of spectators. Teams from the various plants at Gretna, Carlisle and Workington would compete and matches were played to raise funds for the Border Regiment PoW Fund and charities helping wounded soldiers.

◆◆◆

Remembering... Iris Ferguson of Linden House

Miss Iris Ferguson lived at Linden House from 1908 and died when she was 90. She came to live at Linden House adjoining Wellington Place as a child with her parents. They were a well-to-do family and her father worked on the railway. During WW1 Iris's mother looked after wounded soldiers and her father laid on a party for them, putting a piano in the adjoining barn (now part of Victoria Aquatics at 45 Victoria Road). With Mrs Ferguson and Iris staying in the house, a barrel of beer was laid on for the soldiers and a good time was had by all.

When the building of the Magpie was first mooted, she thought she would have to move - but eventually stayed on.

In 1960 Iris set up a bakers shop on Croft Terrace with her friend Molly Cartner from Haltwhistle who lived at 45 Victoria Road. Mike Wood and Jacqueline Barton, former neighbours, had happy memories of those times. She later shared Linden House with her companion, Eleanor Crawford.

Left:: a young Iris with a well-fed cat; centre: blossom time in the garden at Linden House; right: Iris Ferguson with (left to right) neighbours Eleanor Crawford (her companion in later years), Mike Wood, and Jacqueline Barton.

The garden village

The story of Botcherby as a garden village is really the story of four families: the Hamiltons, the Grices, the Fairbairns and the Feddons. As their fortunes blossomed and faded, so the face of Botcherby changed, until today there is little left to suggest they ever existed. It was a very different picture in the 19th and early 20th centuries...

Walking up the hill from Warwick Road on what is now Victoria Road, but was once called Botcherby Lane and then Wellington Place, you are looking at a large part of Botcherby's former horticultural history. On the right-hand side it was nursery gardens all the way.

Fronting Wellington Place were the nursery gardens (later run by Feddons) looking directly across the road to the houses with their long flower-filled gardens. Immediately behind these nurseries stood the Banks Nurseries, used as a nursery ground of over seven acres. In 1880 it was described as touching Warwick Road and running up to the lane which branches off the Botcherby Road, now known as Banks Lane and once the back entrance to St Joseph's Home.

Wellington Place was a Georgian terrace built in the 1820s. Number 5 was the home of some of the Hamiltons who, at one time, owned all the nurseries and whose dwelling house is described as having an acre of ground also used as a nursery.

Continuing on past Mount Florida and onto Durranhill Road (formerly Botcherby Road) stood two sets of adjacent nursery gardens on the right, known as High Gardens and Sombie. Also owned by the Hamiltons, they would eventually become known as Botcherby Gardens, the land on which the housing estate would be built. Botcherby Gardens had a frontage of 639 feet on Botcherby Road with over four acres of fruit orchards on Sombie, with the five-acre High Gardens nursery grounds in front.

The Hamilton family also leased several fields at nearby Rosehill which they used as nursery grounds. It was a vast enterprise.

Opposite these, on the left-hand side of Durranhill Road, is the land known as Croft Nurseries, belonging to the Fairbairn family, but also once owned by the Hamiltons, where, many years later, Charlie Grice and his brothers ran the nurseries, becoming known as Grice's Croft when William Grice built the petrol filling station there.

The nurseries are of particular interest because, in the 19th century, they were really what Botcherby was all about. Apart from the brickworks on Tilbury Road, some houses and farms down Wood Street, the Star Inn on the corner of Warwick Road, the Plough Inn, a blacksmith's shop and Durran Hill House on the back road to Scotby everything was fields and gardens. It must have been a beautiful sight.

The Tithe Register of the township of Botcherby for 1847 gives a concise picture of land usage at that time:

Usage	Acres	Rods (or roods)	Perches
Arable land	296	1	9
Meadow	94	2	10
Permanent pasture	77	2	24
Market gardens	7	0	0
Total for the township	**475**	**2**	**3**

Data: Derek Nash.   1 acre = 4,840 sq. yards; 4 rods(roods) = 1 acre; 1 rod/rood = 40 perches.

Tithes for corn, grain and hay were charged at a rate of five shillings an acre (proportionate for smaller areas) and there were two beneficiaries - Mrs Eliza Lowry of Durran Hill and St Cuthbert's Church. The table below shows how this affected the Hamiltons and Fairbairns, who were to become two of the major market gardeners in Botcherby.

Landowner	Occupier	Map Ref.	Description	Size (Acre, Rod, Perch)			Paid to Eliza Lowry			Paid to the Church		
				a	r	p	£	s	d	£	s	d
Dawson, John	Hamilton, Thomas	87	Stake Meadow	1	2	16		4	9		1	11
Fairbairn, Mary	Rae, James	31	Home and Garden			27						
Fairbairn, Mary	Graham, John	34	Croft Arable	5	1	22		16			6	5
Fairbairn, Mary	Herself	32	Garden		2	4		2	4			
Fairbairn, Mary	Herself	32a	Garden and Buildings		1	6						
Fairbairn, Mary	Herself	33	Garden		1	6						
Graham, John (Butcher)	Hamilton, Thomas	83	Heames Meadow	4	2	3		15	7		1	5
Graham, Richard (Scotby)	Hamilton, Thomas	20	Market Garden	1	0	16		5	4			6
Hamilton, Thomas	Himself	18	Market Garden	4		20		18	7		1	10
Holmes, Catherine	Hamilton, Thomas	44	Market Garden	2				8	10			
Holmes, Catherine	Hamilton, Thomas	44a	Meadow			37						

Data: Derek Nash.   Note there is no mention of the tithes for 44a.

The Hamiltons at Botcherby Gardens

The Hamilton family were the first of the big four, originating in Great Corby. Thomas, the owner of the business, was the son of John and Elizabeth Hamilton. John was born in 1771, died at Botcherby in 1856 at the age of 85 and is described as a gardener. Elizabeth died in 1833, aged 60. Both were buried at Wetheral.

Thomas Hamilton was born in 1796 and married Ann Little at Wetheral Parish Church on 6 February 1828. They raised five children: Dinah born 1831 at Hayton and the four youngest, John (born 1832), Thomas (1834), Elizabeth (1836) and Mary Ann (1839) were all born at Botcherby. Elizabeth died in June 1857, at the age of 20. This would indicate that Thomas owned or leased the nurseries from at least 1832, just after his marriage.

The Botcherby Tithe Map of 1848 shows Thomas owning 18 acres of land, including the two areas known as High Gardens and Sombie. He also had an office in the Greenmarket in Carlisle and leased a number of fields close by for growing produce. As High Garden and Sombie were 10 acres, the other eight acres were the nursery opposite Wellington Place and the Banks Nurseries.

I have not found any earlier origins of Botcherby Gardens further back than 1830.

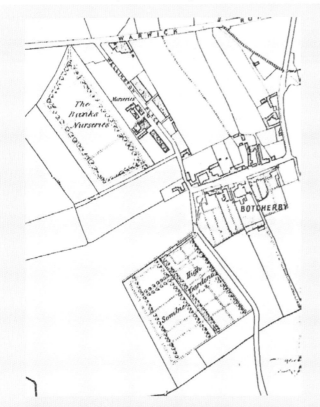

Hamilton's Gardens

Left: map of the Botcherby nurseries in the 19th century, showing the large area they covered. Right: an advert in Arthur's 1880 Directory of Carlisle for Hamilton's gardens and nurseries.

The Strawberry Gardens were established in 1833, as a report in the *Carlisle Journal* on 29 June 1833 relates:

'STRAWBERRY GARDENS:

'These delightful places of summer resort are on the increase in this neighbourhood. Mr. Capstick's garden at Scotby, and Mrs. Galbraith's at Etterby have long been admired for the excellence of the fruit they produce, the great taste with which they are laid out, and the extremely obliging manners of their proprietors. Another garden has been opened this week at Botcherby. The strawberries we have tasted, and can speak for their goodness; neat bowers have been constructed around a green plot in the garden intended for those who love to "trip-it on the green".'

By the following year the paper reported on 5 July 1834:

'STRAWBERRY GARDENS

'We mentioned last year that a new strawberry garden had been opened at Botcherby. This season it *has been very greatly improved. Some delightful bowers have been formed, and the walk much beautified. The fine weather has attracted crowds of people to the spot, and it now forms one of the most pleasant evening promenades in the neighbourhood of the town. On Wednesday evening, the members of the Harmonic Society gave a concert in the garden. Crowds of people flocked from the city and at one time we should think from three to four hundred persons were present. Dancing commenced at seven o'clock, on a green plot which had been prepared for the purpose... music is now in attendance, we believe, every evening, and on Tuesday next there is to be another gala.'*

As its popularity grew, so did the quality of the entertainment. Between 1837 and 1841, Billy Purvis, a famous showman and entertainer, gave theatrical performances there during the fruit seasons. Purvis was greatly admired by Charles Dickens, who is thought to have used him as a prototype for the character of Vincent Crummles, the theatrical manager in *Nicholas Nickleby*. On 15 November 1892 the *Carlisle Journal* reflected back on those halcyon days:

> *'Billy was immense on a Sunday evening during the fruit season surrounded by the ladies and gentlemen of the corps of his theatre at Mr. Hamilton's gardens at Botcherby: Billy resplendent in white ducks, nankeen waistcoat, blue coat, bright buttons and white hat, with a diamond ring on his forefinger with which he emphasised his oracular flow of fun, wit and good humour. Sambo Sutton, a genial negro... a little more pronounced in dress, generally accompanied the great man.'*

In *The Life of Billy Purvis* it tells that, after the Newcastle races of 1834, he and his company - the Victoria Company - were engaged at Whitehaven Theatre for three months before taking Macready's Theatre in Blackfriars Street, Carlisle, for one month. He travelled extensively in the North East, Scotland and Cumberland with his show, and it is likely that he performed at Botcherby during these visits to Carlisle.

This was a time when the re-opening of Vauxhall Gardens in London in 1841 had begun a fashion for pleasure gardens, where people would gather for entertainment and to mix socially in beautiful surroundings. In the days before the development of the railways and day trips, such gardens became popular all over the country and Carlisle was no exception. Year after year glowing reports appeared, showing that Thomas Hamilton was something of an entrepreneur: his gardens were very popular with the people of Carlisle and surrounding villages for many years.

A report in the *Carlisle Journal* on 19 July 1850 says:

> *'Botcherby Strawberry Gardens – These gardens are this season a most fashionable place of resort. They lie at a very convenient distance from the city.'*

The following year, on 4 July 1851, the same newspaper informed the public that:

> *'Botcherby Strawberry Gardens Band of Music will be in attendance at these gardens on Tuesday, 1ˢᵗ, if the weather be fine and if wet not till the following evening.'*

Left: Happy times - the famous entertainer Billy Purvis was a great hit at the Strawberry Gardens in the 1830s
Right: a colourful advertisement for Hamilton's gardens and nurseries.

By 21 July 1854, the *Carlisle Journal* carried the following advert, announcing an exciting new development:

'BOTCHERBY GARDENS

'*THOMAS HAMILTON returns thanks to his Friends and the Public generally, for their former Patronage, and hopes by a respectful attention to Visitors and assiduity in the execution of all orders he may continue to merit their favours.*

'*The gardens will be open every day except Sundays.*

'*T. H. begs most respectfully to intimate that he has now the assistance of his brother, JOSEPH HAMILTON, (Author of the Hamiltonian System of Cultivating the Pine Apple), who will stipulate for the erection of Green-houses, Vineries, Pine Stores, &c. He will also superintend the growing of such Fruits where a Gardener is not kept, at a moderate expense to the owner; will likewise lay out new Gardens; and will contract for the dressing and furnishing of small Gardens with such plants as will display the greatest amount of bloom throughout the season.*'

This expansion may have been the result of Thomas inheriting a considerable sum of money in 1853 from his uncle, Thomas Hamilton Snr, who died at 11 Lowther Street on 22 March 1853, aged 83, and left over £17,000 (over £1.5m today). By a strange coincidence he was lodging at the house of Thomas Tweeddale, the coachbuilder, who died the previous day, aged 68 years. Thomas Hamilton Snr had worked in London for many years as a teacher of the violin and it was said that he was dancing master to King George 111. In Carlisle, he was known as a generous benefactor – the local newspaper *The Citizen* described him as a '*retired toe twirler who is now living very snugly on the fruits of his art.*' He was one of a group of benefactors, including the Fairbairn and Howard families, who supported the building of SS Mary and Joseph's church in Chapel Street in 1824, where he formed a choir.

Joseph Hamilton, introduced in the *Carlisle Journal* advert above, was something of an international celebrity for his expertise in growing pineapples. Born in Cumberland in 1803, by 1832 he was living in Heaton Mersey, Stockport and was married to Susannah who had been born there in 1811. Their son John was born there in 1833.

In 1844 he published the summation of his experience in the snappily titled *A TREATISE ON THE CULTIVATION OF THE PINE APPLE; IN WHICH A SHORT ACCOUNT OF THE MODES ADOPTED BY SOME OF THE MOST EMINENT PINE GROWERS IS GIVEN; WITH A DETAIL OF THE AUTHOR'S METHOD OF CULTIVATING THE VINE AND CUCUMBER, IN THE SAME HOUSE. ALSO, A DESCRIPTION OF THE PINE STOVE USED AT THORNFIELD, AND A PLAN FOR THE CONSTRUCTION OF HOTHOUSES, IN WHICH TO COMBINE THE CULTURES OF THESE PLANTS TO WHICH ARE ADDED, EFFICACIOUS RECIPES FOR THE DESTRUCTION OF INSECTS PECULIAR TO THEM!*

The previous year, he had written to *The Sydney Morning Herald*, giving detailed evidence of his expertise:

'CULTURE OF THE PINEAPPLE

'*Sir, - I offer to your notice a few brief remarks on what I call a new era in the cultivation of the Pine, as it is practised by me at Thornfield. Some of your readers will perhaps remember that in 1840, October 30, No. 200, p. 693 of the Gazette, there is stated the result of several experiments; I also refer your readers to another paragraph written by a Manchester gardener, 1841, No. 252, p. 713; he there stated the fruit of an immense size which he saw growing on suckers. I wish again to draw the attention of your readers to what I consider by far the best system of the cultivation of the Pine. Viz, that of producing fine fruit in a short time from suckers. I cut last summer nine fruit, and their weight was 53 lbs. 7 oz. Avoirdupois; the age of the plants since the preceding fruit was cut, varying from eight to twelve months; the sorts were one Enville, three Montserrats, and five Jamaicas. I have again dressed them, and placed them in the fruiting pit, and I expect next year that they will produce* even larger fruit than they have done this season. I do not hesitate to say, the same plants of the Queen Pine would each produce three fruits in two years and the Montserrats, Jamaicas, &c, would yield one fruit annually, unless some unforeseen accident occur. I have within the last twelve months, cut two fruit from one plant of the Black Jamaica, weighing twelve pounds twelve ounces; a third sucker is making rapid progress, and, in all probability, will not shame its predecessors. I cut two fruit last January, a Montserrat, 4 lbs. 8 oz., a Black Antigua, 4 lbs. 4 oz.; and not many months since the preceding fruit was cut from the same plants; my master pronounced them a first-rate flavour, even surpassing those grown in the summer in the common system. That what I have already stated is a fact, many of my neighbours can testify. Allow me then to ask, what inference can be drawn from such a result, particularly when we consider the trifling expense of growing this noble fruit to that of growing them from crowns or suckers? At any rate, it will be desirable to those who are in some measure dependent on its produce for a living. It is not for me to predestine what may be the result of a few years' practice yet I believe that, ere long, I shall hear that out of a space of 22 feet by 9, 2 cwt. of fruit can be cut annually, independantly of any succession-house. What a sacrifice I have seen during my 20 years' acquaintance with the culture of this plant, by the mistaken notion that, as soon as the first fruit is cut the plant has finished its career, and is of course only fit to be consigned to the flames of rubbish heap; whereas, had it been preserved and judiciously managed, in all probability the second fruit would have far surpassed the first, both in size and quality.

I am, &c.

JOSEPH HAMILTON,

Gardener to F. A. Philips. Esq., Thornfield, Lancashire.

March 17.'

A TREATISE
ON THE CULTIVATION
OF THE
PINE APPLE;
IN WHICH A SHORT ACCOUNT OF THE
MODES ADOPTED BY SOME OF THE MOST EMINENT
PINE GROWERS IS GIVEN;
WITH A DETAIL OF THE AUTHOR'S METHOD
OF CULTIVATING THE
VINE AND CUCUMBER,
IN THE SAME HOUSE.
ALSO, A DESCRIPTION OF THE
PINE-STOVE USED AT THORNFIELD,
AND A PLAN
FOR THE CONSTRUCTION OF HOTHOUSES,
IN WHICH TO COMBINE THE CULTURE OF THESE PLANTS
TO WHICH ARE ADDED,
EFFICACIOUS RECIPES FOR THE DESTRUCTION OF
INSECTS PECULIAR TO THEM.

BY JOSEPH HAMILTON,
GARDENER TO F. A. PHILIPS, ESQ., THORNFIELD, NEAR STOCKPORT.

LONDON:
PUBLISHED BY JOSEPH MASTERS, ALDERSGATE-STREET.
MDCCCXLIV.

Pineapples in Botcherby – Joseph Hamilton's Treatise

At the cutting edge of horticulture, in 1844 Joseph Hamilton published a method of growing pineapples, vines and cucumbers together that brought him wide renown.

Botcherby was obviously acquiring a major player in the cultivation of pineapples and Joseph proved to be as good as his self promotion, as his business flourished.

A further announcement appeared in the *Carlisle Journal* on 29 February 1856. By now Thomas was 60 years old and his father John died that year and it seems that he may have been thinking of stepping back from running the Gardens at Botcherby:

> *'THOMAS HAMILTON, of BOTCHERBY, NURSERYMAN, SEEDSMAN &c., begs to return his most sincere thanks to the Nobility, Gentry, and Public for the most kind support he has received during the 30 years he has been in Business and begs to inform them that the said business will in future be conducted in a more extensive way by his Sons and Partners, under the Firm of HAMILTON AND ROBSON. Botcherby, 21 Feb, 1856.'*

There followed an extensive advertisement for the new company, Hamilton and Robson, indicating the vast scope and diversity of their nurseries and for a shop at Carlisle Market Place for the sale of flowers, fruit and vegetables, as well as their market stall. The Robsons were cousins of the Hamiltons but it appears that the partnership did not survive for long – just a year in fact!

By 1857, the enterprise was undergoing a sea change, as three adverts in the same issue of the *Carlisle Journal* show. The first announces the end of a partnership between the younger Hamiltons and William Robson:

> *'NOTICE is hereby given that the PARTNERSHIP heretofore subsisting between us, the undersigned WILLIAM ROBSON, JOHN HAMILTON, THOMAS HAMILTON, the Younger, and JOHN WILLIAM HAMILTON, as GARDENERS, NURSERYMEN, FLORISTS, SEEDSMEN, and GREEN GROCERS, carrying on business at the City of CARLISLE, and at BOTCHERBY, in the County of Cumberland, under the Firm of "HAMILTONS and ROBSON," was this day DISSOLVED by mutual consent. Dated the Eighteenth day of February, One Thousand Eight Hundred and Fifty Seven.*
>
> > *WILLIAM ROBSON,*
> >
> > *JOHN HAMILTON,*
> >
> > *THOMAS HAMILTON, Junior,*
> >
> > *JOHN WILLIAM HAMILTON.*
>
> *Witness -*
>
> *THOMAS WRIGHT, Solicitor, Carlisle.*
>
> *JNO. NORMAN, Solicitor, Carlisle.*
>
> *'The Debts owing to the Firm of HAMILTON and ROBSON, will be received by Mr. NORMAN, Solicitor, 19, Bank Street, Carlisle; and it is requested that all Claims upon the Firm may be also sent to Mr. NORMAN.'*

It does not seem to have been a particularly amicable ending, as the next advert suggests:

> *'WILLIAM ROBSON begs to say that the SEEDS BUSINESS lately conducted by the Firm of HAMILTONS and ROBSON is now carried on by himself, and takes this opportunity of acknowledging and tendering his thanks for the liberal patronage bestowed upon the late Firm, and hopes to be favoured with a continuum of the same.*
>
> *'W. R. has purchased an extensive Stock of Garden, Flower, and Agricultural SEEDS, which have been selected from the best Growers. He has also made arrangements to Supply the Market with Nursery and Forest Trees, Vegetables, Fruits, &c. All orders shall have his most careful and prompt attention.*
>
> *87, Market-place, Carlisle.'*

Meanwhile, the older Thomas Hamilton seemed keen to dissociate himself from these proceedings. His advert declared:

> *'THOMAS HAMILTON, Senior, begs to announce to his Friends and the Public that he has RESUMED POSSESSION of his GARDEN and PREMISES at BOTCHERBY, where he will carry on his business in all its branches, and where his customers will receive every attention.*
>
> *'He will not have a Shop in Carlisle, but Mrs. HAMILTON will attend the Green Market, as formerly.*
>
> *Botcherby, 19th, Feb., 1857.'*

The phrase 'resumed possession' may also refer to the ending of his venture at Dale Head Hall, situated on the shores of Thirlmere, at the foot of Helvellyn. Today it is an hotel but, in the 1850s, Thomas Hamilton tried to make a success of it as an extensive pleasure garden. We don't know the outcome but, within three years, he was back in Botcherby.

The older Hamiltons seemed to have continued to develop a thriving business at Botcherby for, in *The Gardeners' Chronicle and Agricultural Gazette* dated 13 August 1870, a letter sings the praises of their venture:

*'**Vine Growing near Carlisle.** - If any of your readers interested in the cultivation of the Vine should be passing the border city (Carlisle) and could spare an hour or two, they might see in the establishment of Mr. Thomas Hamilton, Botcherby, a very good specimen of the Black Hamburgh on the extension system, about 50 years of age , nearly filling a good sized vinery. The present crop is a most abundant one, and the wonder is, how they will get it ripened under the circumstances, as there was no preparation at planting, and there seems to be little within its reach to sustain such a crop. There are three other large vineries in this establishment well worthy of inspection. The celebrated Pine and Cucumber grower's (Mr. Josh. Hamilton's) establishment, is near the former, and both places may be seen at the same time; a walk through the latter with this practical grower could not fail to be instructive. He is also an advocate of the extension system, and has had a new vinery erected with a view to carrying out this principle from the beginning. John Taylor, Rose Hill Lodge, Botcherby, Carlisle.'*

But its days were numbered. Thomas Hamilton made his will on 10 October 1870 and died in June 1873, aged 77 years. He was buried at Wetheral on 19 June 1873. He left the bulk of his estate to his wife and two sons, John and Thomas. He also left £750 to his daughter Mary Ann, who had married Joshua Wannop of Brunstock on 27 January 1862 at the parish church of SS Mary and Joseph in Chapel Street, Carlisle. The entry reads:

'Joshua Wannop of Brunstock, son of Thomas Wannop.

Mary Ann Hamilton of Botcherby, daughter of Thomas Hamilton.

Witnesses: Thomas Hamilton of Botcherby, Eleonora Wannop of Brunstock

Lucas Curry [Reverend]'

The Wannops were wealthy landowners and, in 1881 Joshua and Mary Ann were living at Newby Hall, Irthington, with their four daughters and two sons. The 1881 census shows that Joshua was a farmer with 174 acres and four men, and Mary Ann was a farmer with 30 acres and a 'beerhouse wife'. They had five servants.

Thomas's wife, Ann, died aged 74 and was buried at Wetheral on 12 April 1880 and it is after this - after 50 years of successful trading - that things seemed to start going wrong.

The beginning of the end

On 30 August 1880 the *Carlisle Journal* reported an important sale coming up of Hamilton's house, land, contents and the whole business.

The actual sale day is reported on 21 September in the same paper and attendance was sparse. The only bidder was Mr Wilson, agent for one of the building societies who made a total bid of £3,000 and, as no advance on this was made, there was no sale. The dwelling house mentioned was probably 5 Wellington Place. Thomas Wannop, Mary Ann's wealthy father-in-law, saved the day and some of the land, enabling Botcherby Gardens to be kept in the family, as the following report on 4 February 1881 in the *Carlisle Journal* shows:

*'**Botcherby Gardens***

'That portion of the property of the late Mr. Thomas Hamilton, called High Gardens and Sorby (sic), but better known as Botcherby Gardens, Carlisle, consisting of nursery grounds, fruit gardens, vineries, conservatories, greenhouses, etc., and containing about 10 acres has been purchased by Mr. Thomas Wannop, Botcherby for £1800. We understand that Messrs. Hamilton intend to carry on the business as usual.'

But by 20 May 1881 it was reported that Messrs Hamilton were going into liquidation when a sale notice appeared in the *Carlisle Journal* advertising a two-day sale of liquidated stock from Hamilton's. Then on 31 May 1881 the *Carlisle Journal* reported on a creditors meeting to wind up the estate by the end of the year.

The story had taken another strange twist when on 11 February 1881 the *Carlisle Journal* had headlined a court case with the dramatic words:

*'**THE CROFT, BOTCHERBY. APPLICATION TO GET POSSESSION.**'*

Strawberry Gardens forever? Not quite!

Clockwise from below left: hard times - sale notice of Hamilton's as a going concern, 30 August 1880; notice of the sale of houses and land, 21 September 1880; sale notice of plants, exotic and domestic, following the liquidation of the company, 11 May 1881.

FREEHOLD LAND, AND EXTENSIVE, VALUABLE AND LUCRATIVE GARDENER'S, FLORIST'S, FRUITERER'S, NURSERYMAN'S, AND SEEDSMAN'S BUSINESS, AS A GOING CONCERN, IN THE COUNTY OF CUMBERLAND, FOR SALE.

MR. C. P. HARDY has been instructed to SELL, by AUCTION, shortly, the entire BUSINESS, as a going concern, of the late Mr. Thomas Hamilton, of BOTCHERBY. The Estate comprises 18a. 3r. 22p. of superior Freehold Land, on which are erected extensive Vineries, Conservatories, Cucumber and Propagating Houses, Greenhouses, Dwelling House with Out-offices, Stables, Coachhouse, Barns, Byres, Piggeries, Potting and Packing Sheds, Boiler and Forcing Houses, Cottage, Strawberry Forum, &c., &c. The Glass Houses, which are mostly in splendid condition, are filled with the choicest Vines, Cucumbers, Melons, &c., the whole of which have been intelligently cultivated, and the adaptation of the best mode of heating and ventilating at the least cost is very demonstrable. A large portion of the area is covered with fine Forest and Fruit Trees, in all stages of their early growth, for which large orders can be promptly executed. In addition to the foregoing are beautiful varieties of all kinds of Decorative Shrubs and Plants, large Fruit and Vegetable Gardens, and the celebrated BOTCHERBY STRAWBERRY BEDS. Besides these are the growing produce of several fields in the immediate vicinity, held under lease, the goodwill of which will be included in the transfer. Botcherby Gardens are situate 1¼ miles from the Citadel Station, Carlisle, and are an intensely popular institution.—Messrs. Hamilton, the Owners, will show the property, which embraces magnificent building sites. Descriptive Catalogues will be published, and may be had, with further particulars, at the Offices of Messrs. DOBINSON and WATSON, Solicitors, Carlisle.
47, Lowther Street, Carlisle.

PRELIMINARY ANNOUNCEMENTS

BEDDING-OUT, STOVE, AND GREENHOUSE PLANTS FOR SALE.

IN RE-HAMILTON, BOTCHERBY, IN LIQUIDATION.

C. P. HARDY has been instructed by the Trustee, to SELL by AUCTION, in the ALBERT HALL, CARLISLE, on THURSDAY and FRIDAY, the 26th and 27th MAY inst., upwards of 6,000 BEDDING-OUT, STOVE, and GREENHOUSE PLANTS, &c., including Zonale, Ivy-leaved, double and single Tricolor, and other Geraniums, Petunias, Verbenas, Cyclamens, Epiphillium, Truncatum, Camellias, Orchids, Fuschias, Roses, Ferns, Carnations, Harrison's New Musk Azaleas, Tree Ferns, fine Stag's Horn Fern, a splendid Dracæna Australis, &c., &c. Also a Milner's Holdfast Safe, 28in. by 20in. by 20in. Catalogues will be prepared, by which intending purchasers will see the order of Sale, which will be strictly adhered to. The Sale will commence punctually at Two o'Clock p.m. each day, prior to which hour the plants may be seen.
47, Lowther Street, Carlisle, May 11th, 1881.

HARNESS AND SADDLERY SALE

SALES BY PUBLIC AUCTION.

HOUSES AND LAND.

BOTCHERY NURSERY GARDENS.—Yesterday afternoon Mr. C. P. Hardy offered for sale at the County Hotel the nursery gardens belonging to and occupied by Messrs. Hamilton, at Botcherby, near this city. The whole of the nursery, fruit, and flower gardens are 18a. 3r. 22p. in extent, and comprise dwelling house and outbuildings, vineries, conservatories, cucumber and propagating houses, greenhouses, boiler and forcing houses, strawberry forum, and all the apparatus and appliances necessary for carrying on the extensive business pursued by Messrs. Hamilton for a great number of years. The gardens, vineries, &c., are filled with produce, a large portion of the area is covered with forest and fruit trees and shrubs, and the whole is in full working order. Most of the ground is on the west side of the road leading from the Warwick Road to Botcherby, but the house is on the east side, with an acre of ground which is used as a nursery garden. The whole property was first put up in one lot, but no offer was evoked from a company that was not very numerous. It was then divided, the first lot being the dwelling house, greenhouses, vineries, and nursery garden on the east side of the road, the total area being about two acres. For this Mr. Wilson, agent for one of the building societies, offered £600, and nobody advanced on it. The second lot comprised the fruit gardens, which are so well known to all the people of Carlisle and the vicinity, and the nursery grounds behind. The fruit gardens, which open upon and have a long frontage to the Botcherby Road, possess an area of 4a. 1r. 16p., and the nursery grounds behind are 5a. 2r. 33p. in extent. For this Mr. Wilson was again the only bidder, and his offer was £1,400. The third lot consisted of a plot of land also used as a nursery ground, having an area of 7a. 1r. 23p. This ground touches on the Warwick Road and runs up to the lane which branches off the Botcherby Road opposite the new houses which are being built there. Mr. Wilson offered £1,000, and was again left in solitary possession of the field. Mr. Hardy then again tried the property in one lot, and invited an advance on £3,000, the aggregate of Mr. Wilson's bids, but failed to evoke a response. Messrs. Hamilton are lessees of several fields at Rosehill, near Botcherby, which they have used as nursery grounds, and the produce of these fields, still standing, was now offered for sale. No bid was called forth, and accordingly no sale was made. Messrs. Dobinson and Watson acted as solicitors for the vendors.

ESTATE AT HESKET IN THE FOREST. Mr. E. T. Piper

This referred to the land on the eastern side of the road where Croftlands and Grice's Croft Filling Station would stand in future years. It appears that Thomas Hamilton & Sons had owned this land also but had mortgaged it to Andrew Wright of High Crosby (first mortgagee) and Messrs Mackie, Davidson and Gladstone (second mortgagees) for £900 and £500 respectively. The court case was an application that the Hamilton brothers deliver up *'quiet and peaceable possession of the property at Botcherby aforesaid, known as the Croft, including dwelling houses, stables, barns, &c.'* to the mortgagees or to Mr E. F. Fairbairn of Edentown, gardener, the purchaser of the property.

On Thomas's death in 1873 his sons, Thomas and John Hamilton, wished to carry on a banking account with Messrs Mackie, Davidson and Gladstone and they executed a reversionary mortgage to the bank to secure £4,000. That mortgage had full powers of sale. The sale of August 1880 found no buyers and by September 1881 the Hamilton brothers went into liquidation. George Hodgson Dixon was appointed trustee of the estate in October.

The mortgagees then exercised their powers and sold a portion of the property to Mr E. F. Fairbairn for £875 and the two brothers were told that they would have to leave, which they disregarded. Mr Fairbairn had declined to buy the stock of trees and shrubs and the trustee felt that the Hamiltons should therefore be given time to sell them. A lengthy dispute took place in court on the valuation of stock and other offers that were made but disregarded. Obviously the Hamilton brothers and the trustee felt hard done by at the low price paid by Mr Fairbairn. Even the judge seemed put out as he said he had no jurisdiction in the matter and felt it would be unfortunate to spend all the money in law suits. The report ends: *'His Honour entered in his book: - Application dismissed for want of jurisdiction.'* By 30 September the company was in liquidation with the stock in a trade sale.

A further report in the *Carlisle Journal* on 25 November 1881 advertises that 7.5 acres of garden land lately occupied by Hamilton and Sons, Botcherby was to be let either in one or smaller lots. Particulars available from J. Wilson, Builder, Botcherby. It seems that Mr Fairbairn won the day.

John Hamilton was again at the Courts on Saturday 18 July 1885, giving evidence in the case against two youths from Greystone Road and Flower Street charged with stealing strawberries and damaging the gardens. They had been seen by PC Gordon entering from an adjoining field and John Hamilton said he had suffered greatly from such depredations. They were fined 10 shillings and costs with a warning on their future behaviour.

By 15 December 1885 the *Carlisle Journal* reported that Botcherby Gardens were to be let:

> *'Old and valuable strawberry and nursery gardens in occupation of Messrs. J & T Hamilton. 10 acres, 4 large glass houses, fruit trees, vines - newly built dwelling house, stable etc. Apply Thomas Wannop, Botcherby.'*

John Hamilton, the eldest son, may have been in poor health by this time as he died, aged 55, and was buried at Wetheral on 27 December 1886. No record has been found of his brother Thomas: he is not located on the 1891 census and he too may have died by then. Neither brother seems to have married and their housekeeper, their cousin Isabella Robson, died in June 1892 at St Joseph's Home in Albert Street, Carlisle. It was the end of over fifty years of the Hamiltons at Botcherby Gardens and Nurseries.

Wellington Place Gardens

Before leaving the Hamilton family it is interesting to note that, in the 1858 *Post Office Directory of Westmorland & Cumberland*, Joseph Hamilton, described as a 'forcing & exotic gardener', lived at 5 Wellington Place. His brother Thomas is shown as nurseryman, market gardener and proprietor of pleasure gardens at Botcherby Gardens. Joseph had died by the time of the 1881 census and his son John Hamilton, aged 48 and a seedsman, lived at 3 Wellington Place. Also there were his widowed 70-year-old mother Susannah and five-year-old son Joseph, together with his four daughters, Mary, Susannah, Jane and Frances, all aged between 23 and eight and all born at Botcherby.

By then R. Robinson, a working gardener, lived at 5 Wellington Place. In A. B. Moss's *Carlisle Directory 1884* John Hamilton is shown as living at Linden House and trading as a nurseryman and florist, owning Wellington Place Nurseries. In the burial register of the church SS Mary and Joseph in Chapel Street, there is a burial shown for 29 August 1888 of John Hamilton of Linden House. A notice appeared in the *Carlisle Journal* on 2 November 1928 when Messrs Dalton & Son advertised the sale of 5 Wellington Place together with the market garden opposite, with a frontage to Wellington Place of 491 feet and a depth of 154 feet, suitable for building purposes. The market garden was sold to Mr Yeates of Whitehaven (formerly of Botcherby Hall) for £400, but the house was withdrawn at £250. (In later years William Feddon would live at 5 Wellington Place, by then re-named 35 Victoria Road, with his nursery gardens across the road, adjoining the Magpie Inn.)

The advertisement which appeared in the *Carlisle Journal* on 15 December 1885 offering Botcherby Gardens and house to be let from Candlemas 1886 soon had a taker. Thomas French of Wetheral and his wife Mary were the next tenants and also had Stall No. 29 in the Market Hall by 1894. They had two young sons, Robert and John, and employed Robert Roe as assistant gardener.

On 10 July 1891 an advert appeared in the *Carlisle Journal* informing the public that the Strawberry Gardens were now opening daily. Little is known of their period at the gardens but, by 11 July 1899, Thomas Wannop of Linstock Castle was again advertising the gardens to let in the *Carlisle Journal*, and it is noted that they are currently occupied by Thomas French, fruiterer. It was then that William Grice took over Botcherby Gardens.

The Grice family – gardeners, florists and musicians

Tuesday 24 April 1900 was a fresh spring day. It was the day when William Grice walked down the bank from his home at St Ann's Hill, Stanwix to the offices of Saul's solicitors at 23 Castle Street, Carlisle. A tall, lean, bearded figure with an energetic manner, he was eager to start a new chapter in his life – and he did, by signing a lease. His father Samuel, had died on 1 September 1899 and now it was a time of new beginnings.

The lease, for nine years dating from 11 November 1899, was for a market garden at Botcherby. The property consisted of 10 acres, a dwelling house, stable, greenhouses and other buildings and would become the home of William, his children and grandchildren over the next 40 years and more. William was leasing the garden from Silas George Saul of Brunstock, a wealthy landowner and solicitor, at a rent of £70 per year. Saul may have been acting on behalf of the Wannop family, who owned the property from 1881 when Thomas Wannop bought it to save the Hamilton's from losing it. Thomas Wannop died in 1896 aged 90 and his heir William Wannop still owned the property in 1909.

William (or Will as he was called) was born at Houghton Green, near Warrington in 1850 and by 1861 he lived with his parents Samuel and Mary Grice (of Kirklinton) and his three brothers and two sisters at Willow Holme, Caldewgate in Carlisle.

Samuel

Samuel Grice married Mary Carruthers in 1847 at Houghton, near Warrington, before moving to Carlisle in 1853 with their three oldest children, James, William and Martha. Samuel, Richard and Mary were born after they had settled in Carlisle. In 1861, they were living in Willow Holme and by 1871 had moved to Holme Lowe, near Silloth in Cumberland, where Samuel had a nursery garden of 13 acres, employing two men as well as his son Richard. The land had been part of Greenrow Academy (where Stanwix Holiday Park now stands). It closed in 1871 and stood empty for the next 17 years. The market garden and nursery were established and part of the school building was used as accommodation for the 'Carlisle Poor Children's Holiday' scheme sponsored by the citizens of Carlisle.

On 31 August 1888 the buildings and land were sold by auction in the Queen's Hotel, Silloth. They were bought by Joseph Wood, who owned Wood's Bazaar on Silloth seafront, for £2,190. He lived there until his death in 1932.

By September 1896 Samuel, who had moved the family back to Carlisle, had a valuation of his stock at Greenrow nurseries made, which consisted of hundreds of fruit bushes and trees, 30 flower beds and two greenhouses. On 29 August 1899 he made his Will and died on 1 September 1899. His son William had to dispose of his assets at Greenrow. After his father's death, Richard is still shown as a market gardener there in 1901.

The Grices move to Botcherby

Clockwise from top left: Samuel Grice, patriarch of the family who brought them from Greenrow, Silloth to Carlisle; William Grice and his wife, Jean Burnett; a family portrait of William, Jean and their children; the 1900 lease that William signed for Botcherby Gardens.

William

William was a nurseryman all his working life and had nursery gardens at Greenrow nearby. He married Jean Burnett at Annan in 1872 at the age of 21 and they had eight children: James (born 1872), Mary Jane (1873), Samuel (1876), Catherine Isabella (1878), David William (1880), Richard (1883), Martha Ellen (1886) and Margaret Alice (1889). The children had all been born at Greenrow, except James, Mary and Samuel who were born in Annan.

At the time of Samuel's death, the family were living at the Convent Lodge, St Ann's Hill, Carlisle, where William was gardener at the girls' school run by the Society of the Sacred Heart Sisters (now Austin Friars School). It was built in 1891 at a cost of £25,000 and stood in 11 acres of grounds laid out to gardens. William's eldest son, James, was a gardener's assistant, and the younger Samuel was a mason's apprentice.

In 1903 the Sisters left Carlisle to found a teacher-training college in Elmfield Road, Gosforth, and Mary, his eldest daughter, who had joined the Order, moved with them. By 1905 she moved to the Order's mother house at Roehampton, London, and would remain a nun until she died at the age of 92 in 1965.

William worked hard and the gardens flourished. They stretched to where Borland Avenue would be built, the boundary marked by a row of large cypress trees (some of which were still standing in the 1950s.) There were vast orchards of apple trees and every fruit imaginable; rows of long greenhouses, where tomatoes and grapes grew, stood near the house, with beehives nearby in a row.

On 1 February 1909 he signed a new lease, this time with William Wannop of Linstock Castle, a wealthy landowner and farmer, with the rent now £81 per year and the term was on a year-to-year basis. The conditions of the lease were far from satisfactory from William's point of view as, by October 1909, the property was up for auction and advertised as suitable for building purposes!

Unsettling times at Botcherby Gardens

Clockwise from above left: the house at the entrance to Botcherby Gardens before the widening of the lane, by an unknown artist - this would be their home until the building of the estate; the advertisement offering the land for sale as suitable for a housing estate; extract from the 1909 lease making it clear that it ran on a year-to-year basis only; the extent of the gardens leased by the Grices; William Grice in the gardens.

There appears to have been no takers on this occasion but this lack of stability must have been difficult for William and his family: after nearly 10 years the nurseries were well-established in the city, with his children working in different aspects of the business. There was a stall in Carlisle Market where his daughter Alice often worked and a greengrocer's shop at 151 Botchergate run by his son Jim, as well as deliveries made by horse and cart and the sale of produce at their florist's shop in Botcherby Gardens. This was run by daughter Catherine Scott, who was a widow since her husband Nathan's death, leaving her with a four-year-old son William to provide for. An uncle, William Carruthers, aged 78, was employed as a joiner and Mary Logue was a domestic servant.

Alice often worked in the gardens along with the hired help and recalled that she worked extremely hard. There was always something to do: hoeing weeds and sowing seeds, tending rhubarb and raspberries, pruning roses and planting bulbs. She also had a glorious singing voice and had trained to be a professional singer. Locally she took part in many musical shows both at the Waterton Hall and with the Carlisle Musical Society.

CARLISLE OPERATIC SOCIETY.

Alice Grice/Dunn

Clockwise from top left: Alice with her father William; Alice (top left in poster) in 1929 taking the leading role in Amasis, a comic opera; working in the gardens with Maudie, one of the workers; her wedding to Laurie Dunn; 8 Durranhill Road (left), her home after the estate was built; Alice with young Alice in the back garden of the house; laburnum - always a feature in the front garden; Laurie and Alice with their son Father Gerard and his aunt, Sister Mary Grice; Alice in a play at the Waterton Hall, as St Dorothy of the Roses (seated centre).

Alice was a familiar sight cycling up Warwick Road to Our Lady and St Joseph's Church where she sang in the choir.

There were several staff employed in the gardens and in the house. William's fourth son, Richard – or Dick as he was known - worked alongside his father and, on his time off, was to be found playing his fiddle in the Star Inn where the lads of the village met to share 'the crack' and down a pint. On New Year's Day 1923, Dick married Annie Fagan at Our Lady and St Joseph's Church and then lived in the Garden House, where they had a daughter Alicia (also known as Alice) born on 7 January 1927. Dick took over the business on his father's death on 9 April 1927, at the age of 76.

Richard

With Alice Snr now married to Laurence Dunn, Dick and Annie concentrated on keeping the business going. Annie would take on the role of book-keeper and work on the market stall, braving the freezing cold of the stone floors in winter. As well as the orchards and growing flowers and vegetables, they made holly wreaths at Christmas, wedding bouquets for brides, and potted hyacinths and paperwhites. The bulbs were ordered from a travelling salesman who came over from Holland each year bringing his catalogues, and deciding the orders was Annie's speciality. He often received hospitality, staying overnight before continuing his travels to other nursery gardens. Sometimes customers would turn up at the door to buy a stone of potatoes and a cabbage and have a chat. 'Uncle Dick's gardens' as they were known to family and friends alike were a social hub, with parties for the young people at Christmas when everyone gathered around the piano to sing carols and Annie organising her famous parlour games.

Times were changing: Carlisle was a growing city, and the city fathers looked to build new housing. Botcherby was seen as an ideal location. By now Martin Casey of Botcherby Farm had bought the land and then sold it to Carlisle Corporation. A further agreement was signed on 8 March 1930 between Carlisle City Council and Richard Grice. It was a sad day for Dick - he must have known it was the beginning of the end for his nursery gardens. (More details of this are in the next chapter.)

As Botcherby Lane became Durranhill Road and the new housing estate began to take shape, the road widening meant that the Garden House had to be demolished and a new house - 6 Durranhill Road - became Dick and Annie's home amid the remaining land and greenhouses. Next door at 8 Durranhill Road lived Laurie and Alice Dunn with their young son Gerard. These two houses were built behind where the old Garden House stood, and today at the corner of Applewood Close and Durranhill Road, one of the original gate-post trees, under a protection order, still stands.

In the agreement with Richard Grice, the Town Clerk, Frederick George Webster, stated:

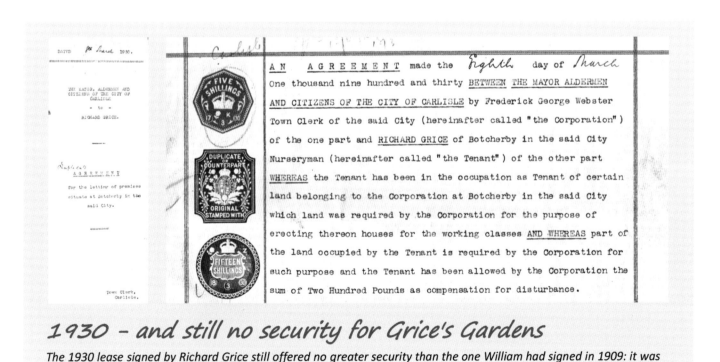

1930 – and still no security for Grice's Gardens

The 1930 lease signed by Richard Grice still offered no greater security than the one William had signed in 1909: it was still on a year-to-year basis - but by now the estate was being built.

Dick, Annie and little Alice – happy times together

Above, left to right: a wedding gift to Richard Grice from the choir of Our Lady and St Joseph's in 1923; Dick at work in the gardens; Annie and young Alice in front of the old house.

Clockwise below from the left: George, one of the workers, sets off on a delivery; family portrait of Dick, Alice and Annie; Alice doing the rounds of the greenhouses with her doll's pram; the young Will and Jim McIntyre on a Norton; Jean Grice/Burnett, Dick's mother, in the gardens; Alice and father Dick among the greenhouses.

'The tenant has been in the occupation as Tenant of certain land belonging to the Corporation at Botcherby, in the said city, which land was required by the Corporation for the purpose of erecting thereon houses for the working classes.'

The Council was taking the land piece by piece: the process had started in the late 1920s with the building of Botcherby Avenue on land outside the nurseries. Dick's family had to watch as trees and plants were torn down, foundations were laid for housing and new roads built. Plans with the deeds show how the area of the gardens decreased: they were still large enough to work but must have looked like a building site as the roads and avenues of the estate increased.

In the lean years of the 1930s, Dick would ensure that his new neighbours on the estate experiencing hard times were not short of vegetables and he took an active part in village affairs, sometimes speaking up for youngsters appearing before the magistrates. These were also the good years when young Alice would reminisce on her great love of the gardens: how she went down to the 'bothy' with her father, banging on a tin to scare away any mice or other undesirables; how she saw no danger in climbing apple trees until Aunt Kate called her down with a grim warning, and how she watched her father tend the beehives, wearing his protective gloves and netted hat. On bitter cold winter days, Annie would clear space in the parlour for Dick to make the wreaths there. With fresh holly and Christmas trees abounding, the carol singers were invited in at Christmas for ginger wine and mince pies. It was an idyllic life for a little girl.

It would end all too soon. As the years went by, Dick's health began to cause concern. He had served with 11th Battalion, Border Regiment and the Royal Welsh Fusiliers in WW1: under fire he had been wounded by shrapnel - some of which could not be removed - and was also in a PoW camp in Germany. My grandfather, Gig Hitchon, would often go to help out his brother-in-law, repairing glass panes in the greenhouses and other work in the busy gardens. It was he who took the photos of young Alice in the gardens with his Box Brownie camera. Dick's health worsened and in the summer of 1939, on the eve of WW2, he died aged 56.

The family were devastated and for young Alice it meant that the plans and dreams that she would train at horticultural college and join the family business would never come to fruition. She did, however, later train to be a florist at Eden Fruit Store in English Street.

She had also inherited a lovely soprano singing voice and would follow her Aunt Alice's footsteps in training to be a singer with Mr Eastwood, performing in Monsignor Smith's musical shows at the Waterton Hall and with Carlisle Musical Society.

Left a widow, Annie was unable to keep the gardens going and, by 1940, she and Alice moved into a house on the newly-built estate at 11 Merith Avenue. Carlisle Corporation took over the remains of the nursery gardens and 6 Durranhill Road became the manager's house when the greenhouses were used to grow plants and flowers for the city's parks and municipal gardens. Mr and Mrs Laurie Dunn continued to live at 8 Durranhill Road for many years and their son Gerard became a Catholic priest.

It was the end of more than a hundred years' history of Botcherby Gardens.

Forget me not

When the golden sun is setting,
And your heart from care is free
When of old times you are thinking
Will you sometimes think of me.
Annie Jane Grice
Christmas Day 1958

Grice Brothers at Croft Nurseries

It was not, however, the end of the Grice family gardening at Botcherby. David William Grice was the third son of William Grice and Jean Burnett and a year older than his brother Dick. He married Agnes O'Neill of Dryfesdale, Dumfriesshire in 1902 - she was living at 13 Grey Street, Carlisle, at this time. In 1911 they lived at 4 Durranhill View, Botcherby.

They had eight sons: Samuel Joseph born 1903, David Patrick (1905, who became deaf and dumb due to meningitis), Charles Arthur (1906), William (1907), Richard James (1911), Robert B. (1914), Archie (1917) and Peter G. (1920).

Archie Hammond had a nursery garden at Upperby by 1897 – he opened the old brickfield ponds as a lake known as Pleasureland on Whit Sunday 1923. When he died in 1928, the Corporation bought it and called it Hammonds Pond, paying £1,850 for 28 acres. David Grice also gardened there. He was a great friend of Archie Hammond, and named his seventh son Archie after him.

At some time after this David, Agnes and their sons lived at Wheelbarrow, Scotby where they ran nursery gardens. They were there in 1929 when their son Archie was killed in an accident, aged 12. In the 1920s three of the brothers went to Australia to work, Samuel, Richard and 18-year-old Charlie. They stayed for four years

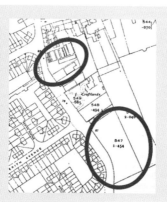

David and Agnes Grice at Croft Nurseries

Clockwise from above left: Agnes and five of her children; the only known picture of David Grice, in the Scotby Cricket Club team in 1925, where he is at the end of the back row – top left; the plan of the gardens let to the Grice brothers, divided into two lots - one part at Grice's Croft, the other opposite 42 Durranhill Road; the house at 42 Durranhill Road; the stall in Carlisle Market.

before returning during the depression days to join the business with their father.

Croft Nurseries, next to Croftlands house on Durranhill Road, were still owned by the Fairbairn family, who leased them out. (The next section deals in some detail with the Fairbairn family.) In 1929, Kelly's *Directory* shows John Garnett as having Croft Nurseries. Soon after this, however, David Grice took over the lease and the family moved to 42 Durranhill Road. With several of his sons, he worked the nurseries and also a large field opposite his home. The business was well established when David died in 1934 at the age of 53.

It must have been difficult but Agnes and her sons kept the market garden going: the eldest son, Samuel, was now 30 and his brothers were in their 20s. Over the years different combinations of the brothers kept the nurseries going, especially Charlie, Sam and Robert, with David, their deaf and dumb brother helping out. Others pursued different careers and Peter the youngest would go to South Africa, where he was a music teacher and professional concert pianist for the rest of his life.

Many people today still remember going to Croft Nurseries to buy a lettuce or a pound of tomatoes. I went there from my earliest days: although I did not live at Botcherby then, I spent every Monday with my great-aunt Annie, and she frequently took me for walks through 'the village' as she still called it. Sometimes she took me to tea with Auntie Mary Mac, who lived with her nephew John McIntyre and his wife Julie in a parlour house at the top of Botcherby Avenue. We had tea in the parlour, on a lovely round polished table complete with embroidered cloth, and it was very genteel and much fun.

My favourite place to go was to see Charlie in the gardens. I remember looking in wonder at row upon row of green tomatoes and grapes hanging from vines in the vast greenhouses. Sometimes it was chrysanthemums – yellow and white and needing great care from any frost or it was a ruinous situation. I would talk to Bobby, the horse, and give him an apple, as he stood looking out of his half-gated stable surveying the world in his retirement.

Best of all I liked to go into the bothy, where flowers such as lavender, and everlasting statice and helichrysums hung in large bunches from ceiling hooks ready to make dried flower arrangements. There were buckets of cut flowers: lupins and larkspur, marigolds, dahlias and roses. This was where bouquets and wreaths were made and the air was aromatic with their perfume. Sometimes there would be a clutch of fluffy yellow chicks running around in the greenhouse to the delight of my young brother.

The Grice Brothers
at Croft Nurseries

Above, from the left: David, not known, Charlie and Robert, with Croftlands in the background; Charlie, Charlie O'Neill and Robert in front of the half-gated stable; the old greenhouses with Durranhill Road in the background. Left: the nurseries from Durranhill Road. Right: Charlie and Robert with the last of the greenhouses in 1954.

Clockwise from above left: a young Sam Grice; Sam (seated left) with his workmates; Sam's children, David and Carmen with the family pet; William Grice (left) worked for a time on cruise liners - this shows him in one of the entertainments organised for the passengers; William's filling station at Grice's Croft in 1961 and all that was left by 2014; Peter Grice, an accomplished pianist and music teacher who found success in South Africa; Mary and Robert Grice at home in Botcherby.

Often David was there too, talking in sign language and making me smile, while Charlie would give me flowers and vegetables to take home to my mother. Charlie and his brothers won many prizes at Carlisle Flower Show for their exhibits and Sam was well known as a local judge at horticultural events. They were also well known in Carlisle Market where they had a stall for many years.

Today Theo Grice, son of Robert and Mary Grice, recalls the time when the land opposite 42 Durranhill Road was flooded and the whole field of chrysanthemums was lost, amounting to 14 weeks' work. It was a hazardous profession.

On 16 February 1961 the *Cumberland Evening News* reported on Botcherby's new filling station to be opened by Mr C.F. Kennett of Shell-Mex and BP the next day:

> *'Sections of Durranhill Road are being widened and this includes the road in front of the new filling station. The blind corner on the right travelling towards Warwick Road, has been eliminated and it is on this site that the new filling station has been built* [erected by Walter Nixon, a builder from Merith Avenue]. *It occupies a small portion of the nursery gardens run by Messrs Grice Brothers.'*

Botcherby Gardens may be gone - but something endures: the tree at the entrance: in the 1900s, the 1920s, the 1980s and today!

It was William Grice who took over running the filling station and it was a successful venture. William was an entrepreneur, owning property and having worked on the cruise boats. 1961 also saw the death of Agnes - or Granny Grice as she was known locally - at the age of 82. In later years she had been a familiar figure standing at the garden gate of her house, greeting passers-by and regaling us children with stories of our Irish ancestors, as she passed out toffees or apples from her apron pocket.

Charlie was the fourth generation of nurserymen in the family and, in May 1962 after the death of his mother (whom he had looked after for many years) he decided to emigrate to Australia. On 21 May 1962 the *Cumberland Evening News* reported the event headlined *'Back to the land of his dream'* – after 34 years Charlie had made a spot decision at the age of 56 to go 'down under' again. For all these years he had corresponded with his friends the Jefferson family of Perth, Australia, and now said: *'They live in the wheat belt and I am told there is quite a demand for men of experience in the nursery world.'*

At the end of 1964 Robert died aged 49, leaving his wife Mary and children Robert, Theo and Marian. Today Theo and his wife Joan still live at Botcherby. In October 1969 Samuel Joseph died suddenly aged 67, leaving his wife Olive and children Patricia, David and Carmen. He was the last generation of the family to be actively engaged in market gardening. Charlie subsequently came back from Australia and he died at the end of 1971, aged 66.

By the 1970s, with many of the brothers dead, the gardens came to an end and, before long, new housing was built on the fertile land of Croft Nurseries. The filling station, too, went and today all that remains is a sign saying 'Grice's Croft'. A sad reminder of happier days.

The Fairbairns – seeds and chicks, Croft House, Croftlands and Croft Nurseries

Fairbairns at Croftlands – 41 Durranhill Road

Above: the entrance to Croftlands 1995 and exterior and interior views today. Below: the beautiful stained glass windows, showing the initials 'GF' and 'AF' (for George and Ann Fairbairn) along with the date of construction, 1905.

Croftlands is remembered by former children of Botcherby as a large spooky house that stood at 41 Durranhill Road behind high red brick walls, the gates never open. It was rumoured that two old ladies lived there and woe betide anyone who tried to venture inside.

Today Croftlands' gates are always wide open and local residents can walk in to admire the lovely bluebell lawns drifting among the trees. Now known as 41 Durranhill Road, run by Croftlands Trust and, since 2013, amalgamated with the Richmond Fellowship, it provides a home for 10 residents experiencing severe and enduring mental health problems who are in need of 24 hour supported accommodation, but do not need admission to hospital.

When I talked to Mandy Wright, then the Project Manager, she described the care available: a short term rehabilitation project, it provides a transition service for those needing support in preparing for a more independent future in the community – which can take up to three years. Each resident has an appointed key worker who will discuss and plan with them any areas of particular help they need and how to achieve this. It is very much a person-centred approach, designed to meet the needs of each individual and help them regain confidence.

Practical support is given in cooking, budgeting and shopping. The residents are involved in many social events, some of these include yoga, dog-walking at the animal refuge, cooking, crafts and Kettlercise, and enjoy going on day trips and outings.

The house retains many remnants of its former glory. Built in 1905 by the Fairbairn family, the lovely stained glass windows and inglenook fireplace are still enjoyed by the residents today.

Edward Frederick

Nursery gardening and chicken rearing were what this branch of the large Fairbairn dynasty was all about. It began when Edward Frederick Fairbairn and his wife Sarah moved from Clapham, Surrey, to Carlisle around 1850. Edward was born in Clapham in 1819, came from a family of seedsmen and nurserymen and, in 1852, started a seed business in Edentown, Stanwix. It was his son George John Alexander Fairbairn, born in Clapham in 1845, who would take over the Croft Nurseries at Botcherby.

George had been working in Ireland and on his return in 1881 - and before he moved to Botcherby - he and his wife, Ann Gunn of Edinburgh, and their young children were living with his father Edward at 4 Eden Street, Edentown at Stanwix. By now his father was retired and the nurseries were being run by George's brother John T.B. Fairbairn.

In 1880 the retired Edward F. Fairbairn bought part of Botcherby Gardens from Thomas Hamilton & Sons. By February 1881, he was embroiled in a bitter court case with John and Thomas Hamilton over possession of the gardens. The full story of this was detailed earlier in the section on the Hamiltons, but it did not deter the Fairbairns from buying even more Hamilton land.

George

The *Carlisle Journal* on 7 January 1881 reported on the sale of part of Thomas Hamilton's gardens at Botcherby to George Fairbairn:

> 'We understand the greenhouse department of these oldest nursery gardens, located at the Croft, Botcherby has been purchased by George Fairbairn, son of E. F. Fairbairn of Edentown, who has for the last eight years been head gardener to the Marquis of Waterford at Curraghmore, County Waterford, succeeded by his brother Robert of London, at Curraghmore.'

Today Curraghmore is still a magnificent estate in Ireland, famous for its arboretum, ancient oak woods and formal gardens, and is open to visitors.

George founded the business of George Fairbairn and Sons, which was carried on at his Town Hall shop and later at his premises at 83 and 85 English Street, serviced by Croft Nurseries. George and Ann had three daughters and two sons, shown in the 1901 census as Sarah Ann (aged 23), Edward George (22), Kate Amelia (19), Georgina (16) and Frederick (13). Kate and Sarah were florists working in the shops and Edward George was a nurseryman, the latter two both born in Ireland. They also had a servant, Mary Irving. (Frederick would later become the founder of the Fairbairn Chick Company.)

They were clearly a success and in the *Carlisle Journal* on 3 November 1899 were advertising the fact:

> 'George Fairbairn and Son, The Croft Nurseries, BOTCHERBY, beg to announce that their PRIZE COLLECTION of CHRYSANTHEMUMS are now in FULL BLOOM, and will well repay a visit. All are cordially invited.'

The Fairbairns lived in a corner house described in George's 1920 Will as *'my Dwelling house or Cottage partly in Wood Street and partly in Croft Terrace Botcherby.'* This must be the house described in the 1901 census as Croft House, standing across from Botcherby Gardens house where William Grice was living and, on its Wood Street side, next to Mayfield where Ernest Carr, a tea merchant, lived with his young family and followed by The Grange, occupied by solicitor William Edwards. Today it is part of Croft Terrace.

In 1920 George was 75 years old and by July had put his business interests up for auction. The *Carlisle Journal* gave notice of the sale on 2 July advertising it as:

> *'The business and nursery of Messrs. George Fairbairn & Sons at Carlisle, Botcherby, Gretna and Annan. Botcherby Nursery and Croft House together with leases of shops in Carlisle and Gretna.'*

On 27 July the paper was reporting on the large attendance for the sale. It appears that Croft House was not sold, as in his Will made in October 1920 he leaves it to his daughter Georgina Gunn Patchett. He named his wife Ann and his son-in-law, Dr Leo Patchett, as his executors. The rest of his estate was left in trust to his wife and daughters, Sarah Ann and Kate Amelia. By now many of the family were living in Croftlands on Durranhill Road, but its history was touched with great sadness for George Fairbairn. It was built on Fairbairn land by George and Ann in 1905 and it is their initials that feature in the stained glass windows which remain today.

Edward George

Croftlands was reputedly built as a wedding gift for their son, Edward George, who was born in 1879 when the family were living in County Waterford, Ireland. He married Annie Eliza Elsworth in 1907 and their son, George Elsworth Fairbairn, was born at Botcherby in 1908. They lived at Croft House in Wood Street in 1911 and it is described as having eight rooms.

Edward George began suffering ill-health and when he made his Will on 10 November 1914, he describes himself as living at *'No. 6 Eldred Street, Carlisle and late of "Croft House" Botcherby.'* He appointed Archibald Hammond, florist, of Upperby as one of his executors, leaving everything to his wife and child. His son George Elsworth Fairbairn would go on to marry Hannah P. Davidson in 1951 and died in Carlisle in 1984 aged 76.

Tragedy was to strike the family, as recorded in the *Carlisle Journal* on 4 June 1915. The report of Edward George's death at the age of 36 makes sad reading. He had been in poor health and was staying in a nursing home at Haydock Lodge, Newton-le-Willows in Lancashire, where he was found hanging from a tree. He was buried at Carlisle Cemetery. We do not know the circumstances that brought a wealthy young man, with a wife and family, a beautiful home and successful business to such a sad end.

Clockwise from above left: Haydock Lodge, the private asylum in Lancashire where Edward George Fairbairn took his life; newly hatched chicks and advert for E. F. Fairbairn; letter heading for George Fairbairn, the nurseryman.

Haydock Lodge, a former mansion house standing in 100 acres, had been opened in 1843 as a private asylum. By the early 1900s it was advertised as specially adapted for the care and treatment of those suffering from mental ailments or of unsound mind. It is described as surrounded by extensive woods and with its own farm. It had gardens and pleasure grounds, lawns for tennis, croquet, bowling greens, cricket and football fields and a golf course. It provided concerts, entertainments, balls and carriages and motor cars were kept for the use of patients. Only the wealthy could afford to stay there, but it could not help Edward George Fairbairn.

His parents, George and Ann, were living at Croftlands at this time and, in June 1926, celebrated their Golden Wedding. Four years later, on 15 August 1930, the *Carlisle Journal* reported George's death at the age of 85. He was buried at Stanwix cemetery. In later years the house was still occupied by the increasingly reclusive Sarah and Kate as the memories below relate.

Sarah Ann and Kate Amelia

The late Mrs Mabel Langhorne, a resident of Wood Street for most of her life, gave an interview to the *Cumberland News* some years ago where she recalled characters of Botcherby:

> *'The two Miss Fairbairns who owned a lot of property in Botcherby at the time come to mind, you could set your clock by them when they used to come round for the rent. They came at the same time every week, but they would change the colour of their hair every week. I remember them coming one week with bright red hair wearing purple costumes and they always had heavily made up faces, they were definitely a sight for sore eyes.'*

James Ord had lived in Borland Avenue since 1938, when he was a small child, and recalls that, as a young man, he was employed to paint the gates of Croftlands. One day Miss Fairbairn came out and said: *'Tell me James are you from the village or the estate?'* It seems attitudes died hard with the Botcherby landed gentry: it was still 'them and us' for the estate residents. Even funnier is the tale of when a boy employed as a gardener at Croftlands in the 1920s fell asleep under a tree – a photo was taken of him and sent to his father! It was too easy just to wake him up.

James Fairbairn at Bramerton Lodge, Wood Street

Yet another branch of the family had Botcherby connections. James Fairbairn owned and ran the Bush Inn in English Street, Carlisle, and had a house on West Walls. He ran a coaching business from the inn and was a Royal Mail contractor and a coach builder and repairer. In 1798 he established the first Catholic Chapel in Carlisle since the Reformation when he converted a building he owned on West Walls. The first entry in the Baptismal Register begun that year starts with the details of his children transferred from Warwick Bridge RC Chapel register. Fr Joseph Marshall came there in 1800 and this chapel became the forerunner of the church of SS Mary and Joseph in Chapel Street built in 1824.

The earliest record of a Fairbairn living at Botcherby is in the 1805 Land Tax returns where James Fairbairn paid 10s 1½d, indicating substantial buildings and a large plot of land. He may have leased land for 14 years on the Garlands Estate, as indicated by documents from 1796. It appears that James and his second wife, Ann Fairbairn, lived in the house which is now known as Bramerton Lodge in Wood Street until his death in 1807, when the house passed to his son James and his wife Mary.

The weather must have been balmy in 1832 when the *Carlisle Journal* reported on 18 August: *'apricots are quite ripe grown in the open air in the garden of Mr Fairbairn of Botcherby.'*

Over the years property was often advertised to let, as in the *Carlisle Journal* on 26 April 1834 when a notice appeared for a house belonging to Mr Fairbairn and adjoining his in Wood Street to be let. It noted:

'A neat and convenient dwelling house; containing a Parlour, Kitchen, Pantry and other conveniences, on the Ground Floor, together with three up-stairs Rooms. The front is enclosed, and the many Improvements lately made in the Village, its convenient distance from Town, the excellence of the different Roads, (good Foot-paths being made the whole way from Carlisle) together with its public Gardens so much frequented , must evidently make it a desirable Residence. On the opening of the Railway coals will constantly be deposited 300 yards distance.'

It seems that this must have been one of the cottages next door to Bramerton Lodge today.

James died at Botcherby in 1835 but his wife Mary Fairbairn continued to live there. She also owned the cottages at 34 and 32 Wood Street plus adjacent fields and orchard. On 20 July 1839 a Notice appeared in the *Carlisle Journal* regarding a sale of property:

'Four valuable Freehold DWELLING HOUSES suitable for the Residence of Genteel Families, situate in the pleasant Village of Botcherby, one mile distant from Carlisle, with Gardens well stocked with the choicest Fruit Trees behind the same, and a Croft in the rear thereof, containing 5A. 2R. 0P. or thereabouts and now occupied by Mrs. FAIRBAIRN and others. The last mentioned property will be Sold Subject to the Life Estate of the Widow of the late Mr. Fairbairn.'

Continuing the family tradition, Mary Fairbairn was a keen gardener - a quality recognised in the local press in February 1844:

'Early rhubarb is now growing in the garden of Mrs Fairbairn of Botcherby, in the open air, a quantity of rhubarb, the stalks of which are nineteen inches in length.'

She lived until the age of 82 and died in 1882, but had sold Bramerton Lodge long before that.

The area of land known as The Croft appears to have stretched from Bramerton Lodge up Wood Street to Croft Terrace and what seems to have been known as Front Street (where the Plough Inn was situated) and as far down as the field where Charlie Grice grew his cabbages - opposite 42 Durranhill Road.

Fairbairn's Famous Chicks

Another grandson of E. F. Fairbairn of Edentown and also named Edward Frederick Fairbairn was the second son of George and Ann, born at Botcherby in 1888. He would start the E. F. Fairbairn Ltd poultry business in 1928 in Caldewgate, Carlisle, and was a pioneer in the production of large numbers of day-old chicks using large cabinet incubators. In fact, he introduced to Great Britain the production and sale of the Secura Cabinet Incubator.

The Fairbairn family had a general farm at Monkcastle, Southwaite and Mrs Fairbairn was interested in breeding

When the Grices left Botcherby Gardens, the City Council ran part of them for a while. One of the managers was a Mr Hitchon who lived at 6 Durranhill Road. These pictures show all that remained after the greenhouses were finally removed - awaiting the development of Applewood Close.

poultry and was looking for a larger incubator than the flat-top type normally available. It was her father-in-law, George, who suggested they obtain a new Belgian incubator that was different in the way it controlled temperature: air was circulated and operated at just under 100° F, whereas the flat-top variety operated at a higher temperature, around 103-105° F. It was produced by a man named Joseph Behaeghe. An incubator of 1,000-egg capacity was soon installed and found to work well. In the 1920s the poultry trade was on the increase and Edward decided to invest in incubators and start selling them to poultry farmers. He arranged with Behaeghe to make them under licence at Enfield and started the Secura Incubator Company. Before long

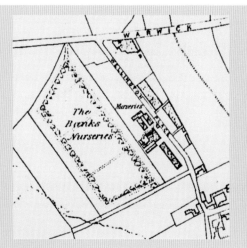

Feddon's Gardens, Victoria Road

Clockwise from above left: a 19th-C. map showing the location of Feddon's Gardens; the gardens in their heyday, during the 1950s (with Botcherby Hall in the background); William Feddon with his delivery van; the view of the gardens looking from the house at 35 Victoria Road with its beautiful borders and planting.
Below from the left: the Feddon family in the front garden at 35 Victoria Road; Mr Feddon continued to work in his gardens long after his retirement.

a factory was opened in Caldewgate, Carlisle, as well as a hatchery.

The company's slogan became well-known as 'Fairbairn's Famous Chicks'. Eventually, by the 1960s, E. E. Fairbairn's (Holdings) Ltd of Northern Ireland would merge with Chunky Chickens becoming Chunky-Fairbairn and later joining with Sterling Poultry Products to form the Ross Poultry Group. Today the Ross Group is part of the global market with products available in more than a hundred countries.

Feddon's Gardens

Many people still remember Feddon's Gardens as the last of the big four nurseries that continued operating long after the others had gone. Sadly, there is very little written about the days of Willie Feddon, so I am greatly indebted to Roger and Pat Atkinson for their recollections of those times - Roger is Willie's nephew.

William was born in Botcherby in 1909 and, as a child, lived in Warwick Road, next to Armstrongs' bakers shop, just round the corner from Charlotte Terrace. He was one of ten children. His father worked for the Midland Railway and his mother was a Hetherington, who died by the 1940s.

In addition to gardening at the former Wellington Place nurseries, opposite the house at 35 Victoria Road, he also had gardens at Scotby and leased land from the Midland Railway beside Durranhill railway cottage where he grew leeks, carrots and rhubarb.

The Feddon family

The Feddons were a large family and had gardens at both Botcherby and Scotby. The two top photos show them in relaxed mood. Top right: they are celebrating a family wedding in the front garden at 35 Victoria Road. On the right is Esther working in Wand Garden Lonning, Scotby, 1961 and, below, in the front garden at 35 Victoria Road. Bottom left is Willie Feddon in his sitting room.

FEDDON'S RHUBARB'S TOO LONG!
MY PASTY WONT GO IN THE OVEN!

Willie Feddon was famous for his longevity and rhubarb, as the cards above show.

He never married and three of his sisters – Esther, Annie and Nellie – lived with him at 35 Victoria Road. Esther looked after the financial side and did the yearly accounts. They made chutney and dried flower posies using Mungrisdale moss, which they took in large baskets to Carlisle market, where they sold their produce on the country benches on Saturdays. His three sisters all died before Mr Feddon. Another sister married George Armstrong who worked at Greenwell Carruthers, the grocers in Warwick Road, and lived in Merith Avenue. They had twin boys, Alan and Tony.

The pictures above show Feddon's Gardens as they were in the 1990s. On the left, Park House, the Magpie and Botcherby Hall can clearly be seen in the background. Eventually the gardens became badly neglected and ripe for the housing development undertaken by Impact Housing, as the four pictures below show.

Before WW2 there was a big demand for rhubarb and Willie Feddon became famous for it. The variety called 'Victoria' was the gold standard for good rhubarb – large fat stems, bright red skin and lack of stringiness and a full tart flavour. But one day while out driving, he came across gardens with a really early variety called 'Timperley Early' – the gardener was reluctant to sell any crowns, but eventually sold two for £5 to him. It was an astute move as it was a variety that could be forced to produce tender pink sticks as early as February. The roots could be split year after year and soon he was growing 15 acres of it. It would be harvested by a machine attached behind the tractor and was hardy enough to survive among the bracken, covered in frost. It was also grown in frames at Armathwaite where boilers were stoked to provide heat - as a result, it would be in Carlisle Market by Christmas. Thirty boxes would be sent by train to Gateshead market by 11pm and would all be sold the next day.

Eventually, in later life, Mr Feddon could no longer manage the gardens on his own and Roger Atkinson helped him for the last 10 years or so. Interestingly, given the coachbuilding connections of Wood Street, Roger Atkinson is a member of the family Atkinson & Davidson who were coach builders established in 1869 by James Atkinson at Cathedral Court, Castle Street. He is a Freeman of the city through the Guild of Shoemakers.

Although there was keen competition between the gardening families, there was also a strong sense of neighbourliness. Pat Atkinson recalls that, when she was expecting her first child, Sam Grice said that if it was a girl he would send her a box of pink roses, but if it was a boy he wouldn't send anything. It was a girl so she got her pink roses – 50 years ago! The Grices also featured in a more mundane way in Willie Feddon's business. Back in 1962 Charlie Grice ordered a Massey Ferguson tractor – there was a waiting list – but before it could be delivered, he emigrated to Australia – so Willie Feddon got the tractor as he was next on the list. Roger Atkinson has just had it renovated and it is still like new: they were built to last in those days!

 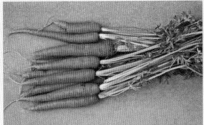 

♦♦♦

Pigeons - fast and fancy

Pigeons have always played an important part in the life of Botcherby - such as Jack Stubbs' favourite Head Case (shown here in 1990 having a rest on its owner) and Mike Hamilton's racing pigeons which were housed in his large shed for many years. He is seen here with Dennis Latimer.

Building the estate, growing a community

It must have come as quite a shock to William Grice when he heard the news. Carlisle City Council were planning to build a housing estate at Botcherby, and right on the land where his house and nursery gardens stood...

The end of Botcherby Gardens

William Grice had developed the gardens since taking on the lease from Silas George Saul of Brunstock in 1899, and had worked hard to make them successful. Now it was all to be destroyed. He was in his 70s and relied on his son Richard, who worked alongside him, to cultivate the land. The land that he loved. There was little that he didn't know about the nurturing of trees and fruit, vegetables and flowers. It had been his life's work.

It was not the first time he had to face the possibility of losing his livelihood as in 1909 there were plans to sell the gardens to build a housing estate. At that time Botcherby Gardens were saved when William Wannop of Linstock Castle bought the land and negotiated a new lease with William.

By 1926 Carlisle City Council was planning to clear slums and old dwelling houses in the city centre and in the Caldewgate area. The city was committed to development, with roads and bridges being widened and new housing estates planned for the outskirts of town. Green fields and rural life were giving way to urban living and modernisation. People needed new homes.

In 1926 Martin Casey, a local cattle dealer, owned a large part of the land at Botcherby, including the nursery gardens. At the beginning of that year he wrote to the Corporation regarding the road-widening scheme. He owned land on the west side of Mount Florida and offered to throw into the deal 387 square yards of land required for the road widening:

> *'Upon condition being that the Corporation relieve him of all charges in respect of street works to be executed on this particular portion of the road and make good the fences adjoining the land in question to his satisfaction.'*

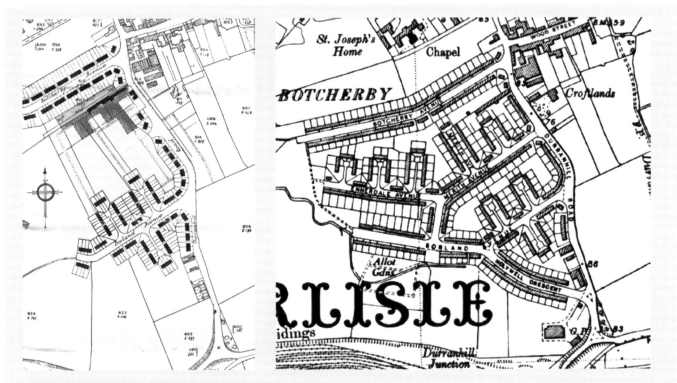

The plan for the estate

Left: the original plan for the Botcherby estate in 1930, showing Botcherby Avenue and Borland Avenue, along with Durranhill Road as the initial phase of the development.

Right: a map from the 1950s showing the completed estate, with Merith Avenue, Ennerdale Avenue and Holywell Crescent.

The offer was accepted and in force by April 1926.

By November 1926 Mr Casey wrote to the City Council again offering to sell land to the Corporation for housing purposes. The proposal was discussed at various committees until finally the Finance Committee, in April 1927, agreed the purchase:

> ### 'Minute 495. Land at Botcherby.
>
> *'A letter had been received from Mr. Martin Casey offering to sell his land at Botcherby to the Corporation... Lying between the River Petteril and Durranhill Road, with a parcel of land on the west side of the River Petteril forming part of Raven Nook and measuring in all 117 acres, together with all buildings erected on the land and all his rights of way over adjoining land for the sum of £11,000.'*

The Finance Committee accepted the offer and applied to the Ministry of Health for sanction to borrow the £11,000 purchase money (over half a million pounds today). On 26 September 1927 the Town Clerk reported to the Housing and Development Committee that he had received:

> *'the official sanctions of the Ministry of Health to the borrowing of the sums of £8,850 and £2,150 for the purchase of land at Botcherby for the erection of houses for persons of the working classes and the provision of playing fields, repayable within periods not exceeding 80 and 60 years respectively.'*

The die was cast and the City Council lost no time in inviting tenders to build the houses and widen the roads. By July 1927 the Housing and Development Committee reported that local builders John Laing & Son and Messrs J. & R. Bell had won contracts to build houses at Botcherby.

One man did not see the demolition of his orchards and nurseries and the end of his life's work, for William Grice died in June 1927 at the age of 76. It was his fourth son Richard, together with his wife Annie and baby daughter Alice, who faced an uncertain future. The City Council made a new Agreement and signed a new lease with Richard Grice on 8 March 1930: he must have known he was signing away his future.

The gardens were taken piece by piece. The area coloured yellow in the Agreement reverted to the Council on 31 August 1930. They paid him £200 compensation for the loss of his orchards and nursery stock. The area of 0.367 acres coloured green on the plan and containing the greenhouses, was leased to him from 2 February 1930 to 1 February 1931 and afterwards on a year-to-year basis (see illustration above). Botcherby Garden

The first street to be built on the estate, Botcherby Avenue remains the longest avenue.

Clockwise from top left: the view from Durranhill Road; a Botcherby Avenue street party in 1946 in the Victory Queen celebration - in the photograph are Barbara Stubbs (née Charters), Rosemary Charters and Marjorie Foster, Gerald Burns and Ethel Burns; heading up the hill towards Durranhill Road; a large group of schoolchildren from the 1940s-50s in a garden in Botcherby Avenue - Pat Nelson is the tall girl on the back row, fourth from the right; the avenue from the Melbourne Park end, with Freshfield Court on the right.

house was to be demolished and the lease states: *'the Corporation agrees to let and the tenant agrees to take the house at present occupied by him until such time as another Corporation house in the vicinity is ready for occupation by him.'* The new house was 6 Durranhill Road.

In the Agreement with Richard Grice, the Town Clerk, Frederick George Webster, stated:

> *'The tenant has been in the occupation as Tenant of certain land belonging to the Corporation at Botcherby, in the said city, which land was required by the Corporation for the purpose of erecting thereon houses for the working classes.'*

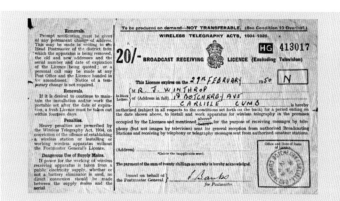

Those were the days... when a radio licence cost £1 in 1949 - and still cost the same in 1960!

Above, left to right: Annie Irwin enjoys a street party in the first cul-de-sac in Borland Avenue; the view from the bottom of the third cul-de-sac today, where I lived at 82.

Above, left to right: looking down Borland Avenue from Holywell Crescent towards the Metal Box; a street party in 1945; Mrs Nellie Conley outside her house at 116 Borland Avenue.

Below, left to right: a street party in the first cul-de-sac, probably celebrating the 1953 Coronation and featuring Jack Irwin; after the haircut at 109 Borland Avenue in July 1949 - Grandas Shane and Atkinson with young Tommy Shane; young Tommy enjoys the back garden of 109.

Bottom, left to right: looking through the window towards 119 Borland Avenue; the triangle - the bus stop was literally on a triangle before the two halves of the avenue were divided from each other; in the early 1950s Freda Bulman, Barbara Charters, Barry Wilson and David Bulman smile for the camera.

This reflected the phased development of the estate, as blocks of houses were gradually built. At the Housing and Development Committee on 25 July 1927 it was reported that John Laing & Son Ltd would erect 14 houses and it is likely that these were at the top of Durranhill Road/Botcherby Avenue. The details were given:

7 blocks of 2 houses having parlour and 3 bedrooms at £826 per block.

Total £5,782 and:

Messrs. J.R. Bell of Carlisle to erect 40 houses:

5 blocks of 4 houses having 2 bedrooms at £1,241 14s per block.

Total £6,208 10s, and

5 blocks of 4 houses having 2 bedrooms at £1,255 per block, Total £6,275.

In addition salaries for the Clerk of Work and others was £456, street works would cost £2,052 and sewers £486. 10s.

Above left to right: the original houses in Durranhill Road were added to with the building of the estate; looking down the road, Florida Stores on the left.

Below, clockwise from the left: two houses refurbished in the original style of the estate; two views of the road today; Alf Hetherington, with Sally the conductress on board, parks the 628 at the Durranhill Road terminus.

The Pryce family

The Pryce family lived at 2 Borland Avenue and, in the 1950s and 1960s, there was a bus stop in front of their house. Anyone from Borland Avenue going into Carlisle to school, to work or just shopping waited there for the bus - so it became a meeting place for children and adults alike. Pictured on either side of the house are Glynis and Alison.

Above, clockwise from the left: sometimes in winter... the avenue looks like this; back in the 1960s this is how it looked - Mrs Clark cutting her hedge at 50 Merith Avenue; the avenue today, looking towards Ennerdale Avenue; the entrance to Merith Avenue from Durranhill Road.

Below, from the left: after the estate was built, Annie Grice and her daughter Alice lived at 11 Merith Avenue for many years - this picture shows Annie in her later years at the front door with me and my brother Gilbert - July 1948; Alice was a regular leading singer in local musical shows - she is fourth from the left in the front row of this production of Monsignor Smith's 'Jolly Roger', playing the part of Dolores; we were regular visitors to their house before we moved to Botcherby - this picture in the back garden is of our parents, Frank and Terry Hitchon, me and my brother.

Over the next four years these committee reports would go on, with tenders being sought, sanctions to borrow money being obtained, contracts given, building inspections made, until finally by 1932 all 558 houses were erected.

The first street to be built was nearing completion in July 1928 when it was named Botcherby Avenue. It was the longest street in the estate stretching from Mount Florida to Melbourne Park, where a footpath was erected from the bottom of the avenue across the park, with a bridge over the river Petteril to Melbourne Road and Greystone Road.

By March 1929 the next street to be completed was named Borland Avenue, after Councillor Matthew Borland for his work on the Housing and Development Committee. These two avenues might have been called the 'top and tail' of the estate, before the land of the nursery gardens in between was built on. By September 1930: *'it was resolved that the new street between Durranhill Road and Borland Avenue be named Holywell Crescent.'* On 30 October it was reported that *'the schedule of completed houses to date is 3,013, a new contract for 100 houses has been set off.'* This total included houses built in other parts of the city.

In January 1931 Merith Avenue was named, and by September 1932 it was reported that all roads were cut and foundations laid and Ennerdale Avenue came into existence. The estate now had all its names! But not

ENNERDALE AVE

1953 Coronation party

'I remember there was a large tent marquee on the land behind the houses off the first cul-de-sac in Ennerdale Avenue, where the adults and children celebrated the Coronation with a big party. There was plenty to eat and drink. I seem to remember quite a few were drunk.'

Jack Stubbs

Top left: the children at the party included Jack Stubbs, Jack Buckley, Sylvia Graham, Shirley Brown, Barry Fern and Joyce Stubbs. Top right: the adults at the party included Tommy Burgess, Mrs Burgess, Mrs Crosbie, Mrs Stubbs, Jackie Baty, Jackie Galbraith and Norman Ethridge. Above: Ennerdale Avenue boys in the 1950s. Below: four views of the avenue today.

all of its numbers: there are six house numbers missing at the top of Holywell Crescent, opposite the old CWS dairy, as the numbering starts at 13 Holywell Crescent.

Of sewers and sub-stations

Building an estate is not just about bricks and mortar – it is also about roads, cast-iron fire ranges, sewers, shops, electricity, telephones, post boxes, road signs and bus routes. All of these things exercised the discussions and decisions of the councillors over these years.

The main public sewer ended at Tilbury Road. On 27 April 1928 the Town Clerk reported to the Health Committee as follows:

*'**Minute 600**:.. submitted correspondence between Messrs. R Forster & Sons of Botcherby and the Surveyor intimating that... they were prepared to pay the annual loan charges amounting to the sum of £37. 6s. 0d. per annum, in necessary extensions of the public sewer from its present termination at*

Tilbury Road, such sum to be paid until the rates collected from the new houses equal the annual loan charges and to be proportionately decreased as houses are erected.'

Above: Holywell Crescent in the 1930s and the same view today. Below clockwise from the left: off on a coach trip - Mr and Mrs Shriner, Mrs Archibald, Mr and Mrs Maddison, Mrs Wilson and Tom Armstrong; the bus terminus in the 1980s; the 24 bus waiting at the terminus in the 1950s; Brian Alford, Mary, Doreen and Ralph Maddison, Jacqueline Keeler, Maureen Glendinning, Sylvia and Colin Dodds, Anne Kelly; David Maddison, unknown and Jim Wilson.

The Seat

If you walked straight ahead from the top of Holywell Crescent towards Durranhill Road, you came to a triangular piece of grass with a metal bench, known as 'The Seat' and to the left of this was an area with some trees known as 'The Tip'. In the 1950s, it was a favourite meeting place to play for boys like Brian Smith, Ralph Maddison, Ian Boyd, Mike Kelly and Ron Maddison (above right). Above left is how it looks today, with Eastern Way crossing over it.

The offer was accepted and the sewer to serve the estate cost £525.

The committee reports went on, as J. & R. Bell won the contract to erect a transformer sub-station for electricity supply at a cost of £213 18s and a telephone kiosk was erected in the garden of 2 Botcherby Avenue.

The Path

In May 1929 the building of a raised footpath from Botcherby Avenue to Melbourne Road at a cost of £1,500 was approved. As all the tenders received exceeded this cost, it would be built by direct labour, and the Surveyor would decide how many electric lamps were required to light it.

In January 1934 costs were worrying the councillors and it was suggested that a privet hedge might be used to give the footpath shelter. The Surveyor submitted an estimate to the Highways and Streets Committee of the cost of erecting an oak weather-boarded fence along both sides of the footpath from Botcherby Avenue to the river Petteril at cost of £580. As the existing iron railings would be unnecessary they could be used at Heysham Park, thus reducing the actual cost to £400, and this was agreed by the Council in February 1934. 'The Path' as it became known still stands today.

Its route is now changed as the course of the river Petteril was altered in 1961 but for many years it has served Botcherby people as a quick route to the south end of Carlisle. Men going to work at Cowan and Sheldon or the LMS Railway Company, children going to school and mothers pushing their baby prams on the way to town. Not to mention 'the lads of the village' making their merry way home after a Saturday night on the town.

The main route into Botcherby via Victoria Road and Durranhill Road was still in its 'village state' and too narrow for the increase of vehicles and numbers of people now travelling.

Widening the road meant procuring small parcels of land along the route and in July 1930 the Surveyor reported that in order to obtain access from the Durranhill Road to the new 60-ft wide road being made through the estate, it would be necessary to acquire a narrow strip of land forming the embankment to Durranhill Road belonging to the LMS Railway Company. The strip was 295 feet in length and was supported by the embankment. In return for an agreement that the Council would maintain it in perpetuity, it was conveyed to the Council.

The Path across Melbourne Park

The boarded path across Melbourne Park in its heyday! Clockwise from the right: local and school teams played regularly on Melbourne Park - this picture shows Jack Stubbs and team mates from the St Nicholas Arms, 2nd Division Winners, Sunday League, 1968. It includes Botcherby boys in the back row: Leslie Bell (2nd from left), Barry (Butch) Wilson (4th), Jack Stubbs (5th) posing in front of the old boards which were meant to protect from wind and rain!

Below, Mrs Proudfoot and her young children enjoying the play area beside the Path; 1950s map showing the route of the Path across the park to Melbourne Road.

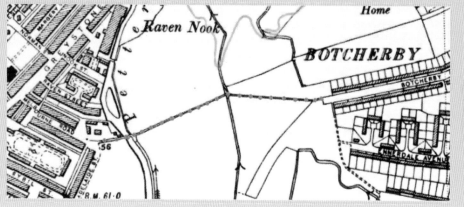

By September 1932, with tenants living in the houses, the Housing and Development Committee agreed to request the Highways and Streets Committee *'to expedite the commencement of the scheme for the widening of Victoria Road, which in its present narrow state, is a source of danger to traffic approaching and leaving the Botcherby Housing Estate.'*

Some entrepreneurs were quick to see opportunities, and Miss Fairbairn applied for permission to build two

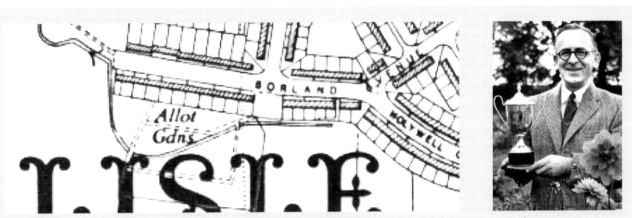

The allotments

Allotments have always played a big part in the life of Botcherby.

Clockwise from above left: 1950s map of Borland Avenue and Holywell Crescent, showing the beck emerging at the end of Holywell Crescent and flowing behind the houses until it wandered through the allotment gardens; William Taylor with his Prize Dahlia Cup; the Botcherby Paddock Allotments today, Botcherby Hall in the background.

shops opposite Botcherby Avenue in December 1931. The Surveyor reported rather frostily that this would be *'in contravention of the Town Planning proposals for the widening of Durranhill Road opposite Botcherby Avenue. Resolved: that permission be not granted.'*

Mr J. W. Thompson had already converted one cottage at the junction of Wood Street and Victoria Road into a shop and he too was informed that the Town Planning proposals would require the building to be set back and that *'any cost incurred to altering the premises at the present time or at any time after... will not rank for compensation when the roadway is widened.'*

Allotments for all

Allotments were not a new idea when Carlisle City Council promoted them in the 1930s, as new housing estates were built on the outskirts of the city. In fact they were started in 1807 by the Bishop of Bath and Wells and the *Carlisle Journal* reported on the success of the venture on 1 February 1834 telling its readers that the Bishop had let *'small allotments of land subject to the following rules: for potatoes and vegetables only; no more than one rood of land per person; no sub-letting and an annual rental of 10 shillings.'*

Carlisle took to them in a big way as, by 1843, Messrs Peter Dixon and Sons of Shaddongate Mills had set aside parcels of land in Shaddongate and at Warwick Bridge as gardens for 130 of their work people. With the General Enclosure Act of 1845 provision of allotments was made *'for the purposes of exercise and recreation and for the labouring poor.'*

This was a voluntary scheme for landowners and employers and only later did it become compulsory. With the extension of the scheme to other parts of the city and villages, the *Carlisle Journal* published letters of advice to novice gardeners, one advising, *'dig deep, manure well and clean thoroughly by burying weeds.'*

By 1908 the Small Holdings and Allotments Act made local authorities responsible for the provision of allotments and this gave rise to schemes to help the unemployed. One of these was to infill the disused reservoir on Harraby Hill, thereby creating 27 allotments for rent at five shillings a year.

World War One brought an increased need for home-produced food and the Cumberland and Westmorland Home Food Culture Scheme promoted this by *'contributing to natural food supplies by allotments.'*

By the 1930s the city saw a large development in the numbers of allotments, their popularity increased with the effects of the depression and unemployment. The new housing estates set up organisations such as the 'Botcherby Housing Estate Allotment Society' and gardeners took pride in their produce. The allotments were on land between the houses.

The Mayor, writing to the *Cumberland News* on 14 January 1939 explained that, since the inception of the scheme seven years before, seed potatoes to the value of £700 had been distributed when 2,816 people were unemployed. He was appealing for £100 to keep up the scheme for the 225 cultivated allotments.

World War Two saw a huge expansion of the scheme as the 'Dig for Victory' campaign got under way. At a meeting at the Town Hall in December 1941, the Mayor presented Certificates of Merit to allotment holders, emphasising: *'the Government's appeal to women to play a larger part in food production by taking allotments.'* *'Women,'* he said, *'were good at gardening.'* By May 1942 Carlisle had 732 wartime allotments and at a meeting of the City Horticultural Society it was reported: *'that 32 tons of lime and 238 loads of manure had been delivered to allotment holders,'* but that shortages of fuel were preventing further supplies.

> *Botcherby was a good place to grow up in during the 50s and 60s. A place with real people. Which means it wasn't perfect. But it had heroes in every house and felt like a community. Since then I've moved away from those roots. But my life has been shaped by the values I learned there. I'm from Botcherby and proud of it.*
>
> Gil Hitchon

In the 1950s it was said in Botcherby that railwaymen were good gardeners as so many of them liked to be out in the fresh air tending their vegetables, and they were proud of their neat rows of lettuce and carrots. There was also an abundance of free fertiliser – indeed when the milk cart's horse had been on its delivery rounds, Mr Whitfield of Borland Avenue would be straight out with his shovel and barrow, and feeding his soil. The best soil in Carlisle where the vegetables flourished along with the gladioli. Other times he got loads of manure delivered and spent a pungent afternoon shovelling away!

In fact, most avenues on the estate had their own allotments. In Ennerdale Avenue, they ran from behind the house in the first cul-de-sac to the bottom of the road and also to the top of Merith Ave and out to Durranhill Road. They also extended through a cut in Ennerdale to the back of the houses in Botcherby Avenue and to the bottom of Botcherby Avenue. In Ennerdale Mr Baty, Elsie Baty's father-in-law, was very organised and had his area wired off with concrete posts. Robert Grice also had a block. At the start of Borland Avenue, Joe Hetherington had one opposite his house where he grew fruit - there were three allotments behind the two even-numbered cul-de-sacs. People also had pigeon lofts and kept hens and rabbits, as well as growing fruit, vegetables and flowers. At the far end of Borland Avenue (where the Metal Box later built a car park), there was another allotment through which a beck meandered. This came down from Durranhill, along the back of the houses in Holywell Crescent - where it was underground - emerging where Borland Avenue started, opposite the Triangle. Jack Stubbs remembers his Auntie Ethel, who lived at 91 Borland Avenue, losing her shoe in the mud when the beck flooded into her garden - a recurring risk in this area where houses had steps down to sunken back gardens. Eventually, the diverted beck from the end of Holywell Crescent was buried in pipes, to get rid of the problem.

Today, the allotment scheme is still popular with Botcherby people and there are three allotment sites between Borland Avenue and Merith Avenue. In addition the Botcherby Paddock Allotment, in the area between Willow Park and Victoria Road, is also well cultivated.

Brief lives – some of the people who made Botcherby a community

Doreen Hutton, Botcherby's world-class swimmer

Doreen Hutton's success as a champion swimmer is still recalled by Botcherby people today. Had she been in her prime right now, she would have been a star performer on national TV sports programmes: that's how much she achieved in a few brief years before WW2.

She lived at 6 Botcherby Avenue, learned to swim in the river Petteril down Johnny Bulldog's Lonning, and had her first competitive swim in 1935 as a member of the Border City Swimming Club - she was only 12 when she swam in the Northern Counties Amateur Swimming Association (ASA) 100-yard junior ladies championship for under 16s.

She was soon making headlines and, over the next few years, went on to great success winning many championships and being twice Border City champion while still under 14. In 1936 she first represented her club in an English championship at Wembley and between that year and 1940 she won many Cumberland and Westmorland championships.

By 1939 she was swimming in the ASA championships in Minehead where she was a surprise winner. A local

  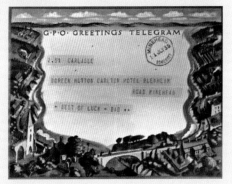

Botcherby Avenue's very own swimming star!

Top row: a young Doreen Hutton with her earliest swimming certificates. Middle row: medals for the Cumberland & Westmorland Swimming Association 220 yards freestyle championship and second place in the Northern Counties ASA 220 yards freestyle - both 1938. Bottom row: congratulatory telegrams for her following her ASA success in Minehead, 1939.

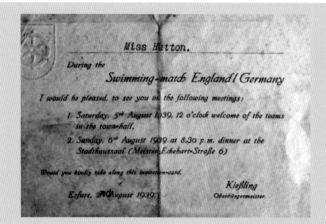

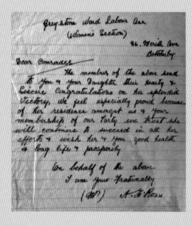

England v Germany, and bright hopes cut short by war

Like so many lives, Doreen Hutton's rise as a swimming star was changed dramatically by the outbreak of WW2 - but not before she had competed for England in Germany in August 1939, for which she received a medal (top right). Her fame at home is evident from the glowing letter (bottom left) sent to her by Mrs Rose of 86 Merith Avenue on behalf of the Greystone Road Labour Association (Ladies Section). The central picture shows Doreen and her family on the doorstep of their home at 6 Botcherby Avenue. After the war, she continued to compete but, as the certificate (bottom right) shows, never quite attained the same dizzying heights again.

paper reported how she *'confounded the prophets when she defeated the two fancied candidates, Daisy Wheway and Helen Yate, in 440 yards in 1 min. 49 4/5 secs.'* Another expert commented: *'Miss Hutton possesses the most devastating last length speed I have ever seen from a girl over this distance.'* She was clearly a very special talent. She also won the Argenta International Trophy at Blackpool after a number of close finishes in previous years.

By now she had left Brook Street School and was working at West End Dryers and Cleaners in Silloth Street and Globe Lane, Carlisle, where her father was a partner.

In August that year, as the war clouds gathered over Europe, she swam for England against Germany in Erfurt, the capital of Thuringia, and beat her German opponent in the 400-metre freestyle event. As the *Cumberland News* recorded:

'IN ACTION AGAIN TO-NIGHT

'Fresh from her swimming triumph in Germany, Miss Doreen Hutton, the Carlisle champion, was accorded an enthusiastic reception at the Citadel Station when she arrived home on the Royal Scot from London this afternoon. She had left Germany about ten o'clock on Monday morning and when she alighted from the train in Carlisle she looked remarkably fit.

'On the platform were a number of Doreen's proud relatives and friends, including Doreen's father and mother, grandparents, her sister Annie and brother Tommy, her aunt Mrs J. Hutton, and her cousin Kenneth. Those waiting to offer congratulations also included members of the staff of West End Dyers and Cleaners...'

The *Carlisle Journal* had its own take on the story, quoting Doreen as saying:

'What am I aiming at next? Well I'm going to try and retain the 220 yards championship of Cumberland

and Westmorland at the Baths to-night. I am swimming for England against Denmark at the Empire Swimming Pool, Wembley, in a fortnight's time, but I'm afraid I can't hope to win there.'

There was a strong sense of a firmly grounded young woman in the statement - she knew she would probably be racing against the Danish multiple world-record holder! However, she was given a great welcome home back in Botcherby and invitations came in thick and fast for her to attend swimming galas all over the country on the back of her success in Germany.

Only the outbreak of WW2 in 1939 and the cancellation of the 1940 Olympics, originally scheduled for Tokyo but then changed to Helsinki, prevented her from becoming an Olympic swimmer.

For many years she worked at Marks and Spencer's in Carlisle, continuing her passion for swimming and helping disabled children learn to swim. She died at the age of 92 on 23 July 2015.

Ted Beckett, poet and author

Another notable former resident of Botcherby Avenue is the author Ted Beckett (writing as Terence Ted Beckett). His family moved into 33 Botcherby Avenue when he was just two years old and he spent his formative years there. His book *The Cannibal mouse*, dedicated to his late son Philip, gives a lively account of life in Botcherby and the local area between the 1940s and 1960s - for anyone wanting to take a stroll down memory lane to Botcherby as it was, this makes fascinating reading. Ted has also published a number of other works of poetry, essays, family history and memoirs.

The Simpsons... among the first residents of Ennerdale Avenue were the Simpson family, comprising Joe and Isobel Simpson with their baby daughter June, who wrote an affectionate memoir of their life and times there

Isa Bella (Isobel) Mackie was born in Motherwell and worked in Glasgow, but would often visit her brother and his wife in Carlisle. Joe Simpson was born in Corbridge and his family moved to a market town near Carlisle when he was still a boy. He fought and was injured in WW1 and finally settled in lodgings in Carlisle. His sister was married to Isobel's brother and that's how he met her, during one of her visits from Glasgow. He was immediately taken with her Parma Violet perfume and nicknamed her 'Lady Isobel' - a name that endured as their romance blossomed. They married in May 1931 and just over a year later, baby June was born.

They moved into Ennerdale Avenue from Denton Holme in April 1933. June describes the scene:

'They put their few belongings into a small van driven for Joe by one of his mates and moved to 50 Ennerdale Avenue, Botcherby. The house was a semi-detached and on a corner site at the bottom of a steep cul-de-sac of other new houses. It had a very small garden back and front with a much bigger triangular plot at the side with privet hedges. There were two upstairs bedrooms and a small bathroom but this contained only the bath and water tank. Downstairs there was a living room with a door leading to the stairs and the front door. There was a big kitchen range in the living room for heating the water and oven. The kitchen had a long cupboard built into one wall, a gas cooker, a porcelain sink with brass taps and a door to the recess formed by the stairs for use as an indoor coal bunker. The water closet was outside the back door but built into the house. There was also a wash house with a cold water tap and a gas fired wash boiler, this was on the other side of the back door.'

The rent for the new house was seven shillings and sixpence per week.

'All the families at Ennerdale Avenue were first tenants... you could always tell the railway men by their nice gardens and clean windows. They were employed, earning a wage and had time off and a spare shilling... but many of the men were out of work and with big families to support ... the avenue was known locally as Quality Street because in 1933 Albert Worley, a projectionist at the Lonsdale

Above, left to right: the Simpsons and friends in the garden at 50 Ennerdale Avenue, around 1946 (left to right: Annie Riddle, Isobel Simpson holding young Myra Riddle and Joe Simpson); Albert and Alice Worley at their home at Brisco.

Right: Miss Wolledge, the dancing teacher; dancing queens - little June Simpson with friends Muriel, June and Lilian in the garden of Miss Wolledge's house, 1935.

Cinema, had the only car on the estate at the time. It was a Ford with perspex windows. The Worleys had lived in an old house, The Poplars, in Wood Street and now rented 52 Ennerdale Avenue.'

Their neighbours, the Worleys were waiting for their new home, Westgarth, a converted dairy in the small village of Brisco but - even after they had moved there - the friendship with the Simpsons endured. Another close family to the Simpsons were Annie and Walter Riddle. Isobel and Annie became lifelong friends and, when Annie's baby Myra fell seriously ill, Isobel nursed her back to health.

These were hard times for men to find work that lasted for any length of time and Joe travelled far and wide to make ends meet, always on the lookout for permanent work, having to make do with odd jobs. His perseverance finally paid off when he became works joiner at Morton Sundour Fabrics, the textile factory in Denton Holme - a job he held for the next 25 years. With a regular wage coming in and a secure job, they gradually added to their furniture, piece by piece, from Vaseys furniture shop in Fisher Street, paying it off weekly, the way that most folk had to at that time.

They were also the days of making your own entertainment, and June's mother was keen to give her the best start she could:

'She even took June, then only three, to a dancing class, pushing the black push chair across the path, over the fields to a select little group run by a young woman called Miss Wolledge. June was the youngest there along with another three year old called Alma Atkinson from Durranhill Road. The girls all wore the same outfits and Isobel made June's herself, a short tunic in soft grey velvet with side splits and a satin top in blue with matching knickers. Joe bought special little crescent shaped toe taps and screwed them into the sole of June's shoes and for toe work Isobel bought a small pair of ballet shoes and stuffed the toes with cotton wool to make them fit.'

The dancing class would have disbanded when Miss Wolledge left the area but Lillian Ryecroft, one of the older students, decided to keep it going with only a few girls from the Botcherby area. She held the classes in her mother's living room and outside on the concrete of their back garden if it was fine.

As there was little or no traffic in Ennerdale Avenue for a long time, the families got to know each other quite well and June's memoirs read like a *Who's Who* of the street: Browns, Brysons, Charters, Cricketts, Currys, Etheridges, Feddons, Forsyths, Fosters, Frasers, Granhoffs, Greigs, Grices, Irvings, Lawsons, Littles, Macbeths, McColls, Percivals, Riddles, Ryecrofts, Sinclairs, and Youngs alike, all come to life in the pages of *Lady Isobel*.

I am indebted to June M. Dunn for permission to use this information from her (as yet) unpublished memoir of her mother, here and in the rest of this book. Hers is a very personal account of the life and times of working people in Glasgow and Carlisle in the first half of the 20th century, and is a treasure trove of detail for any social historian wanting to know what it was really like during those difficult years.

Remembering... Joyce Proudfoot – a tragic accident in Botcherby Avenue in 1940, still fresh in the memory after many years

Tragedy struck the Proudfoot family on 12 January 1940, when seven-year-old Joyce Proudfoot died in the Cumberland Infirmary as the result of a terrible accident at the family home at 95 Botcherby Avenue. She was the eldest daughter of John and Edith Proudfoot and her funeral service was held at St. Andrew's Church where she had been baptised on New Year's day 1933. The newspaper report on the inquest into her death makes sad reading, as does the letter of condolence from Norman Street school.

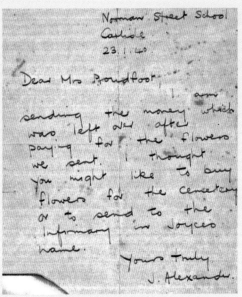

CARLISLE GIRL SCALDED
UPSET TEAPOT OF BOILING WATER

An inquest was held in the Cumberland Infirmary on Saturday by the Assistant Deputy Coroner, Mr Gaunt, on Joyce Proudfoot, aged seven, daughter of Mr and Mrs J. Proudfoot, 95 Botcherby Avenue, Carlisle. The little girl was scalded when she upset a teapot, which had just been filled with boiling water, over herself.

Mrs Edith Proudfoot, the mother, stated that about nine o'clock on Tuesday last Joyce and the other children were playing in the kitchen. Witness went into the back kitchen to fill the teapot with hot water to make some tea for the children before they went to bed. She had filled the teapot and was on the way to the kitchen. Just as she was going through the door Joyce came running towards her with her head down. Witness called on her to be careful, when she raised her head and knocked the teapot out of witness's hand. The hot water went over the little girl, who was in her night attire. Witness stripped her, put olive oil on the scalds, and took her to the Cumberland Infirmary, where she died on Friday.

Dr J. H. Roberts, house surgeon, stated that the child was admitted to the Infirmary suffering from scalds on the back and neck. She died from shock as the result of scalds. A verdict of death from shock due to scalds, accidentally received, was returned.

May Nixon, long–serving Lonsdale usherette

'TRIBUTES TO "MOVIE STAR" MAY' was the headline in the *News & Star* on 22 October 2005, when Kelly Eve paid tribute to May Nixon, who had died the previous Sunday at the age of 85. Mrs Nixon was thought to be Cumbria's oldest cinema usherette.

The great-grandmother worked at the Lonsdale Cinema on Warwick Road for more than 50 years, and only retired at the age of 83. She is famously remembered as the lady who told Mick Jagger of the Rolling Stones to get his neck washed! She met all the stars who appeared in live performances and collected stacks of signed photos, including Jimmy Shand, Lonnie Donegan and Johnnie Ray.

Christine Graham, the Lonsdale manager, recalled how Mrs Nixon got cinema-goers to sing *Let the Rest of The World Go By* before the screening of *Out of Africa*. Border TV presenter Eric Wallace once described her as the *'pre-show entertainment'*. She was also a favourite with children going to the ABC Minors on a Saturday morning.

She was married to the late Walter Nixon and had a son John and a daughter, the late Anne.

May Nixon at the Lonsdale over the years - top left shows her beside the manager, Mr Scott-Buccleuch and, bottom right, she is surrounded by some happy customers at an ABC Minors show.

Her daughter-in-law Marie recalled, *'The cinema was her life. She also kept goats, hens and geese in a big allotment at the back of her house on Merith Avenue until around ten years ago.'* Latterly she would visit the Metal Box social club to play bingo, and the girls from the club including Elsie Baty would push her there in her wheelchair.

Donald Lightfoot – amateur boxer, railwayman and top broadcaster in Zambia and Zimbabwe

A well-remembered Botcherby man is Donald Lightfoot who began his working life as a clerk at Carlisle's Citadel Station and rose to become Director-General of the Northern Rhodesia Broadcasting Corporation. A bright intelligent boy he left Brook Street school at 14 to start work and during this time he seemed set for a career in professional football, playing for Carlisle, Workington, Queen of the South and Glasgow Rangers, mainly for the second-string sides. A serious leg injury ended his footballing career at a time when he was climbing the ladder with people like England international Jackie Sewell.

He carried on with boxing and won the Northern Counties bantamweight boxing championship. He also became involved in youth work and in 1947 represented Britain at a Youth Congress in Czechoslovakia.

In 1948 at the age of 21 he emigrated to Southern Rhodesia working on the railways at a little station out in the boondocks. He soon headed to Northern Rhodesia to Lusaka where he went into broadcasting as a sports commentator for the Central African Broadcasting Corporation. He soon rose to the top and by 1963 was the future Director-General tasked with the complete re-organisation of Northern Rhodesia's radio services.

Avenue thoughts – memories of Merith Avenue

In 1995, after Alice Grice had long left Merith Avenue, she wrote the following poem Avenue thoughts which was published in Poetry Now. I think it reflects how she felt about the place that she called home.

I walk along the avenue past the tidied
Gardens with their smiling, red-jacketed gnomes,
Well-brushed paths, closed-up garden sheds
And trimmed, plant- filled garden beds.
Red-bricked and put-away homes.
Quietly awaiting their sun-setting people
Arriving briskly from high road, town and steeple.
A quiet anonymous people.

The old black collie dozing behind an iron-closed gate
Raises his head for a short-sighted peep
Then - 'You are not the one I seek.'
And down goes his head again, in sleep.
Neatly clipped hawthorn hedges, all spring-shaded green
Their May flowers splashing in starry white
Burnt-summer fences behind which, the summer laughter Is heard.
And shining windows, uncurious and curtain –patterned bright.
A happy anonymous people.

Home they are coming, sounds can be heard
Back to their nesting at set of the sun
Within the song-silver of an even-tide bird
Hurrying gatewards, their work is all done,
Up the neatly-brushed paths and the still friendly gnomes
Patting the dog and reviving their homes.
A constant anonymous people.

The people who live in the bricked avenue
In their semi-detached homes with a loved garden view
A hardworking, good-natured, enduring band
Perhaps you're the last of the reasonable few?
Dear, quiet, anonymous people of the land.

Alice Grice

February 1995,

©P. Hitchon

Interviewed in *The Sunday Mail* on October 27 1963 when on a visit back home, the paper headlined '*You would hear a sonic blueprint for a radio service if you could tune into his brain.*' Donald commented,

> '*I intend the new Northern Rhodesian service to be something worthwhile. It's going to be truly national and will cater for everybody. We have a hard-working nucleus of black and white radio men here. Multi-racialism is no problem to us...we discovered a long time ago that we can't do without the other fellow.*'

In 1964 the country declared independence and became Zambia. Donald was at the top, becoming well known internationally as Director-General of broadcasting services and was awarded the OBE. Later moving to Southern Rhodesia, which became independent Zimbabwe in 1980, he ran a public relations and advertising business in Salisbury (Harare). In Africa he met Anne Huntingdon from the well known Gretna bus company family and they soon married. He was a close friend of Bobby Robson, England's former football manager and of former England player and sports writer Ivor Broadis. On his death Ivor told the *Cumberland News*:

> '*Donald had a natural bent for broadcasting. He was the equivalent of Lord Reith at the time. He was very keen on sport and entertained many famous personalities in his African home, when they were touring out there.*'

His cousin, John Hughes, remembers him with great affection when as a small boy, Uncle Donald gave him his first tricycle. His sister Dorothy married a military man who became a brigadier and British Consul in Bulgaria.

Josephine Cummings – Holywell Crescent's own psychic who used her natural gifts to aid good causes

Mrs Cummings is something of a legend in Botcherby and today she is recalled with affection by many. She lived at 4 Holywell Crescent, near the bus stop and opposite the Co-op Dairy in a house that had all its original fittings, including the black-leaded fireplace and outside toilet.

She was the daughter of Carlisle's first Labour Councillor, Scott Parker of Denton Holme, and was a very clever woman who gave up the chance of extended education to help the family finances.

When she died at the age of 78 on 15 February 1987, the *Cumberland News* on 20 February headlined their article: '*Woman of compassion and talent.*' for that is what she was. She possessed the gift of 'second sight' and used it to give help and guidance to a large number of people who sought her skills. Her clients were from all walks of life and included entertainers, medical and business people, many who became friends. Initially she used tea-leaves for her readings but, as she became well known and her workload increased, she found cards more convenient. Even those who perhaps went along very sceptical were often astounded at her insights.

Her family always came first and it was after her retirement in 1974 that she had time to use the psychic powers that she had always possessed. Turning down an offer to set up a commercial business, what little money she made was often given to charity. Financial gain was never her motive for making her talents available to the public, but rather a warm-hearted response to public demand.

In his book *Over the Garden Wall* Donald Scott recalls the time when he worked at the Co-op in Botchergate with Mrs Cummings:

> '*There was also a piano in there and when we were having tea I'd play while she told everyone's fortunes. She was very good and people were staggered by the things she told them. I reckon she was psychic. She predicted that I would be famous and appear on television and radio, long before I was doing anything like that... that prophecy first came true with early musical broadcasts on Border Television's early evening Focus programme.*'

Today her daughter Joyce remembers that, when her workload became onerous, she would spend weekends with her at Cotehill and her granddaughter, Jenny, sees her as a counsellor who was giving help and understanding to people.

Mike Notman, the successful photographer with a keen sense of humour and an eye for the unusual shot

Mike Notman lived at 76 Borland Avenue in the 1950s: his father was an engine driver and his mother worked at Her Majesty's Theatre. He attended Creighton School. His interest was photography and began with his first job at Hayley's chemists and photography business in Abbey Street where he learned about developing and printing. This was followed by a job with John and Peter Barker's Border Press Agency before setting up a freelance photographic enterprise with Eric Scott-Parker. He was noted in his early days as a man who was professionally ahead of his time. When most commercial photographers preferred studio settings Mike looked for a different viewpoint and took some exciting pictures. A Licentiate of the Master Photographers Association (LMPA) he preferred to take subjects outside and groups would be taken at the Cathedral or straddling the cannons at The Citadel, or sometimes he would take shots from above using a high-lift 'cherry picker'.

He married Margaret Harrison in 1975 and they had a son and a daughter. He created Studio North when he was 40, developing a successful business until he retired in 2005. He became an acclaimed specialist in wedding photographs and portraits doing much work in Gretna and won awards from both Fuji and Kodak. He photographed everyone from President Eisenhower to Brigitte Bardot, but many of his pictures were lost when the *Carlisle Journal* premises were burned down in the 1960s.

Many will also remember him for his delicious sense of humour and for being a practical joker who once, somehow, managed to get a parrot drunk at a posh function in Newby Grange! Mike died on 25 September 2012, aged 69. His daughter Rachel Notman is also a talented photographer becoming an LMPA in the Master Photographers Association. She worked alongside her father who encouraged her to develop her own style and innovative ideas and took over Studio North on her father's retirement.

George 'Sailor' Wise – the genial giant who became a friend to the top entertainers of the 1960s

I remember George when he was a teenager and lived next door at 80 Borland Avenue with his mother and sister. A jolly, good-natured boy he attended Creighton School and would be out early in the morning on his bicycle doing his paper round. It is said that he was given the nick-name 'Sailor' when one morning he didn't have time to change into his school uniform and wore a roll-neck sweater to school and someone said he looked like a sailor and the name stuck. His first job was as a clerk on the railways at Gretna Green and later he went to work at Stead McAlpin, the textile printing works at Cummersdale.

At over six feet tall and 17 stones of muscle and bone, he was a force to be reckoned with when he worked as a bouncer at the Cameo Ballroom, County Hotel and the White Heather Club at Kirkbride. He became a legend in his lifetime as he was known to sort out any trouble with sweet reason, but if that failed he took appropriate action. He was often employed as minder to the stars, when they came to Carlisle, Cliff Richard and the Beatles among them.

More than a genial giant, George made friends with many of the visiting stars and people like Karl Denver and Guy Mitchell were regular visitors to his home whenever they were in town. He was also celebrated in song, when Humble Pie recorded *Big George* written by local band member Greg Ridley, who played bass in the group.

He became firm friends with international singing star Guy Mitchell and, with his wife Shirley, went to work for Guy in Nevada where he managed the singer's affairs for a couple of years. He was well known and respected in Carlisle and wrote an entertainment column for the local newspaper, 'Get Wise with Wise'.

In 1974 he and his family moved to the Thornaby-on-Tees area where he was latterly a partner in a jewellery firm but retired early due to ill-health. He died in the late 1990s at the age of 61. He was married to Shirley for 41 years and had two daughters and a son. He is remembered with great affection in Carlisle. Sadly Shirley also died in December 2014.

Remembering... the Borradaile family

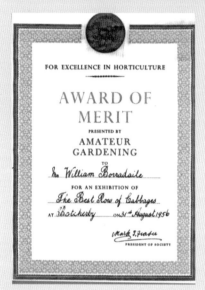

In 1940 the Borradaile family lived at 6 Charlotte Terrace - they had lived there since the turn of the century.
Clockwise from top left: a group photo taken around 1916-17, shows some of the occupants of the terrace including Mary Cook (top left), Edith Borradaile (top middle), Martha Borradaile (top end), sisters Florrie and Hannah Borradaile - (one behind the other, bottom left), William Feddon (bottom middle), the Armstrong brothers, who once had a baker's shop round the corner (bottom right) and George Greenhow (bottom far right); a more formal group showing the family, dated from the 1920s; a lovely picture of Hannah Borradaile at Botcherby School in the 1920s - note her neat haircut and boots; William Borradaile is seen holding one of his grandchildren - also in the photo is Armstrong the Bakers van and the filling station on Warwick Road – in the 1940s; William was a keen gardener and won an Award of Merit presented by Amateur Gardening for the best row of cabbages in August 1956.

Pete Hoban remembers... Charlie Grice

Charlie Grice was a gentle and kindly man, no less gifted as a musician than as a gardener. The parlour at 42 Durranhill Road was alive with music when guitar sessions were on. Pete Hoban, today a well-known entertainer, has good memories of Charlie. He recalls that it was Charlie who first taught him to play the acoustic guitar when he was 15 years old and went to No. 42 for lessons in 1955. Pete says, 'One thing that stuck with me, Mr Grice was a market gardener and worked the land and had stubby fingers – yet the way he could play the Spanish acoustic guitar was inspirational.' Several boys went for lessons and some dropped out, but Pete had a determination to succeed in music. He recalls his brothers buying him a harmonica and then an acoustic guitar with steel strings at Dias's Music Shop. Among the highlights of his career are joining Phil and Pam Bayne in 1969 when they were looking for a third member of their band The Runaways. Pete was with them until 1973, then did solo work. By 1982 he had joined Cliff Eland, fronting the 16-piece big band and, with Cliff's sudden death in 1995, band members continued with a memorial band under the name Big Band 95 and were a big hit. Today Pete sings with the Roz Sluman Quartet and Smooch Band, continuing his extraordinary and successful career. But he has never forgotten Charlie and his first guitar lesson.

Back to the land of his dream

CARLISLE MAN SAILING TO AUSTRALIA

A 56-YEAR-OLD Carlisle market gardener, the fourth generation of a family of nurserymen, emigrates on Wednesday to Australia—the land he has dreamed about returning to for 34 years.

family business and managed to carry it on into better times.

That was when their father, the late Mr David Grice, was alive. He died 26 years ago, leaving Charles to look after his mother. Mrs Grice died very recently and Charles made a spot decision to go "down under." He sails on Wednesday.

FRIENDS AWAIT HIM

Mr Grice will be met at Fremantle by a family with whom he has corresponded since they...

Pete Hoban and Charlie Grice

Clockwise from left: newspaper report on Charlie Grice's plan to move to Australia in 1962; Charlie raises a glass Down Under; a young Pete Hoban with his acoustic guitar; Pete today - still on top form; Pete in the 1970s at the Gilsland Spa Hotel with Maurice Irwin on drums.

Mrs Marsh, Holywell Crescent's own expert with the Indian clubs

Mrs Marsh lived in Holywell Crescent and was grandmother to Brian and Eileen Smith, who lived a few doors down from her in the 1950s-60s. A pleasant lady with a round happy face, she wore her grey hair in a bun. Many years ago the *Cumberland News* featured photographs of her displaying her great talent – performing with the Indian clubs and I believe her granddaughter Eileen did some lovely drawings of her at that time. Unfortunately, I have not been able to trace more information or a photo of her, but I think she will be well remembered.

Carmen Smith and Botcherby's first children's lending library

It was with great sadness that I attended Carmen's funeral on 27 June 2013. She had achieved much in her life and Christ the King Church at Harraby was packed with family, friends and colleagues. My thoughts went back to happier days when we were children. The days in the early 1950s when, with her parents Sam and Olive Grice, she lived with Granny Grice at 42 Durranhill Road. Carmen started a children's library in the parlour and a few of us loaned books for each other to borrow. We had great fun seeing what was available each week – perhaps a *Mickey Mouse* annual, *Black Beauty* or *Ballet Shoes*. Carmen kept everything in order and, for a time, the library flourished and we enjoyed reading such scarce treasures... sweet memories. Carmen is seen here with her husband Greg.

Jack Stubbs remembers the Botcherby that was... across three generations

Jack Stubbs and his wife Barbara (née Charters)

I first came to Botcherby in 1946. I used to stay with my Aunt Ethel and Uncle Carl Hodgson, who lived at 91 Borland Avenue, at week-ends and school holidays.

It was still a comparatively new housing estate, having been finished in 1933, the year that the Magpie Inn and the Co-op were built.

To a young boy brought up in Tait Street, with only a small backyard to play in, it was a whole new world, every house had a front and back garden and, in those days, everyone kept them tidy, unlike today. The Second World War had just ended and the community spirit, developed during the War years, was very much in evidence. Sadly this would decline in later years.

Botcherby then was surrounded by green fields and meadows and woodland. There were ponds, open streams (we called them becks) and marshes. It was like living in the country. To children it was an adventure playground, always something different to do. Trees to climb, for bird nests and chestnuts, swings hung from them, were great fun. Some kids today destroy them before they are fully grown, sad to say.

The railway sheds and sidings, where we could collect engine numbers, or play in the old defunct steam engines waiting to be scrapped. We took steam engines for granted in those days, every train was pulled by one, and the Midland and the North-Eastern Railway companies, running side-by-side, parallel behind Borland Avenue and Holywell Crescent. We saw and heard many famous steam engines, before the decline of the historic age of steam.

The river Petteril, with its Bay for swimming and fishing - we caught lamprey with forks tied to brush poles. Melbourne Park for football, cricket and other sports. Also the ghosties and the old ash tip. Johnny Bulldog's Lonning and the Army Camp, the Clay Pits and Scotby Three Fields, and the Eden Marsh were other places to play. There was an abundance of wild life around Botcherby. The great crested newt was common, as were toads and frogs, rabbits and hares. The song of the skylark, never heard now, reed buntings, linnets and chaffinch, just a few of the many species of songbirds to be seen, as well as duck, snipe, curlew and grebe, just a few of the many water birds then to be seen.

Once a young boy, now a grandfather, I have seen many changes over the years, some good, some bad. I have many happy memories, have met fine and good people over the years. And here in Botcherby I met my wife. I don't regret for one moment coming to live in Botcherby all those years ago.

Jim Wilson, founder member of BRAG and Botcherby Forever

Jim Wilson of Borland Avenue was well known in Botcherby, and became a founder member of the BRAG and Botcherby Forever Community Groups. The Fairbairn family of Croftlands owned a substantial amount of property as well as their horticultural and chicken production enterprises and Jim was employed by them as a rent collector. He also worked for Simmons Furniture Store in Botchergate in the 1950s.

Botcherby characters remembered – part 1

She was the Queen of Botcherby.
Mrs Elsie Baty was her name
And our Elsie will live forever
In the Botcherby Hall of Fame.

They came from all over Cumberland
To Mrs Cummings's house in Holywell.
After reading tealeaves in their cup
Their future fortune she would tell.

Long before they were world famous
The Beatles she did scold
'You want to get your necks washed'
By May Nixon they were told.

Harry drove the milk float
Helped by Sally the milk lass
Delivering milk from her pram.
The bottles then were made of glass.

The barmaid in the Magpie Inn,
The one and only Betty Kinnear.
She would refuse to serve a customer
Slightly drunk from too much beer.

Michael Walsh and David Postill
Are indeed a special breed
Always there with their expertise
In your hour of need.

In the Magpie Sidney Gill yodelled
And sang a song or two.
His younger brother Willie Gill
Well he loved the lads in Blue.

And Dennis (Darcy) Latimer
On him you could write a book.
They came from miles around
Just to simply have a look.

Kevin Beattie could have played
In front of the Liverpool Kop
But he and David Geddis
Both played at the very top.

I don't know if Sailor Wise
Ever went to sea
but formidable as a doorman.
Take it from me.

Jack Stubbs

Philip Bayne, co-founder of The Runaways, the top country music duo in the Borders

Philip Bayne lived at the bottom of our cul-de-sac, at 62 Borland Avenue, and I can remember him standing at the window in his front room practising his guitar-playing and singing. All those hours of practice stood him in good stead as, in 1966, he went on to found the successful country-music group called The Runaways with his wife, Pam, originally performing as a duo.

Philip had previously played in Hod & the Shakers and The Hotrods. Pete Hoban joined The Runaways in 1969. Initially they performed mainly in youth clubs and folk clubs, eventually earning bookings at the larger clubs and halls in Cumbria and the south of Scotland. They also ran their own folk club in Gretna with regular guest artists. Highlights of these years included appearances at the London Palladium in 1977 and Wembley in 1978.

In the tough financial climate of the 1970s and 1980s, many clubs were failing and venues for fulltime musicians were in decline. Around this time, Pam and Phil took over her family's photography business in Gretna and this gradually absorbed much of their efforts as they were bringing up their three daughters, Kas, Angela and Alison. They also ran a successful and - at times - controversial country and western programme for Radio Cumbria.

In 2001 Pam and Phil appeared at the Sands Centre in Carlisle with other local artists such as Olly Alcock in a show supporting the New York 9/11 appeal.

In an interview with the *News and Star*, in March 2011, Pam recalled that:

> 'In spite of the business taking up so much time, we still found time to get together with other musicians and joined forces with Dave Midgeley, Bob Hinkley and Kenny Blowman – who had been known as Backbeat. Ali was also singing with us at this time.'

Their passion for music has endured and 2016 saw them celebrating 50 years of making music together, still as popular as ever.

The noble art of boxing in Botcherby

Boxing was a popular sport locally and Alan Morland of Wood Street recalls the days when he and Jack Baty boxed at Jim Patterson's Boxing Booth at Carlisle fairground. Jack, the late Elsie Baty's husband, was a marvellous gymnast and others recall the Sunday-morning boxing at the Joiner's Arms pub in Byron Street when his father John Baty, known as 'Gentleman John', won a prize of a sack of potatoes which he carried off home over the Path to Ennerdale Avenue.

Joe Winthrop and Tex Williams, two others who fought professionally, are also well-remembered.

Joe Winthrop

Joe 'Jackie Moran' Winthrop was a professional boxer who was active between 1933 and 1948. He boxed middleweight, light-heavyweight and heavyweight and took part in 37 professional contests. In 1937 he fought and beat Jack 'Cast Iron' Casey at Newcastle. Casey was a British middleweight boxer who held the British (Northern Area) Middleweight Title in 1932 taking the title from 'Rochdale Thunderbolt' Jock McAvoy, who went on to be British Middleweight Champion. Casey's career stretched from 1926 to 1942. Moran is remembered in Botcherby as he famously fought and drew with Bert Gilroy the Scottish Middleweight Champion, who was noted for his style, gameness, punch and toughness. In later years Joe Winthrop was often seen enjoying a quiet pint in the Magpie.

Tex Williams

Tex Williams – real name John Corrigan – had been boxing since his schooldays in Liverpool, but first took the sport seriously when he came to Hadrian's Camp in 1949 as a five-year regular soldier. He had lost his parents in the Liverpool blitz and lived in an orphanage until he was 15. Tex was a welterweight and fought his first professional fight in 1953, knocking out Syd Cameron of Edinburgh in the first round at the Eldorado Stadium in Edinburgh to win his first £10 purse. He is remembered as marrying Jean Harkness of Botcherby at the end of 1950.

Training regularly at the West Tower Street gym, he was managed by Jim Turner of Blackpool. His manager Charlie Graham emigrated to Canada in 1954 causing a hiatus in his career, but when new trainer Pat Haley, a well-known Carlisle former professional boxer, became his trainer in 1955 his career took off. He went into the ring on Mr W Little's first boxing bill at the Queen's Hall, Carlisle, beating Malcolm Tiffany in the first round. His career continued throughout the 1950s with matches at Tower Circus, Blackpool, Northern Ireland and Birmingham.

Left: Tex Williams in his prime. Centre: Joe Winthrop at his fighting weight. Right: Joe in later life was a regular at the Magpie.

What is it and where is it?

Locally, it's said to be a gatepost that marked the entrance to fields at the bottom of Wood Street - fields that have long since disappeared with the building of Eastern Way. The picture on the right shows part of the road leading to Casey's Farm - this was once part of Tilbury Road but now forms an extension to Wood Street.

Please Miss!

Botcherby has a proud history of schools from the 18th century up to and including today. But what happened to the first one?

Botcherby's first school

It was a lucky day when Derek Nash began researching the history of Bramerton Lodge, his home in Wood Street, for he came across information in the land transactions that led to the new discovery that Botcherby had a school as far back as the mid-18th century!

Bramerton Lodge appears to have been built around 1800 but, in conveyancing documents for the land, an abstract of title entry for 1 December 1753 shows the Will of Joseph Atkinson and his bequest of money for the building of a school at Botcherby with some conditions attached. He left his wife Jane Atkinson, *'His best dwelling house at Botcherby and one half part of the Orchard for her natural life'* - but the bequest goes on to say:

> *'He gave his kind friends Joseph Bowman at Botcherby aforesaid and John Holme of the same place, carpenter, the sum of twenty Pounds in Trust to be applied towards building a school house at Botcherby aforesaid with convenience also for the school master to dwell in provided the said building was undertaken in two years time next after his decease and that the owners of estates in Botcherby contribute such further sums as would be necessary for making the said house convenient for use. But in case the said owners of Estates did not contribute such further sums as would be sufficient to complete the aforesaid building within two years after his decease he did thereby order that his said trustees should return the said sum of twenty Pounds to his Executor thereafter named.'*

These men were among the great landowners of Botcherby. Joseph Atkinson was a shoemaker and a Quaker who lived at Botcherby and had extensive land holdings. He sold land in Wood Street to James Fairbairn who would build the houses which became Bramerton, Bramerton Lodge and the associated buildings. Joseph Bowman, also a Quaker who lived in Wood Street, was a friend of Margery Jackson who in 1783 made him the main beneficiary of her Will.

Information on the school is sparse, but Hodgkinson & Donald's map of 1774 shows a building on land which

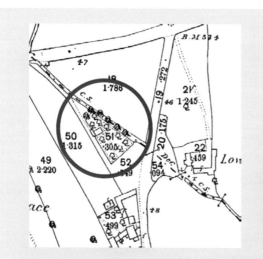 

Botcherby's first school

Left: 1864 map showing the location of Botcherby township's first school near to Wood Street and the brick works. Right: today the area where Botcherby's historic first school was built is a nondescript place on Eastern Way where it joins Warwick Road and the bottom of Eden Park Estate.

can be identified as that left by Atkinson for the school. By 1860 Whellan's *History of Cumberland and Westmorland* notes: *'Botcherby... on the northside of the village is a small school for children of both sexes which will accommodate about 50 pupils; average attendance about 40. It is supported by the quarter-pence of the scholars.'*

It is described in the 1861 Morrison Harrison & Co. *Directory*, as a day school being run by Daniel Twentyman, who had been running it since at least 1847, as noted in the Mannix & Whellan *Directory of Cumberland* for that year, and probably since 1835. Little is known about Dan Twentyman: he lodged at Botcherby with Mrs Jane Bulman, a farmer, and her son Joseph, and on 18 August 1864, at the age of 61, he married Isabella Fisher, then aged 40 at Wetheral Parish Church. Isabella was the daughter of Mary and Joseph Fisher, who worked as a husbandman or free tenant farmer. Whether or not his marriage was happy, we don't know but on 13 October 1865 the *Carlisle Journal* reported that he appeared at the County Court:

'A SCHOOLMASTER'S BEER – W MOFFET v. DAN TWENTYMAN

'This action was to recover the sum of £1. 9s. 3d. for beer alleged to have been consumed by Dan. Twentyman, the well-known Botcherby schoolmaster. Mr. McAlpin appeared for the plaintiff, and Mr. Wannop for defendant. The plaintiff keeps a public-house in the village, and the defendant had a running account for beer, which was sent out to him. Whenever he got spirits he drank them on the premises and paid for them as he got them. Defendant's wife said she paid for every drop of beer that came out of the house, and added that on one occasion she caught her husband drinking out of lemonade bottles in the garden. – Verdict for plaintiff.'

As an interesting aside, on 8 May 1863 the *Carlisle Journal* reported on a meeting of the Carlisle Consistory Court regarding the planned gallery for Upperby Parish Church (Botcherby was in that parish at the time) which stated that *'the children who attend Botcherby School on Sundays need to be considered.'* Mr Cory of Bramerton Lodge designed the gallery and the plans are in Carlisle Archives, but Canon Jim Hyslop, rector of the church today confirms that it was never built.

By 10 February 1871 the *Carlisle Patriot* reported on a presentation that took place in Botcherby School House in Mr Cory's grounds:

'For some time a Sunday school, gathering almost every child in the village has been carried on by Mrs Cory, her family and the Misses Norman. A collection having been made amongst the scholars and their parents, it was determined to spend it on a silver biscuit tin, with a pencil case for Mr Cory... The presentation was made by Rev. G. F. Head in the name of the people.'

The Misses Norman were also part of a prominent Botcherby family, living in Wood Street and were daughters of Mary Fairbairn's solicitor.

We do not know whether this event marked the closure of the school, as it isn't mentioned in the report, but the school appears to have played a large part in the educational and social life of the village throughout these years.

Daniel Twentyman, the schoolmaster, died on 15 December 1875 aged 72, and on 30 October 1877 the *Carlisle Journal* reported on a court case between the trustees of Botcherby School and Mrs Isabella Twentyman of Botcherby and Edward Parker of South Street. The action was one of 'ejectment' as, since her husband's death, Mrs Twentyman refused to give up possession of the premises to the Trustees. The arguments went back and forth with Mrs Twentyman saying that her husband left it to her in his will and that they had the property for 39 years. Mr Norman, trustee, said he had known it for at least 40 years and, up to Mr Twentyman's death, it was used as a school. He thought the rent would be £6 a year. It was then explained that, on Mr Twentyman's ill health, it was converted to a dwelling house, but they never lived in it themselves: it was let to another party in the village.

Mr Cartmell admitted that there was no deed, and produced a letter in which the writers stated that the house, which had been a school for so many years, should continue for that purpose and not be let as a dwelling house:

'"The probability was that Botcherby would have to provide a school before long, as there was not any other accommodation." His Honour: "But they have had 40 years possession and paid no rent" Mr. Wannop said that the property was let for £5 a year. He could show nothing in favour of his case but possession.

TO THE CHARITY COMMISSIONERS of ENGLAND and WALES.

In the matter of the School Site situate at Botcherby in the Parish of St Cuthbert Without Carlisle in the County of Cumberland and

In the matter of "The Charitable Trusts Acts 1853 to 1891".

We hereby apply to the Charity Commissioners for an order establishing a scheme for the administration of the Charity.

Dated this 14th day of October 1897.

JOHN NUTSFORD. BOTCHERBY ⎱ Members of the St Cuthbert With-
RICHARD GRAHAM.BOTCHERBY ⎰ out Parish Council.

That a Scheme to the following effect should be established for the administration of the Charity viz For the sale of the piece of ground on which there formerly was a School and garden but which is now and has for a long period laid open and waste and which contains according to the ordnance survey .305 and is No 51 on the Map of 1889 and of the adjoining waste land containing according to the Ordnance survey .549 and numbered 52 on the said Map and giving all necessary and incidental directions in relation thereto and for the expenditure of the money arising from such sale in and about the enclosing raising levelling and laying out for the use of the inhabitants of Botcherby Township of another portion of waste ground which is the property of the said Township and is bounded on the North by the main road leading from Carlisle to Warwick Bridge and o the East by the Highway leading to Botcherby Village on the South b: land now or late of Joseph Hamilton and Sons and on the West by the Botcherby Hall Estate and which contains according to the Ordnan Survey .398 and is No 42 on the Ordnance Map of 1889.

Roll and attendance figures for Botcherby School

Year/quarter ending	Roll	Attendance
Reported to attendance Committee on 13 Nov. 1905	102	not stated
Year to 31 Mar. 1921	122.14	109.14
Qtr 31 Dec. 1923	69.3	65.72
Qtr June 1926	42.7	35.96
Qtr Dec. 1926	27.5	22.5

Left: proposal to the Charity Commission for the sale of the first school's land and the purchase of a different plot, which became the site of Botcherby School (now the Community Centre).

Above: some figures showing the growth and decline in the number of pupils at Botcherby School over the years. Source: Derek Nash's research.

'His Honour advised the plaintiffs to pay the widow £20 for the house, and adjourned the case till the next court.'

No trace of a further court case can be found and it is possible that the matter was settled out of court. Isabella did not live very long after her husband, as she died in November 1878 at the age of 54 and was buried at Carlisle Cemetery.

There is no further mention of the school until an entry in Moss's *Carlisle Directory 1884*, when Miss M. Knipe is running a day school at Botcherby and J. F. Dodd, assistant schoolmaster, lives at Park House on Mount Florida.

By 1897 it seems that the school no longer existed and a trustee body was established by the Parish of St John's Church, Upperby. John Augustus Cory was a Trustee along with the vicar and two other gentlemen. Their aim was to apply to the Charity Commissioners for permission to sell the land next to the school. Correspondence flew back and forth setting out the case for the sale and the questions raised, and the request was finally accepted with conditions.

A report on 18 May 1897, *Botcherby Wasteland Committee to the Upperby Parish Council* commented on the state of the land at the time and recommended steps be taken *'to stop the common tip for filthy rubbish'* and going on to propose that the *'water course to be cleaned out and that the whole site be nicely levelled.'*

On 4 June 1898 a letter states: *'A piece of land at Botcherby a part of which a school, known as the Botcherby School formerly stood'* and gives the area and valuation as £50-£60. The charity that was established by the Church was called 'The Charity known as Wasteland in the said District' referring to Botcherby.

On 14 October 1897 members of the St Cuthbert Without Parish Council, John Nutsford and Richard Graham, made an application to the Charity Commissioners:

'That a scheme to the following effect should be established for the administration of the Charity viz.

For the sale of the piece of ground on which there was formerly a school and garden but which is now and has for a long period laid open and waste and which contains according to the ordnance survey .305 and is No. 51 on the Map of 1889 and of the adjoining waste land containing according to the ordnance survey .549 and numbered 52 on the said map.'

The object of applying to the Commissioners for permission to sell the land was to raise money to pay for the:

'Enclosing, raising, levelling and laying out for the use of the inhabitants of Botcherby Township of another portion of waste ground which is the property of the said Township and is bounded on the North by the main road leading from Carlisle to Warwick Bridge and on the East by the Highway leading to Botcherby Village on the South by land now or late of Joseph Hamilton and Sons and on the West by the Botcherby Hall Estate and which contains according to the Ordnance Survey .398 and is No. 42 on the Ordnance map of 1889.'

It was a great surprise to look at plot No. 42 on the Ordnance Survey map and find that it is part of the site where Botcherby School is located - this opened in 1900 and today houses the Community Centre. So it seems that education in Botcherby has been there for a very long time.

This is confirmed in *Carlisle Journal* 20 April 1900 which reports that the school site was to be sold to provide the price for an elementary school.

These discoveries tie in well with the educational revolution that was taking place in 1891 when the Assisted Education Act came into force, and was a hot topic for school boards and managers. The Act proposed that there should be free education for children, replacing the fee paying system and a government grant to schools of 10 shillings for each child attending would be paid.

Botcherby School, Mark Two

This school has been part of the Botcherby scene for more than a hundred years and has had a long and varied history, being very much part of the lives of its residents. Here I give its story.

Plans submitted by the architect A. W. Johnstone for the building of Botcherby School and Master's House at the bottom of Victoria Road were approved by the Carlisle Rural District Council, Health and Water Committee on 8 March 1899. The school was formally opened on 15 March 1900, and the following day the *Carlisle Journal* reported on the celebratory tea and concert which took place when Mr John Wood, the owner of Bramerton Lodge, presided over the concert. It was the Upperby School Board who erected the school as, at this time, Botcherby was still part of Upperby Parish and schools were built or sponsored by the church.

The following report in the *Carlisle Journal* on 16 March 1900 gives many interesting facts about the school and the village:

'BOARD SCHOOL FOR BOTCHERBY

'Yesterday a new school, which has been erected at Botcherby, by the Upperby School Board at a cost of about £3000, was formally opened. Just over two years ago a petition signed by 80 ratepayers of Botcherby, headed by Mr. Richard Graham, was laid before the Board, in which it was pointed out that there was great need of a school for the children of the village, who were at that time estimated to number 70. Owing to having to walk long distances in bad weather to the nearest available schools, such as Brook Street and St. John's, much illness was caused, and as new houses were rapidly being built, the need of a school in the village would become yearly more necessary.

'The Upperby School Board, on receiving the petition, took up the matter energetically, and the result has been the erection of the new school and master's house near the corner of Warwick Road opposite the Star Inn. Mr. A. W. Johnston, Castle Street, was the architect, and his plans have been skilfully carried out, so that the appearance of this corner of Botcherby has been greatly improved, while the roadway in Wellington Terrace has been considerably widened. The school, the master's house, and part of the playground occupy a site in Wellington Terrace which was purchased by the Board for about £600. The rest of the playground is on "No Man's Land" an area of about 1,700 square yards, which was conveyed free to the Board by the Upperby Parish Council. "No Man's Land" was for many years an unsightly place on Warwick Road , but it has now been levelled up and enclosed with a nice wall so

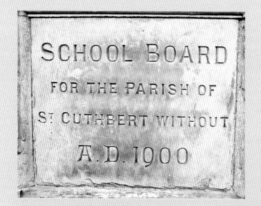

Clockwise from top left: foundation stone for Botcherby School, dating from 1900, before the village was merged with Carlisle; the school around 1907; the schoolmaster's house; the girls at the school in 1920. Below: more pictures from the school in 1920 - bottom right, front row - second left Edith Borradaile, centre Mary Feddon.

as to give a spacious recreation ground for the children attending the school.

'The school itself is well built, airy and light. It has accommodation for 196 boys, girls and infants. There is a large room 69 feet long by 23½ ft. wide; a classroom 22½ ft by 21½ ft; two lavatories, vestibules, &c. The building has been done with Botcherby bricks, with red stone dressings, the contractors being as follows:- Messrs. James Baty and Sons, Botcherby, builders; Mr. E Musgrove, Court Street, joiner; Messrs. Ormerod and Son, Close Street, plasterers; Mr. J. Kellet, slater; Mr. N. Foster, Lowther Street, plumber; Messrs. Nelson and Sons, Botchergate, painters and glaziers; Messrs. Joseph Wharton and Sons, Mary Street, ironwork; Mr. John Corbett, Corporation Road, heating apparatus.

'The schoolmaster's house contains six rooms and has been erected according to the requirements of the Education Department. The total cost of the buildings, &c., exclusive of the site, has amounted to about £2,500, while the cost of the school alone works out to about £10 per head of the accommodation. The Board borrowed £3,200 with which to do the work, and the present rate in the parish is 3d. in the pound. There are two other schools under the management of the Board, one at Upperby and the other at Stoneraise. Mr. F. A. Shaw , the master at Stoneraise, has been transferred to the new school at Botcherby. Miss Shepherd has been appointed assistant mistress of the new school; and Mr. Shaw's *place at Stoneraise has been taken by Mr. Adams. The formal opening of the new school was attended by Mr. Gill, Scuggar House, chairman of the School Board; Mr. J. W. Nicholson, vice-chairman; and Mr. Richard Graham, one of the members of the board.*

'Later in the day the parents of the children in Botcherby attended a tea, which was followed by a concert, presided over by Mr. Wood, Bramerton Lodge, at which an amusing programme was contributed by the Border City Minstrels and Mr. Nutsford, ventriloquist. The committee by whom the arrangements for the tea and concert were made was composed of Messrs. Richard Graham, Fairbairn, Shaw, James Baty, Nutsford, J. R. Matthews and Joseph Robson.

'The school is open on Monday next for the children, and it is expected that there will be one hundred in attendance the first day. There are 45 infants in Botcherby who have not hitherto attended any school. To those and the rest of the children the school will be conveniently near. No fees will be charged, and the school has been well furnished with desks, books, maps, apparatus, pianoforte and other necessaries.'

The first pupils duly attended on 19 March 1900 and the school Log Book states:

'Opened and commenced directives in this school.

Staff – Frank Armstrong Shaw. (Headmaster Mixed)

Elizabeth Shepherd. (Mistress of Infant Dept.)

Mixed Dept.   Boys 21)

Girls 15)

70

Infants Dept.   Boys 20)

Girls 14)'

The Log Book contains lesson plans, staff appointments, transfers and terminations and agreements on holidays. Besides reporting on everyday events such as the boiler breaking down and the weather and its impact on attendance and minor damage to two windows, it gives a fascinating insight into the life of the school and its development.

Cumberland Education Committee Minutes in July 1907 show that the *'Rev. F. L. H. Millard enquired about the charges and conditions for the use of Botcherby Council School for the purposes of a Sunday School'* and his letter was referred to the Managers of the school for a reply. The following year, in November 1908, it is minuted that Botcherby Evening School had 100 students and that HM Inspector approved the appointment of a Superintendent and that the Headmaster had applied for some payment for his work.

By 20 November 1912 the School Management Committee Carlisle (Extension) Order 1912 recorded that the maintenance of certain schools had been taken over from 9 November confirming that the City Council was responsible for Botcherby School. This was at the time of the city boundaries being extended to include Botcherby.

April 1913 saw 194 pupils on the School Roll with the caretaker's salary rising from 7s per week to 15s per week *'with approval to procure all the assistance required.'* On 16 December 1914 the Head Master's salary was fixed at £177 per annum and a free house equal to £15 per annum was made available, this being the maximum for a school of this size.

During those years the school experienced normal staff turnover and there is nothing recorded regarding the issues that the school was shortly to face.

But the 1920s began to see a slow decline in the numbers of children on the school roll. In December 1921 the School Management Sub (Reorganisation of Schools) Committee states *'Standards 6 and 7 at this school consist of 16 children who require the services of a separate teacher.'* The resulting outcome was that those children were transferred to Brook Street School; one teacher was placed on Reserve Staff and the teacher of Domestic Science was given one month's termination of her contract.

The first indication of closure is in the minute of the Education Organisation Committee 9 December 1925 which comments on the *'Diminished attendance at Botcherby School'* and proceeds with a resolution to transfer the Head Master and two other teachers of Botcherby School to Upperby Junior School. Miss A. E. Pickering, Assistant Teacher to be in temporary charge of Botcherby School.

On 25 August 1926, the School Management and Organisation (Joint) Committee comments on the *'Meagre Attendance'* and the *'Cash incurred'* with a recommendation to the Board of Education to *'Close the school as early as possible.'* The City of Carlisle Council commented on the proposals in the minutes of 12 October 1926 but, on 18 January 1927, the School Management Committee agreed to close the school. The final day was Friday 21 January 1927.

It is not clear why there was a fall in attendance, as this was about the time when Botcherby Estate was in the early stages of development. The authorities also seemed to have lingering thoughts about the building for, in January 1928, the School Management Committee sought consent from the Education Committee to rent 8.058 acres of a field to be used as a school playing field. Consent was granted and, later that year, it was agreed to erect an iron-railing fence estimated to cost £400, and to install a games shed on the field at a further cost estimated to be £50.

Some years later, part of the field was used for the Warwick Road widening scheme. Decisions still hovered in the air as the Carlisle Corporation Minutes of 11 July 1928 report agreement to re-open the school. However, the meeting was also made aware that the ultimate decision was vested under the 1921 Education Act to the Education Committee. On 2 November 1929 the *Cumberland News* reported that the school was re-opening, but by 1932-33 the City Minutes record that it was agreed to re-open for younger children in the winter term.

During the long years of its official closure the school had been made good use of by a number of groups, including a venue for Labour Party meetings. In preparation for war, it was used by St John's Ambulance and the Red Cross Society for air-raid training and the storage of equipment.

1938 saw a new turn in the school's fortunes as, on 28 January, the *Cumberland News* reported on a meeting of Carlisle Education Committee. Mr W. Goody said:

> *'The thing which interested him in particular was the use to which the Botcherby School was now being put. It appeared to be utilised every available night in the week and as the building was under the jurisdiction of the Education Committee he thought consideration might also be given to the conversion of the school into a community centre. A host of organisations were using it and the need was very great.'*

This high usage is reflected in the scale of charges agreed in June 1938:

> *1 room 3/6d (including 1/- for the Caretaker)*
>
> *1 room 3/- for ten meetings (including 1/- for the Caretaker)*
>
> *2 rooms 6/- (including 2/- for the Caretaker)*
>
> *2 rooms 5/- for ten meetings (including 2/- for the Caretaker)*

At the time the City Council were looking at the lack of community centres in all areas of the city, but there had been no general development plan at the time when the estates were built. The concerns were summed up in the statement: *'There had been a good many appearances in the various Juvenile Courts and this did not reflect great credit on the youth of the city.'* The lack of positive activities for young people was leading to problems.

The school had not been used as a school in a good while; the boiler was out of action and the walls running in water. Botcherby children were travelling to schools on the edge of town.

Soon, everything was to change.

People power – Botcherby mothers take control

The headline on the front page of the *Carlisle Journal* on 9 December 1938 thundered:

> **'City Mothers Take Action – Botcherby School Protest Meeting**
>
> *'Botcherby mothers are up in arms about the conditions their children are exposed to in attending the local elementary school. They want the school... re-conditioned, and free bus conveyance provided for all the children to and from the school every day.'*

It was a case of 'people power' and a 'Botcherby Parents' Council' had been formed with 50 mothers attending a meeting at Durranhill Road and electing three parents (Mrs Shepherd, Mrs Cotton and Mrs Rose) to approach the City Education Authority on the matter. Mr Frank Ashton, Director of Education, was invited and attended the meeting. A committee consisting of two parents from every avenue in Botcherby was appointed as there

Clockwise from top left: the school in 1936; pupils at the school around 1945; inside the school in 1957 (Cumbria Image Bank); Botcherby School Committee 1958-59 - left to right - Jimmy Bennett, Maggie Winthrop, Jim Spalding, Mrs Glendining, May Egglestone, Ian Iveson, Dot Fern, Mr Ellis, Mrs Scott, Jim Spedding, Mrs Thompson, Mary Johns, Mrs Halliburton, Muriel Spedding, Mrs Gourley, Frances Bennett and baby Maxi Spedding in front.

were complaints that previous requests for improved conditions had no result.

The next step was to hold an open protest meeting the following Wednesday afternoon to which City Education officials, all the City councillors and the Ward representatives were invited.

> *'One of the leaders in the parents' agitation told a Journal reporter that their action was representative of all classes of residents in Botcherby and had no political bias."The school badly needs redecorating," she said, "and the path leading to it is often flooded, although it was repaired and built up at one time. This entails a big detour four times a day for little children up to seven and eight years of age and to send them to school by bus is an expensive business for parents with three or four children."'*

This refers to the high-fenced Path that ran from the bottom of Botcherby Avenue across Melbourne Park, with its bridge over the river Petteril, emerging on Greystone Road with access to the local schools: Norman Street, Brook Street, St John's and St Cuthbert's, involving a four-mile walk each day.

Botcherby's dads support their wives

The headline in the following week's *Carlisle Journal* on 16 December 1938, again thundered out the news:

> **'We Demand! Fathers Support Botcherby Mothers**
>
> *'Four members of Carlisle City Council listened to spirited speeches expressing the "seething discontent" of Botcherby mothers at the local school yesterday afternoon, when the newly-formed Botcherby Parents' Council formulated and unanimously carried the following demands to be sent to the Carlisle City Council and Education Committee:*
>
> > *Free transport for all Botcherby children travelling to and from their respective schools.*
> >
> > *The re-conditioning and opening of Botcherby School.*
>
> *'The meeting was presided over by Mrs. M. Spears and the large gathering of mothers present revealed a deep and spirited sense of grievance with which all Councillors expressed complete sympathy.'*

Mrs A. E. Rose outlined the two demands, criticising the general lack of social amenities in Botcherby and, most glaring of all, the lack of school provision in the district. The mothers present made full use of the free discussion, complaining about the condition of the bridge along the Path the children used. Discontent was also expressed about inequality in bus fares for children attending the various schools. *'When we get the new schools at Botcherby, then we will consider swimming pools and new Town Halls!'* declared one mother.

Of the men present, one complained that his child had twice been knocked down on the Path by a cyclist, contending that the Path was a definite danger. Another man strongly advocated a collective school strike to secure their demands. Mr John Minns, representing Aglionby Ward, contended that the school should not have been closed until better alternative facilities had first been provided.

The arguments rolled on: Mr Goody said that the entire matter was a question of human needs and the present position in Botcherby was one of the most shocking things that had occurred in Carlisle. Mr Thomson pointed out that *'suburban facilities had been lost sight of in the rapid growth of the city... at present, Botcherby, although an important suburb of the city, was only "an oasis in the desert".'*

The issue was certainly exercising the minds of the Education Committee, as the next headline in the *Carlisle Journal* on 2 June 1939 indicates:

'Botcherby School Controversy: Final Decision Not Yet Taken

'Criticism of the passing of three varying resolutions at as many meetings of the City Schools Management Committee concerning the advisability of re-opening Botcherby School was voiced at a meeting of the City Education Committee held in the Town hall on Wednesday:

'"The Committee is playing with the sincerity of Botcherby mothers in this matter," declared Mr. Edgar Grierson, "and I warn the Committee that unless something is done the parents will refuse to send their children to school. I would like nothing better, if nothing were done for these children."'

And so the discussions and arguments went on, until the following week when a further event in this long saga appeared in the *Carlisle Journal* headlined on 9 June 1939.

'Botcherby Parents: FOUR HUNDRED SIGN PETITION

'About four hundred parents in the suburb have signed a petition to be presented to the City Management Committee when it meets this afternoon to further consider the question. It was unanimously endorsed at an open-air meeting held at the corner of Botcherby Avenue and attended by a large number of parents.'

The petition was blunt in its demands, stating:

'We the undersigned parents of Botcherby, energetically protest against the action of the School Management Committee in rescinding the decision to re-open Botcherby School as a temporary measure, and its failure to make any arrangements for free transport as contained in our last resolution submitted to the Education Committee.

'We also support a further resolution to the effect that any attempt to send our children to Lowther Street School, unless free transport is provided will be met with the fullest resistance.'

Mrs A. E. Rose of 86 Merith Avenue, gave the meeting a lengthy review of the agitation and Mr Grierson expressed his support and sympathy at the lack of action by the Education Committee:

'I will convey your petition to the Schools Management Committee tomorrow... there were 158 children in Botcherby up to six and seven years of age who could attend the local school if it re-opened. The initial capital expenditure of re-opening and maintaining the school would be £1,800 a year, the annual cost thereafter would be £1,000.'

The bitter taste of success

Well, they won!

But not quite everything and, on 23 June 1939, the *Carlisle Journal* reported that the mothers were far from satisfied. The cost of bus fares for older children travelling to town was not met and the school was only being opened for 5- to 7-year-old children - it was felt that including up to 9-year-olds would have been better.

There was disappointment that the 10-year fight had not resulted in an all-age school and fears that a new school would not be built.

'We are glad to have the school opened for the little ones, they have done us a good turn. But the older kiddies are not benefitting much. I would like to see a new road made across from Borland Avenue to Sybil Street. It has been talked about for ten years but we have not got it yet.'

The next day, 24 June 1939, the headline in the *Cumberland News* told the story:

'WHY IT WAS DECIDED TO RE-OPEN BOTCHERBY SCHOOL:

Not due to Threat of Strike by Parents.'

Reporting on the meeting of the Carlisle Education Committee on 22 June it said:

'The Chairman (Mr. Herbert Atkinson) stressed that they had not yielded to threats of a school strike – a statement which was questioned – and after some discussion in which the need for speeding up the erection of new schools was stressed, the Committee approved the scheme by a large majority, only two voting against it.'

This was a time of change for education in Carlisle as the school-leaving age was to be raised to 15 years of age on 1 September 1939, which meant an additional 150 children had to be found places. By moving the 150 Botcherby infants who attended Norman Street school to Botcherby School and making other adjustments, 150 places for seniors were created at Brook Street and St John's Schools! New housing estates such as Harraby also meant an influx of children, and new schools were being built at Currock with a further school being planned on the eastern side of the city, but not yet built. The arrangements were but a temporary expedient, and even though £1,350 was spent on the re-opening, Botcherby School was regarded as obsolete.

The war years saw the school used by evacuees and by children from other schools who worked the 'double shift' system. Miss Nancy Robinson was appointed as teacher at Brook Street Girls' School on 1 February 1943. She recalls how they shared their classrooms with St John's School, as part of St John's was used to store ammunition. School sessions were 8.30 to 12.30 and 1.00 to 4.30 with the school week being shared.

The 'off' session was spent at Botcherby School (which did not operate as a school then). There were 55 pupils in the class and they didn't all attend the 'off' sessions. Occasionally they used Melbourne Park on Sports Days and played netball in St John's school yard. In 1956, Miss Robinson was appointed to Pennine Way Infants' School for its opening term but, as the building was not ready, the children were bussed to Botcherby School for temporary classroom space.

Soon Botcherby School would have a new use and a new life as it became Botcherby Community Centre.

The school that never was

Had WW2 not intervened, today's map of Botcherby might look very different. Re-organisation of the city's schools was a hot topic. Sniping would go on between councillors at the Education Committee meetings, at the delay in the Surveyor's Department (who were engaged in Air Raid Precautions [ARP] work) in progressing the Currock Schools. It was suggested that the Surveyor needed further assistance, with Dr G. Sheehan supporting this because it was a step towards getting new schools for Botcherby.

Carlisle Archives hold a letter from Frank Ashton, Director of Education, to W. J. C. Baty of Blackwell Vale, Carlisle, dated 29 March 1939, headed *'Compulsory Purchase Order – Baty's Land at Botcherby.'* It went on to say that *'land is required for a school site – Senior School in the Eastern area'* and comments on an urgent need for Secondary School accommodation. A statutory questionnaire regarding title, mortgages and occupiers was completed by Mr Baty. The occupier was J. B. Hind of 24 Chiswick Street, Carlisle.

An undated plan, drawn by Percy Dalton, the City Engineer and Surveyor, shows the extent of the school site. It was behind the south side of Wood Street and faced Durranhill Road and the housing estate.

It appears that the war put an end to the plan for Botcherby's new school, as there is no follow-up correspondence, and the school was never built.

St Cuthbert's Catholic Community School

An entry in St Patrick's School log book on 2 October 1871 gives us the beginnings of the story of St Cuthbert's School. It was made by the Head Teacher, Jane Burton:

'On Friday I resigned charge of this school in order to undertake the management of St. Cuthbert's which will be newly opened on Monday next.'

In 1870 the proposal was to provide places for 250 children but, by November 1871, HM Chief Inspector C. H. Parez reported that the school had recently opened and gave the following pupil numbers:

Boys	Girls	Infants	Total
116	116	118	350

This made it the largest Catholic school in Carlisle, with St Patrick's and St Bede's having a total of 179 pupils and 264 pupils respectively.

These few words must have been sweet music to the ears of Rev. Luke Curry of SS Mary and Joseph's Church in Chapel Street (later to remove to Warwick Square as Our Lady and St Joseph's in 1893). He had worked long and hard to establish Catholic education in the city, and had frequently met with stone walls from officialdom. Now, with the exception of the Infant classrooms, the school was open. It would last for a hundred years.

The school was built on the corner of Union Street (now Rydal Street) and Fusehill Street, a red-brick Victorian building, today the site of St Cuthbert's Court.

This was a time that saw great expansion in school building brought about by the introduction of the Elementary Education Act 1870 in England and Wales. After years of development with the Industrial Revolution bringing factories to the towns, it became apparent that, if Britain was to remain at the forefront of manufacturing in world trade, it needed an effective education system. Initially the Act provided for education from the age of five to 10 years, but by 1880 attendance was made compulsory for children until they were 12 years old. A system of School Boards was set up to run the schools and the Boards could pay the fees for parents who were too poor to pay. It was not until 1891 that education became free for both Board and Church schools.

Not everyone thought it was a good idea. There were fears that education would lead ordinary working people 'to think' and to realise the hardships in their lives, often living in poverty and squalid conditions, leading to revolt. Some factory owners feared that children in school meant the loss of cheap labour at work. Others feared 'mass indoctrination' of the children. The more enlightened realised that a workforce who could read, write and do arithmetic had to be a benefit to their workplace.

The developments went ahead and with the Balfour Education Act in 1902 new legislation abolished the School Boards and replaced them with the Local Education Authority, who also had secondary education in their remit for the first time. So this was the background to the opening of St Cuthbert's.

In 1879 Canon George W. Waterton came to Carlisle on Canon Curry's retirement. He took over as Chairman of the Governor's of St Cuthbert's and as a member of the Carlisle School Board. The Infants' classrooms were completed and by the early 1900s evening classes were established.

By 1884 my great-great-aunt Mary Graham was Headmistress, her sister Ellenor was a pupil teacher and, before the end of the century, my grandmother, Mary Shane, was a young teacher at the school. She would recall the very hard times that working families experienced then, with poorly paid work, bad housing conditions and little health care. In those days, long before the welfare state, tiny children would often arrive at school cold and hungry and with inadequate clothing, but would soon be warmed up for the day with hot soup.

The school went on to teach thousands of children and many of the names of its teachers still resonate through the decades until today. Names from the post-WW2 period include Miss O'Connor as Headmistress, followed by Miss Mary Brett and Mr John Lett. One of the most popular teachers was Miss Lily McBride and others, including Miss Ciappazonni, Miss Win Owens (later Mrs Loughran), Miss Tess Kelly (who married local vet, Charlie McNulty), Mr Vincent Fitzsimons – known as 'Pop', Miss McCaffrey, Miss Nutter, Mrs Barr, Mrs Reid and Mrs Miles are well remembered.

After Miss Brett retired, Mr John W. Lett took over as Head in 1954 and was to remain with the school until after its transfer to the site at Botcherby in 1972, thereby becoming the last Head of the old school and the first of the new school.

The new site at Botcherby had been bought from Botcherby cattle dealer Martin Casey by the Catholic authorities in the 1940s. The fields stood on the hill at the top of Victoria Road and close to St Joseph's Home. During the war years, the 1944 Education Act had been legislated and this brought in the tripartite system of education, with three types of secondary schools: grammar schools, secondary modern schools and secondary technical schools. Children were assessed for their most suitable school by the 11-plus exam. Free school milk

Old St Cuthbert's School

Above, clockwise from top left: schoolteachers and priests outside the school in Rydal Street, early 1900s - on the back row, 3rd from the right is Mary (Polly) Shane, my grandmother, and Canon Waterton is seated centre - on the right of him may be the Head Teacher, Mary Graham; two pictures from St Cuthbert's archives of classes in the early 20th century; a school trip to Silloth in the 1950s - teachers include Miss Mary Brett, Miss Owen, Miss Ciapazonni and Miss McCaffrey - Botcherby girls include Eileen Farish, Antoinette Kirk, Barbara Charters, Carmen Grice and the author.
Below: Mr Lett and Father Harrison flank this 1954 photo of Standard 1 class. Among the Botcherby pupils were Kenneth McKnight, Alex Nocter, John Sheridan, Angela Reid and my brother Gil.

was provided to all pupils under the age of 18 and the Act brought about an expansion in education for women who would go on to higher education.

In April 1947, Monsignor Richard Lawrence Smith, now the parish priest at Warwick Square (and just returned from his post with the British Council Control in Germany where he reported on conditions in the British Zone of Occupation), wrote to Frank Charnley, Director of Education. He offered to put the site at Botcherby at the disposal of the Local Education Authority for the building of a new St Cuthbert's school. The old school had served its purpose, but with no room for expansion and with primitive outside toilets it was badly in need of replacement. It was not to be and it would take another 25 years for a new school to be built when, in 1970, permission was given by the Department of Education to plan a replacement school.

On Wednesday, 30 August 1972, a great day dawned when the Rt Reverend Bishop Pearson, Auxiliary Bishop of Lancaster, led the Official Blessing and Opening ceremony at the school – now known as St Cuthbert's Catholic Community School. Large numbers of guests and parents attended, and the parish priest Fr Frank

Moulding invited all the head teachers in the city, along with the Mayor, MP, Officers of the city and representatives from other denominations.

With the old St Cuthbert's school demolished and the site at Rydal Street vacant, consideration was given to the idea of erecting thirty flats for the elderly on it. The parish approached Help the Aged Housing Association, who undertook the project and leased the site from the church, whilst the Parish Priest retained allocation of 50% of the new flats. Today Anchor Housing Association run the development, and the old school is but a memory.

Mr John Lett was well known as the forthright Headmaster of St Cuthbert's School for nearly thirty years. He came to the old school in 1954 and would remain until his retirement from the new school in 1983. He is quoted as saying that he had what he called *'a consuming final interest in education.'* He said at the time of the move to Botcherby that he couldn't sufficiently emphasise the joy and anticipation this gave him.

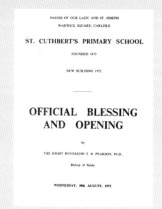

St Cuthbert's Catholic Community School

Clockwise from top left: the sign and the new school and nursery on Victoria Road; the commemorative programme for the opening and blessing of the school; the school entrance; the nursery; the opening ceremony for the new nursery showing (from left to right) Monsignor Gregory Turner, Chair of Governors and Parish Priest of Our Lady and St Joseph's Church, Ian White, Head Teacher, and Eric Martlew, MP; Barbara Stubbs preparing meals at the school; and the school football team in 2002.

The new school at Botcherby went from strength to strength as the challenges of the National Curriculum went ahead and sporting activities were developed, including clubs for swimming, gym and fell walking run by the PTA. School Governors played an increasingly important role in all aspects of running the school and as former Chair of the Governors, Derek Nash says:

> *'The education service, like many other areas of public life was undergoing considerable change and well loved highly skilled and dedicated teachers, particularly Heads were being bombarded with change. Simply put they were being forced into becoming managers not teachers - the role that they joined the profession for. We were in danger of losing the children, and our living Lord under this barrage of change. The role of School Governors changed too: no longer was their role one of a smiling face at concerts and sports days, fund raisers, mini bus drivers: no, they were to become managers, in commercial terms non-executive directors, and critical friends of the school.*

> *'A huge challenge, development plans, budgets, nursery schooling, inspections, national curriculum, policies and procedures, staff appointments, although Aided Schools were already responsible for the recruitment and employment of their teaching staff. The reduction in support from the County Council and the Diocese increased the demands on heads and governors.'*

The school's Mission Statement begins with the words 'Let Your Light Shine'. School activities over the years reflect this ethos, as a glance through reports in the local newspapers show. In March 2004, Head John Turner invited parents and those living in the area to attend a meeting to be involved in a new development plan for the school saying, *'We are hoping for a good turn-out because we want our development plan to reflect the needs and ideas of everyone in this community.'*

The same year saw the children planting 60 trees in the school grounds as part of National Tree Week celebrations and the following year the Conservation Club planted 500 daffodil bulbs around a specially-created garden, along with a wildlife haven, bird boxes and pond.

More recently, in October 2013, there was a visit from Dudley the Elephant, when Mr Hunter from ESH Company (who were building new houses on the site of the former Borland Avenue flats) talked to children on how to stay safe around building sites. And on Wear Pink Day, Mr Blobby helped members of the PTA, staff and children raise £150 for the Breast Cancer Campaign - a great time was had by all. The Cyclewise event saw pupils gaining certificates for learning how to ride their bikes safely. These are just a few of the activities that make this a true Community School.

The Ofsted inspection report in September 2013 stated:

> *'The school is a calm and welcoming place where the views and talents of all individuals are respected and nurtured. Consequently, children feel safe and morale is high.'*

The late Ian White followed Mr Lett as Head and in 1993 wrote these words:

> *'Visitors to the school see the motto "We work together, we pray together, we play together" at the main entrance. These words summarise what we set out to achieve at St Cuthbert's. We want the school to be a welcoming place where the children, staff and parents feel comfortable as part of the school family.'*

With the retirement of Head Teacher, Pauline Moss in December 2015 new developments were ahead. The school governors along with the governors of St Margaret Mary's Primary School at Upperby began looking at ways to maximise benefits to both schools and protect their long-term viability. This would build on the links between the two schools already established as part of the Carlisle South Primary Cluster (CASPA). St Cuthbert's had 108 pupils on roll and St Margaret Mary's 239 pupils. Proposals were put forward to form a Carlisle Catholic Federation from 1 September 2016.

Jose Hodgkins was appointed as temporary Head Teacher for three-and-a-half days per week, and Fr Anthony Gaskin appointed the new Chair of Governors at St Cuthbert's. He told the *Cumberland News* on 16 March 2016 that: *'Federation of these two schools is a great chance to pool our resources... The schools will keep their local identity, and they will be better working together with a single governing body and a single headteacher.'*

A formal consultation document was issued on behalf of the two governing bodies who had voted to proceed to public consultation with a six-week consultation period ending on 25 April 2016.

By 22 July 2016 the *Cumberland News* reported that the federation of the two schools had been given the go-ahead by the Diocese of Lancaster and the Department of Education had agreed.

Chris Wilkins, the present Head Teacher at St Margaret Mary's School was appointed to take charge of both schools from 1 September 2016. Mr Wilkins said: *'I'm really excited about working for the two schools. St Cuthbert's at Botcherby has absolutely fantastic potential and parents should be really pleased that their children go there. They have small class sizes, beautiful buildings and staff know all their children well.'*

Writing to parents of St Cuthbert's School, Mr Wilkins said: *'I want to bring stability to the school after several years of change.'*

After 145 years, the school looks forward to new developments in the 21st century. I think Jane Burton would have been very proud to see how it all turned out.

◆◆◆

On the buses...

The United Bus Company ran two bus services from Carlisle to Botcherby – in the 1950s and 60s these were the No. 30 and the No. 24. The buses were red double-deckers with a driver and a conductor to dispense the tickets. A well-known Botcherby man was Inspector Graham who would catch the buses at random to inspect passenger's tickets. The buses at this time had no doors and anyone could hop on and off with ease.

The No. 30 went from the Town Hall via Botchergate and Greystone Road onto Warwick Road, up Victoria Road and then round Botcherby estate via Durranhill Road, Merith Avenue and the triangle at the corner of Borland Avenue. The Terminus was at the top of Holywell Crescent opposite the Dairy.

The No. 24 left the Town Hall and went straight down Warwick Road to Botcherby and it turned on Durranhill Road outside Florida Stores and went back up to the terminus opposite Croftlands, and was a much quicker service into town.

The school buses were single-deckers especially for children going to schools near Greystone Road – Norman Street, Brook Street, St John's and St Cuthbert's. One of the best known conductresses was Sally who stood no nonsense from the children and expected good behaviour and politeness. On summer days children often spent their bus fares on ice lollies and walked home across the Path on Melbourne Park.

Later the Ribble took over the service with modern single-decker buses and were changed to No. 628 with the terminus on Durranhill Road.

A faithful community

Today, Botcherby is best known for one historic church, St Andrew's - but it was not the first church in Botcherby. Just across the road, all that is left of the first, 250-year-old village church is a wall with historical arched windows and a door...

Bramerton Lodge Chapel

Bramerton Lodge Chapel stands at the bottom of the garden of Bramerton Lodge and still stands thanks to the tenacity of Derek Nash who fought for its conservation when plans were announced for it to be demolished and replaced by housing. Councillor John Robinson argued for the barn's preservation but failed to get enough support from the Council's Planning Control Sub-Committee. Bizarrely, although Wood Street had been made a Grade II Conservation Area in 1968, the barn had been excluded from this, presumably because its historic connection with the local faith community was not fully appreciated at the time.

The struggle divided opinion among Wood Street residents and made the headlines in the local press. Finally a decision was made and reported by David Guide in the *Cumberland News* on 4 July 1986:

> 'A compromise solution has been reached in a barn preservation dispute affecting residents in a Carlisle suburb. The rear wall of the... building will remain, to preserve the view enjoyed by some people living in Wood Street. But the rest of the building will be demolished by Allan Builders, who plan to construct four homes for first-time buyers on the site.'

The barn building formerly known as Botcherby Village Church is believed to have first been used for worship in 1867, when arched windows and fireplaces were put in the barn to enable church services and Sunday school to be held there.

When St Andrew's opened, seven oak benches, made of wood from the land of Bramerton Lodge, and the reading desk from the barn were given to the church.

Botcherby's moveable church

We do not know for certain in what year the barn chapel closed but, on 16 November 1888, an advert appeared in the *Carlisle Journal,* placed by H. Higginson, Architect of 24 Bank Street, Carlisle, inviting tenders for the erection of a movable wooden church at Botcherby for the Rev. W. M. Shepherd. On 30 November, the paper reported:

> 'A wooden church is about to be erected at Botcherby, near this city... a movement has been on foot for the erection of some place of worship for the village, where services might be held in conjunction with the parish church, St John's...until a permanent edifice is erected. The site, consisting of 713 square yards, has been given by Captain Farrar and stands on the high ground behind Botcherby Mansion, and on the corner of the highway and the road leading to the mansion.'

Described as a neat little edifice of wood and slate, the plans give details of the size and structure:

> 'It will consist of a nave, 40 feet by 25 feet, accommodating 176 persons; a chancel, 12 feet by 10 feet; a class room and a minister's vestry, each 10 feet square; and a porch 12 feet by 4 feet. The whole fabric will stand on a stone-base at the ground level, and a particular point in its construction is that it will be movable... the cost of the whole work will be £239. 15s, that being the sum for which the sole contract has been let to Mr Reed, joiner. About £200 has been raised already by subscription.'

The church is likely to have moved on to another parish after the erection of St Andrew's Mission Church in 1890.

Two other chapels used to serve the community in the village, one the Chapel at St Joseph's Home and the other at Durranhill Convent.

Bramerton Lodge Chapel and the battle for its survival

Above, clockwise from the left: the chapel in May 1940, when Bramerton Lodge was owned by the Simpsons; the remains of the chapel after the demoliton work and before the new houses were built; three pctures of the garden side of the barn - the first, from the 1980s - shows the original doorway which was replaced by the window, shown centre. Below, clockwise from the left to right: Derek Nash and his wife, Tess, campaigned to save the chapel when it was threatened by new developments in 1986 and two example of how the local press reported it; how the barn looked in the 1980s and how it looked after the conversion work was completed.

Battle of the barn splits neighbours

Save barn bid bites the dust

St Andrew's Church and Parish Hall

The old and beautiful red-brick gem stands tucked away on the north side of Wood Street: St Andrew's Mission Church. It was designed by architect Henry Higginson to seat 70 people and opened on 25 July 1890 at a cost of £600 and has served the community well. It was linked to St Aidan's Church on Warwick Road and followed the Anglo-Catholic tradition. It has a notable East Window showing the Greek letters representing the words 'Jesus Christ' and in between is the Holy Dove representing the Holy Spirit.

There were many beautiful artefacts in the church commemorating Botcherby people. The altar cross is inscribed: 'St. Andrew's Mission Church Botcherby. In memory of John Barnes who died 23 May 1925'. A tablet on the wall tells us that John Barnes was a diocesan lay reader who gave many years of faithful service to the church. The brass Missal Stand is 'The Children's Offering' and the Processional Cross commemorates Tom Henderson who died in 1949. The Collection Plate was originally 'presented to Christ Church [on Botchergate, and demolished in 1952, becoming a quiet park] by William Thompson, Churchwarden and Server, Easter, 1929'. Members of the parish had embroidered a beautiful altar cloth and made tapestry kneelers for the benches, including some by Marie Hall for 'Jack' and 'Elsie'.

Other items of note are the tablet on the North Wall commemorating 'Richard Graham who died January 16th 1906, aged 79 and has worked for 14 years for this Mission Church'. There is also the list of names of men who died in the Great War – now 100 years ago, and a priest's copy of the Book of Common Prayer that was given on 2 June 1953 - Coronation Day.

The church has a long and varied history and celebrated its Golden Jubilee in July 1940 during WW2, when the Bishop of Carlisle, Henry Williams, spoke on the meaning of history:

> 'When we think of fifty years of parish life there is one thing that comes to all of us. We cannot estimate what God has done for us, and I suppose the real history of St Andrew's is not to be found in parochial letters or records nor can it be gathered fully from the memories of those who have worshipped here... True history was written in the Book of Life... the true triumphs of this church are only discernible in eternity.'

During the 1950s and 60s, Mrs Bell was the church organist and her husband Herbert is remembered as a keen fisherman.

The Carlisle Floods in January 2005 had a devastating effect on the Warwick Road area with many people having to move to temporary accommodation. St Aidan's was forced to close due to flood damage and this saw a huge increase in the congregation attending St Andrew's. People squashed into seats and the collection tin had never seen so much money.

St Andrew's Church

Clockwise from top left: the original plan for the mission hall; the proposed front elevation; the church in the 1950s and how it looked in the 1890s.

Rev. Richard Oakley, vicar at both churches said: *'It certainly makes things a bit more intimate and gives us more of a sense of togetherness... it is wonderful to see a church so full.'*

Kathleen Morland, the sacristan who cared for the church said: *'The singing is wonderful now... because we are just a small church if there are 50 people in here it is packed. We can fit in around 70 if they squash into the seats. It is a lovely sight.'*

St Aidan's opened again in July 2005 and St Andrew's congregation returned to a dozen people.

Alan and Kathleen Morland are now retired from their duties at the church. They have many happy memories of their time there, when Kathleen spent 25 years as sacristan and Alan tended the beautiful gardens. Kathleen succeeded Mabel Armstrong as sacristan, while Alan was a freelance photographer whose work appeared in *Country Life* and other major magazines.

By May 2007, the congregation at St Aidan's returned the compliment by welcoming St Andrew's parishioners when their church had to close due to falling masonry from part of the ceiling. Rev. Oakley said:

> *'We don't know how long the church will be closed but it shouldn't be too much of a problem... an inch and a half piece came down – that could have killed someone. The congregation at St Andrew's is very small - 12 to 16 people –but they are very faithful.'*

By August, with the appeal only two weeks old, £4,200 had been donated. It had emerged that the insurance company would only pay for the clear-up costs and not the ceiling repairs and so £7,000 needed to be raised. Parishioners rallied round with coffee mornings and jumble sales, even auctioning a painting of the church, and Rev. Oakley expressed his hope that an opening service would be held at the back end of the year.

By October the local press reported that Rev. Oakley said: *'We've been overwhelmed by the support we've had... the thing about Botcherby is that everyone thinks that it has problems, and it has, but it is actually a community. There is a bigger community in Botcherby than there is in other parts of Carlisle.'*

He also held regular meetings with a residents' group at the Metal Box social club to build greater links between the church and community.

It was Carlisle Housing Association who enabled the church to hit its target of £7,000 with a donation of £2,500 in November that year. Rev. Oakley expressed his delight: *'This donation puts us where we want to be... we want to have a service for the whole community.'*

That wish came true at the beginning of December when a Mass was held at St Andrew's to celebrate the re-opening: prayers of re-dedication were said and a thanksgiving service for the Botcherby community was held.

Rev. Oakley retired in 2011.

More recently, the church came under threat of closure as the congregation dwindled. Supported by the Diocese of Carlisle, the Rev. Steve Donald was given the task of turning around the church by 2014. One of his parishioners, the late Elsie Baty, who attended the church for 51 years commented: *'This is such a lovely street for it to be in. Some churches, if they've got that secret ingredient, go like the clappers and people love to go.'*

Rev. Donald was hoping that many more people would love to come to St Andrew's, as much as the older residents did, and set up a development group. He said, *'St Andrew's is going to be the mission church to Botcherby. Botcherby needs its own church on its own territory because it's a village. Our slogan will be: "Your village church, support it, come along to it".'*

The death in May 2014 of the 89-year-old Right Reverend John Satterthwaite, Bishop of Gibraltar in Europe, reminded some Botcherby people of his service at St Andrew's as a young curate attached to St Aidan's in 1954. He is remembered with affection and went on to great things in the Anglican Church. He played a major part in strengthening his church's relations with those of the Roman Catholic and Orthodox traditions and also in establishing a strong Anglican presence in continental Europe, travelling extensively in both Western and Eastern Europe and coping ingeniously with constraints imposed by the Iron Curtain. He eventually returned to Carlisle in his retirement.

In 2015 the church, with its link now to St John's Evangelical Church on London Road rather than St Aidan's Anglo-Catholic tradition, was in a state of flux. The old practices were giving way to the new as Rev. Donald

Rogation Days

These are days in the Christian calendar when processions are held and the Litany of the Saints are read, praying for protection from disasters. The major day is on 25 April with minor days being celebrated on the weekdays preceding Ascension Thursday. In Botcherby, the celebration took the form of a service at St Andrew's and a procession up Wood Street and through Clark's Field (now Eden Park estate). The photographs date from 1953.

St Andrew's in bloom

This photographic essay by Alan Morland shows the church and its surroundings at their colourful best.

Now retired, Alan and his wife, Kathleen, worked for many years to support the church: she as sacristan, he as gardener.

It's sad to think that we may never see it looking so beautiful again - but Alan's photographs give us a lasting memory of how it once looked.

tried to breathe new life into the church. As benches were turned sideways to create a large space for activities and sacramentals were removed, it seemed important to record the way things were. Plans are now proposed for alterations to the church, making it more 'user-friendly' – it will entail removing the organ and building kitchen and toilet facilities, as well as providing disabled access and removable seating to create space for social activities.

Work started in December 2015 on Phase One of the alterations and by May 2016 the changes to St Andrew's were well under way and Phase One had been completed. The organ has been removed and there is now a kitchen in place, and also a toilet for disabled visitors. Two of the original wooden pews have been retained.

It is hoped that St Andrew's will once more become a hub of the community.

St Andrew's Parish Hall

St Andrew's Parish Hall, standing near Grice's Croft and the Coop Store, where Sinclair Court is today, was dedicated in December 1949, during the incumbency of the Rev. W. Edmondson-Jones (1939-51). It became the scene of many local celebrations, as parties and wedding receptions were held there on high days and holidays.

Above, clockwise from top left: the interior of the church, ancient and modern; the church committee in 1952; members of the St Andrew's Guild say goodbye to the Rev. Alan Holt in the garden off Bramerton lodge, 1945 - standing: Doreen Wood, Rhoda Gourley, unknown, Mrs Sinclair, Mrs Harrington, Mabel Langhorne, Mary Thompson, Mrs Towers; seated: Mrs Tallentire, Mrs Susie Baty, Mrs Holt with daughter Hillary, Rev. Alan Holt, Mrs Meall, Mrs Bell and Mrs Ruddick.

Below, clockwise from the left: front and back of the scented card (advertising the exotic Phul-Nana perfume) - selling for three pence per brick for the new parish hall; the Quality Street award for 1998; The Rev. Steve Donald, the current vicar; the church organ; portrait of the Rt Rev. John Satterthwaite, once a young curate at St Andrew's.

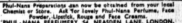

151

St Andrew's Hall

For many years St Andrew's Parish Hall, located between Croft nurseries and the Co-op shop, was the centre of most of the formal community activities in Botcherby.

Clockwise from top left: two pictures of local residents at the opening service of the hall in 1949; two pictures of the Hitchon family and relatives in the 1960s; Mr Johnston, the vicar, outside the hall with Grice's greenhouses in the background; a group of Botcherby residents at a wedding reception?

Mabel Langhorne remembered:

> 'We built the church hall brick by brick. We would go round all the houses in the area selling scented cards for one penny (the exotic Phul-Nana perfume) - each penny would buy one brick. We would also go round collecting flour and sugar, not by the pound but by the spoonful, or what anyone could spare. We were lucky if someone gave you half a dozen eggs. We would then return to the church hall and weigh it into pounds to sell off to make money for the church.

> 'We held Sunday school meetings every week, they were very well attended up to eighty young children in the hall, and the same again of older children in the church... I also ran my tanner hop – I had an old wind-up gramophone to play records on, it was open to all the children in the area... one night three ten year old lads turned up, the Atkinson brothers with a wash-board, a tea-chest with a broom handle and string attached to it. They went on to play and the children were mesmerised... sitting on the floor and staring at them playing.'

Another group to meet in the hall was the Women's Fellowship, where the catering was done by Frances Bennett.

St Joseph's Home

St Joseph's Home (or Botcherby Home) became a landmark. It was built on land acquired in 1892 by Canon George Waterton of Our Lady and St Joseph's Church in Warwick Square for the Roman Catholic order of the Little Sisters of the Poor. The Sisters had been in Carlisle since 1880, providing shelter and care for the infirm and elderly of all denominations at premises in Albert Street, off Victoria Place. They soon had to expand and by 1884 were in premises in Milbourne Street, off Caldewgate. In 1893 they moved into the new home at Botcherby. They soon had 70 residents and, as 1897 was the year of Queen Victoria's Golden Jubilee, the Mayor of Carlisle provided a celebratory meal for the entire house and gave a donation of £30.

The invasion of Belgium by Germany on 4 August 1914 saw the outbreak of WW1 and, because of its treaties with the Belgians, by 11pm that night Britain had declared war on Germany. Thousands of refugees poured out of Belgium, and many of them came to Carlisle. One of these families stayed with the Little Sisters at Botcherby Home. Father Gerard Van Maele and his brother, Father Arthur, were young men, aged 14 and 23 years respectively when they came from West Flanders to Carlisle with their mother and two sisters in 1914. Their aunt, Sister Arsena of St Paul was a Little Sister at the Home at that time, and the family were given refuge there until 1919. Gerard attended Carlisle Grammar School and was employed at Carr's biscuit factory from November 1916 until April 1918. On 19 September 1969, the *Cumberland News* reported that the two brothers had returned to visit St Joseph's Home, for the first time in 51 years.

By January 1932, with the development of the housing estate and the number of Catholics moving there, the usual 7am Mass for the Sisters was supplemented by a Sunday Mass for the estate's residents at 9.30am. This was very well attended by over 100 people. A priest would come from Our Lady and St Joseph's to celebrate the Mass and meet the residents.

The large distinctive red-brick building with its long driveway from the entrance on Warwick Road was surrounded by extensive grounds, including apple orchards. Inside there was high-quality accommodation for the residents and a beautiful chapel. The Sisters (or The Little Twisters as some jokingly called them) were well known in the community and, in the 1950s, Sister Josephine and a companion often called house to house on Saturday mornings to collect alms for the upkeep of the Home and for their work in the community.

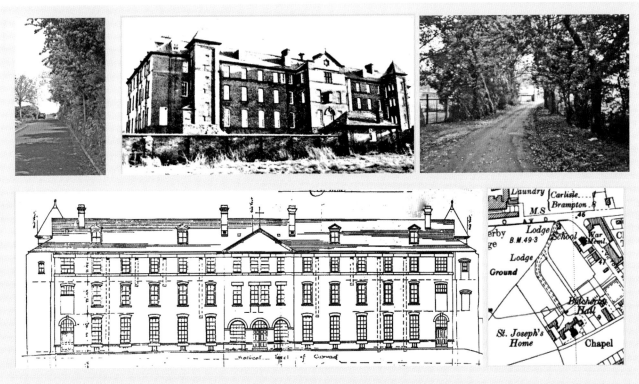

St Joseph's Home

Clockwise from above left: Banks Lane, leading to the back of St Joseph's Home, the usual route for Catholics going to Mass on Sunday mornings; an early photograph of the front of the home; the drive from Warwick Road leading up to the home; map showing the location of the home, alongside Botcherby Hall; elevation of the front of the building.

The community also contributed in more practical ways as Brenda Burgess, an early resident of Ennerdale Avenue, recalls: she went to Botcherby Home every Sunday in the 1950s and helped out by peeling a bucketful of potatoes for the residents' dinner.

The Little Sisters were also a familiar sight at Carlisle United football ground where they would stand with their collection bags at all the home games. The donations were put to good use and in the hard times of the 1930s, 40s, and 50s, many families benefited from the Sisters' help.

On 29 December 1939, the *Carlisle Journal* reported on local events held to celebrate the first Christmas of the war:

'BOTCHERBY HOME

'A quiet but happy Christmas was spent by the 94 aged poor at Botcherby Home. On Christmas Eve each inmate received a small present from the Mother Superior. The Christmas dinner consisted of soup, chicken, mashed potatoes and vegetables, with plum pudding and a glass of wine. Afterwards each man received a gift of an ounce of tobacco, a pipe and a box of matches, while each woman was given sweets and chocolate.

'Dean Fleming and the five priests of the parish were warmly received when they arrived to wish the inmates a happy Christmas.'

FATHER DOBSON

The month of October has brought changes in the parish staff. Father Dobson goes to the Cathedral in Lancaster. We thank him for all his good work over the past five years. He has spent much time with his people at Botcherby and gained the affection and respect of Catholics and non-Catholics alike. We beg God's blessing on all his future work and hope he remembers us sometimes in his. In his place comes Father Betram Taylor—no relation of Father Michael Taylor who until recently was at St. Bede's. We welcome him to the parish and assure him that he will find friendliness and happiness in his work with us.

LITTLE SISTERS OF THE POOR

FLAG DAY

SATURDAY, 21st MAY, 1960

Everything depends on having an army of flag sellers. Please help us.

All willing to help, for however short a period, should get in touch with Father Walmsley at Botcherby Home, who will be most grateful for their assistance.

THE LITTLE SISTERS HELP **EVERYONE AND ANYONE**

THIS IS OUR CHANCE **TO HELP THEM**

Clockwise from top left: interior of the chapel looking to the choir; the exterior of the chapel at the rear of St Joseph's Home; advert for a flag day in May 1960 to raise money for the Little Sisters of the Poor; the chapel looking towards the altar (Carlisle Library); 1961 cutting from the Carlisle & Cumberland Herald - a fond farewell for Fr John Dobson, who had a massive impact on Botcherby and is still remembered with affection and respect today.

By 1959 the home was a hub in the community, as each week a priest from Our Lady and St Joseph's continued to say Mass on Sundays. A lonning (now Banks Lane) beside the Magpie Inn led to a door at the back entrance for local people to attend.

In February 1959 Father John Dobson held a meeting of 25 parishioners to discuss how the community could meet and mix more with people of all faiths. A great idea was put forward – why not have an Open Day to let local people see the work they were supporting at Botcherby Home? The Little Sisters, conscious of the support they received from Botcherby people, thought it a grand idea. One thousand invitation cards were printed and hand-delivered - and, on a lovely Sunday afternoon in June 1959, well over 500 non-Catholic friends accepted the invitation and went to a beautiful tea at the Home. This report from the *Carlisle & Cumberland Herald* describes the afternoon.

'Botcherby Home

'On Sunday afternoon, June 21st, the Little Sisters held an open-day at St Joseph's Home, and generously - perhaps rashly - threw a free tea. It was a scorching day and literally hundreds accepted their invitation, so that at one stage the crockery was insufficient to cope with the combined thirst of the visitors, all were immensely impressed with what they saw, and the residents thoroughly enjoyed their share of the limelight. It was a splendid idea, and many non-Catholics came away with a new idea of the Sisters and the wonderful work they do. Every Christmas Day the Mayor and Mayoress tour the City's institutions, the hospitals, the homes for old people and the like. It is always of Botcherby Home that they speak afterwards, so deep is the impression it makes upon them. Nor was it different with the vast crowds that thronged the corridors and filled the drive on this Sunday. Perhaps, now, there will be wide support for improving the surface of the lane that leads to the Little Sisters' drive.'

The following September the 'Botcherby Campaign' began with a month of prayer and the decision to have a series of 10 informal weekly talks to be held at the Little Sisters' Home. The first talk was on the 'Daily Life of the Little Sisters' and other talks covered the whole outlook of the Catholic faith. Introductory letters were sent out followed by a personal visit to everyone and 139 people said they would like to attend. The first talk began on Wednesday, 7 October 1960, and 80 people attended. By the next week it was 90 people. So it went

The beginnning of the end for Botcherby Home

'In December 1989, the stables and outbuildings were demolished to make way for houses and a little piece of Botcherby's past history had gone. I took some hurried photographs before they disappeared.
'During the Little Sisters' time, the gardens and graveyard were immaculate. My photographs show the graveyard overgrown, unkempt and untidy, the crosses and statues worn and disfigured with time.'

Jack Stubbs

– a friendly atmosphere where people got to know more about each other: it proved very popular with Catholics and non-Catholics alike.

Today people at the Community Centre still remember the framed pictures of the Sacred Heart of Jesus made when Fr Dobson and Dr Leo Johnston set up a temporary picture framing business. They sold large pictures for 7s 6d and small ones for 5 shillings - in today's money 37p and 25p – good value from more than 50 years ago!

Other events took place: there were flag days, church meetings and garden fêtes – where on one occasion in the 60s the highlight of the afternoon was when a penned sheep, the subject of a competition to guess its weight, tired of all the attention and took off down the drive towards Warwick Road. It was hotly pursued by the men of the parish and returned to its pen looking very disgruntled, much to the embarrassment of its young keeper (the author!). But Fr Bertram Taylor picked the winner and the sheep was happily returned to its green fields.

When the Little Sisters left Botcherby Home, the nuns and chaplains in the graveyard were re-buried in Carlisle cemetery; once the outbuildings had gone, work began on the development of Willow Park.

Christmas was special, and at Midnight Mass the nuns would begin by singing *O Holy Night* and were noted for their high-voiced singing (which the congregation struggled to match). It was often standing room only, as people crowded in. By 1964, the Sisters had a resident chaplain when Canon Matthew McNarney, a well-known Carlisle-born priest retired there, and became a familiar figure until his death in 1975. The Canon used to keep chickens and would go to Casey's farm to get oats to feed them – however, John Casey would say that oats were for people, not chickens – so the Canon's chickens had to make do with corn!

Father Philip Casey would spend holidays at his brother's farm and, when he wanted to say Mass at Botcherby Home, he would just turn up, in spite of Mrs Casey's pleas for him to make arrangements. One morning he wanted to say Mass at 6am and climbed over the back wall – it was reported that the Sisters got a great fright at this unexpected intruder!

The sad end of Botcherby Home

By December 1976 it became apparent that Botcherby Home was no longer viable and would be put up for sale. The Lancaster Diocese bought the building, putting it on the market. The parish bought the chapel for £12,000. The 40 people living there were offered accommodation in other homes run by the Sisters in Lancashire and Scotland. Speaking on behalf of Bishop Pearson of Cumbria, Fr Francis Moulding said:

> 'St. Joseph's Home has become part of the Carlisle scene. The people of the city and the whole of this part of Northern England and the South of Scotland have supported and valued it. The Sisters in the Botcherby Home feel the loss of the Home deeply.'

But the local community did not give up easily, and by May 1977 the press reported that the Home might be saved by a group of people in the area who hoped to raise the £60,000 needed to buy the building and continue to run it as a home for the 40 old people. Fr Moulding, as parish priest of Our Lady's in Warwick Square, was co-ordinating the effort and asking for volunteers who would be willing to work in the home.

It was not to be, and the Sisters and residents had to move. After that the home had a chequered life and eventually became the Edenside Nursing Home.

Local historian, Jackie Stubbs says:

> 'In December 1989 the stables and out-buildings were demolished to make way for houses and a little

The end

On 6 October 2002, fire finally destroyed what was left of Botcherby Home. Bill Boak took these powerful photographs showing the destruction of a place that had once been at the centre of the local community.

piece of Botcherby's past history had gone. I took some hurried photographs before they disappeared. During the Little Sisters time the gardens and graveyard were immaculate. My photographs show the graveyard overgrown, unkempt and untidy. The crosses and statues worn and disfigured with time.'

By 2002 the nursing home had closed and developers made a planning application to demolish the building and erect new housing. Before that could happen, at lunchtime on Sunday 6 October 2002, fire engulfed the building.

The next day, the *News and Star*, gave dramatic front-page coverage to the massive blaze under the headline *'Inferno'* and reported that the fire could be seen 17 miles away in Gilsland. The blaze was thought to be caused by arsonists and broke out in the roof void of the chapel at the rear of the four-storey building.

Residents at nearby Willow Park expressed their concerns. Pat Grunwell, Chairman of the Willow Park Home Owner's Association, said, *'We have been on for years to get it demolished... I've seen people on the roof taking slates...'* Thieves had stripped it of electrical cable, pipes, slates, doors, wood panels and oak floor boards, leaving a rubbish-filled void which had become a den for drug users and down-and-outs.

A few days later John Kidd, who recalled attending Mass with his brothers and sisters in the chapel in the 1960s, called for a small memorial garden incorporating the statue of St Joseph and the child Jesus to be built. The familiar large white statue had survived the flames, in its niche high on the outside wall. Mr Kidd said: *'Perhaps a small garden area... with a plaque recording the history of the building... it should include the statue of Christ off the front... It is a vivid memory of my childhood. The nuns seemed to do a lot of work in the Botcherby community and I remember my father being given clothes... We can't turn back the clock but we can do something about the future.'*

It was the end of an era, soon the demolition workers moved in, and St Joseph's was but a memory.

Durranhill Convent and Lodge

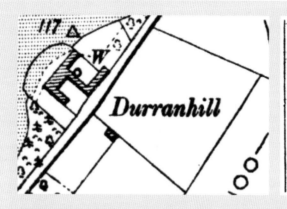

Durranhill House Convent

Above, left to right: 1901 map showing the extensive area covered by Durranhill House; 1857 advert for a boarding school for young ladies there. Below: left to right: the courtyard and entrance to the house; the chapel.

Richard Lowry was a solicitor with offices in Castle Street, Carlisle and, in 1811, he commissioned architect Peter Nicholson to design a villa for him at the top of the hill amid the rural landscape of Durranhill Road - on the back road to Scotby. The villa faced north with landscaped gardens and magnificent views. Further improvements were made in the 1830s and viewed from Durranhill Road: it had a courtyard extension leading to a five-bay façade added to the back of the original house. In 1841 67-year-old Lowry died in a fall from his horse and was buried in Wetheral graveyard. His daughter Miss Mary Anne Lowry inherited the house and, by April 1842, the house was advertised to let. In March 1856 it was again advertised to let for three years. On 23 May 1856, the *Carlisle Journal* reported that Miss Julia Blanche Thompson had taken it to open a Ladies Boarding School and, by 9 January 1857, it was announced that the school would open on 19 January 1858. Miss Lowry was living at the house at the time of her death in 1887 aged 65.

She left her estate divided into three shares between her godson, Mr P. C. Howard of Corby Castle, the St Vincent de Paul Society, London and a legacy to build a new church in Warwick Square, where Our Lady and St Joseph's Church - opened in 1893 - replaced the old building in Chapel Street. In her Will, Miss Lowry also left instructions that Durranhill House should be used for religious purposes, but this was not as straightforward as it might have been!

Coincidentally, the Marquis and Marchioness of Bute, wealthy patrons of other orphanages, had opened a residential home in Lochwinnock, in Scotland, to care for young women of school-leaving age, who had spent their childhood in orphanages and who had no accommodation to return to. The home was managed by Sister Ethelburga and the Sisters of the Sacred Hearts of Jesus and Mary. The Superior-General of the congregation at that time, Sister Winefride Tyrell, wrote to the Bishop of Hexham and Newcastle requesting permission to open a second, similar home in Carlisle. With the support of Canon George Waterton, parish priest of Our Lady and St Joseph's, this was agreed.

However, Mr R. B. Brisco, a distant heir of Miss Lowry who lived in Canada, contested her will and won, which meant that Durranhill House would have to be purchased from him if the residential home was to be opened. The house was sold to the Sisters for £4,000: Lady Bute loaned the money, with half to be repaid within fifteen years. It opened on 6 March 1906 as the 'House of Providence, Durran Hill' with Sister Ethelburga and six sisters, and the first school leavers arrived from Edinburgh, Ayr and Wigton. As little state support was available, the Sisters set up 'income generating projects' to make the home self supporting. One of the projects was a laundry service to local people and hotels and another was glove making. Mr Gibson of Dumfries supplied several knitting machines and trained the young women to become skilled glove makers. By September 1906, Sister Ethelburga was seeking advice from Fr S. Canning of Stonyhurst College in Blackburn on the subject of laundry irons and his reply throws light on the Sisters' drive for self-sufficiency:

'Dear Sister Ethelburga

'A reliable acetylene burner has not yet been brought out, so acetylene will not do for the laundry irons. But if you adopt acetylene for lighting purposes you might easily put on a small pipe to the coal gas main for the irons. If you are likely to make your present resting place permanent I should certainly advise you to be your own gas makers. The process is perfectly simple, the light is infinitely superior to ordinary gas.

'There is no danger which is not found in coal gas, and at the present price of Carbide the cost works out at 2/9 per 1000 ft. The cost of the plant with a cheaper holder – good enough however to last some years – would be about £18, the piping will be about the same for coal gas; as far as possible none but iron pipes should be used – smaller diameter for Acetylene than for coal gas...

S. Canning SJ'

Canon Waterton wrote many letters in sorting out the problems of setting up the convent and, at the same time, was arranging the transfer of the Chadwick Industrial Memorial School from Newcastle to St Ann's Hill (now Austin Friars School site), as well as the acquisition of the Little Sisters of the Poor Home at Botcherby. By 1907 the Canon was in poor health and he retired to Durranhill Convent where he died on 6 February 1911. His words of the convent, *'I believe that they will be able to keep themselves with the proceeds of this*

Above, left to right: Sister Winefride Tyrell; the inside of the chapel; the letter from Queen Elizabeth, the Queen Mother, thanking the convent for its efforts in WW2. Below, left to right: residents and staff with Canon Waterton in the early 20th century; the statue of the Sacred Heart in the courtyard.

Holy Wash Tub.' would prove to be true. The Chapel was built during the time of the Canon's residency in 1909.

By October 1911 most of the original girls had found employment or set up their own businesses and so Bishop Collins wrote to the Superior General in Chigwell to ask if the Sisters could change the registration of Durran Hill House so that they could accept women with learning disabilities. This would enable the convent to accept girls who lived in two residential homes run by the nuns in Liverpool, to come to Carlisle to receive skills training. With the change of registration approved by the authorities, girls from Hillingdon School and Allerton Priory school were among the first to come to Durranhill. This change was significant in the later running of the convent.

One of the most interesting items that has survived from these early years is the visitor's book from 1914 to 1958, which contains reports of the Annual Inspections by the Board of Control Inspectors, giving a detailed picture of the life and work of the girls living there. Durran Hill House was now a Certified Institution under the Mental Deficiency Act 1913: it followed a Royal Commission report of 1908 which estimated that out of a population of 32 million British inhabitants almost 150,000 (0.46%) were considered 'mentally defective'. It recommended the establishment of a Board of Control which would oversee local authority efforts aimed at 'the well-being of the mentally defective'. Today the language and provisions of the Act sound Victorian and insensitive, when what was needed was sympathetic legislation to care for vulnerable people. The Act remained in effect until it was repealed by the Mental Health Act of 1959.

One of the earliest reports on 24 September 1914, where the girls are described as 'patients', tells of these early years in war-time:

> *'The patients are employed mainly in the laundry where outside work is undertaken, but up to the present, to an insufficient extent to pay expenses, about ten patients were employed there this morning. About six patients were employed in the Sewing Room where there are a dozen knitting machines: the patients were making gloves for the troops.'*

Other training focused on keeping poultry, gardening and baking bread, with instruction in the 3 Rs in the afternoon. There was also time for recreation, as piano-playing and dancing took place in the Recreation Room almost every evening and the girls were learning how to play basket ball. The adjoining Golf Club placed their grounds at the Convent's disposal on Sunday afternoons for exercise.

Botcherby characters remembered – part 2

Barry Brayton played for Carlisle United.
Brent Hetherington done the same.
Hughie McIlmoyle lived in Wood Street,
A true legend in the football game.
He just simply didn't work Mondays,
For that was Big John Postill's creed,
And the bowling green was sacred ground
According to Skip Jackie Reid.
He knew so many people
And Tommy Towns really was a gent.
Archie accompanied him when he sang,
Although his spoons were rather bent.
Chris Proudfoot (happy days)
Managed the Magpie football team.
Never happy when they lost,
When they won his face would beam.
The Magpie had its share of characters
And I say that with a wink,
For most of them were at their best
When full of State Management drink.
Remember when Steven Ulrich

Ate Jimmy Grieg's giant leek.
He won the bet of a fiver,
But was off work for a week.
Jackie Sheridan in the Magpie Inn
Poured his drink down a Wellington boot
He was made to drink every single drop
Because Paddy was quite a brute.
Jackie Reid was a real character
And could make things disappear,
But nine times out of ten,
It was someone else's beer.
In the Magpie one evening
All was quiet still
Except for someone snoring.
It was my old pal Willie Gill.
So many lovable characters
Passed through the Magpie door.
Their memories remain,
Sadly they come no more.

Jack Stubbs 1987

Everything was inspected and the meals, bedrooms, premises all received good reports, with the final comment: *'I was favourably impressed with the management.'*

By 1920 Sister Cecilia Cullinan had succeeded Sister Ethelburga and the number of girls had risen to 62. By 1926 the report says:

'A well-lit and airy room has been erected at the end of the recreation hall which accommodated six girls who are engaged in clog-making and boot-repairing. This new industry being taught to some of the girls by a Mr Watson of Carlisle, who voluntarily gives up some of his time weekly to attend the home and instruct the girls.'

Left to right: programme for the opening of the Shalom Wing in 1996; the author with Sister Rosemary Clerkin, who provided valuable information on the history of the convent and the Sisters of the Sacred Hearts of Jesus and Mary; 2002 thanksgiving mass for 96 years of service.

The Inspectors continued their visits through the years, noting details of the numbers of girls (usually about 65) and reporting on all aspects of their life and welfare. Sometimes suggestions were made for improvements to facilities in the workrooms or for additions to the girls' recreational activities, and these were always provided by the nuns. Dr Gerald Sheehan was Medical Officer in 1938 and, when he died in 1953, he was succeeded by his sister, Dr Kathleen Gillow.

Again, on 29 December 1939, the *Carlisle Journal* was reporting on the wartime Christmas festivities:

'DURRANHILL INSTITUTE

'Early Masses at 7.30 and 8 o'clock were celebrated at the Durran Hill Institute on Christmas morning. The inmates spent the rest of the day listening to the wireless programmes, and going for short walks.

'The dinner consisted of goose, mashed potatoes and green peas, followed by plum pudding, custard and fruit. A tea party was held and afterwards carols were sung. Each girl received a present and a gift of money.

'A visit to the pantomime has been arranged for January 6th, and later in the evening the girls will be treated to a special cinema show which is being held in their own Hall.'

The newspaper obviously liked to call people 'inmates'!

The war continued and in 1941 the Inspector noted:

'The Institution differs from others which take girls of a similar type, in the religious basis for all its activities. The Chapel is kept open and girls can go there when they wish, as well as at regular services.'

The Chapel was also open to the public and many Botcherby residents went there to hear Mass.

In 1942 the girls were doing their bit for the war effort and undertaking darning and mending for troops stationed nearby. By 1943 Monsignor R. L. Smith was chaplain and by the end of the war it was said: *'This homely like Institution has not suffered from war conditions, nor has it allowed difficulties to curtail its activities or lower its aims.'* During WW2 a letter was received from Queen Elizabeth (who became Queen Elizabeth, the Queen Mother) thanking the Community for their work.

The social side of life was not neglected as, throughout these years, it is reported that the girls went on outings to Silloth and Blackpool, shopping trips, cinema visits, to see the circus and pantomime, and suitable plays and concerts. They wore colourful summer dresses of their own choice.

By 1950 the playing field used for the girls' recreation was permanently lost to them when the Army built married-quarters housing on it, and the girls then played ball games in the yard. The dormitories and day room were now overlooked and the report notes:

> *'Owing to the proximity of the Army Married Quarters frosted glass has been fitted to the lower portion of the windows overlooking these houses... unfortunately it rather detracts from the general appearance of these rooms.'*

1954 was a year of development, with the re-decoration of the Chapel and parts of the house; new flooring was laid in the kitchen and the wall re-tiled. A new playing field and a brick pavilion had been built for recreation. After 45 years' service in charge of the knitting room, Miss Cooper had retired and her work was taken over by one of the Sisters.

Friends and relatives of the girls could visit whenever they wished, as there were no fixed visiting days. As most of the girls' family homes were in north-eastern England, quite long journeys were involved to make a visit.

The last entry in the record book is dated 9 October 1958 and notes that Reverend Mother Cecily Ford was in charge, assisted by seven Sisters. Also employed were one domestic, one gardener and one handyman.

By now there were 68 women living there but it was an ageing population and, while 35 women worked in the laundry and 12 in the knitting machine room, a small group of elderly women did light domestic duties in the mornings to keep them ambulant.

The report notes:

> *'A fair number of these patients are able to go to their own homes for short holidays. This is not a young group; however, and it will be appreciated that several of the elderly members are now without relatives. The Reverend Mother hopes that a few suitable parents will agree to their daughters being accompanied by a guest occasionally.'*

It was just after this time that a branch of the Legion of Mary was set up in Botcherby, meeting weekly at St Joseph's Home under the direction of the chaplain from Our Lady and St Joseph's. It was a small group of young women who volunteered to help in the community, and among their activities was spending recreation times with the girls at Durranhill, chatting, listening to music and even practising the latest dance crazes – the Madison and Cha-Cha-Cha - and a lovely time was enjoyed by all. In fact quite a bit more fun than some of the group's other activities: cleaning the corridors and choir at the Little Sisters and polishing wooden floors with heavy 'bumpers' and rarely meeting the nuns' high standards!

The years rolled by and, in 1983, Margaret Thatcher's Government adopted a new policy of care, after the publication of a series of reports which set out the benefits of ending institutionalised care and re-settling people into small community-based establishments or caring for them in their own homes.

It was due to this new legislation that, in 1990, a Life Plan programme was introduced to prepare some of the women to move out into independent living in the local community. Some moved to sheltered housing at Arnwood House, others to an ordinary house in Geltsdale Avenue bought by the Congregation, and in all cases they were supported by staff and later by Glenmore Trust. Those who needed more health care remained at Durranhill Home with en-suite single rooms and a programme of care supported by social workers. Major renovations were made in 1994 when the convent was registered under East Cumbria Health Authority as a Nursing Home for 37 residents, and a manager was appointed. By 1997 the decrease in the numbers of Religious Sisters meant that they could no longer keep Durranhill open, and the women were placed in suitable care homes locally, along with friends where possible.

Durranhill Home closed in 2002 and was sold to property developers Senator Homes. By 2004 the property had been converted into homes known as Waterton Court – in recognition of the man who did so much to secure its beginning 96 years before.

Durranhill Lodge

Durranhill Lodge stands on the road up the hill that led to the convent: a former mid-18th century farmhouse, it is inscribed above the entrance 'REBUILT 1870', which seems to refer only to the roof and chimney stacks. The building with its adjoining barn was listed in 1994.

Durranhill Lodge

Left to right: Durranhill Lodge in the 1990s; Durranhill Road, leading up to the convent; Durranhill Lodge today.

In its beautiful rural setting, the house was occupied by the Taylor family for over 50 years and they were a great support to the Sisters at Durranhill Convent. Mr and Mrs Taylor and their children, Connie, Dorothea, Lawrence and Donald were all involved in the Botcherby community. Mr Taylor was a familiar sight driving the white laundry van, going on his rounds collecting dirty laundry from establishments in Carlisle and the surrounding area, and returning it fresh and clean from the Convent laundry service. On his retirement, his son Donald took over the laundry run.

His good friend John Scott Foster recalled in 1999:

> 'Mr and Mrs Taylor were an excellent couple. Donald was very much a Botcherby man and a Magpie man, Geordie Greenough, Syd and Alf Monk were among many of his drinking cronies... he could turn his hand to any job, always willing to help. He grew up with Ian Irving and Ray Millican in Lawson Street area. Donald became very much involved with the Sisters in the Home and did sterling work driving to various places as required.'

Connie is well-remembered in Botcherby, when as a young woman she worked in the Co-operative store on Durranhill Road, with her blonde hair and bright smile greeting the customers. She and Dorothea would later work in Binn's department store. The family left Durranhill Lodge in the early 1990s on Donald's retirement. Connie has told me that she left Lawson Street when she was 12 to live at Durranhill and that Lawrence also drove the laundry van. She is very pleased about the book and said her Dad would be tickled pink about being in it.

Kingdom Hall – a 'new' addition

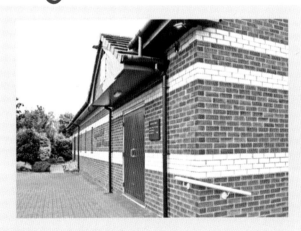

In 2002 a purpose-built Kingdom Hall appeared at Pasture Walk, Durranhill. It was the new headquarters of the Jehova's Witnesses. The denomination was founded in the USA in the late 19th century under the leadership of Charles Taze Russell and has over 130, 000 members in the UK. Members of the movement are probably best known for their door to door evangelical work, where they offer Bible literature and the opportunity to take part in Bible study discussions. The Witnesses do not have a special creed as other Christian religions, but base their beliefs purely on the text of the Bible. The Witnesses do not celebrate Christmas or Easter.

The Village Inns

No village would be complete without the local inn – the central meeting place for a pint and a gossip – and, over the years, Botcherby was no different...

The Plough Inn

Despite the ambiguity of the maps showing its location during the 1860s, we can be fairly sure that the Plough Inn stood at the top of Mount Florida – next to what is the Post Office today.

It has been many things in its existence, from a butcher's shop to the place where the Durranhill murder inquest was held. Cyril Brown, the butcher who had the shop for many years and lived in Merith Avenue, told local historian Jackie Stubbs that the deeds to the inn were kept in the bank, as they were written on animal skin and very fragile. It would have been a large building, stretching downhill - the frontage has been made into flats and rendered, but they would have been brick originally. Anywhere called an 'inn' meant you could go and demand a bed for the night. Look at the building on the map, it is clear that long stables at the back could have housed coaches and horses.

It is thought that the Plough may have been a staging post in the old days on the route of the only way over to Harraby by way of the Durranhill crossing. It originates at least from 1828.

Ward's *North of England Directory 1851* throws new light on the Plough, as it shows that it was originally named the Sun Inn and the landlord was George Johnston of Botcherby, but within 10 years it had been renamed the Plough.

By 24 April 1854 it was advertised to let in the *Carlisle Journal* as *'an old-established beer shop at Botcherby with entry at Whitsuntide'* along with a very desirable dwelling house and garden.

The Carlisle Express & Examiner reported on Annual Licensing Day, which took place at the Courts on Saturday

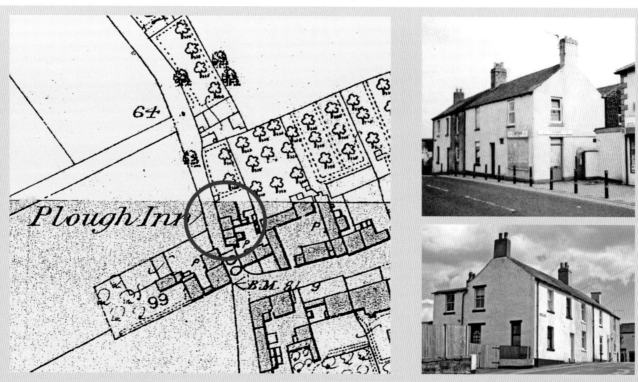

The Plough Inn

Located at the top of Mount Florida, the Plough Inn (circled in red) flourished throughout much of the 19th century. As the two pictures show, some of the buildings that were part of it remain standing today.

September 6, 1862 that, after severely reprimanding several publicans before granting their spirit licenses, the magistrates heard another application:

> 'At the close of this routine, Mr. Wannop applied, on behalf of Mr. Thomas Dodd, for a spirit license to The Plough Inn beerhouse, Botcherby. A memorial in support of the application, which had received the signatures of nearly every householder in the place, was presented to the Bench. Mr. Wannop said that Mr. Dodd kept the house for thirty-five years, and in the whole of that long period not a single complaint had been made against him. Lately, much inconvenience had arisen from the want of accommodation in the rising locality, particularly at the time of the investigation of the circumstances connected with the Durran Hill murder [committed in 1861], when it was the subject of special complaint by the jury. The court was soon after cleared for the Bench to deliberate; and on the re-admission of the public it was stated that the magistrates had decided to grant a spirit licence to the house.'

The *Carlisle Patriot* on the same date also reported that 'the inhabitants of Botcherby wished a licence to be granted and produced a petition signed by almost every householder in Botcherby.'

Thomas Dodd and his wife, Mary-Ann, are shown on the 1861 census as aged 39 and 37, with three children.

By 1864 the Plough was 'To Let' and was taken over by William Moffat and by October 1866 the following advert appeared in the local paper:

> **'PIGEON SHOOTING AT BOTCHERBY**
>
> 'William Moffat, of the Plough Inn, BOTCHERBY, begs to inform his friends and the public, that he intends having his Annual PIGEON SHOOTING on Monday, the 12th day of November 1866, when he will give TWO GUINEAS to be SHOT FOR AT PIGEONS, and the Entrance Money added to the Prize. Single entries, 3s. 6d.; Double Entries, 5s. Each Shooter allowed a Dinner Ticket out of the Entrance Money. Double Guns to stand at 18 yards, and Single Guns to stand 21 yards from the Trap. 80 yards Boundary.-shooting to commence punctually at 11 o'clock.
>
> 'Dinner on the Table at Five o'clock.- a Ball in the Evening as usual.'

The Star Inn, a.k.a. Dixon's Arms and the White Star

On the corner of Warwick Road and Victoria Road stands a building known today as the Warren Guest House, and in bygone days it served the community well as a pub. In 1855 it was called Dixon's Arms and described as being at Botcherby Lane End (before Victoria Road was built). It then became the White Star and finally the Star Inn. Many a night in the 1920s the villagers had a pint and listened to Richard Grice playing the fiddle as they relaxed after a long day's labour.

Life did not always go smoothly for the innkeepers of Botcherby as the following shows.

A report on Licensing Day appeared in the *Carlisle Express and Examiner* on 7 September 1861:

> 'There were three applications from beer-house keepers for spirit licences: from Thomas Todd [sic], of the Plough Inn, Botcherby; from Archibald Hoodless, of Kingstown; and from George Stubbs of Dixon's Arms, Botcherby Lane End. The whole of the applications were dismissed, the notices of them not being in conformity with the law. Stubbs, who appeared to be partly in a state of inebriation, harangued the Bench at some length, and concluded by saying that he did not care whether his application was granted or not, and that he should not care if all the public houses were done away with. This was the tenth annual application made by Stubbs for a spirit licence.'

Mr Stubbs was not deterred by the unhelpful magistrates for, on 12 February 1864, the *Carlisle Patriot* reported that he was before the magistrates for selling spirits without a licence:

> **'WEDNESDAY, FEBRUARY 10.**
>
> (Before W. N. Hodgson, Esq.(in the chair), P. J. Dixon, Esq., and Jos. Ferguson, Esq.)
>
> **'SELLING SPIRITS WITHOUT LICENCE**

'George Stubbs, beerhouse keeper, Botcherby Lane-end was charged on information laid by Thomas Walby, excise officer, for that he did, on the 15th day of January, at his beerhouse, sell one glass of rum and one glass of whiskey without having the spirit licence.

'Mr. Geo. Whitehead, excise officer, conducted the case for the prosecution; and MR. WANNOP appeared for the defence.'

It was the word of George Hinckey and Michael Creegan against Jane Ann Stubbs, daughter of the defendant, and his wife Mrs Stubbs, who both denied that they had served spirits to the men. After lengthy cross-examinations, Mr Wannop denied that any spirit had been served. *'He contended that the men were drunk and had been told by other publicans to say that they got spirits there.'*

'The CHAIRMAN said he did not like the manner in which the two men had given their evidence; but still they would have to convict the defendant and he was only sorry that they could not mitigate the penalty which was £12 10s and costs.'

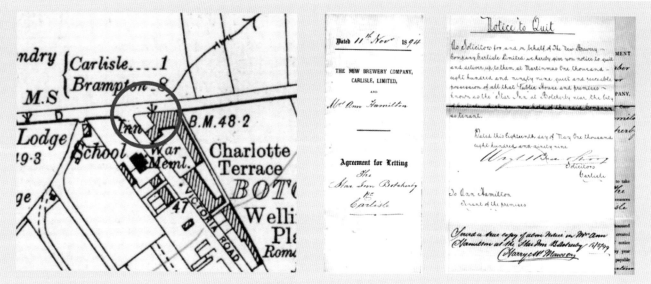

The Star Inn

Above, left to right: 1927 map showing the location of the Star Inn (circled in red); 1894 lease between the New Brewery and Ann Hamilton; notice to quit served on her in 1899. Below, clockwise from the left: four views of the Star Inn, then and now; Edmund Bulman was the landlord shown standing in the doorway - today it is the Warren guest house.

In 1869 the *Carlisle Patriot* was advertising the long-established inn for sale and by 1884 Henry Reay was the publican and having no better luck than George Stubbs, as the following report in the *East Cumberland News* on 26 January 1884 shows:

> **'THEFT OF A HEN**
>
> *'Isaac Armstrong, an elderly man, was charged with stealing a hen, belonging to Henry Reay, of the Star Inn, Botcherby, on the 3rd instant. Mr Errington appeared for the prisoner. Prosecutor stated that the prisoner and another man came to his house on the day stated, and the prisoner went into the yard, where there were about forty hens kept. Both men left about 11 o'clock. Witness missed a white hen some hours afterwards. He suspected the prisoner, and gave information to the police. Margaret Johnstone, a dressmaker, Botcherby, said that as she was returning to Carlisle from Botcherby at nearly one o'clock, she saw the prisoner leave the yard door of the Star Inn with a white hen which he had caught from among several others. He followed witness, with the hen under his coat, until he turned to go down the Botcherby Mill walk, near Petteril Bridge. She watched him and saw him kill the hen by twisting its neck. He then went to Carlisle. Mr Errington... said it was the prisoner's first offence. Mr Harrison, by whom he had been employed, informed him that the man bore an excellent character, and was most trustworthy... The Bench found the prisoner guilty, and sentenced him to imprisonment with hard labour for six weeks.'*

According to Bulmer's *Directory* of 1884, it was called the White Star but this name seems not to have been used. By 1891 Mrs Ann Hamilton, aged 57, was the innkeeper. On 11 November 1894 the New Brewery Company, Carlisle, issued a lease to her at a yearly rent of £30 to be paid half-yearly at Martinmas and Whitsuntide. The terms of the lease were strict:

> *'And also will not permit any cardplaying or gambling whatever upon the said premises , or keep the same open for the sale of drink during unlawful hours... And also will purchase exclusively from the Company all ale, beer and porter(whether in cask or bottle) to be consumed upon or sold off the said premises.'*

By 18 May 1899 she was given Notice to Quit:

> *'As Solicitors for and on behalf of The New Brewery Company we hereby give you notice to quit and deliver up to them at Martinmas One thousand eight hundred and ninety nine quiet and peaceable possession of all the Public House and premises known as the "Star Inn" at Botcherby near the City of Carlisle.'*

The inn closed on 3 December 1933, the night before Harry Redfern's newly built Magpie Inn opened. The staff just moved up the hill!

When Carlisle and District Tramways Company was formed and registered in November 1906, they published their plans for the tramway, showing No. 2 route started at the Courts and terminated near the Star Inn.

The Magpie Inn

It was the blossoming of the new housing estate that caused the Magpie Inn to be built. A modern pub with good facilities and closer to the estate was seen as essential. The Star Inn had served the village well, but its location on the corner of Victoria Road and Warwick Road was not convenient to the new estate.

Now, with the continued development of the Carlisle and District State Management Scheme (SMS) since its formation as the Central Control Board (Liquor Traffic) in 1916, and its wartime measures to curb the drinking of the Gretna munitions workers, new ideas were coming to the fore. A Royal Commission on Licensing (England and Wales) sat between 1929 and 1931, and members of the Carlisle Scheme submitted statements. It was apparent that Carlisle's drinking problems were over but the Scheme, which had been an 'experiment' in 1916, was now a successful manager of Carlisle's public houses.

The conclusion of the Commission was that: *'Public ownership should be applied elsewhere in circumstances which will submit the system to a further test both in a social and in a financial sense.'* In other words, the Scheme was a success and should be extended to other areas.

At the time of the inception of the Central Control Board in 1916, Harry Redfern was Assistant Director of the Survey of Greater London, a group who were charged with compiling lists, sketches and photographs of historic

Magpie memories across 80 years

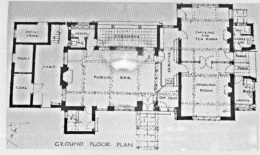

Clockwise from above left: the Magpie taken from the flat above Park House in the days when red double-decker buses were a common sight in Botcherby; the modern inn sign; plan of the ground floor (photographed in situ after the 2013 closure); in the mid-1950s, manager Fred Thomson pulls a pint, watched by his wife and Jack McQuigan, barman, with Jock Scott in the background - Jack was something of a character, recognisable by his short-cropped hair and broad belt - he carved his own pipes and was also an expert bowler - Fred was manager for 14 years; lined up and ready to go - a view of the bowling green in 1945; the Magpie shortly after its closure in 2013; Harry Redfern, architect of the Magpie and the State Management Scheme; how it looked at its opening in 1933. Below, clockwise from the left: in the 1970s, manager John Jack plays the one-armed bandit watched by Alf Hetherington - he was manager for 14 years with his wife Dot - Alf was a driver on United buses and drove for the Magpie on trips away; ready for the off - a group photo before another Magpie trip; regulars in the bar, 1986; looks like the 1960s - but what's the event?

Above, clockwise from the left: Ducks Thompson, Darcy Latimer, Keith Bulman and Jackie Reid enjoy a game of dominoes; more satisfied customers; Jack Stubbs voted 'Local Hero' by Magpie regulars, 1988; collection card/voting slip for 'Local Hero'. Below, clockwise from the left: Archie Stevenson bursts into song watched by a young-looking Paul Johnston and Raymond Patt; John Dawson - the Falcon - manager in the early 1980s; Ronnie Nanson reads the Magpie book, Nat Taylor in the cap, his son Barry next to him - Nicky Taylor in the foreground - Ged Smith and Bert Berry at the bar; Herbie Kerr, Ian McManus and Paul Johnston.

Below, clockwise from left; Jack Rook, Tommy Towns, Jack Stubbs and Norman Mark were runners-up in the first round-robin three-way rinks final in 1986; but was she a regular?; the Squire Tommy Towns and Jimmy Murray; John Carruthers and Big Bert Daddley - two ex-Royal Navy stokers - at the 1987 pensioners' party; office full, 1986; Ronnie Millar in quiet mode.

buildings and ancient monuments to be preserved. The 54-year-old Redfern was appointed Chief Architect to the Central Control Board (later the State Management Scheme) and would retain this role for the next 33 years.

His name would become synonymous with Carlisle and the surrounding area's inns and public houses, as he transformed many and built new ones. He said: *'Inn design is subtle and difficult,'* and all his skill, his belief in the principles of the Arts and Crafts movement, and his brief to make the model inns of the 1930s customer friendly were seen to perfection in Carlisle.

The Magpie Inn, with its striking black and white livery, opened on 4 December 1933 and has become one of Botcherby's landmarks. Its location on the hill going up to Mount Florida and in front of Botcherby Hall was largely dictated by availability of land.

Land was often an issue in Botcherby at this time. The building of the estate and widening of Victoria Road impinged on other properties. The Magpie was to be no different. Willie Feddon had long owned the former Hamilton nursery gardens which ran from the houses next to the Community Centre, up the hill towards Mount Florida, and was to lose part of them to the proposed bowling green of the new pub. Interestingly, the retaining wall is said to have been built of stone from the old jail in Carlisle.

Dr Philip de Mello of Botcherby Hall was also involved. In 1931 the Finance Committee of the City Council had negotiated with him to: *'Throw part of his land into the highway for the widening and improving of the Warwick Road/Victoria Road area.'* Locally, it was said that he had bought Botcherby Hall to protect the Little Sisters at Botcherby Home (which stood alongside the hall) from being too close to the inn! He must have felt under threat as the SMS indicated that it was prepared to purchase approximately 4,278 square yards of land fronting Victoria Road at an actual purchase price of £4,333. It was also prepared to purchase and remove the Hall buildings and pay the Corporation on that account.

When the problems relating to the site were resolved, Laing's began to build the pub that was to become home-from-home to many of the men of Botcherby, playing its part in establishing this new community. It became a vital meeting place and, in the days before television, computers and all the entertainment that we take for granted today, had many social activities. The site dimension was 140 ft by 275 ft and about half of the space was given to the bowling green.

It is a handsome building, set between two deep grassy banks, with the paved terraces and steps leading to the once-magnificent bowling green. Inside there were open coal fireplaces, a tea room and smoking room, as well as the public bar. A verandah overlooked the bowling green and gardens, and a wide forecourt provided a car park. The opening was a day of celebration as the Manager, Mr Herbert Smith, and his staff from the Star Inn opened to the public. Mr Smith was later killed in the Gretna air raid of 1941, when the Masonic Hall was bombed, and his brother Harold Smith took over as Manager.

Sport was a key feature of life for the Magpie's punters, with thriving bowls and darts teams. Originally there was no provision for a dartboard as, under SMS rules, there had to be supervision by the Manager, but this did not deter the would-be darts players and they would carry a dartboard down the hill to the Community Centre and take their drinks with them. But by 1949 plans were submitted by Joseph Seddon to the SMS showing a glazed enclosure to the verandah where, during the bowls season, a set of folding doors in the wide centre opening could be opened back flat to the inside wall. For the rest of the year, with the doors closed, the verandah could be used as 'darts alley'. Harry Redfern approved the plan and work was completed by 14 October 1949. The issue of gambling was ever a fear to the Manager and, due to the problems of supervision on busy weekends, it was stipulated that no darts could be played on Friday, Saturday or Sunday nights.

Darts alley also held a famous seat, a wooden bench said to be made from the timbers of the dreadnought battleship, HMS *Iron Duke,* named after the Duke of Wellington, which had been built as the flagship for the Grand Fleet in 1912 and which fought in the Battle of Jutland in 1916. After seeing service in WW2 it was sold for scrap in March 1946 and Magpie customers could sit on the bench to watch the bowls and reflect on its past glories!

There were musical entertainments and singing competitions, coach trips, a bowling team which played in the SMS bowls competition and a football team: something for everyone. By 1971 Mr John Jack had been Manager for three years and this was an anxious time, as the government were about to de-nationalise the

Bowling at the Magpie – the glory days

Above, clockwise from the left: an early successful team but year unknown; class of 1960 - we mean business - D. Gordon, not known, Ivor Bell, Tommy Towns, John McLelland, Joe Fawcett, Albert Wilson and Gordon Towns; game on!; a tense moment for Jack Stubbs, Tommy Towns and the home supporters; another winning team - but what year?; chairman Jack Stubbs with the Greenall Whitley Bowls League winner's trophy in 1987. Below, clockwise from the left: the 1987 winners of the Greenall Whitley Bowls League; a ticket for the presentation at the West End Club, Silloth; on the night, Mike Hamilton leads the way; SMS Bowls League William Little Cup, Division One, Sealed Handicap Champions 1974 - the Magpie shared it with the Near Boot Inn; game over, time to go home; SMS John Downie Cup, Division Two, Sealed Handicap Champions 1979 - the Magpie won it outright.

SMS and sell the pubs back to private enterprise. In August 1971 Mr Jack told the *Cumberland News:*

> *'A public house is more than just a place where people can buy a drink or two; it should be a social and community centre where the customers can all "muck in" and get to know one another.'*

The football team too had its days of glory and in 1970 won the Cumberland Sunday League Cup, a beautiful trophy which graced the bar along with other sporting trophies.

The focal point of communal activities was the social club, with 60 members, and the club for women. Over 200 people would crowd into the two bars at weekends often overflowing onto the verandah and into the gardens. The annual Carnival Day celebrations saw the pub full.

After 80 years of providing a friendly and sociable venue for Botcherby's residents, the award-winning inn was under threat of closure on 3 June 2013. The owner, Barnsley-based Oakwell Brewery, was closing all of

Nineteen Eighty Seven

In Nineteen Eighty Seven
The Magpie were the best.
That year we were Champions
Below were all the rest
Colin Dodds played superbly
At least that's what he said.
Les Metcalfe was another
Bowling to the head.
Jack Stubbs, he was the Chairman,
Tommy Towns the Captain bold,
The Working Mens got silver,
The Magpie took the gold.
Geoff Thompson played at number one
Finding a perfect land.
Jack Rook and Jackie Buckley
Drawing either hand.
Norman Mark and Bob Walton
Were Committee men
Along with Jackie Nanson
Seven times we won with ten.
Paul Nugent bowled impressively
For the Magpie team.
Willie Queen and Gordon Towns
Playing like a dream.
Big Jimmy Hetherington
Also done his bit.
Mainly due to him
The Pontoon was a hit.
Chamois Davis made his debut
In the form of Clifton White
But like Colonel Gadaffi
Talks a load of sh***.
There was Johnny Carruthers
What a smashing lead.
Who played in all positions?
That man was Jackie Reid.
The West End Club was crowded

On presentation night,Not a sign of trouble,
Not a fight in sight.
Mike Ham and Big Mike Irwin
At the Farrier were tight
And I don't mean their bowling.
Three men beat their rink that night.
Sam Clarke, he was so proud of us,
I say that with a wink,
The only Manager that night
Not to buy his team a drink.
Sam Clarke, he was not happy
When we left him out
If only he could bowl
The way that he can shout.
The stage was full of Magpie folk
Singing with the band.
"You'll never walk alone" they sang
And it sounded grand.
Bob Nanson done the business,
So did brother Ron.
Arthur Nanson was another
Whose bowling was spot on.
Homeward bound upon the bus
Full of happy chatter,
Sandwiches were handed round
On Bob Nanson's silver platter.
Willie Winthrop bowled through minefields,
Hoping for a wick.
Big Harry played his part as well
When he got out of nick.
Thanks to all involved that year
A bowler's seventh heaven.
In years to come they'll talk about
That year of Nineteen Eighty Seven.

Jack Stubbs 1988

its 30 pubs nationwide due to financial problems. It was hoped that a new buyer could be found before that date. Landlord Anthony Evans and his partner Sharon Gibson, took over the pub a year previously, after returning to the UK from Greece, and had worked hard to provide social amenities: darts and pool competitions, as well as summer competitions on the bowling green. The pub was a winner, being crowned the Spring 2013 'Pub of the Season' by the Solway branch of the real-ale outfit CAMRA, and in November 2012 won the prestigious English Heritage CAMRA conservation honour. The pub is a Grade II listed building.

No buyer was found to pay the £425,000 asking price and, on Sunday 2 June 2013, the Magpie held a big party before closing its doors for the last time. The *News & Star* reported the event on 3 June. Around 200 people, most in fancy dress, attended the party with DJs from Manchester and a 15-piece brass band entertaining the crowd. Anthony Evans said that his regulars had been very supportive:

> 'It's going to kill them if we close. Some have been drinking here for 50 years. The brewery has had a couple of people interested but it's not what the brewery is willing to accept.'

Councillor Robert Betton who launched a petition to save the community pub said they had more than 100 signatures. He said: *'It's getting bigger and it's on Facebook as well. Just through talking with the locals, letting them know it's the last night, they think it's a shame and they don't want it to close.'* He was also going through various channels to apply for grant funding and hoping that someone would step in to buy it.

There was a palpable sense of shock in some of the comments reported from the regulars.

2013 – 2016... best pub, closure and rebirth!

The past three years have seen the Magpie go through massive change - in Spring 2013 it was awarded 'Pub of the Season' by CAMRA's Solway Branch only to close later that year. Left is the closing event and the 'for sale' signs were soon in evidence. Towards the end of 2015 came the welcome news that it had been bought by Samuel Smith's Old Brewery and the doors opened once more for business in January 2016.

Dave Collins from Freshfield Court had been drinking in the pub for 20 years and liked the banter and the fact that there was no trouble, commenting: *'It makes you wonder where all the lads will go for a pint.'*

Paul Johnston said it had been his local for the past 48 years and added: *'We were all gutted. It's been terrible and a lot of people just can't believe it.'*

Perhaps the last word should go to David Queen of Holywell Crescent, who had used the pub since 1969 and whose mother Clara was a barmaid there for about 20 years. He said: *'It was the atmosphere and the characters. On a weekend, when Carlisle United were playing, you couldn't get through the door. By 2.50 p.m. it was empty and after 5 p.m. it filled up again. It's just a brilliant place.'*

That seemed to be the general agreement – a brilliant place – which had impacted on the lives of Botcherby residents from 1933 to 2013. But the story doesn't quite end there...

'The Magpie spreads its wings again!'

This was the headline in the *Cumberland News* on 22 January 2016, just as this book was being finalised, and it brought great news to Botcherby people. For the Magpie had been bought by the Yorkshire-based Samuel Smith's Old Brewery of Tadcaster and was set to reopen soon. Councillor Robert Betton told reporter Matthew Cobb that:

> *'It's great that one of the Redfern pubs is reopening because it's got history behind it. In the past it was really good to go down there and play bowls or darts... people in Botcherby were disappointed when it closed, but I'm sure they'll all be absolutely delighted that it's going to reopen, as am I.'*

Another former regular, John Jordan of Durranhill, commented: *'It's somewhere we always met. I've got a lot of friends who went in there... it'll be good if everyone gets back together at The Magpie.'*

On Wednesday 10 February 2016, the *News & Star* reported on the reopening with Laura and George Parsons from Glasgow running the pub and receiving a warm welcome from the locals. *'It's all about conversation and the real fire which is a big hit. The Botcherby people were pleased to see the pub reopen.'*

With its three separate rooms, they will host bingo every second Monday (with tea and cakes) and on a Sunday afternoon. There will be quiz nights, and pool and darts will be started. Future plans include tables outside in summer, barbeques and opening the bowling green again. It had been a busy weekend on that Sunday with fans ahead of the Carlisle United's FA Cup tie with Everton. Laura said: *'It was mental. We had one or two buses here. George is going to speak to some of the away clubs to let their fans know that we are here.'*

So Harry Redfern's lovely pub lives again and Botcherby people couldn't be happier to regain this hub of the community.

Outliers

Three other public houses have an association with Botcherby, although not strictly within its boundaries: the Petteril Bridge Inn, the Beehive and the Harraby Inn.

Clockwise from top left: map and pictures showing the location of the former Petteril Bridge Inn on Warwick Road; the Beehive in Warwick Road, virtually opposite the site of the Petteril Bridge Inn; three pictures of the Harraby Inn, at the junction of Harraby Grove and London Road - the old photo shows it in its original use as a private house, Harraby Grange.

THE FORMER
PETTERIL BRIDGE INN
BUILT BEFORE 1855
A LICENCED PREMISES UNTIL
1917 WHEN IT WAS CLOSED
BY THE STATE MANAGEMENT
AND SINCE HAS BEEN
A PRIVATE RESIDENCE

Petteril Bridge Inn

Long before the housing estate was built, the journey from Carlisle to Botcherby village could be broken at the Petteril Bridge Inn. As the map shows, it was located at Brunton Place - almost opposite the Beehive - and can be found in local directories from 1855 to 1914. In the 1861 census, Carlisle-born Joseph Glaister was the innkeeper but by 1891, Charles Barker from Todmorden, Yorkshire, was shown as the victualler. It finally closed under the SMS in 1917 and has been a private residence since then.

The Beehive

Mention pubs in Botcherby during the 1950s and you could only have been talking about the Magpie or the Beehive - which has been going strong since the 1870s, surviving floods and hoards of visiting football supporters, en route to Brunton Park. It was probably a farmhouse originally, but in 1872 it had a full licence under Robert Irving and was owned by the Iredale Brewery. Over the years it has been improved by extensions, alterations and refurbishments, the most recent being a result of the December 2015 floods in Warwick Road.

The Harraby Inn

Long before the Harraby estate was built, the road from Botcherby to the main southern route out of Carlisle came out at what is now called Harraby Grove. The old Durranhill Road that led there is now closed off, but at the corner with London Road, the Harraby Inn still stands. Formerly known as Harraby Grange it was a working farm and, in the 1890s, belonged to Miss Mary Ann Lowry of Durranhill House. After her death it was let and in 1913 the Cavaghan family came to reside there, close by their factory on the site of the former Shield House. They lived there for over 40 years and today Cavaghan and Gray have new premises on the Durranhill Industrial Estate. The property became a public house on 23 June 1949, acquired by the SMS. The *Cumberland News* waxed lyrical about it: '*Harry Redfern, the architect, had to exercise considerable ingenuity to adapt the premises to their new use but has done so very successfully.*'

◆◆◆

Remembering... Kim Nicholson

 **Environment Agency**

Environment Agency
Eden and Petteril Flood Defences

In Memory of Kim Nicholson
Area Manager 2002 - 2007

This river flows, a glimmering path of moments.
Carrying our dreams and memories,
Our tears of joy and sadness,
Whispering onward through eternity

A poignant reminder to a recent attempt to stem the force of flooding can be found on Botcherby Bridge: it is a plaque dedicated to the memory of Kim Nicholson, the Area Manager of the Environment Agency who oversaw the rebuilding of the defences after the 2005 floods. She grew up in the Carlisle area and worked all over the world before returning to work in Cumbria and the Environment Agency in 2002. She was responsible for the first response to the floods and subsequently played a major role in fast tracking the building of the new defences. Sadly, she died of cancer in 2007. Tony Dean, North West Regional Director of the Environment Agency, paid a heartfelt tribute to her:

> '*Kim was one of the few people I have met who managed the almost impossible feat of being an exceptional leader and manager, but also liked by everybody she worked with, which is different from mere respect.*'

Shops, street traders and industry

By 1933 most of the houses on the estate were let and families had settled into their new homes in this leafy environment. As the houses filled up with new tenants, the estate came alive with new shops and small businesses opening up...

The village shops

A new purpose-built store for the Carlisle South End Co-operative Society Ltd opened in 1933 on Durranhill Road, next to Miss Fairbairn's home at Croftlands. It was large and spacious and John Hunter is remembered as working there in later years, as well as Connie Taylor.

Further down past Croftlands stood a grocer's shop, Florida Stores, opposite Merith Avenue, where it still stands today. In the 1950s it was owned by Hannah Wannop, a bright-eyed, rosy-cheeked lady who wore a green overall and smartly served her customers, assisted by the equally bright-eyed Betty Nugent. In later years the shop was owned by Mr and Mrs Vipond and later by the partnership of Freddie Rudden and Mr and Mrs Harrison.

At the top of Mount Florida stood the shop and Post Office on the corner at 1 Wood Street and, in its early years, it boasted a small library for estate residents. In 1938 it was run by Mrs Rose Greenop. By the 50s and 60s it was run by Stanley and Dorothy Banks and its later claim to fame was when ex-Carlisle United footballer Barry Brayton took over - sadly Barry passed away in 2015, as this book was being prepared.

In 2008 the Post Office, now owned by Louise and Linda Ruddick who had spent a lot of money in improving the counter services, was under threat of closure. The Post Office Users Consultative Committee issued a

Above: the changing face of Botcherby Post Office over time, and the late Barry Brayton, who ran it for many years. Below, left to right: Victoria Aquatics on Victoria Road, run by Maureen and Michael Robson for the last 35 years; Park House has housed many types of shop over more than half a century; the shops in Croft Terrace have been the hub of the community from the earliest days of the estate - this was how it looked over 20 years ago.

Consultative Document setting out in detail its efficiency targets and its arguments for closing certain branches, suggesting that Greystone Road Post Office was the one that Botcherby residents should use.

Above: the Co-op was the largest shop in Botcherby for many years, following its opening in 1933. After it closed a number of different businesses occupied the premises, including Edgar Bros - today it stands empty, secured against all comers. Below, left to right: all that remains of Tom Clark's butchers shop at 5 Wood Street; Florida Stores has served the community for over 70 years; on the corner of Croft Terrace, the Op Shop meets a wide range of needs when people are stuggling with the increasing cost of living.

The local community was galvanised into action: Derek Nash wrote a letter in response answering each of the arguments point by point and found there was a number of errors in the document's statements. The letter was taken up by Eric Martlew MP, and there was support from many other local bodies and with the leadership of the Botcherby Residents' Action Group (BRAG) a protest was organised. There were scenes of delight as the news came through that the residents had won the day and Councillor Robert Betton, Chairman of the Group, writing in the *News and Star* on 26 June 2008, thanked all who had helped saying:

> *'It is local people who work together within resident's groups that make their voices heard and make things happen to improve their areas by working alongside other people in authority as has been proven by Botcherby Post Office being kept open.'*

The Post Office continues to serve a wide community today.

Round the corner stood Tom Clark's butcher's shop at 5 Wood Street and opposite, at 6 Wood Street, was William Parr, the greengrocer, whose house and garden adjoined the shop (now demolished and a vacant lot). Mr Parr was a busy, hardworking man, and Mrs Parr a tall, gentle, graceful lady who wore her hair in plaited ear-buns. Their two tall sons, Stanley and Denis played cricket on Eden Park field to a high standard.

Barbara Millican recalls war-time shortages:

> *'Word would get around that Mrs Parr had got in a supply of oranges. We had to grab the ration books and rush up to the shop where Mrs Parr would supply a fixed number of oranges per ration book and mark the book with an indelible pencil so that it could not be rubbed out by cheats!'*

After WW2 when bananas once again appeared in Mr Parr's shop, there were long queues!

Stan Kitchin ran Coronation Stores on Mount Florida in 1940, with a Hairdresser and Beauty Parlour adjoining: this was in the Park House building opposite the Post Office. Within a few years he moved to 4 Wood Street next door to Mr Parr, and stood in his white overall selling groceries and dispensing ice-cream cornets to little girls who thought what a kind, jolly man he was – not realising that their mothers were paying! I believe this shop later became the Silver Grill. In 1940 the small shop adjacent to the Post Office at the top of Mount Florida was Northern Butchery Stores run by Mr T. Cowen.

It is thought that Park House was once a farmhouse and it appears to have been rebuilt over the years, as it was further out on the old Botcherby Road before the road-widening of 1933. The outhouses behind were once a barber's shop and it was variously run by Alec Watson as a general grocers and, later - as Park House Stores - by Joe Rowley in the 1960s. Once known as The White House, it has been a wine market, a pea-packaging company and today is Simply Food & Drinks, a convenience store.

Over the years there were a number of shops on Croft Terrace and the former Croft House, on the corner with 2 Wood Street, became a fish-and-chip shop in 1938 run by William Little and, after the war, by the Smith family. Miss Iris Ferguson from Linden House ran a bakery with her sister Molly and, in time, a bookmaker set up shop.

Slightly further down the hill, at 39 Victoria Road, lived Miss Mabel Clark who provided another service, that of tailoress. She worked at home, making clothes for top people, and was regarded as quite a character when she was seen riding about on her motorcycle which was something very new at the time.

As well as the shops, there were regular street traders and delivery men. In her memoirs, June M. Dunn recalls her mother Isobel Simpson buying produce:

> 'Milk and eggs were delivered daily by a red-faced jolly man with a high pitched giggling laugh, he wore a butcher's striped apron over a white overall and a flat cap. His name was Joe Fell from Rose Hill Farm near Durranhill. He collected his money every Saturday like most of the other traders as this was the day after Friday pay day for most of the workers, but those not working paid every day.

> 'Freddie the fishman had a pushcart with the fish in boxes on a bed of ice, winter and summer. He wore a woollen muffler and mittens. Isobel said his fish was good and bought herring to fry or pickle, or cod for pie and fishcakes on Friday... she rushed out the moment she heard Freddie's bell and loud shout of "any fish, fresh fish, any fish, fresh fish".'

The 'Tattie Wagon' was a horse-drawn, long, open farm cart with metal poles across the top and a canvas cover for bad weather. It was driven by a big man who wore small round rimless spectacles and was known as the 'Big Fella' and a dwarf named Little Jimmy. Jimmy would hoist himself onto the cart and then *'hanging*

Clockwise from top left: horse-drawn ashcarts were a familiar sight well into the 1950s; the knifegrinder and his partner were a familiar sight back then (both CN - The Cumberland News); Ringtons Tea was delivered to houses in horse-drawn carts too, before they were displaced by smart liveried vans; Bill and Heather Kilpatrick, of the Beeches B&B in Wood Street 1994; the lamplighter (CN - The Cumberland News); Miss Anne Clark, who worked from home as a seamstress; Eleanor Rollo of the Robin Trust charity shop, Wood Street, 1994; advert for John Liddle's taxis in Borland Avenue.

JOHN LIDDLE — MOTOR PROPRIETOR
Telephone 1252
166 BORLAND AVENUE, BOTCHERBY, CARLISLE
LIMOUSINE FOR WEDDINGS AND PRIVATE PARTIES.
TAXI-CARS FOR HIRE.   DISTANCE NO OBJECT

on to the metal struts he swung across the cart like a monkey among the boxes and passed things down for the Big Fella to weigh out on the big brass scoop of his weighing scales.'

The Ringtons Tea and Coffee man called weekly in his distinctive high two-seater horse-drawn carriage with a hooded top:

> 'His seat at the front was of black quilted leather. The whole outfit was painted in dark green and gold and black and the driver wore a green and black uniform and the horse was glossy and decked out with gleaming brass and shining leather. The wheels of the carriage were very big with long painted wooden spokes and there was a high step on either side and the children used to hang onto it and annoy the driver. He had a long whip but only pretended to use it.

> 'In the summer months an old man and woman were seen pushing a small cart with a grinding stone, worked by a foot pedal. They both wore black clothes, flat hats and mittens and old boots and they called "knives to grind, scissors to grind" and the old woman knocked on doors and the man sharpened the knives and scissors for people. When the old woman died he pushed the cart himself and when he died no one else came.'

There were two ice-cream men touring the estate in those early days. One had a bicycle with 'Eldorado' painted on the sides and he sold water ices in packs and loose wafers. But of all the reminiscences I have heard the one almost everyone mentioned was of the 'Monkey Blood Man'. Here June M. Dunn gives her memory:

> 'The favourite with the children was an Italian, the "Monkey Blood Man", a big fat dark jolly man with a horse-drawn cart. The cart had open sides and the top had cut-out shapes around the edges and was painted white with coloured patterns all over it. Inside there were deep metal tubs for the ice cream, a metal scoop to make the ice cream balls for the cornets, and a holder for the wafers that slid them off onto paper servers when the ice cream was sandwiched between them. There was a glass bottle with bright red sticky raspberry or strawberry syrup inside and the man would ask the children, "You lika da monkey blood ha?" and sprinkle the syrup over the cones, then throw back his head and laugh and the bright cotton scarf tied round his neck jiggled about with the laughter.'

June liked the 'Eldorado' ice cream the best but always had a small cone because of the 'monkey blood'. Cornets cost a half penny and a squirt of 'monkey blood' an extra half penny.

The estate was well served by the traders and almost every need catered for, with the coalman making weekly deliveries, a rag-and-bone man giving away balloons or goldfish to children who ran indoors to find some rags, often grabbing the nearest thing which might turn out to be mother's favourite cardigan, and angry words would be exchanged as she sought to retrieve it.

Joe Hetherington ran a mobile shop from his house at the end of Borland Avenue in the 50s, and there are distant memories of a converted bus which served as a fish-and-chip café, with seats upstairs and a drive around the estate for the customers. There was a taxi service run by Mr Liddle of Borland Avenue. In other words – just about everything that anyone needs.

Those at the bottom of the hill were served by Armstrong's bakers on Warwick Road just before the turning into Charlotte Terrace. The shop at 5 Victoria Road opposite the Community Centre was the one-time bus office and became Botcherby Stores owned by Mr Broughton in 1950 and was later known as Warwick Stores, run by Bill Fennelly in the 1960s.

And if you are looking for a beautiful blue-faced angel fish or perhaps some brightly coloured Japanese koi carp for your garden pond, you will find them further up the hill, at Victoria Aquatics, 45 Victoria Road. Here Maureen and Michael Robson have been in business for 35 years and are well known among fish aficionados who travel from all parts of Cumbria and south Scotland in pursuit of their hobby.

As Maureen told Roger Lytollis reporting in the News & Star on 10 March 2016, 'It's advisable to know a bit about it before you start. We always give people advice if they want it.' There are different types of fish: marines live in the oceans and are hardest to keep and need a saltwater aquarium, whereas tropical fish, who live in freshwater rivers and lakes, need suitable freshwater fish tanks where they are a delight to watch.

The popular koi carp seen in many garden ponds lie dormant at the bottom of ponds in winter, before emerging in summer as brilliant flashes of colour and pattern. Care has to be taken to put the right fish together - otherwise they fight.

Michael has served three generations of customers and his son Glen is now involved in the business also. Fish have been his passion for over 50 years and he says: *'It's the colours and they've all got character about them.'* Maureen says, *'It's a very enjoyable hobby.'*

Today, one of the best supported shops is the Op Shop on Durranhill Road, run by volunteer relief manager Lynn Taylor and a team of volunteers. There are a number of Op Shops in the Carlisle area which are operated by the Carlisle Diocesan Charity Shop Network. The shop is a help to residents on fixed incomes who find themselves struggling with the cost of living. The need for such shops has become more pressing over the last five years with welfare reforms, such as the bedroom tax introduced in the government welfare reforms in April 2013, affecting those on low incomes. Tenants face cuts in the amount of housing benefit they receive if the have a spare bedroom in their social housing. This presents real problems as George Cornish of Sinclair Court and Secretary to the North West Tenants and Residents Assembly commented in the *Cumberland News*: *'We have a high proportion of people that will be virtually destitute. There aren't any one-bedroom places to put them.'*

The Op Shop is doing its bit to help people out.

The CWS Dairy

The CWS Dairy on Holywell Crescent was opened in 1932 and became a familiar landmark to the residents of the new estate, as well as providing employment in the area. Children in Holywell Crescent and Borland Avenue recall lying in bed in the early hours of winter mornings listening to the crash of milk churns being loaded up from wagons, and the milk being transformed into bottles in crates, ready to be sent off on deliveries. The dairy was built in a good position, close to the main road and transport services. The City Minute Book of 1931/32 tells the story:

> *'The Town Clerk reported negotiations with CWS as a result of which the Society were prepared to purchase for £1000 four acres of land fronting to Durranhill Road for the purpose of erecting a Milk Dairy Building.'*

And then confirms that:

> *'permission be granted to the Co-operative Wholesale Society Ltd to erect a chimney of less height than 100 ft. in connection with the Milk dairy Building proposed to be erected by them adjoining Holywell Crescent.'*

In May, the Mayor, Alderman Thompson, went to London to finalise the sale of land to the CWS and by October a licence was granted for the pasteurisation and sale of pasteurised milk. Over the years the dairy went from strength to strength and, as one of the first depots established in the area supplying bottled pasteurised milk to CWS locally, it would eventually increase milk production and supply Co-ops in Tyneside and in West Cumbria.

Arthur Sanderson, the former Chairman of Cavaghan and Gray Ltd, has good memories of Botcherby Dairy:

> *'Many Botcherby people worked at Cavaghan and Gray's. At first it was a bacon factory only and then moved into food production. It made convenience food such as cauliflower cheese, Cumberland pie and mashed potato. The milk was supplied by the CWS dairy at Botcherby. We went there automatically. The chap who ran it was from the north-east named Jim Brough. Cavaghan and Gray had a factory cricket team and we heard he was a high-standard player in Alnwick. At first he said 'no' –he was too old, but was persuaded and played. He did very well and was very competitive. He lived in the dairy house on Holywell Crescent.'*

After more than 60 years, milk production came to an end. On 23 June 1995 the *Cumberland News* reported:

> *'The Coop's Carlisle milk bottling operation will close on July 29th with the loss of 29 jobs... The decision was taken because production at the Botcherby Creamery had fallen dramatically in recent years.'*

By 2004 it was acquired by Dairy Farmers of Britain and was used as a milk distribution depot until the farmers' co-operative collapsed in June 2009. The building remained empty and there was a fire in the old boiler room in June 2010. Firefighters said the premises were not secure and asked the police to ensure the building was locked to prevent unauthorised entry. After this most of the buildings, apart from the office and reception, were demolished later that year.

Nature soon took over and the site became the home of newts, frogs and bats, with kestrels and hawks in the woods, where copses of silver birch and goat willow trees flourished amid the remains of the former buildings and hard-standings.

Botcherby CWS Dairy

Clockwise from top left: aerial view of the dairy; Robsons 'Border Duke' carrying Botcherby dairy milk churns; the dairy when it was operational; collecting the milk in churns (CN - The Cumberland News).

By 2013 the creamery site was still standing derelict and a proposal was put forward to the planning authorities to build residential housing on the redundant industrial plot. Developer Top Notch Contractors Ltd proposed to build 41 three-bedroom houses, 23 two-bedroom houses and two four-bedroom houses. Outline planning permission was granted by Carlisle City Council's Development Control committee on 15 November 2013 - but not everyone agreed, as Councillor Robert Betton told the *News and Star* on 16 November 2013:

> *'The people of Botcherby don't want this massive scale development... It will be a rat run –a dangerous rat run. Meaningless traffic is going down there now. I have contacted the police and speeding is an issue... People in Botcherby are suffering because there is a lack of one- and two-bed housing.'*

The site stands close to Durranhill Bridge serving Eastern Way and, to the south, the Durranhill Sidings still stand beside the Carlisle-Newcastle and Carlisle-Settle-Leeds railway lines. To the west is a field and the Crown Bevcan factory and to the north the houses fronting Holywell Crescent. Network Rail have indicated that, although the sidings and headshunt track are currently unused, they may be re-activated at any time, and this needs to be taken into account. At the time of writing building work has not yet started. One of the conditions of the planning approval is that the developers contribute more than £100,000 to sports and play facilities.

Two images of the dairy manager's old house and all that remains of the dairy today - a site ripe for development.

The Metal Box factory

Talk to any of the men and women who live in the Botcherby area and many of them have worked at the Metal Box factory. They speak of the camaraderie, the friendships and the memories. The factory became a major employer and, with its social club, a popular meeting place after work. The multinational company of today sprang from modest beginnings.

Hudson Scott and Sons had been a long-established company in James Street, Carlisle. It started when Caldbeck-born Benjamin Scott (born 1764) opened for business in July 1799 in a shop at 27 English Street – on a site near where the HSBC bank stands today. He set up a successful business as a printer, bookseller and stationer and by 1832, on his retirement, the business was taken over by his nephew, Hudson Scott. Hudson made great strides in developing the business and took advantage of the technical knowledge which was becoming available in lithography with the advent of steam litho presses.

The Metal Box

Above: Benamin Scott, founder of Hudson-Scott; the factory at the end of Borland Avenue - a major part of the community since 1956. Below, clockwise from the left: sample of their fine decorative boxes; brochure for 1992 open day; a celebratory can of ale; sample of a four-shift calendar, 1983; how the plan of the factory looked in 1992.

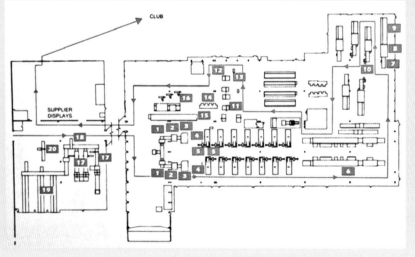 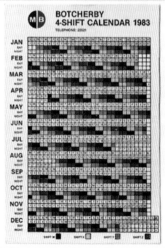

By 1868 he transferred the business to his two sons, Benjamin and William Hudson Scott and in 1869 the firm moved to the James Street premises. The rest, as they say, is history, with the company surging forward in the development of tinplate decorating, and supplying Carr's of Carlisle with tinplate sheets for their popular fancy biscuit boxes. At this time Hudson Scott's did not make their own tin boxes, but would do so from 1886 onwards with greater expansion of the premises. They employed their own artists in the Drawing Room and the colourful designs appeared on boxes and metal advertising plates used by national and international companies, such as Cadbury's chocolates, Peek Frean biscuits, Jacob's cream crackers, Kardomah tea, Brown and Polson cornflour, Yardley's talcum powder and Buchanan's Scotch whisky.

By 1922 Hudson Scott's had merged with two other companies and became Metal Box and Printing Industries Ltd with a head office in London. The company continued to expand acquiring works in Newcastle, Worcester and a tinplate works in south Wales. In America the art of canning fresh vegetables and fish within hours had become an important business and American Can began looking for a foothold into the British market. They did not succeed but Metal Box Company Ltd (as it became in 1930) came to an agreement with Continental Canning by which they had exclusive rights to buy their sophisticated machinery and thus became the unrivalled supplier of cans in England. The first factory to use the high-speed automated lines for Open Top production was built in Worcester.

In 1935 Carnation Milk condenseries at Milnthorpe and Dumfries created work for the manufacturing of Vent Hole Milk Cans and this saw the start of Open Top lines at the Carlisle factory. During WW2 the company played its part in the war effort and was heavily involved in the production of items as diverse as boxes for army ration packs, millions of metal sheets for Ministry of Food Dried Milk tins, fake boot polish tins that contained a spool of trip wire for minefields and making equipment used by the balloon barrage in the battle against the flying bomb.

In the time of austerity after the war it was apparent that James Street premises had limitations as far as expansion went because the site was surrounded by the railway station and the river Caldew. As there was a large increase in demand for open top cans it was decided to build a new factory.

Botcherby became the site of the new Open Top factory and the first issue of a new works magazine in February 1957 describes the event:

> *'Operations started at Botcherby with site clearing in September 1955 and the first line went into production on 19th November 1956. At the time of going to press three lines are in operation and, it is hoped, that all six will be finished and running by some time in March. Of these six lines four will run most of the time on milk cans and the other two on open top, though two of the lines have been designed to run either type of can, so that we can run three on milk and three on open top should the need arise. We hope to produce each year something in the region of 350/400,000,000 cans. In addition to the can lines we shall be having an Open Top press department of three presses capable of making some 300,000,000 open top ends each year.'*

The factory was built on a vast site at the bottom end of Borland Avenue giving room for potential expansion. The site had been swamp land with a rat-infested tip on the west side, but had the advantage of a railway running along the back of the site, and this was used for the transportation of cans to the factory's main customer, Carnation in Dumfries, until it pulled out in the mid 60s.

The works magazine report ends on a high note:

> *'The company has set its usual high standard in working conditions at the new factory and the canteens and surgery should be the last word. We have had automation for a long time. The thermostatic controls in our solder baths are an example of automation. Must we then consider that our jobs are in danger? On the contrary, more people are going to be employed at Botcherby than are employed at James Street.'*

Local people were soon undergoing training to run the Venthold and Open Top lines and, in 1960, an Apprentice Training Centre was built where training schemes were available to school leavers. The factory became very busy and a two-shift system was in operation where 12-hour shifts, seven working days per week, were in operation to keep up with demand. It was considered revolutionary when a beer-can line was installed as no-one drank beer from cans in those days!

It was a serious blow to Botcherby when Carnation decided to produce their own cans, but good news came

Durranhill Industrial Estate... old and new

Above, clockwise from the left: open for business; Cavaghan and Gray, and an advert for their products; World Group Services; adverts for Robertsons bread and their factory (Carlisle Library); Border Televison studios (Carlisle Library)and their logo.

Above, clockwise from the left: advert for Robsons Border Transport, their workshops (Carlisle Library) and two of their distinctive fleet; Top Notch Contractors; Porter Engineering (Carlisle Library); more development opportunities; R. Hind, motor body works (Carlisle Library); Cumbria Coaches - to let.

out of bad, and led to the decision to expand the production of beer and soft drink cans. From 1966 onwards Botcherby became the number one beer-can factory with full-time shift work. By 1981 the factory almost doubled in size when it undertook further production for the brewing industry and a new Training Centre was built outside the main factory.

As technology advanced there were developments to meet changing market demands in the drinks industry, from Soudronic welding to Plastic Obrist bottle caps, and in 1988 the company invested £5 million to increase production. By 1989 Metal Box Company merged with Carnaud of France to form CMB Packaging and restructuring of the management took place, changing the name to CarnaudMetalbox.

Crown Holdings took over in 1996 and renamed the Botcherby plant Crown Bevcan UK. with a major investment of £9 million upgrade in 2011 to increase the production capacity of the existing beer lines. This was followed by a further £2 million to create SuperEnd, for the ends of cans. The factory produces billions of cans every year for major players in the drinks industry and employs over 300 workers – who still affectionately call it the 'Metal Box'. Today the site is almost three times the size of the original factory.

Durranhill Industrial Estate

The names are so familiar to Carlisle people: Robson's Border Transport, Cavaghan and Gray, Coulthard's, Simonacco, Robertson's Bakery and Border Television, just a few of the companies who made their base on Durranhill Industrial Estate.

With the gradual development and growth of the city after WW2, Carlisle City Council published the *City of*

More from Durranhill Industrial Estate

Above, clockwise from the left: advert for William Coulthard & Co.; Thompson's Accident Repair Centre; more units in Stephenson Road; Ruddick's Parcel Delivery Service (Carlisle Library) Carlisle Window Systems. Below, left to right: the new Fire Station; Cumbria Constabulary North Area HQ.

Cowan and Sheldon and the Botcherby boys

Cowan and Sheldon were a world-renowned firm of crane builders - their products were on docksides and navy yards across continents. Founded in 1846, they moved to St Nicholas, off London Road in 1857. Many of those employed at the Carlisle works lived at Botcherby and they could be seen regularly wending their way to and from work across the Path at Melbourne Park. The picture above left shows Botcherby boys Cyril Charters (centre foreground) and John Jamieson among a team of painters. Above right, Cyril Charters is busy painting while in the background is the 15-ton travelling crane driven by his son-in-law, Jack Stubbs.

Carlisle Development Plan, 1950. The Council realised that planned industrial expansion was essential to the city's growth and economic stability and was anxious to attract new industries to the area. However, it knew that the previous *ad hoc* arrangements, where factories were often built adjacent to housing, with unpleasant effects on living conditions and with no room for industrial expansion, was no longer acceptable. The Council therefore embraced the post-war idea of building out-of-town trading estates, on often-derelict or unused land and where communications were better.

Today Carlisle City Council is the ground landlord for seven industrial estates in Carlisle with a further six in private ownership. One of the Council-owned estates is Durranhill Industrial Estate which came into existence in 1951. Known at that time as Harraby Trading Estate, it stands 1.5 miles from both Junctions 42 and 43 of the M6 on the northern side of Eastern Way. A 1951 photograph shows the estate with only two units occupied, Coulthard's and Hind's, but as it developed and more companies moved in Botcherby people would find employment there.

It was in 1936, on the advice of his accountant Noel T. O'Reilly, that Stan Robson changed the small haulage company that he operated from his Ashley Street home into a limited company, Robsons (Hauliers) Ltd, and bought an old Post-Office yard on the old Durranhill Road, later moving to larger premises across the road. This was the start of Stan Robson's connection with Durranhill and by 1956 the business moved into purpose-built premises on the industrial estate. The haulage wagons with their personalised names such as 'Border Raider' became a familiar sight at Botcherby's CWS Dairy and in the county. The company remained at Durranhill until 3 November 1980 when Robson's Border Transport Ltd was sold for £2,100,000 to United Glass.

Border Television began broadcasting from its studios on the estate on 1 September 1961, after the start of the national independent television network in 1955. It covered a vast area from the Scottish Borders to West Cumbria and the Isle of Man and its programmes and presenters were to become favourites with the viewing public. Initially all programmes were in black and white but by 1970 some were in colour - it would be 1972 before it became all colour.

One of the favourite programmes was *Lookaround* and presenters such as Eric Wallace and Fiona Armstrong were household names. Derek Batey was a national star with his successful husband and wife game show *Mr and Mrs,* and Toni Stoppani, the Border TV chef, brought out his own cookery book for his fans. In the 70s the Border TV pantomimes directed by Harry King were popular and raised money for local charities. National celebrities, such as Terry Wogan and Jimmy Young, would make guest appearances in the filmed sequence, as well as local celebrities.

It would all end too soon and, on 24 February 2009, the *News and Star* reported that the final *Lookaround* show from ITV Border studio would be broadcast that night. A cost-cutting merger with Tyne Tees meant that a 15-minute slot, broadcast with the regional evening news programme from Gateshead and covering Cumbria and south-west Scotland, would replace it. It marked the end of an era for Cumbrian television. Carlisle City Council bought the studio with plans to develop it and re-model the industrial estate as part of the Renaissance project. By 2014 the site was cleared of all buildings and put up for sale.

On 21 May 2009 the City's new police station on Durranhill Trading Estate was officially opened by Councillor Reg Watson OBE, Chairman of Cumbria Police Authority. The £8m state-of-the-art building replaced the former headquarters in Rickergate, which had become too small. When the Great Flood of 8 January 2005 wreaked havoc, it was decided to replace the building with a modern divisional police headquarters. The elegant, landmark building in Rickergate had opened on 17 April 1941 when the Police Service moved from their 100-year-old base in the old Town Hall and West Walls. The new site incorporated the Fire, Ambulance, Weights and Measures services and Magistrates Court which were all under the command of the Chief Constable, until the Fire Service's nationalisation during the war years.

By July 2012, the new Carlisle East Community Fire Station opened. A 72-year-old brass fire pole, which came from the old fire station in Rickergate has pride of place in the station.

2015 saw exciting developments for the estate, with work due for completion by October 2016. The £2.25m makeover comprised funding of £2m from Cumbria Local Enterprise Partnership and £250,000 from the Homes and Communities Agency.

On 22 July 2016, the *Cumberland News* reported on the opening of the new Locke Road, giving access to the site from Eastern Way. In addition there are improvements to the electrical infrastructure and landscaping.

Heather Bradley, Carlisle City Council's portfolio holder for economy, enterprise and housing said: *'The investment has given the estate a major boost and we are already seeing significant new investment into the estate. Three of the four sites created on the former Border TV site are now sold.'*

The M6 comes to Botcherby...

The first section of the M6 (the Preston Bypass) was opened in 1958, but it took until 1970 for the most northern stretch, past Botcherby, to be completed. These pictures show work under way near Scotby. Its arrival spurred the development of Rosehill Industrial Estate.

Rosehill Industrial Estate

Rosehill Industrial Estate is another of the seven industrial estates in Carlisle for which Carlisle City Council is the ground landlord. It is located one mile east of the city centre, off Warwick Road on Montgomery Way, and is adjacent to Junction 43 of the M6 motorway. It is on the site of the former Durranhill Army Camp and covers an area of over 20 hectares. The Borderway Mart opened there on 23 August 1974, after the H&H Group moved its livestock auction mart from Botchergate.

On 16 April 2015 the *News & Star* reported that the Group had embarked on a £5-million plan to redevelop five acres of land currently used as car parking between Montgomery Way and Eastern Way, after acquiring the land from Carlisle City Council. It took three years for the transfer process before the council could sell the land as it was designated as 'public open space'. The development will be between 40,000 – 50,000 sq. ft and will accommodate a mixture of commercial, retail and rural-based enterprises in about 10 units. There will also be a 350-space, pay-and-display public car park. H&H has created a 400-space car park on its own land at Rosehill, so there will be more than the current 600 space capacity overall. The enterprise will create 50 jobs.

Many other companies have found the benefits of business on the estate due to its proximity to the M6 motorway and its easy access to southern Scotland - factors that continue to attract new enterprises, whatever the economic climate.

Rosehill Industrial Estate

Above, left to right: the walk from Warwick Road to Scotby Road via tin sheets and the big tree at the entrance; the bigger picture - signs of a passing era as the industrial estate begins to take shape; Borderway Mart. Below clockwise from the left, Rosehill today: the Auctioneer restaurant; Cartmell Shepherd, solicitors ; the VW dealership; the Shepherds Inn; Armstrong Watson, accountant, business and financial advisers; Pioneer foodservice - just a few of the businesses operating there.

The Second World War

Since 1908, until the building of a new course at Aglionby in 1939, Durranhill had been the home of Carlisle City Golf Course. It was now redundant but, no sooner had the thud of golf balls died away, than the sound of the military moving in disturbed the peace at Durranhill...

From Golf Club to Army Camp

Golf has always been a popular sport in Carlisle and the first game recorded in the city was in 1876, when Grammar School teacher Mr Baillie laid out a 10-hole course on Binnings Field near Strand Road and 36 boys played for the honour of being school golf champion.

By 1885 the Carlisle & Silloth Golf Club had opened at Silloth, but soon Carlisle's keen golfers found this too far to travel, and a separate Carlisle City Golf Course was opened at Durranhill on 22 October 1908. This remained the situation until a new golf course was built at Aglionby and opened on 1 May 1939, just a few

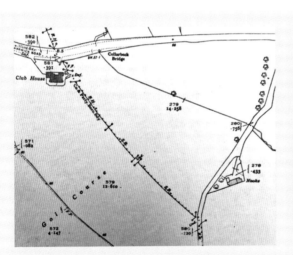 

Carlisle City Golf Club at Durranhill

Clockwise from above left: map of the area covered by the golf club 1920 - 1935; the club house, off Warwick Road; list of officers of the club, 1923-24; layout of the holes and distances involved.

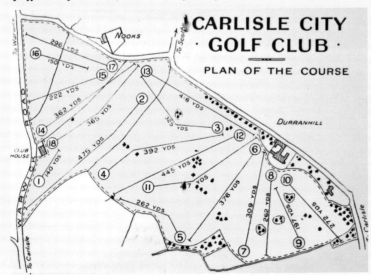

months before the beginning of World War Two (WW2). The old Durranhill course was not out of service for long, however, as the Army soon had another use for it.

Durranhill Camp became an Infantry Training Camp for the Border Regiment: the land was taken over in October 1939 and work went ahead building the camp. The Golf Club House became the Officers' Mess and the camp's entrance was on Warwick Road. Within the perimeter fence there was a complex of wooden huts, storage sheds and concrete magazines, around a parade ground.

It was ready for occupation by 1940. Colonel P. J. S. Watson was on the staff when war broke out in 1939. The *Cumberland News* reported on 23 December 1960 that Gordon Grant enlisted with the Border Regiment and was one of the first recruits stationed at Durranhill Camp: in 1941 he was commissioned to the Royal Scots Fusiliers.

After the end of WW2 the camp was used as a training facility for recruits undergoing National Service and was known as 34 Personnel Transit Centre (PTC). National Service would continue after the war, until it was ended for those born after 1 October 1939, and call-up ended on 31 December 1960.

John Barker recalls his days at Durranhill Army Camp following his call-up for two years' National Service on 2 October 1947. He had recently qualified as a teacher and worked at Harrington Junior School, he says:

> *'Durranhill Camp was then an army primary training centre run by the Border Regiment and was responsible for the six-week initial training of several hundred national servicemen from much of Lancashire, Cumberland and Westmorland. The army was then aiming to improve its image and was known as Monty's New Model Army, named after Field Marshal Montgomery, then Chief of Staff.*

> *'At Durranhill, the national servicemen arrived with their first day's pay (four shillings) safely in their pockets, and were kitted out, given army-style haircuts, drilled incessantly, learned to handle a rifle and Bren gun and made physically fit. The climax of the six-weeks' training was a route march from Burgh by Sands back to camp.*

> *'After Durranhill the national servicemen were sent to complete their training to the various army regiments and corps they had been chosen for. Carlisle was then very much a garrison town with many hundreds of other soldiers stationed at the Castle and Hadrian's Camp, with RAF men at 14 MU, Silloth, and Kirkbride and with Fleet Air Arm men at Anthorn. A popular NAAFI club for all three services operated on the site of the present Civic Centre car park. Durranhill Camp closed in the fifties but was re-opened later as a station for an Army artillery regiment before finally closing in the sixties.'*

(14 MU or 14 Maintenance Unit, formerly RAF Carlisle, was a major employer in the city and provided storage and distribution of critical supplies for RAF units throughout the country. It closed in September 1996.)

For the first six weeks, national servicemen (i.e. while they were at Durranhill) were all members of the Army's General Service Corps (GSC) before joining their regiment or corps. The Border Regiment, with its chapel in Carlisle Cathedral and base in Carlisle Castle, was influential in the city and many families had links with the regiment going back several generations. The late Sir John Burgess, former chairman of Cumberland Newspapers, served in the regiment during the war and ended his career as a colonel. The regiment had been part of the D-Day landings and was evacuated from Dunkirk.

By 1949 discussions were being held about the camp's future and the Secretary of State for War said the site was required permanently for military occupation and there was no prospect of release for civilian housing. The *Cumberland News* reported on 6 August 1949 that *'it was partly used by the Territorial Army as a training centre and partly as an Army Education Centre and it was intended to establish married quarters at the camp as well.'*

By 1951 the married quarters had been built and a succession of regiments were based at the camp. Albert Pollard of Clayton-le-Moors in Lancashire recalls his time at the camp in September 1953, serving with 59 Heavy Anti-Aircraft (HAA) Regiment, Royal Artillery:

> *'I spent the three months before Christmas of that first year training to be a useful soldier and then we had a passing out parade. This would be around the middle of December 1953. The whole parade of three troops were paraded on the barrack square to be inspected by the Brigadier.*

> *'The weather was a little wet, to say the least, and the local paper sent a photographer to record the event. The parade went ahead in the rain and the photo in the paper had a headline something like,*

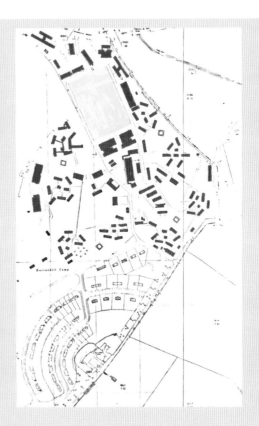

The Army comes to Durranhill

Above, clockwise from the left: Durranhill Camp looking in from Warwick Road; the camp plan, showing the buildings in red and the parade ground in yellow, with the married quarters outlined in blue, surrounding Durranhill Convent; 1947 passing out parade. Below, clockwise from the left: the parade ground; the camp from Warwick Road; the decaying entrance gate; looking towards Warwick Road from the parade ground - these last three pictures, by Bill Boak, date from April 1969, by which time the Army was long gone.

> "The recruits paraded like true veterans in the rain." They should have said, "Like true weterans," - that would have been more appropriate.'

The young soldiers training at Durranhill Camp in the 50s had to watch their step when they were off duty as Albert Pollard recalls:

> 'Those were the days when the bobby used to walk around. One night we were walking back to camp after a good night out and singing the good old songs. Out of the dark came a flash of light and a great big policeman. He warned us that singing in the streets was a little anti-social and we should not repeat it if we knew what was good for us. Although we were four or five to his one we did as we were told. I wonder if it would happen like that now.'

The 'bobby' in question was probably PC Blenkinsop, well remembered from the good old days in Botcherby. He is described as the village policeman who *'had a kind heart and a hard hand.'* He was a very large man, lived in Botcherby Avenue and did a good job of law-keeping.

In 1956, world issues again loomed large for the village when, at the time of the Suez Crisis, Theo Grice recalls army tanks painted yellow and red going past Grice's Gardens from Durranhill Camp.

It was reported in November 1958 that, after two-and-a-half years at Durranhill, 32 Medium Regiment Royal Artillery was off to Hong Kong and 39 HAA Regiment was taking over. With the departure of the 39th in February 1960 the camp was now empty.

The War Office special board met in 1961 to decide the future of the camp and it concluded that, with no further military use for the site, it could be sold off. Carlisle City Council considered the purchase of the site from the Ministry of Defence in 1965 and by 1968 had finalised negotiations, paying £67,000 for it. A scheme for housing and industrial development had been formulated for this prime site on the outskirts of the city.

Discussions were going ahead to enable the auction marts to move here from the city centre and this came about when the Borderway Mart opened on 23 August 1974. The following years would see further development and extension of the site when in 1993 Carlisle City Council sold the mart site for £1 million, and Rosehill Business Park was built.

The camp was a familiar place locally, part of the Botcherby scene and many of the Botcherby boys have memories of it. The back of the camp was marked by the wood and old path by the beck, that had gone through the golf course from Scotby Road and now had a wire fence to enclose the camp. There were two 30-yard shooting ranges and a favourite game of Jim Ord and his 12-year-old friends was to jump the beck and go over the wire fence to get the spent bullet cases. The Physical Training Instructor (PTI) in red and black, would chase them as they ran off and jumped the beck. He shouted at them *'Don't come back'* and chased them along the beck to the clay pits and they ran off in fear into Johnny Bulldog's Lonning. But fear soon dissipates in a 12-year-old – and they were back!

Even delivering the camp's newspapers was a fraught job! A friend of Jim Ord was Joe the paper boy whose round covered Wood Street, Tilbury Road and the Army Camp where there were strict instructions to check in at the Guard House. Once, when he went across the square parade ground to the Sergeant's Mess with the paper, the Sergeant Major bellowed, *'Put it in the Guard room in future!'* No-one was allowed on the parade ground.

The walk up Scotby Road and around Three Fields, ending up via Tilbury Road to Warwick Road was a favourite, and now part of it was on the perimeter of the camp. Courting couples would meander along the green countryside and children would fish for 'tiddlers' in the beck. Sometimes the young ladies of Botcherby would stand at the wire fence and chat to the soldiers, who seemed very exciting. Keeping the camp spick and span was a priority and the local priest in the late 50s visiting the camp recalls seeing the soldiers painting the fire

  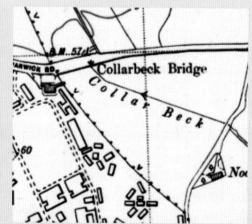

The path that ran alongside the Army Camp, between Warwick Raod and Scotby Road was a favourite walk for courting couples. Here Barbara Stubbs (née Charters), in best 1950s fashion, stands on the path with the camp fence on the right. The middle picture shows where the kissing gate was and the map shows the camp perimeter and Collar Beck.

buckets and painting kerb stones white, after having cleaned off the old paint. A soldier's work was never done!

Today the former camp's military history is recalled in the names of the roads that make up Rosehill Industrial Estate, names which resonate to past glories: Wavell Drive, Montgomery Way and Alanbrooke Road.

Air Raid Precautions Service (ARP)

The housing estate had been completed by 1933 and, with the development of shops and inn, school and churches, the new community was settling down into a normal way of life.

By 1939, when people might have hoped that the hard days of the depression, with its unemployment and grinding poverty, were over, the country was drawn into WW2 and six years of battle and bloodshed.

Suddenly the estate was depleted of men as calling-up papers were received and recruitment into the Army, Navy and Air Force raced ahead. Men who had fought in WW1 shook their heads in sorrow and disbelief that once again Europe was at war with Germany and the country's young men were on the front line. Not all could go: some, such as the railwaymen, were in reserved occupations and needed to keep the country running; others were exempt for health reasons. But in some way or another everyone became involved in the war effort.

June M. Dunn in her memoir of her mother, *Lady Isobel*, describes the community involvement, as her parents, Isobel and Joe Simpson, who had lived at 50 Ennerdale Avenue since 1933, played their part.

> *'After some discussion about how they could "do their bit" towards the war effort, Joe and Isobel decided to join the ARP (Air Raid Precautions Service). So along with Sammy Charters, Willie Walls and others from Botcherby estate they enlisted in Carlisle and were told that their local base would be in Wood Street. The base proved to be the conservatory of one of the fine old houses on the same side of the hill as the Poplars where the Worleys had lived and next to the house of the police chief... It was a tall building with windows set high in the brick walls and heating pipes round the floor and a grapevine across the ceiling.*

> *'All the uniforms and equipment arrived in wooden crates and boxes and there was much paperwork in signing for and checking everything off from endless lists... They both did a few hours weekly on duty, Isobel a couple of afternoons when June was at school and Joe in the evenings and on a rota for overnight duty. The uniform consisted of a big black overcoat and white tin helmet with W in black on the back and front and an arm band of white with a black W. Isobel said that she was not going to wear the overcoat, such heavy and rough material, or the helmet, but she would wear the armband and carry the helmet... At this stage of the war the heating pipes were still in use. The conservatory was warm and the grapes green and juicy and within her reach. She was able to deal with all the paperwork involved and the telephone. No Council house in Botcherby had a telephone, the only public call box for the entire estate was at the top of Botcherby Avenue so the telephone presented no problems for her as she had learned to take calls during her early years in domestic service. She helped with the distribution of uniforms and leaflets from the base, sorting out and posting invoices and receipts.*

> *'Joe helped with the gas masks, every adult and child was given one and Joe had to make sure that they were carried when outdoors at all times, and fitted correctly. He carried the masks in a big bag, all kept in strong cardboard boxes with carrying straps. He usually took June with him on these sessions as many of the children were afraid of the black masks with the rubbery smell covering their faces and the strange noise when they breathed. June did not really like the mask but, with the other children, they quickly turned it into a game and were like little black faced piglets running around, snorting and rubbing their round filter snouts together. There was a special mask for babies it covered them all over and fastened under the legs. Most of the babies and smaller children screamed with terror when the masks appeared, but Joe was very patient with them and their anxious and often cross mothers and fathers who were themselves worried about the war.'*

But it was not all work for the wardens: Joe Simpson was a good darts player and joined the Botcherby team who played matches against warden teams from other centres: *'The local championship contest was held in the warden's centre based in Durranhill dairy – June went along as a spectator and when they left after the match the night watchman sometimes slipped the odd small bottle of cream to one of the players.'*

John Casey of Botcherby Farm on Tilbury Road was also a warden and his daughter Eileen recalls, as a small child, seeing him in mask and helmet. Walter Riddle of Ennerdale Avenue worked as a pattern maker at Cowan Sheldon, the cranemakers, and joined the Home Guard. He was doing training in Leeds and narrowly escaped injury during an air raid when a large plate-glass window shattered in the bomb blast.

Wounded soldiers from Fusehill Hospital celebrating a tea party outside the old Star Inn pub, 1940s - seated at the front in the beret is Chris Proudfoot, a man who worked tirelessly for local football in Botcherby over many years; commemorative certificate from Taukkyan War Cemetery, Burma, for Fusilier James Wilson, husband of Nora and son of Thomas and Sarah Agnes Wilson, who died on 1 June 1944.

Children of war, evacuees at Botcherby

Like most other towns in Cumbria when WW2 started, Carlisle had its share of evacuees, some from London and some from Newcastle. They were billeted out with local families and Stan Sullivan recalls those days. Stan was born in 1933 and lived with his family in Botcherby Avenue. Here he recalls his friend Ronnie Whitfield, an evacuee from London where V2 bombs were being used, who stayed with the Sullivan family for 4½ years until the end of the war:

> *'While playing I met a boy the same age as myself who told me he had been evacuated from London. He was staying with his Aunt and Uncle who were living in Botcherby Hall with a Doctor de Mello, a black man. May Stark was an opera singer and with her husband John, ran a butcher's stall in the Covered Market. I took the boy Ronnie Whitfield home and my mother made us a meal. I asked Mrs Stark if Ronnie could occasionally stay at our house and Mrs Stark agreed.*

> *'Ronnie started to spend all his home time in our house, eventually staying there day and night until the end of the war. I recall my mother was in tears one day, she had just received a letter from Ronnie's mother saying how much Ronnie liked living with us and asked my parents that if she was killed in the Blitz would we care for Ronnie and gave a signed document giving my parents' permission to adopt Ronnie. He was already treated as one of the family, he went on our annual holidays together and my mother bought his clothes when she bought mine. When the war ended we took Ronnie back to London, he hadn't seen his Mother since 1940. His Father was away and had been divorced. They lived in a large terraced house in London W1, it was undamaged. We never saw Ronnie again and only heard from him once – he was a postman.'*

Stan also recalls going over to Botcherby Hall with Ronnie where they played on Dr de Mello's car –a Wolseley. By then Dr de Mello was partly blind and always wore a bowler hat.

An interesting report appeared in the *Carlisle Journal* on 29 December 1939 when a Christmas party was held in Botcherby School for evacuee children:

> **'Christmas Party For Catholic Children From Tyneside**

> *'An enjoyable party was held for 117 Roman Catholic evacuees from Walker in the Botcherby School, which had been gaily decorated for the occasion, on Wednesday afternoon. A well-laden Christmas tree, provided by Colonel Elwes, Warwick Hall, occupied pride of place in the big room, and from it*

every child received a useful present. Games were played, interspersed by community singing. During the afternoon a visit was received from Mrs. Rose, Chairman of the Central Committee.

'Miss Monroe, Headmistress of the Walker Catholic Girls' School, supervised the general arrangements. Sweets were provided for the children by Father J. McDonald, St Anthony's, Walker, while the gifts were given by the teachers themselves. Apart from the gifts, the expenses were borne by Newcastle City council. Catering arrangements were discharged by Messrs. Armstrong's, Botcherby.'

Fusilier James Wilson

Botcherby people were kept busy with their war work but eventually the years of worry and hardship came to an end. June M. Dunn writes:

'Sammy Charters was the first person to rush over to Joseph Simpson's house at 50 Ennerdale Avenue and tell Joe that they could take down their wooden ARP plaques and use their helmets as hanging flower baskets. The war in Europe had ended in May 1945... It seemed that everyone in Carlisle was in the city that night celebrating in all the pubs and gathering in groups singing and dancing with arms linked up to the Town Hall... They arrived at the Town Hall, people were crowded everywhere – on the steps, the balcony, the canopies over the bus stands, perched on the cross bars of lamp posts, all a happy jostling throng... Joe leapt into the crowd with Clarrie Rudden and started a conga round the Mayor's Monument... raincoat flapping he led the dancers round the Town Hall square, in and out of the monuments and up and down the steps... June looked at Joe leading the conga with Isobel and half of Carlisle behind him – she had never seen her parents like this before and did not know what to think.'

Above left: Olive Naylor (centre) of Merith Avenue worked in munitions 1942; the NAAFI in Carlisle provided an important opportunity to escape from the pressures of war, with its cafeteria, lounge, games room, tavern and ballroom.

Sadly, at another house in Ennerdale Avenue, the Wilson family would not feel in the mood for such celebrations. Fusilier James Wilson was with the 1st Battalion of the Lancashire Fusiliers fighting in the Burma Campaign when he lost his life on 1 June 1944. He was 26 years old. His parents were Thomas and Sarah Agnes Wilson and he married his wife Nora Thompson in 1937 and had three sons, Alan, Brian and Jimmy. He rests in the Taukkyan War Cemetery in the Yangon (formerly Rangoon) region of Myanmar, as Burma is now called. I am proud to publish his Roll of Honour in this book.

The fighting in the Burma Campaign in 1944 was among the most severe in the South-East Asian theatre of war. The Japanese had conquered Burma in early 1942 and, by 1943, the Allies created South East Asia Command with Admiral Louis Mountbatten as Commander-in-Chief. It involved British Commonwealth, Chinese and US forces against the forces of the Empire of Japan and the Indian National Army. Battles were fought along the borders of Burma and India and Burma and China, and the campaign lasted from January to November 1944 with victory for the Allies.

Taukkyan is the largest of three war cemeteries in Myanmar and it was begun in 1951 for the reception of graves from four battlefield cemeteries which were difficult to access and could not be maintained. The cemetery now contains 6,374 Commonwealth burials of WW2. To such men we owe our freedom today.

War brides, a wartime love story

Botcherby had seen all the trappings of war reflected in its small community. There had been queues for food rations at Miss Wannop's stores on Durranhill Road, and at the butcher's shop at the top of Mount Florida; the ARP met in a house at the top of Wood Street; air-raid shelters stood in many houses and gardens and life in general had been one of hardship, although the spirit of neighbourliness and camaraderie saw everyone through.

Carlisle was half empty, with many of the men away serving in the Armed Forces: others were in reserved occupations. The women carried on and brought up their families supporting each other, often doing a wartime job, as well as looking after the children.

Young teenagers travelled into Carlisle to work, in the shops, factories and offices. In their spare time they were often looking after the younger children or helping their mother in the house and garden. Or they were part of the Girls Training Corps and other Youth Movements, designed to train and entertain young people during difficult times.

Dances in Carlisle were popular, as military men stationed at Durranhill Camp, Hadrian's Camp or Anthorn Naval Base mingled with young local women to the music of live bands.

One of these girls was Kathy Clark who lived at 50 Merith Avenue with her parents, George and Mary Clark. She and her friends would go to the dance at the Cameo ballroom in Botchergate every week and meet up with servicemen from Canada and other parts of the world. The authorities encouraged dances, cinema and theatre as a good form of morale boosting for the troops, as well as the local community. One of Kathy's friends from this time writes: *'Kathy was the smallest of the group, with a pert face and a dainty figure. She had an almost doll-like look but wore a slightly quizzical expression with one eyebrow lifted teasingly.'*

Arthur Douglas, a saxophonist, played all the wartime hits, with his Victor Sylvester-style band, and was a great favourite at the Cameo as well as at the NAAFI Club in Rickergate (now the Civic Centre car park). It was great fun, with bright lights and music contrasting sharply with the streets outside blanketed in darkness, with police and wardens patrolling the town to make sure that no one left a light showing which might attract enemy aircraft.

Dance was Kathy's great love, and tap dancing was her passion from the age of eight, when she first put on her shiny black tap shoes. She was just 17 when she saw a visiting theatre company performing at Her Majesty's Theatre on Lowther Street. She pleaded with the producer for a job and, after a quick audition, he gave her one: a two-week engagement in the chorus line of a flashy energetic production of *Malibu*. A few nights later she was sitting perched on her suitcase in the corridor of the packed midnight train to London. She was on her way. For Mr and Mrs Clark in Botcherby, it must have been quite a shock, for Kathy hadn't asked their permission - she had just left a note, knowing that she would not have been allowed to go. *'I knew they wouldn't let me go,'* she said. *'But I just had to.'*

It was 1943 and London was no longer under heavy bombardment from Germany, although there were still night raids from fighter-bombers. The tide of war was slowly beginning to turn, with the RAF carrying out daytime bombing raids on Berlin and German U-boats being withdrawn from the North Atlantic.

In an interview that she gave in Canada in 2005, Kathy recalled that she and 14 other dancers were packed in an old house up the road from the theatre and for two weeks she listened to the wail of air-raid sirens. The earth trembled each time a bomb made a hit. For a few terrifying nights the group huddled in the small air-raid shelter buried in a corner of the backyard. It was uncomfortable and the dancers didn't get much sleep, but it was safer than the house. *'I was tired,'* she said, *'I danced on my nerves most of the time.'* Kathy may have felt fearful but noticed that the seasoned Londoners barely flinched at the sound of the wailing sirens.

The theatre looked drab on the outside - lack of supplies meant no coloured advertising posters showing photos of the show, just a bleak building. But the crowds flooded the theatre every night and inside it was like Aladdin's cave. The stage was alive with dancers in colourful costumes, swirling and twirling to the rhythm of the band as it struck up and played the latest tunes. Kathy recalled her costume in detail - a short, deep pink dress made of satin and covered in beads and lace. The sound of her tap shoes clicking in unison with the other performers was moving. On the stage she felt charged and her fears of the chaos outside barely resonated.

The happy-ever-after war bride

Above, left to right: Kathy Clark and Marc Coupal in 1947; Her Majesty's Theatre, Lowther Street, where a stage-struck Kathy talked herself into the chorus of a musical in war-torn London; Kathy and Marc in later years, still very much a love match.

Left: the best of friends Kathy with Alice and Annie Grice. Kathy and Alice had a friendship that stood the test of time.

When the curtain fell on the last show she packed up and left for Carlisle. She got a job at a toy shop and, on free evenings, went to the local dances. It was here, across a crowded room, that her eyes met those of Leading Seaman Marc Coupal, a Belgian-Canadian, and the two spent the night dancing. *'Marc could not speak any English, but he could sure dance, and had a charming smile. I think that's why I married him. He was a marvellous dancer.'* Kathy recalled.

LS Coupal was part of the Canadian Navy and it is likely that he was based at RNAS Anthorn, sited at a remote village 13 miles west of Carlisle. (Originally a WW1 landing strip, the site was re-instated by the RAF at the beginning of WW2 as an emergency landing ground for RAF Silloth. The Royal Navy took over the site in December 1942, building RNAS Anthorn, eventually being commissioned in September 1944 and given the title HMS *Nuthatch*. The base closed down in 1958.)

Over the next two weeks they laid the foundation of a relationship and, when Marc left for the North Atlantic, they wrote cheerful letters to each other. She knew nothing of the dangerous life the young sailor faced in a warship navigating the icy waters, the sea battles and the death toll.

Their romance grew as they kept up their correspondence, until they decided to marry when the war ended. LS Coupal travelled to London for the Victory Parade and to meet his young fiancée. When they were reunited they decided to miss the celebrations and travel back to Carlisle to be married. Three hours after the ceremony LS Coupal left for Halifax, Nova Scotia.

Six months passed before Kathy Coupal, leaving behind family and friends, stood on the deck of a cattle boat, looking back at her country and forward to a new life in Canada. *'I wasn't so sure of myself then,'* she remembered. But now after 60 years of marriage, she knew she made the right decision.

'I've had a good life,' she said, *'I did everything I liked and wanted to do.'*

Kathy and Marc finally settled on Vancouver Island where they brought up their two daughters, Jacqueline and Kim. Over the years they would visit Botcherby many times to see her parents and her brother, and catch up with her oldest friend, Alice Grice.

Theirs was a wartime romance that stood the test of time.

Sadly, I received the news of Kathy's death on February 13 2014. As her Memorial Card says *'Marc and his beloved Kay are finally together again, undoubtedly dancing up a storm in the heavens.'*

Prisoners of War at Durranhill

It began with a few stories: people had memories of hearing about some Prisoners of War (POWs) wandering around the village - memories of a camp of Nissen huts on the high bank behind the Durranhill Engine Sheds below the Durranhill Road, which crossed the railway bridge to London Road, but few facts seemed to exist.

Jack Stubbs had heard of it, and obtained two signed testimonials of its existence. Jack recalls that one old chap told him that the bus drivers would drive off if they saw the Conscientious Objectors coming to catch the bus.

'Some people said the prisoners were German, others that they were Italians, but all agreed they had a diamond shape on their brown uniform. They played football against the Magpie Inn at Melbourne Park and on their own pitch in the Camp. Other people said they worked in the farmers' fields and on the land. Mabel Langhorne remembered them going to St Andrew's Church in Wood Street and recalled they installed a spotlight that shone on the choir. One old soldier told me that it was called Camp Warwick.'

In her statement, Mrs Graham of 103 Borland Avenue said:

'Prisoners would walk past my window with patches on their backs going to the fields. There was a Prisoners' Camp at Durranhill, one day the soldiers were looking for a prisoner who had escaped from the camp. They were looking in all the gardens for him and the fields. I was getting in my washing when I noticed the curtain move in my wash house. I ran to the soldiers and told them it could be him and if it was a young soldier lad, I told them not to be hard on him, he was just young. They were always going to the fields.'

Dick McLaughlin of Rosevale, Harraby gave this statement to Jack:

'The above named recalls very well the Prisoner of War Camp at Durranhill Road. He was on leave from the Army and played against the football team of POWs at Melbourne Park. In the game he was left with a broken arm. He recalls it was a spill-over Army Camp before the POWs were there. The NCC [Non-Combatant Corps] were billeted alongside, also Bob Crickett had a pig farm along the side facing the Durranhill shed. The year was 1945 when he played.'

More recently, Audrey Harker recalled her memories for me:

'During the WW2 the camp at Durranhill on the Harraby Road was occupied by 'Conchies', Conscientious Objectors. My friends and I used to go up there as there was a lot of scrub land good for playing and would on occasions stop and talk to the soldiers in the camp. In those days, of course, nothing untoward was attributed to this. The men were away from home and their own children and kind to us.

'Later, at the end of the war, the German prisoners awaiting repatriation stayed there... Then Polish troops were there. Also, afterwards, for a short while, the Indian wives married to our troops who had been stationed in India and had married local women were housed there pending being found proper accommodation. It was very amazing seeing these exotic ladies in colourful saris walking to our village shops.'

James Ord told me that:

'When the Germans came they kept everything spotless and they had a football ground. Just after the war finished they could be seen on Scotby Road collecting brambles – they were always smart. There was a fellow worker at the Metal Box factory, Siegfried Wolfe, who had stayed on here after the war and married a Carlisle girl. This was because he was from East Germany where the Russians took over.'

These were the memories that fired my search for information on Camp Number 696, Warwick Camp, Durranhill Road, Carlisle - there seems to be little recorded history on it and little 'official' information.

Barbara Millican, who had been born in Durranhill Railway Cottage on 3 August 1933, and moved to 57 Borland Avenue in 1939, emailed me from Australia with more information about her father, William Millican:

'At the outbreak of war my Dad did not pass the medical for the forces so was drafted into the Auxiliary Fire Service (AFS) later renamed the National Fire Service (NFS). I don't know how many fires he attended but after one where a woman was burned to death my Dad was so sickened by it that he stayed in the depot and became the cook. My mother was a cook... she would walk all the way from the cottage to work as cook at Dr Hartley's private nursing home on the top of Stanwix Bank. My

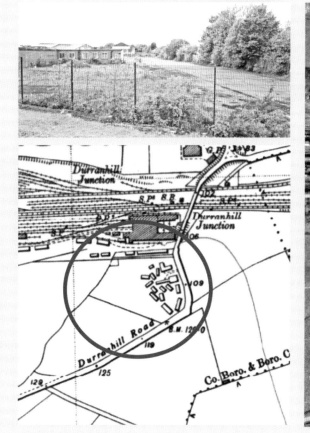

Botcherby's POW Camp

Clockwise from top left: Petteril Bridge ordnance depot in WW2, adjacent to the POW camp; Durranhill railway shed with remains of the POW camp visible at the top of the embankment; May 1948 aerial photo showing the camp (circled in red) located just off Durranhill Road, with the CWS dairy and Durranhill railway sheds clearly in view; a contemporary map showing a similar view; all that remains today of the camp, overgrown and fenced off.

mother would write recipes for my Dad to cook for his fellow firemen and the meals were so good the men preferred to keep my Dad cooking for them than going out fire fighting. My Dad took a St John's ambulance course... but anyone having an accident would call on my Dad for help before paying a doctor.

'When he came out of the NFS my Dad got a job with the garrison engineer and was in charge of a team of about six German POWs from Durranhill camp. He would take them to various Ministry of Defence properties to do repairs, etc. At Christmas 1947 the UK Government said that German POWs could be invited into private homes for Christmas Day. My Dad brought his team home. One asked if I would become the pen pal of his daughter who was my age and I agreed. In 1951 I went to Frankfurt am Main to visit her and her family. When the other men heard that I was going I was invited to their homes too. I was in Berlin BEFORE they built the Berlin Wall.'

Botcherby in the 1940s and 50s was still a rural area, despite the building of the estate in the 30s. Its farms and surrounding fields would be seen as an ideal location for the POW camp; work was available on the land, in the farms and at harvest time. Eileen Casey whose family lived at Botcherby Farm on Tilbury Road, recalls her mother telling her of Italian POWs marching to Durranhill Convent every Sunday to attend Mass. At Christmas they played carols on musical instruments and sang *Silent Night* in beautiful harmony. Towards the end of the war they helped on Casey's farm and would make toys for the children - a beautiful wooden doll's house in traditional style was a particular favourite.

Warwick Camp was just one of over 600 POW camps set up all over the country by the British Government to house enemy troops captured in the theatres of war. They would be processed in a holding area, in Belgium or, later, in British-occupied France where they were treated for disease, searched and questioned. On their arrival in Britain, prisoners were assessed and interrogated for any useful war information, particularly on German weapons and machinery, and then graded according to their military importance and sent to an appropriate camp.

The different nationalities of the men at Warwick Camp reflected the course that the war was taking. In 1939 there were just two camps in Britain and the first prisoners were rescued U-boat crews, but by 1948 there would be 600 camps. Gradually there were German prisoners and, by mid-1943, camps began to fill up following the victories in North Africa, when Italian and German prisoners were captured. The Allied invasion of western Europe in 1944 saw more German and other eastern and Polish men who had been forced to join the German army captured: they were transported on large barges (along with wounded Allied troops) across the English Channel to major ports where they were sent by train to one of the nine Command Cages to be interrogated. The Command Cages were at racecourses, such as Kempton Park, or football grounds, such as Preston North End's ground. Prisoners were then sent on to camps. As Britain upheld the Geneva Convention, prisoners were treated fairly.

Those on farm work such as hedging, ditching and harvesting came under the direct command of the farmer who employed them. Their time was also filled with activities such as lectures, classes in learning English, handicrafts, woodcarving and making toys for local children and playing sports. The work and activities were optional but most prisoners chose to take part to pass the time.

The prisoners were well fed and received medical care, but still suffered the anguish of being separated from their families with little or no news. However, their treatment was far better than prisoners held in many other parts of the world.

Men who were Conscientious Objectors, either on grounds of religious beliefs, such as the Quakers, or those who objected to warfare as a means of settling international disputes, faced social stigma. They were tested by Conscientious Objection Tribunals, chaired by a judge, who could grant full exemption, exemption conditional on alternative service, exemption only from combatant duties, or dismiss the application. Those directed to non-combatant military service were allocated to the NCC where they could work in clothing and food stores, in transport, the Royal Army Medical Corps, ambulance service, fire fighting and agriculture and farming. It seems that those men at Warwick Camp were in the latter category.

At the end of the war all of Europe was in chaos: Germany had no government and no peace treaty could be signed. The country was therefore divided into zones occupied by the British, American, French and Russian armies. There were millions of prisoners of war of all nationalities awaiting repatriation to their home countries, and it would take until 1948 before the immense task of processing and releasing all the prisoners before repatriation, could be achieved.

Denis Perriam records further information on the camp in the *Cumberland News,* 26 April 2014. The new 1946 Ordnance Survey map, shows not only the group of 16 huts, but also huts of the Central Ordnance Solway Depot arranged alongside the railway. As men were repatriated after the war the huts became useful vacant property and the Director of Education made enquiries about the possibility of using a hut for Botcherby Youth Club, but was told none were available. After discussions on whether Carlisle City Council could use it for housing, the Finance Committee were told in December 1947 that *'this camp will continue to be required for War Department use for some time.'* By 1950 it became redundant to War Department requirements and negotiations began which saw the Territorial Army use the site *'for erecting permanent garages for training vehicles'* on a 99-year lease. By 1956 a new Territorial Army (TA) Centre was built there costing £120,000, but by 1966 the site was redundant. By then, peace had returned to Botcherby.

.♦♦♦

Ghosties and other strange events!

No book about a village as old as Botcherby would be complete without recounting some of its best-loved stories of those unexplained events, handed down through the generations, and brought out for an airing whenever a few get together chatting about old times. The legends of the ghosties!

At Durranhill railway cottage, where Mrs Emmerson the gate-keeper was murdered in 1861, a ghostly lady walking with a lamp was seen. Here too, on the old road to Harraby where the old Carlisle to Newcastle bridge was knocked down, Jack Frost the 'Ice Man' was reportedly seen about. Tales are told of young people going across the old Durranhill Road to Harraby to the Argyll cinema or later to the Cosmo dance hall, as it became, and feeling spooked as they returned to Botcherby. On the dark wintry nights with the wind howling in the trees, there was many a quick sprint to reach the safety and houses of Holywell Crescent.

After the Little Sisters of the Poor left Botcherby Home, it was said that the organ in the chapel would start playing of its own accord and occasionally a fleeting figure of a nun would appear. This must have been around the time when, with the gatehouse and stables demolished, the Sister's graveyard was cleared and the graves removed to Carlisle cemetery, where no doubt, the nuns now rest in peace.

Park House on Mount Florida is said originally to have been a large farm cottage occupied by a man and his wife and children. The building later changed, was rebuilt and had different uses - it was an ice-cream parlour in the 50s, a wine shop, Alec Watson had a Spar-type shop in the 60s, and Joe Rowley had the shop before moving over to Croft Terrace. Legend has it that the spectre of Margery Jackson, the Carlisle Miser, wearing her long cloak and clogs would be seen around Park House, still haunting the district where she once lived, perhaps searching for old sovereigns that she may have hidden away and long-forgotten. Some years ago local tenants also reported seeing her in surrounding council properties and applied for moves from the houses.

A more recent claim to fame came when two staff at the now-named 'Simply Food & Drink' store saw a strange recording appearing on their CCTV screen on the night of 23 February 2010. The *News & Star* reported the mysterious event on the 25 February 2010. Trish Nolan and Sonya Hird were working when a mysterious apparition appeared on the screen (shown above), like a white mist drifting in and out of the shop almost ten times in one hour. Workman had been renovating a flat opposite also reputed to be haunted and may have disturbed the spook.

The manager, Mrs Sue McKie told the newspaper that the ghostly goings-on continued into the weekend: 'I don't believe in ghosts but I can't explain what is happening. There have been some strange things going on.' Footage showed 14 appearances on Saturday and 7 on Sunday and concerned company bosses arranged for a medium to visit the store. Before long it was not just a Botcherby event, but a global event as 20,000 people downloaded the images from the *News & Star* website. 57 people sent in possible explanations ranging from a spider crawling in front of the lens causing out of focus images, the reflection of lights from passing cars or was it Margery Jackson up to her old tricks again! The mystery still hasn't been solved - what do you think?

Floods and flood defences

As schoolchildren in the 1950s and 60s, it seemed exciting to have floodwater swirling around the platform of the bus at the bottom of Victoria Road. Today, we see only the devastation and misery that flooding regularly brings to Botcherby...

Centuries of flooding take their toll

We have seen in the story of Ambrose Holme how flood waters devastated the area of Botcherby township for hundreds of years. The high floodwater levels of the meandering river Eden and the river Petteril would gather force in outlying eastern villages before sweeping all before it onto the flat meadows to Botcherby, Walkmill Fields and the bottom of Victoria Road.

The vivid reports go on through the centuries. In 1570 there was a breach of the Eden near Carlisle. In 1771, 1794 and 1809 newspapers headlined *'the worst floods in living memory.'* By 1822 it was reported that the storm and blast were worse than 1771 and in January 1851, the *Manchester Guardian* reported on the worst floods in Carlisle since 1822.

Sometimes there was fun to be had, as when in 1893 the old river channel froze over after the floods making a skating pond and the local paper reported that *'hundreds go to the pond on the Botcherby Road but they are a good stretch from the city.'*

1918, 1925, 1929 and 1931 were also bad years for flooding in Botcherby. There were also concerns about flooding by Carlisle City Council in 1925, when consideration was being given to building a housing estate at Botcherby. As the Highways and Streets Committee reported on 22 May 1925:

> *'The Committee together with Councillors Mrs. Buchanan, Fitzsimmons and Tassell visited the district of Botcherby which is liable to flooding when the Rivers Eden and Petteril are in flood, and conferred with certain residents of the district as to the effects of the flooding.'*

In August 1956 Victoria Road and the grounds up to Botcherby Hall were under water and, by the late 60s and early 70s, flood-prevention schemes were being proposed.

By 1961 it was decided to change the route of the river Petteril behind Greystone Road and through Melbourne Park and on 8 September the *Cumberland News* published a photo of the new river and the old dry river channel. Even this was not enough to stem the flow of water and a severe flood in October 1961 caused considerable damage to the new course of the river. It was reported that repairs would cost £27,000.

Further reports in the paper on 21 February 1969 detail a multi-thousand pound scheme being prepared by the River Authority.

2005: a flood to remember

The worst floods since 1822 deluged Carlisle on Saturday, 8 January 2005 and made national and international news. Now, over a decade later, people still recall the horror of that night and the months that followed.

The weather had been wet and windy for some days, with storm damage and floods forecast. A number of unusual factors came together to create the devastation. There had been exceptionally high rainfall in the previous 36 hours when the equivalent of two months' rain fell on Carlisle and the rivers were at bursting point. This, combined with hurricane force winds of up to 110 mph across Cumbria, drove up already-high tides in the Solway estuary and unleashed the terrible torrent of water.

In the early hours of that day all main routes into Carlisle were impassable and the flooded Willowholme electricity supply plant, feeding 15 sub-stations, was powerless, cutting supplies to 70,000 homes. The spread of the water was inexorable as more areas of the city succumbed to the rising levels.

Floods from 1918 to 2005

Above, clockwise from the left: Botcherby floods, September, 1918, looking down Warwick Road towards the Star Inn; heading for the shelter of the Star Inn in spite of the floods; the view from the Waterworks in September 1918, looking across to Botcherby, with Warwick Road, the Steam Laundry and St Joseph's Home in the distance; puddles are for playing in - Victoria Road, 1968.

Below, left to right: the 2005 floods at the river Petteril, Melbourne Park, make the bridge to the Path barely passable; emergency services in action on Mount Florida, battling the floods at the bottom of Victoria Road, 2005. Both pictures courtesy of David Ramshaw.

A huge emergency operation was put into effect as officials from the police, fire and ambulance services, Environment Agency, United Utilities, mountain rescue teams and the local authorities met at Cumbria Police Headquarters at Carleton Hall, where the Gold Command strategy of removing threat to life and protecting people was under way. The emergency planning room at Carlisle Castle had been in operation during the night and the coastguard appealed on local radio for anyone with boats to volunteer their services for evacuation. The RAF offered two Sea King helicopters to help.

Radio Cumbria was wonderful, and people listened on battery-operated radios as their only link to find out what was happening. Warwick Road, Victoria Road and Eden Park were badly flooded but Botcherby estate was saved, as so many times in the past, by the hill up to Mount Florida. Willow Park was under six feet of water and 35 residents were forced to leave their homes. Jimmy McGowan would later recall, *'We lost*

2005 floods on Melbourne Park, looking towards the Lakeland Gate Premier Inn and Warwick Road; help on its way - at the bottom of Victoria Road, a boat heads off to evacuate a trapped resident, 2005 - both images courtesy of David Ramshaw; Charlotte Terrace top left aerial view of the 2005 floods.

everything. The water got right up to the ceiling. The fire brigade brought a dinghy and they broke the window to get our neighbour out.'

Around 500 homes in Warwick Road were evacuated by boat. The fields across Melbourne Park were under water, as the river Petteril flooded the meadows and the only access to Botcherby was by the bridge there.

There were many stories of heroism that day, not least among Botcherby people as the *Cumberland News* published lists of those nominated as 'heroes' shows. Soon, portable cabins were set up alongside Botcherby Community Centre, where valuable computers and equipment in the youth wing were lost under four feet of water. By early March they were back in business, providing support to the community. Gill Jones, the manager was soon organising drop-in sessions for those forced to move out of their homes. By the end of August 99% of the refurbishment of the centre was complete, with improvements for disabled access.

It would take up to two years for things to get back to normal, as some flood victims experienced problems with cowboy builders, insurance claims and illness caused by stress.

After the deluge

It was obvious that the city needed flood defences - and fast - and the *News and Star* reported on the start of work on 16 May 2006. The two-year, £12m Eden-Petteril scheme began with a sod-cutting ceremony by flood victims Mary Wilson and BBC Radio Cumbria's Belinda Artingstoll, both of Warwick Road.

The flood defence programme would see embankments along the two rivers re-built and raised, making them higher and wider. New flood walls were built and drain-down sluices to drain away any trapped water quickly. The scheme was planned to reduce flood risk to 1,500 properties in the Warwick Road and Botcherby areas. The project also included building a recreation area at Melbourne Park to attract new wildlife, and improvements to the Eden created a better habitat for fish and other aquatic life. The Environment Agency said the new defences would protect the area for years to come.

Carlisle's MP Eric Martlew said:

> *'I am absolutely delighted that this work is starting. It will protect homes and properties in the areas of the rivers Eden and Petteril. The £12 million given by the Government will ensure that flood defences will be built to such a standard to withstand the deluge experienced in January 2005.'*

December 2015 - the same old story: rescuers at work again, saving residents from their flooded homes in Victoria Road; the footbridge in Melbourne Park is at risk again. Both pictures from David Ramshaw's book 'The Carlisle Floods 2015 with recollections from 2005'.

The Eden-Petteril flood alleviation scheme was the first part of a £36m programme to improve the city's flood defences.

Not Again! December 2015: Storm Desmond does its worst!

After the devastation of the 2005 floods and all the money spent on defences, the people of Carlisle almost believed they were safe from future floods. The evening of Saturday 5 December 2015 saw that belief waver. After 70-mph winds and flash flooding on the previous day, the *News & Star* headlined on Saturday, *'Worst Yet to Come'* – how true it was. The Environment Agency issued a severe flood warning for the city indicating that river levels were expected to rise dramatically overnight. By 9.00pm, with the Eden and Petteril overflowing, Rickerby Park looked like a lake and Botcherby Bridge was closed amid fears that it would be swept away.

There was to be no escape - within a few hours, Tesco's at Rosehill was under water; Newman School was

Alex Proudfoot's record of the floods in December 2015

When Storm Desmond devastated Carlisle in December 2015, Alex Proudfoot decided to make a record of its impact. These pictures provide a permanent record of those difficult days. Above, left to right: Tilbury Road, looking across Eastern Way to Wood Street; Ron Maddison's back garden under water on Eden Park Estate.

Below, clockwise from the left: Warwick Road looking towards Petteril Bridge; Charlotte Terrace looking out to Warwick Road; the Warwick Road Bed Centre was one of the worst hit businesses; no respite - looking down Warwick Road towards the Lakeland Gate Premier Inn.

More of Alex Proudfoot's record of the 2015 floods

Above, clockwise from the left: every picture tells a story - and they're all too familiar - the recurring problems faced by Botcherby Community Centre and the residents of the lower part of Victoria Road. Below: two views up Warwick Road, looking towards Tesco's and Rosehill.

wrecked and areas of Warwick Road, Melbourne Park, Victoria Road, Willow Park, Kingfisher Park and Eden Park at Botcherby were submerged - as well as many other areas of the city. As the day went on it became an even worse situation than in 2005, with flood levels reaching 20 inches higher than at that time. But at least the flood defences had given a short breathing space when some people managed to move possessions from their homes upstairs: it was little comfort.

The devastation was enormous as, once again, the rescue boats were out and helicopters surveyed the damage. The emergency services were magnificent as always and received help from rescue teams around the country, including soldiers from the 2nd Battalion of the Duke of Lancaster's Regiment. Reception centres were set up at Greystone Community Centre, Morton Community Centre and Richard Rose Morton Academy, and locals donated goods to help the victims – food, clothing, toys and blankets– the spirit of Cumbria was alive and well.

As Carlisle people faced their difficulties with courage, television pictures of the beleaguered city flashed around the world and families worried about the safety of relatives tried to make contact. The Prime Minister, David Cameron, chaired an emergency meeting of COBRA, the Government's crisis-response committee, on Monday 7 December and, hours later, came to Carlisle to see the devastation, where he praised the heroic work of the emergency services and described what he had seen as *'absolutely heartbreaking'*. He pledged that the Government would do all it could to help. On Monday 21 December, the Prince of Wales visited Carlisle and toured the devastated areas, visiting residents on Warwick Road and expressing his concern.

The outlying districts did not escape, as Rickerby, Warwick Bridge and Crosby-on-Eden were among those badly affected (as reported in the *Cumberland News* on 11 December). Mike Fox, Chairman of Low Crosby Flood Action Group who helped secure improved defences, commented: *'The amount of rain was quite exceptional. If the defences hadn't been here I think things would have been far worse... The one thing we all know is water will find a way.'* Ayesha Weston, Head teacher at Crosby-on-Eden Primary school, clearing up the flood damage with staff, said: *'We're just devastated... we can't keep doing this. We really need some Government action.'*

The events were catastrophic to Cumbria and, on 7 January 2016, the *News & Star* reported on a delegation from the county giving evidence to the influential Environment, Food and Rural Affairs Committee in Parliament the previous day, where it was described as a *'horrendous situation just before Christmas.'*

In the meantime people got on with cleaning and clearing, talking to insurance companies and loss adjusters and hoping that this time will be the last time they have to suffer such traumatic events.

By May 2016 Cumbria County Council, with support from the Environment Agency, issued a detailed analysis of the events in the draft *Carlisle Flood Investigation Report*. The report identifies areas of flood defence failures and these included the river Petteril overtopping defences upstream of Botcherby Bridge, which acted as an obstruction. This caused flooding on Riverside Way, Greystone Road, Tullie Street and Warwick Road. Some local residents were pictured at Botcherby Bridge with a protest placard saying: *'This dam must go,'* claiming that the arches were too low and forced the water back into Melbourne Park, around defences and into their homes.

The report recommended among other things that the defences around Botcherby Bridge be reviewed, as well as the pumping station at Durranhill Beck. Meetings of the Flood Forum have been set up with local residents to gain local knowledge of the events and discuss the report. With the promise of £25m given to the city by Government it is hoped that more effective defences can be provided.

Lest we forget...

The end of 2016 and all seems back to normal in Warwick Road - but not quite. Work continues on the refurbishment of those houses still not ready to be lived in again. And round the trees is a grim reminder of the devastation of one year ago - the blue ribbons (circled in red) were placed there by community police to show the height that the floodwaters reached.

Let's bring back the Carnival!

Jackie Stubbs is something of an expert on Botcherby Carnivals, after all he appeared in 1949 dressed in top hat and tails and escorting his sister, Joyce...

This is what Jack has to say about it:

> 'The Botcherby Carnival especially in the 40s and 50s was a great social occasion for the people of Botcherby. For young and old alike, a real family fun day full of community spirit.

> 'A young local girl would be crowned carnival queen and would reign for the following year. She and her attendants would then travel around the streets on the back of a decorated horse-drawn cart or wagon followed by floats and happy laughing people, many children, some in fancy dress marching to the music of the bands which led this Mardi Gras stylish procession. There would be side-shows and stalls, fancy dress competitions, sports, egg and spoon, sack and wheelbarrow races. In the evening there was a carnival dance in Botcherby school for the adults and teenagers.

> 'Many willing helpers gave time and energy, both male and female. It must have taken months of planning to make the carnival such a huge success. In its hey-day people came from miles around to see the Botcherby Carnival.'

In the early days the horse-drawn carts would be loaned by local farmers and, later, lorries would be used, but without the same character. The 1946 Victory carnival was the first of many and on that occasion Pat Fearn(later Twentyman) was the first Queen.

1946 Victory Queen celebrations – where it all began

To celebrate the end of WW2 the people of Botcherby decided to have a Victory Queen in 1946 and Patricia Fearn was crowned Victory Queen by Isa Graham, the Mayor of Carlisle, at the top of Botcherby Avenue. Norman Foster was her pageboy and her attendants were Anne Wilson and Margaret Scott. Pat Fearn later married Geoff Twentyman, who played for Carlisle United and Liverpool FC. Pat was also a county ladies bowler. The Victory Queen celebrations were so successful with street parties, flags and bunting, etc, it was probably where the idea of the Botcherby Carnival was born.

There were changes over the years - in the 1940s and 50s Mr Gill was the main organiser and after his death, Elsie Baty and Irene John's grandmother took on the job. There were different venues, sometimes Clark's field or Botcherby School and also different bands would play. Mr R. C. Jeffrey of 50 Borland Avenue played the bagpipes and often practiced in his garden wearing full kilt, with the sound resonating around the avenue. He was a member of the Scots Pipe Band and one year they led the Carnival procession. He had a son Alec and in the 1950s lived next door to the Charters family in the first cul-de-sac.

The following pages are a pictorial celebration of those happy times.

1940s – Sports Day and Carnivals

Clockwise from the left: an early carnival celebration; Botcherby sports day 1948 and a big crowd awaits the competitions in Clark's field at the back of Charlotte Terrace - among Botcherby notables watching are Mary 'Mac' McIntyre and Annie Grice (circled in red); two views of the first official Botcherby Carnival in 1948. Among the participants were Isa and Alison Graham.

Carnival in the 1950s

Above, left to right: an early carnival outside Botcherby school, photo with Doreen Atkinson as Queen, Ronnie Wilson as the pageboy, and Patricia Graham is the little girl freezing with her coat on - also shown is Christine Atkinson and Mavis Metcalf, the tall girl next to the pageboy; inside the grounds of Botcherby School in the early 1950s, getting ready for the carnival; taken outside the old lean-to at the back of the school, left to right - John Liddle, George Routledge, Mr Hounslow, Annie and George Hunt, drummer and accordionist unknown, ? Pat Blair in the front.

Below, left to right: in the early days, horses from local farms and businesses were used to pull the floats; the carnival procession in Wood Street, early 1950s; Mr Sid Gill with his horse and cart with the queen and her attendants about to take part in the procession around the streets of Botcherby.

Above, left to right: 1953 was a special year for the carnival as it coincided with the coronation of Queen Elizabeth II. Ann Ditchburn[née Wilson] was the Botcherby Coronation Queen and is shown here with her attendants in Botcherby Avenue, including her pageboy, Brian.

Below; each street had its own celebrations - this ticket and programme was for the Borland Avenue celebrations on 16 June 1953. Note that Alice Grice, from 11 Merith Avenue, was the star singer in the programme.

BORAVE CORONATION FUND	
★	
To Celebrate the Coronation of	
H.M. Queen Elizabeth II.	
A DINNER AND SOCIAL EVENING	
will be held in the	
CO-OPERATIVE CAFE, CARLISLE	
TUESDAY, 16th JUNE, 1953	
AT 7-15 P.M.	
This Ticket is not Transferable.	

COMMITTEE

Chairman—Miss P. BLAIR

Secretary—Mr. L. KEEN

Treasurer—Mr. J. LIDDLE

Mr. A. METCALFE

Mr. W. READ

Mr. T. HOUNSLOW

Mr. G. CLARK

Mr. T. GRAHAM

Mr. D. RICHARDSON

Mrs. E. ROUTLEDGE

Mrs. S. LATTIMER

Mrs. P. HURST

Mrs. K. WILSON

Miss H. HURST

PROGRAMME

DINNER

Toast: " THE QUEEN "

DANCES

1 QUICK STEP
2 OLD FASHIONED WALTZ
3 Miss ALICE GRICE (SOPRANO)
4 PAUL JONES
5 LADIES CHOICE (REQUEST)
6 GAY GORDONS
7 FOXTROT (SPOT)
8 MODERN WALTZ
9 DASHING WHITE SERGEANT
10 CANADIAN THREE STEP
11 MILITARY TWO STEP
12 Miss ALICE GRICE, (SOPRANO)
13 QUICK STEP (LADIES CHOICE) ELIMINATION
14 ST. BERNARD WALTZ
15 LADIES CHOICE (REQUEST—SPOT)
16 SLOW FOXTROT
17 SCHOTTISCHE
18 PAUL JONES
19 QUICK STEP
20 LAST WALTZ

AULD LANG SYNE

"THE QUEEN"

Master of Ceremonies: Mr. M. PATTINSON
Music by IVAN HUNTER AND HIS BAND

More on the Botcherby Carnival in the 1950s

Above: two photos of the street parties that celebrated the 1953 Coronation. The picture on the left includes Mrs Bulman and her daughter, Freda.

Below, clockwise from the left: Irene John Carnival Queen in 1958 with Betty Harold, Shirley Brown and Anne Nixon also on the float; Alice Brown as Queen, Prince White as her pageboy. June Bell, Joyce Hunter, Irene Skinner, Evonne Page, Margaret Murray, Helen Cartwright and Rosemary Charters as some of her attendants, in the 1950s outside Botcherby School; a large group of participants in the fancy dress competition in the carnival in 1955 - the little mandarin girl showing her second prize centre right is the late Mrs Mary Jones (née McCabe), a Botcherby girl herself who gave many years of sterling service to our community as a support worker in the Botcherby Community Centre; another view of Alice Brown as Carnival Queen.

Carnival outside St Andrew's, 1955–56

A carnival photo outside St Andrew's with Linda Hope (née Underwood) as the Queen. Her small attendant is Joyce Underwood, the chimney sweep is Maureen Murphy (née Underwood). Also in the picture are Noeline Little (née Underwood), Mildred Walsh, Eileen Shackley, Anne Nanson and Pauline Turnbull. Note the old railings and wall round the church before St Andrew's Close was built.

Carnival 1959

Six photos from the Botcherby Carnival of 1959.

Above, from top left: Pat Allen, the dance teacher, oversees things; Ann Kelly is the Queen in the centre, but three Queens are shown in total.

Below are three pictures of the parade floats carrying the Queen and attendants plus a fourth of the fancy dress competition - Irene and Lesley Scott are in this picture - they were the daughters of Mrs Agnes Scott, who was caretaker and secretary of the school for many years.

Carnival in the 1950s or 60s

Right and below right: two pictures from the same carnival - but when was it and who are the Queens? Can you name other people in the pictures?

Below left: this Carnival Queen on her float is Lily Lahey of Borland Avenue - but what's the year?

Carnival in the 1950s, 60s and 70s

Above, clockwise from the left: the Queens and their attendants in the grounds of Botcherby School; a procession going down a cul-de- sac in Borland Avenue - but when and who?; the announcement of the Carnival Queen; a fancy dress parade.
Below: a selection of carnival floats and a group enjoying the sunshine in the grounds of Botcherby School.

Below: a selection of photos from the 1970 Botcherby Carnival, including the procession of the Carnival Queen.

Carnival in the 1970s

Above: scenes from the 1970 Botcherby Carnival, featuring Elsie Baty (centre and right) who was a tireless worker for the carnival and the community over many years. Below: a couple of photos from the 1975 event.

Let's bring back the carnival

What happened to the carnival?
Someone was heard to say.
They used to come from miles around
For Botcherby's special day.
It typified the spirit
The community once had.
That it is no more
Makes many people sad.
Many willing helpers
Gave time and energy
To make our own carnival
The pride of Botcherby.
The young girls as attendants
Looked lovely and serene,
But the VIP of the day
Was the local girl crowned queen.
Ladies in waiting,
Page boys looking grand,
Floats adorned with flowers,
And the marching band.
Fancy dress parades,
Side stalls full of fun,
Egg and spoon and sack races
For the kids to run.
A happy family fun day
Enjoyed by everyone.
Let's bring it back again.
It never should have gone.

Jack Stubbs 1994

Photo is of Lily Lahey as Carnival Queen, 1950s

The beautiful game

Ask anyone in Botcherby about local footballers and the names come tumbling out. Well of course Kevin Beattie and David Geddis – Botcherby's heroes really. And didn't Hugh McIlmoyle himself once live down Wood Street – and so many, many more.

Kevin Beattie went to St Cuthbert's school; the late Barry Brayton had the Post Office; even the legendary Bill Shankly crowned the Carnival queen one year . And then there was the late, great Seamus O'Connell. All great men and all well remembered...

The teams

It began many years ago with schools and amateur teams, including Botcherby FC and the Magpie Inn team. Then there were the Botcherby lads who turned professional and Carlisle United players who lodged with landladies in Borland Avenue – football memories all the way.

Raffles Rovers, Brook Street and St Cuthbert's

Above left: Raffles Rovers 1944-45 - back: far left - John Robert Aldersey, coach and founder, centre - Jake Kelly, far right - Arnold Crickett, cousin of Norman; front (l. to r.) - unnamed, Arthur Rowlands, Norman Crickett, Ronnie 'Ginger' Thompson, Johnny Bell. The five named players are all from Botcherby. Arthur, Norman and Ginger signed for Carlisle United in the 1947-48 season, Arnold emigrated to the USA. Above right: Brook Street School 1946 - back (l. to r.) - Mr Ball, Mr Halle, ? Wilson, ? Morigan, Norman Etheridge, Eric Michael, ? Walker, Alan Percival, Head Mark Graham; front (l. to r.) - Gordon Coupe, ? Galbraith, Ian Atkinson, Norman Crickett, Ron Thompson (Capt.), Derek Dixon, Arnold Crickett (Norman's cousin), Ron Wardlow, Laurie Irving. Five from Botcherby went to Brook Street and played for Carlisle Schoolboys, the pick of local talent.

Below, left: Raffles Rovers 1947-48 - back (l. to r.) - George Davidson, Arnold Crickett, ? goalkeeper, Kenny Henderson, Norman Crickett, ? Banks, John Robert Aldersey; front (l. to r.) - Denis Quinn, ? Douglas, Alec Hutchinson, Derek Dixon, Iggy Galbraith. Below right: St Cuthbert's School 1964-65 - back (l. to r.) - ? Tully, ? Murray, Mr Rafferty, ? Farry, ? Cummins, ? O'Mahony; front (l. to r.) - ? Brown, ? Andrews, Kevin Beattie, ? Rafferty, J. McAlindon, John Hamilton.

Botcherby FC through the years

Above, clockwise from top left: earliest known photo of Botcherby FC, taken outside Botcherby school - from their young age, they may have been pupils there; the badge of honour; Botcherby FC in 1934; the team that played in a tournament in Liege, Belgium in 1977 - from the back: Dennis McNeill, Sid Gill (manager), David McKnight, Ian Proudfoot, John Jamieson, Bobby McNeill, John Hamilton, Gordon Bone, Hugh McCluskie, Ronnie Lowther (referee), Steve Bell, Tommy McLean, Rob Pattinson, David Redpath, Ian Gray, Danny Carruthers; celebrating at the Cosmo in 1977 as runners up in the Sunday Morning League, 2nd Division - back (l. to r.): John McLean, Brian Redpath, John Hamilton, Ronnie Maddison, David Guy, Ian Porter, Norman Mark, John Jordan - middle (l. to r.) - Ian Proudfoot, Johnny McNeill, Norman Haynes (deceased), Sid Gill, Gordon Bell, Bobby McNeill, Peter Gill, David McKnight - front - Hugh McCluskie; the 1992 team: back (l. to r.) - John Johnston, Gary Anderson, Tom Johnston, Brendan Cherry, Mark Moffat, Shane Stubbs, Mike Clarke - front (l. to r.) - Stu Windsor, Frank Walker, Paul McCrea, Gerald Sloane, Paul Johnston, Kevin Dixon, David Christie, mascot Amy Walker.

Below clockwise from the left: 2002-2003 team: back (l. to r.) - Lee Ingledow, Ian Matthers, David Carrigan, Simon Elston, Mark Quinn, Si Phillips, Alan Jamieson (coach), Richard Fidler, Tom Johnstone, Adam Pratt, Craig Simpson; front (l. to r.) - Danny Ibbotson, Adrian Gatkin, Willy Williamson, Paul Johnstone, Billy Kenny, Stu Windsor, Rob Edmondson, Ste Bell. Missing: Roy Holliday, Scott Skinner, Paul Lewis; the under 18 team, 2002-2003, winners of the Consolation Cup; the squad for 2003-2004 season; left: 1999/2000 Second Division Runners-Up Medal, right: 2000/2001 First Division Runners-Up Medal.

Raffles Rovers FC

On 22 August 2008, the *News & Star* featured the 1944 Raffles Rovers team and stirred many memories. Raffles Rovers FC was founded in 1944 by John Robert Aldersey, who ran a Salvation Army scout troop based in Shady Grove Road. His son Ralph Aldersey recalled how he took up a bottle contract with British Rail to clear unwanted glass bottles from trains in the Upperby Carriage and Wagon Shed. This helped finance the football teams. John ran under-16 and under-18 squads over a number of years in the Carlisle Youth League and he also organised the Senior Raffles United Team. With little money available he got the first black and amber strip from a second-hand shop in Caldewgate. Over the years, the team proved a great launch pad for much of Botcherby's aspiring footballing talent and was a rich recruiting ground for Carlisle United.

The most famous photo shows the first season the team played in 1944-45 and there are a number of Botcherby boys in the team. Norman Crickett, one of the team, has given me photos and memories of the well-known faces on the photo: Ronnie 'Ginger' Thompson, who went on to play for Carlisle United, and Jake Kelly standing tall in the centre, who became a BBC TV journalist.

Some of the Raffles Rovers lads were also in the Rydal Recreation Team run by Billy Shannon, who also ran the Boy's Brigade at Rydal Street Church and played for the County Shield – Under 21. Jackie Stubbs and Norman Crickett were part of this team.

Stuart Campbell told the *News and Star* on 2 October 2004:

> *'Those were the early days of youth soccer in Carlisle. Home games took place in Bitts Park but before any games took place the goalposts had to be carried from the park-keeper's house over to the far corner of the park and then erected. There were no nets in those days, and afterwards we'd have to take the posts and return them to the house. I wonder how many teams would do that nowadays.'*

Botcherby FC

Botcherby has had its own football team from the early part of the 20th century. The first image of it dates from 1914 and shows a group of schoolboys outside Botcherby School. Over the years, its fortunes have waxed and waned (as happens to every football team). The past decade or so amply demonstrates this. At the moment, it plays in Division 3 of the Carlisle City Sunday League but, back in 2001-02, it finished as runner up in the Premiership, having achieved successive promotions in the previous two seasons. Since then it has had an up-and-down existence, even suspending its activities for a while but, as the photos show, it has had many proud moments and contributed massively to community life in Botcherby.

Carlisle United FC

Carlisle United has a long history and began life as Shaddongate United, who had headquarters at the Duke of York pub and played at Willow Holme in 1902: by 1903 they had moved to play at Millholme Bank near Boundary Road. In 1904 the club decided to change the name to Carlisle United and move their HQ to a more central location at the Fish and Dolphin in St Cuthbert's Lane.

They were originally competing in the Cumberland Senior League and in May 1905 made history when they became the first ever club to win the Cumberland Senior League Championship and the Cumberland Cup. They successfully applied to join the Lancashire Combination League in 1905 but, after the league's re-organisation in 1909, the club entered the North Eastern League, replacing their reserve team who had previously played in the league.

They also planned a new ground on Devonshire Park (today the location of Newman School). In 1905 the *Carlisle Journal* published an advertisement for tenders to lay down a playing pitch and 'a*lso for work in enclosing the ground and building a grandstand for Carlisle United Association Football Club.'*

The ground and stand were built to hold 16,000 people but, by 1907, the club was on the move again to a new location on the north side of Warwick Road, in spite of petitions by the residents who feared the value of their property would deteriorate and *'cause an intolerable nuisance owing to the crowds whose conduct and language is most undesirable.'* The building went ahead and Brunton Park opened on 31 July 1909 with a sports meeting and bands playing. The first to use it was the Cumberland and Westmorland Wrestling and Athletic Association with events of wrestling, racing and cycling. Carlisle United officially moved in September 1909.

Carlisle United were crowned champions of the North Eastern League in 1922 and, when the first team left to join the Football League, the reserve team resumed its place in the North Eastern League. On 4 June 1928 a delegation from Carlisle United attended a Football League meeting in London to hear the results of a vote on their application to join. With the second highest number of votes, they were admitted.

When WW2 broke out in 1939, national and regional competitions were suspended and Carlisle United only played local football. After the war ended Ivor Broadis was appointed as player-manager. Aged only 23 at the time, he remains the youngest manager ever appointed in the Football League.

Botcherby's connection with Carlisle United goes back to these early days and some of its most notable players are given below, along with those who found fame further afield.

The players

Ian Atkinson

He was born in Carlisle in December 1932 and lived in Holywell Crescent. After playing for local clubs he joined Carlisle United in September 1952 as an inside forward. In 1955-56 he was joint top scorer for Carlisle, along with Alan Ashman, netting 17 league goals. In all he played 123 games for the Blues scoring 54 goals, until he left in March 1957 to join Exeter City. Ian Atkinson died in 1995.

Kevin Beattie, David Geddis, Robin Turner – stars of Ipswich Town

Kevin Beattie was born on 18 December 1953 and lived in Botcherby Avenue. In his book *The Greatest Footballer England Never Had: The Kevin Beattie Story,* he describes his early life in Botcherby and how he began

The Magpie's football teams – and some rugby too!

Above: left - the team that won the Cumberland Cup in 1969-70; right - with the cup, back - T Bone, R Proudfoot, B Wilson, D Warwick; middle - J Monaghan, D Blyth, R Little, H Irving; front - S Proudfoot, B Neal.

Below, left - back: H McCluskey, B Redpath, L Bell, G Bell, G Bone, I Proudfoot, D Ivison, front: S Gill, D McKnight, K Shackley, C Birrell, R Pattinson D Snelgar; right: the Botcherby team that competed successfully in the 1974 Great Fair seven-a-side rugby tournament. Holding the shield is Colin Bee. Middle row: Gordon Bone, Rob Pattinson and Trevor Ford. Front row: Barry Notman, Alan Bell, Barry Cowton and John Hamilton.

playing football on the local playing-fields with jumpers on the grass for goal posts, and practising his skills to perfection. Kevin Rafferty, his teacher at St Cuthbert's School had encouraged him from his first day at school by giving him a football to play with. He went on to play in the school football team as goalkeeper, a position his father Tommy had played in amateur football, even having a trial with Aston Villa. Soon Kevin was playing centre forward and scoring on average two goals per game. Mr Rafferty had put together a good team which went a full season undefeated, until the day they met their local rivals in the cup final and they lost the match 3-2.

Although he passed his 11-plus exam for the Grammar School, he went to St Patrick's RC school, where he played for the school side and also for the local amateur club, Blackfriars, managed by Mr Rafferty. By the time he was 14 he started to play for the Magpie team who played in the local league: his father played in goal and Kevin was a striker. He was an all-round sportsman, becoming school sprint champion and covering 100 yards (now 91.44 metres) in 10 seconds flat – and wearing his football boots!

His dream was to become a professional footballer and one of his heroes was Hughie McIlmoyle, who had once scored 44 goals for the club in a single season. Mr Rafferty spoke to Carlisle United, but as there was no junior side then, it was not to be. Schooldays ended on a high note with scoring two goals in the cup final and winning the schools' cup.

After doing a number of jobs locally and playing for St Augustine's on Saturdays and Blackfriars on Sundays, he was approached by a Liverpool FC scout. Bill Shankly was manager at this time and after a trial Kevin was told he would be given a contract. When he returned to Liverpool, no one met him at the station and, at 15 years old and with only the clothes he stood up in and no money, and believing that Liverpool had changed their mind, he used his return ticket and went back to Carlisle. He thought it was the end of his dream. Within days he was approached by another scout for Ipswich Town and, after a trial game, was told by Manager Bobby Robson that he would offer him a contract as an apprentice professional footballer which he accepted. Liverpool FC had by now discovered the reasons for his non-appearance there, but it was too late, much to Bill Shankly's annoyance.

At Ipswich Town, and by now playing as a defender, his career went from strength to strength, from his first match with the first team in 1972-73 season against Manchester United at Old Trafford, until the 1977-78 season when Ipswich Town won the FA Cup at Wembley, beating Arsenal 1-0.

Of Beattie, journalist Peter Hill recalls:

> 'Beattie was phenomenal as a youngster... he could hit the ball from one end of the field to the other with hardly any back-lift. He was extraordinary... he is the only youngster I can remember who beat me in the sprint competitions we used to hold... These impressive physical attributes have carried Beattie to full England honours and Geddis who is only 20 was this week called up for the England 'B' tour, New Zealand, Malaysia and Singapore.'

David Geddis was born on 12 May 1958 and would become another of Botcherby's famous professional footballers. Educated at St Cuthbert's and Newman School in Carlisle, after playing for England at youth level, in 1976 he went to play for Ipswich Town at the age of 18. His talent was recognised when leading goal scorer Trevor Whymark was injured against Norwich City on Boxing Day 1977: Geddis replaced him in the line-up and remained in the side. This brought about one of his greatest achievements when he was one of the youngest players ever to make an appearance in the FA Cup final as Ipswich beat Arsenal at Wembley on 6 May 1978. Geddis delivered the cross which led to Roger Osborne's winning goal.

On 12 May 1978 Peter Hill writing in the *Cumberland News* reported:

> 'John Irving a 28 year old qualified football coach, is part of a two man team that has searched out and developed some of the North's best young footballing talent and sent them off to East Anglia. Ipswich scout John Carruthers finds players and Irving, whose own football career was cut short by injury, works on their weaknesses. Two of the players to have come under their wing, David Geddis and Kevin Beattie starred in last week's outgunning of the Arsenal... both of them had natural talent it was just a question of building them up physically and trying to overcome what few weaknesses they had... In David Geddis' case there was no need to push him... David was absolutely determined to make the grade. He was a clean-living lad and fully deserves the success he has had.'

On Cup Final day and beyond Ipswich went wild, with celebrations and family parties echoing scenes across

Carlisle United

Above: two pictures from 1909 showing action from an early match at Brunton Park against Newcastle United reserves. The Steam Laundry chimney and Warwick Road houses are in the background.

Below, clockwise from the left: Andrew Burns playing in goal for Carlisle United in the early 1900s; postcard of Carlisle United challenging for Lancashire League championship; the Cumberland team around 1900 with Andrew Burns in goal; the Carlisle United team that earned the famous 0-0 draw against Arsenal at Highbury on 6 January 1951 - the team included two players from Botcherby, Norman Coupe (back row, far left) and Geoff Twentyman (back row, second from right); 'Carlisle - Rovers 1918' is the only information we have on this WW1 team.

the town as supporters and fans saluted this fine achievement.

Geddis was transferred to Aston Villa in 1979 for a fee of £300,000 and the following season won a League Championship medal by being one of the 14 players that Villa used that season. 1983 saw a move to Second Division Barnsley where he scored an impressive 24 goals in 45 starts. By 1985 he was sought by former Villa boss Ron Saunders at Birmingham City. He became a firm favourite with fans due to his contribution to the promotion winning campaign of the 1984-85 season.

In January 2002 Sir Bobby Robson brought in Geddis to work as coach alongside John Carver at Newcastle United. He would later become coach to several teams and scouted for England manager Sven-Göran Eriksson and the English FA at the 2006 World Cup in Germany.

Robin Turner was the third Botcherby footballing star to play for Ipswich. Born on 10 September 1955 he was an FA Youth Cup Winner in 1972-73 at Ipswich Town and played for the senior team from 1975 to 1984 as a striker. He was a Charity Shield Runner-up in 1978-79. In 1984 he signed for Swansea City and in 1985 for Colchester United and, a year later, for Bury Town.

Botcherby's three Ipswich players turned film stars in 1981 when Paramount Pictures made *Escape To Victory,* a film directed by John Huston. The famous cast included Sylvester Stallone, Michael Caine, Max von Sydow and Daniel Massey and also starred famous footballers including Pelé, Bobby Moore and Mike Summerbee.

In the footballing scenes, Kevin Beattie was stand-in for Michael Caine and other Ipswich Town players, including David Geddis and Robin Turner, were featured. The film is an exciting story about Allied Prisoners of War who are interned in a German prison camp during WW2. Coached by an English Captain (a former professional player for West Ham United – played by Michael Caine) they agree to play an exhibition match against a German team, only to find themselves involved in a German propaganda stunt.

Freddie Blackadder

Born in January 1916, he lived at 48 Durranhill Road and played for Queen's Park in the Scottish league before joining Carlisle United in April 1938 where he played centre half. He eventually became trainer of the reserve team until he left in September 1946.

Barry Brayton

Barry was born in Carlisle on 29 September 1938 and played for local teams until December 1959 when he joined Carlisle United as a part-time professional, being signed by manager Andy Beattie. He played outside-right and made 161 League and Cup appearances for the Blues scoring 35 goals. He is remembered at Brunton Park, where in May 1962 a crowd of 12,660 watched him score the club's second goal in their 2-0 win at home to Chester, securing the club's promotion to Division Three. He went on to win a Division Three Championship medal in 1965 after playing 20 games in a successful season. In February 1967, he joined Workington Reds.

Barry is very well remembered in Botcherby as owning the Post Office on Mount Florida from 1970 for more than twenty years. He died on 20 January 2015. Paying tribute to him in the *News & Star* on 22 January 2015, Ivor Broadis said, *'Barry was a ball player. I thought a lot of him as a player because he didn't waste the ball.'* Former team-mate Hugh McIlmoyle said: *'He was a good player and a really nice fella, who was good company to be with.'*

Andrew Burns

Andrew Burns was one of the earliest players for the club and was a goalkeeper for the first team in the 1906-07 season. He married Mary Armstrong in 1909 and was a well-known local chimney sweep, later living with his family at 38 Botcherby Avenue. He became Barbara Stubbs's and Rosemary Hartley's grandfather.

Jackie Cape

Jackie Cape lived at 56 Merith Avenue and was born on 16 November 1911. He was a centre forward and before the war played for Penrith and Carlisle United in the 1929-30 season, playing 15 matches with two goals. Described as an exciting winger, he was sold to Newcastle United in January 1930 to subsidise the rebuild and covering of what was once the 'Scratching Shed' side of Brunton Park, opposite the main stand and the paddock area. (This was demolished in the 1990s.)

Cape played 50 matches, scoring 18 goals at Newcastle United before going to Manchester United in January 1934, playing 59 matches with 18 goals. He then moved to Queens Park Rangers in June 1937, playing 61 matches and scoring 12 goals. He then went to Scarborough in 1946, before moving to Carlisle United in the October, where he played three matches. He died on 6 June 1994.

John Charles CBE

William John Charles was born on 27 December 1931 in Swansea and became rated by many as the greatest international footballer ever to come from Britain. He was inducted into the Football Hall of Fame in 2002.

Standing at 6ft 2in., he was nicknamed 'The Gentle Giant.' He began his senior career with Leeds United, playing from 1948 to 1957 where, in 297 appearances, he scored 157 goals. He later played for Juventus, Roma, Cardiff City, Hereford United and Merthyr Tydfil, becoming player-manager at the last two. He was also a Welsh International from 1950 to 1965, making 38 appearances and scoring 15 goals. He also played for the Great Britain team against Ireland in 1955 and, in 1958, played for Wales at the FIFA World Cup in Sweden.

His link with Botcherby came between 1950 and 1952, when he served his National Service with the 12th Royal Lancers at Durranhill Army Camp and is remembered playing football on the Co-op field (now Walkmill estate). The Army allowed him to turn out for Leeds, but also saw to it that he played for them and, in 1952, Charles skippered his side to win the Army Cup.

Botcherby's footballing hall of fame

Ian ATKINSON

Kevin BEATTIE

Barry BRAYTON

Andrew BURNS

Jackie CAPE

John CHARLES

Joseph Norman COUPE

Norman CRICKETT

David GEDDIS

David GEDDIS, family and friends

Brent HETHERINGTON

Joe LAIDLAW

John MCALINDON

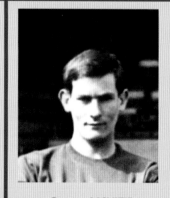

George MCVITIE

Seamus O'CONNELL

On his retirement he received many honours and in the foreword to Charles's autobiography, Sir Bobby Robson describes him as 'incomparable' and classed him among the all-time footballing greats such as Pelé, Diego Maradona and George Best. He died in February 2004.

Joseph Norman Coupe

Joseph Norman Coupe served as a Corporal in the Royal Marines in WW2 and took part in the D-Day landings. Born in 1924, he played rugby for his school before signing up with the Marines when he was 17. He lived at 130 Borland Avenue and, after the war, played for the local Swifts until 1947 when he signed for Carlisle United. He stayed with United under Bill Shankly's managership until 1951 when he transferred to Rochdale. One of his greatest footballing moments was when he was in the Cumbrian side that held the mighty Arsenal to a famous goalless draw at Highbury on 6 January 1951. The FA Cup third-round tie was watched by a crowd of 57,932 – the biggest ever to watch Carlisle on a league ground. (Only Wembley has hosted a bigger Carlisle crowd.) The Magpie Inn was close to bursting at the seams that evening as fans celebrated in the time-honoured way. The bulk of Norman's 35 appearances for the Blues came in his final season. After their heroic match at Highbury, the Division Three North team welcomed the Gunners back to a packed Brunton Park on 11 January, with more than 20,000 fans cheering them on. Excitement ran high in Botcherby that afternoon as Arsenal won 4-1, but all agreed that United had done well against such a team.

Ivor Broadis, former Carlisle and England player would recall:

> 'Norman joined the club just after I left for Sunderland. They went to Highbury and no one expected them to have a chance, but they got a draw and brought them back here. It was a great Arsenal side. I'd say that draw at Highbury was one of the greatest games in Carlisle's history. Norman was a left full-back. He was strong and he had a good left foot... I can tell you he was a powerful fellow who took no prisoners.'

After leaving Carlisle, Norman played football for Rochdale and Workington and then changed his allegiance to rugby league at Workington Town and supporting the creation of Carlisle's own rugby league team. His golfing prowess was well known at Carlisle Golf Club where he would play off a golf handicap of four. He worked as a panel beater at the city's County Garage and later was employed at Metal Box. Norman died in April 1998.

Norman Crickett

Norman Crickett is part of a well-known local footballing family. Norman himself played for Brook Street School, Raffles Rovers and Carlisle United, where he played from 1952 to 1956 as an outside right. His cousin Arnold also played for Brook Street and his uncle Billy Crickett of Ennerdale Avenue played for Carlisle United before the war – they won the Cumberland Cup and the League Cup that year and Norman recalls *'it was a lovely trophy with a football on top.'*

Brent Hetherington

Born 6 December 1961, Brent played for Carlisle United and lived at Botcherby. Remembered as playing as striker against Liverpool FC on 7 January 1989 at Brunton Park with a result of 3-0. He played for United between 1987-89 and scored 28 goals in 71 appearances in League, FA Cup and FL Cup matches.

Joe Laidlaw

A North-Easterner, born in Whickham in 1950, Joe Laidlaw was a crowd favourite during his four years with Carlisle United. An energetic midfielder, he started his football career with Middlesbrough, before joining Carlisle United in July 1972 and living in Botcherby. He played a key role in the 1973-74 team that gained promotion to Division 1 and was top goalscorer the following season, with 14 goals. In all he played 171 league and cup games for Carlisle, scoring 48 goals. He moved to Doncaster Rovers in 1976 and subsequently played for Portsmouth, Hereford United and Mansfield Town.

John McAlindon

John McAlindon was born on Christmas Day 1930 in Botcherby. On growing up his footballing career began with the Carlisle Catholic Youth FC, followed by a stint with Penrith Amateurs. On 19 May 1948 he joined Celtic FC and, by this time, had also trained as an electrician. In those days of modest wages, it was prudent for footballers to have a trade to fall back on.

His first senior competitive game for Celtic was two years later, when as centre forward he scored two goals against Hearts in a 2-2 draw. Charlie Tully had a hand in setting up each of them and, from that day on, they

Botcherby's footballing hall of fame

Hugh MCILMOYLE *Left to right: McIlmoyle in his playing days with Carlisle; with the author at the launch of the Carlisle United video in 2002; the statue outside Brunton Park shows McIlmoyle heading for goal in typical striking fashion. It was unveiled in 2005.*

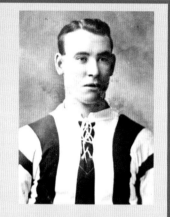

Charlie PARKER | Arthur ROWLANDS | Jackie SCURR | Ron 'Ginger' THOMPSON

Robin TURNER | Geoff TWENTYMAN | George WALKER | George WHITELAW

became firm friends. Other friends were Sean Fallon and Bertie Peacock. John was there when Jock Stein was a player and again when he returned as manager in 1965.

He never became a regular in the first team and his time at the club was interrupted by National Service in 1954. He married his wife Lucy in 1960 and they had four daughters. At 5ft 11in., he was a fast lively player but was seen mostly as an understudy to John McPhail. He was loaned out for a time to Worcester City and, when his playing days with Celtic were at an end, he had a brief time with Shrewsbury Town. While there he sustained a cartilage injury which ended his playing career. He returned to Glasgow and Bob Kelly brought him back to Celtic Park as maintenance electrician. He is said to have relished the job. Known as Johnny Mack, he was the man staff sent for when any kind of practical work was required about the stadium. He carried special responsibility for the floodlighting. Between 1948 and 1957 he played 16 league games scoring 7 goals.

He also played in the Scottish Cup and the League Cup. John died on 10 February 2002, aged 71, having served at Celtic Park for over forty years. He was buried at Dalbeth cemetery in Glasgow where his memorial is inscribed: *'A kind and gentle man.'*

Hugh McIlmoyle

Hugh McIlmoyle is linked to some of Carlisle United's most successful years in all four divisions of the Football League. He was born in 1940 at Port Glasgow and came South to join Leicester City where he was a controversial selection at centre forward in the 1961 FA Cup final against Spurs' double-winning side. In 1963 he began his long relationship with Carlisle United, joining from Rotherham United.

During his first spell at Carlisle from 1963-65, he scored a total of 51 goals in 88 appearances (including the phenomenal 1963-64 season when he bagged 44 goals) before signing for Wolverhampton Wanderers. Following a spell at Bristol City, he was back from 1967-70, when he scored 36 goals in 82 matches. After playing at Middlesbrough, Preston North End and Greenock Morton, he was back again in 1974-75 during United's one memorable season in Division One. This time he scored just twice in 19 games. With the end of his career in sight, McIlmoyle returned briefly to Greenock Morton in 1975-76 before finally settling down in Carlisle and living for a time in St Andrew's Close, off Wood Street in Botcherby.

A statue was erected in his honour outside Brunton Park in 2005 and rumour has it that, when the floods of December 2015 hit Warwick Road, the rising waters stopped when they reached the statue's grounded foot - proving what we always knew: McIlmoyle walks on water!

Frank McKenna

Born in Blaydon in 1933, he joined the Blues from Leeds United and was another of the Borland Avenue lodgers. In 1957-58 he scored once in 15 appearances, and in 1958-59 hit the net 10 times in 31 games before moving on to Hartlepool United at the end of that season.

George McVitie

A right-winger, George McVitie was born in Carlisle on 7 September 1948, and lodged in Borland Avenue. He had two spells playing for Carlisle United, from 1965 to 1970 where he made 128 appearances and scored 21 goals. After playing for West Bromwich Albion and Oldham Athletic, he returned to Carlisle from 1976 to 1981 making 198 appearances and scoring 20 goals. After leaving Carlisle in 1981 he played for Queen of the South for one season.

Seamus O'Connell

Seamus O'Connell was born in Carlisle on New Year's Day 1930. Although his family lived on Warwick Road, they are remembered as attending Sunday mass at the Little Sisters of the Poor chapel at St Joseph's Home, Botcherby. His father ran a lucrative cattle-dealing business and Seamus worked in this. These commitments, and the low maximum wage paid to professional footballers at the time, meant that he chose to remain an amateur player.

An inside-forward, he joined Chelsea FC making his spectacular debut on October 16 1954, playing against Matt Busby's Manchester United side at Stamford Bridge, London. The game would never be forgotten as O'Connell equalised United's opener, and he struck his second goal when the score was 6-3 to the visitors. He completed the hat-trick, but United won 6-5. The 56,000 spectators went wild. Matt Busby had tried to persuade O'Connell to sign for his side as a professional. Six months later he was in the team that won Chelsea the League Championship. In total, he played 17 games for Chelsea and scored 12 goals.

He later played for leading non-league team Bishop Auckland, helping them win the FA Amateur Cup in 1955 and 1956. He played for England at amateur level and had games for Crook Town and Carlisle United as an amateur towards the end of his career. Later he moved to Spain to run a bar, where he died in February 2013 at the age of 83.

Charlie Parker

Born 1 September 1891 at Seaham, Charlie Parker played for local clubs in the area until, in 1913 at the age of 21, he signed for Stoke, playing in a half-back position. A popular player with the club's supporters, he helped Stoke regain their League status in 1914-15. He remained there throughout WW1 and, after the war, one of his career highlights was to play in England's 2-0 win against Wales, at the Victory International on 8 October 1919 at the Victoria Ground, Stoke.

Much to the annoyance of Stoke fans, he was sold to First Division Sunderland in 1920 for a fee of £3,300 and would stay there until 1928, making 245 league appearances. He joined Carlisle United for the 1929-30 season as player-coach and made 9 appearances for the team. He lived in Botcherby where he was a popular figure. He ended his footballing career with local North-Eastern teams and died in 1969 aged 78.

Arthur Rowlands

One of the 133 people who lost their lives when the MV *Princess Victoria* sank off the coast of Northern Ireland on Saturday 31 January 1953 was Arthur Rowlands. It is a tragic story.

Twenty-one-year-old Arthur was well-known in Botcherby and lived on Durranhill Road. Always keen on football as a boy, he played for the very first Raffles Rovers team in the 1944-45 season, along with other Botcherby lads. He later played for Carlisle United. He also had a few matches with the Belfast team Distillery and played inside-forward in the Bangor Summer Football League for Trinity Old Boys.

Stuart Campbell recalled those early footballing days to reporter Chris Musson of the *News &Star* on 2 October 2004 after seeing a photo of the team published:

> *'I know most of the Team, Jake Kelly was a well-known journalist for Look North and worked at Sellafield. Arthur Rowlands lost his life returning to Northern Ireland after a spell of leave when the ferry sank in the Irish Sea during a gale. I remember it well. It was a sad loss, and Arthur was a brilliant player.'*

A craftsman attached to the REME at Palace Barracks, Holywood, County Down, he had been home on leave to Botcherby, and had married Maureen Henderson of Carlisle just two days before travelling back on the MV *Princess Victoria.* He was returning to his regiment prior to a posting to the Middle East.

The North Channel is a treacherous stretch of water between Scotland and Northern Ireland, only 21 miles across from Stranraer to Larne. On that fateful Saturday morning the weather was so severe that today it is still remembered as the 'Great Storm', affecting the United Kingdom and leaving 300 people dead and a trail of devastation in its wake. A total of 178 people were on board the roll on/roll off ferry, with its car deck and its gated open stern to allow cars and lorries to be driven off. Within an hour of setting sail from Stranraer the ship was in trouble. The BBC had been issuing weather warnings for the Irish Sea area since the previous evening and by 6am on Saturday gale warnings were broadcast. The Captain decided to sail and at 7.45am the ship began its journey down Loch Ryan and into the open sea, where the full force of the storm hit the ship.

Over the next few hours the ship struggled to survive but, with the stern doors breaking open, water began to flood the car deck and affect the stability of the ship. The situation worsened as the engine room flooded. Calls for assistance were sent, life jackets given out and the life boats prepared. In spite of other ships in the area trying to help, it was to no avail and the *Princess Victoria* was lost at 2pm. Three lifeboats and some rafts were in the water and survivors clung to them. Only 44 people survived. Today memorials to those lost stand in the towns of Stranraer and Larne.

Even after more than 50 years, the tragedy of the *Princess Victoria* is still remembered by local people. Stephen Farley recalled to the *News & Star* on 31 January 2012 how he should have been on the ferry, returning to Northern Ireland to continue his National Service with the Royal Army Medical Corps. Arriving at Carlisle station an hour early to catch the boat train to Larne, he bumped into a friend who wanted to buy him a drink in the Caledonian pub on Botchergate. When he arrived back at the station he had missed the train by five minutes and he ended up bedding down at Carlisle Castle. The next morning the sergeant told him of the loss of the ship. Stephen says:

> *'Now I go to Carlisle Cathedral to pay my respects and say a prayer for those who died. I ended up getting to Larne. I went the next day on Victoria's sister ship Margaret. I remember as we went by we all lowered our heads and it was very sombre. The flag was lowered too.'*

Jackie Scurr

Born in North Shields in 1940, Jackie Scurr was another of the Borland Avenue lodgers during his time with Carlisle United. A forward/midfielder, he joined from Arsenal in 1960-61 season and was part of the successful team that won promotion from Division Four the next season, under Ivor Powell. In all he played 15 league games and three FA cup matches, scoring once. He later played for King's Lynn, Cambridge United, Bedford Town and Stotfold.

Ron (Ginger) Thompson

Ron Thompson was born on 20 January 1932 and was brought up in Ennerdale Avenue where, at an early age, he liked nothing better than to kick a ball around. He sang in the Cathedral Choir, attended Brook Street School, where he was made captain of the school's football team, and then got a place in the Raffles Rovers team. When Bill Shankly, Carlisle's manager, advertised for a new 'A' team and 300 turned up for trials, Ginger soon caught his eye and remembered the Scot with respect: *'Shankly was the best. There won't be another. He worked us hard and was always on your back. You dared not mess about and I liked that.'*

At first Ginger was playing part-time and working for a local engineering works, but when the Third-Division Blues drew against First-Division Birmingham City in the FA Cup and his boss wouldn't give him time off for the replay, he left and went full-time at United. He and George Walker, a team-mate, set up a building and welding business and never looked back. Those were the days when professional footballers were on a maximum wage of £12 a week - nothing like today's high salaries - and most had to have other employment to earn a living. Ginger recalled that in his Army days, 60 years ago, he was in the same regiment and Army team as Jack Charlton.

His career at Carlisle United lasted from 1951 to 1964, playing wing half, and he set the appearance record of 374 matches. In 1975 he and George Walker set up Carlisle City Football Club and the senior team has been a member of the Northern Alliance league since then. By 1990 a junior section was set up with an under-18 team and today there are three senior sides, 14 boys teams and four girls teams. The club has received the FA Charter Standard Community Club award and has a school partnership link with Kingmoor School. No small achievement for a man who has never rested on his laurels: *'I never think about all that. For me you just played and played and that was all there was to it. I always needed that challenge in me. I still do.'*

Geoff Twentyman

In 1949 Carlisle United was the first club to appoint Bill Shankly as manager and it was here that he met local player Geoff Twentyman, whom he would later sign as head scout at Liverpool. Geoff was born on 19 January 1930 and had played for the amateur club Swift's Rovers before joining Carlisle United in 1947. Noted for his ability to lift both the team and the fans in the quest for success, his work in defence was exceptional. He married Botcherby girl Pat Fearn in 1952 and, by 1953, was bought by Liverpool for £10,000. He returned to Carlisle in 1963 and later became player-manager at Morecambe, before returning to Liverpool to work with Bill Shankly. Geoff died in 2004.

George Walker

George Walker was born in Sunderland in 1934 and died in Carlisle in August 2012. He was a well-liked player at Carlisle United and was one of the stars of the United team that won its place in Division Three for the first time in 1962. His goal in a 2-0 promotion-clinching win against Chester on the final day of the season secured his place in club history.

The inside forward lodged with Mary Thompson in the cul-de-sac at 31 Borland Avenue, as did other United players over the years, including George Whitelaw, Jackie Scurr, Frank McKenna and Joe Laidlaw, and was well thought of on Botcherby estate. He joined the Blues from Bristol City in 1959 and would go on to make 164 league appearances for United, scoring 53 goals from 1958 to 1963. When his playing days ended because of a broken leg, he formed a building business with friend and team-mate, Ginger Thompson. They also established Carlisle City Football Club together in 1975. His son Andy told the *News and Star* on 14 August

2012: *'Him and Ginger loved a battle on the pitch but they were always gentlemen too. We're all very proud of him and what he did.'*

George Whitelaw

George Whitelaw was another of the players who lodged in Borland Avenue when he played for Carlisle United. He sported a cropped haircut and was known as something of an eccentric: he was a force to be reckoned with on the pitch and a great entertainer.

Born in Paisley on New Year's Day 1937, he played centre forward. He started his career with St Johnstone in 1955, followed by Sunderland, Queens Park Rangers, and Halifax Town before signing with Carlisle United from 1960 to 61 where he played 34 games, scoring 10 goals. He left for Stockport County in 1961 and went on to play for Barrow, St Johnstone and Stenhousemuir until 1965. He retired in 1965 having made 238 appearances and scoring 81 goals. He died in 2004.

◆◆◆

Remembering... Bill Shankly OBE

Bill Shankly is something of a legend in Carlisle and his achievements with Carlisle United and Botcherby footballers are still talked about today. The pictures above show him in his pomp as Liverpool manager and the day, at some time in the 1950s, he crowned the Carnival Queen at Botcherby.

Born in 1913, one of five footballing brothers, he began his professional playing career with United in the 1932-33 season, when they were playing in the Third Division North, with their reserve side in the North Eastern League. He made his debut playing for the reserves, and at the end of the season, they won the North Eastern League Cup, defeating Newcastle United reserves 1-0 in the final. He made his senior debut on 31 December 1932 in a 2-2 draw against Rochdale, totalling sixteen appearances before spending the rest of his career at Preston North End, who won the FA Cup in 1938.

He served in the Royal Air Force during WW2 and went into football management in 1949, after the war. Returning to Carlisle United as manager from 1949-1951, he transformed the club's league position. In the 1948-49 season Carlisle were struggling in the bottom half of the Third Division North and finding it hard to attract southern-based players to come north. That season they finished 15th in the league: by 1949-50 they improved to 9th and were 3rd by the end of the 1950-51 season. One of his young players was Geoff Twentyman who later transferred to Liverpool and after retirement became chief scout there, working with Shankly.

In 1959 Shankly became manager of Liverpool taking them from the Second Division to the First Division by 1962. Liverpool won the FA Cup Final in 1974 and Shankley announced his retirement a few weeks later. His criteria for success in football management was: 'I could speak common sense about the game and I could spot a player.' He died in 1981 at the age of 68.

Whatever happened to Tom Clark's field?

By the 1950s developers were looking to build more houses at Botcherby, and Tom Clark's field, opposite the Magpie Inn on Victoria Road was a suitable size for a new estate. The picture shows a Rogation Day procession through it in 1953, with Tilbury Road in the background – all distant memories now...

Eden Park estate

Applications to the City Surveyor for the development of this estate had first been made in April 1952 but nothing further seems to have happened until 1959, when Border Engineering Contractors Ltd, a Whitehaven-based company, made application to build an estate comprising 44 pairs of semi-detached houses and six bungalows.

The application was approved, subject to detailed layout and building plans for houses, streets, sewers and street lighting. In particular, the floor levels of the housing had to be to the satisfaction of the Council, to safeguard against flooding.

No new vehicular access would be allowed from Charlotte Terrace or Warwick Road, with the only entry being from Victoria Road. This was to prevent any congestion on Warwick Road near its junction with the proposed Ring Road and Victoria Road, ensuring the safety and free-flow of traffic.

The Council also stipulated the planting of trees and shrubs and grass verges to enhance the appearance of the estate. Concern about the Ring Road was also evident in the final stipulation:

> 'The estate is to be fenced off at its eastern boundary to the Council's satisfaction from the triangular piece of land required for the proposed Ring Road situate between Tilbury Road and the estate boundaries, in order to preserve the line of the proposed Ring Road and to prevent vehicular access to the estate from the Ring Road.'

The 1959 *Abstract of the Title of Border Engineering Contractors Ltd to Freehold Land situate at Botcherby in the City of Carlisle* gives the following information: the land had belonged to the Farrer family for many years and, at least since 1898, had been held by different family members until, finally, Phillip Tonstall Farrer of London sold the land to Horace Wills Mawson, solicitor of Bank Chambers, Bank Street, Carlisle in 1936.

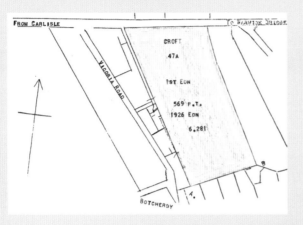
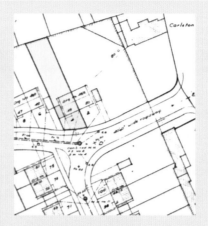

Eden Park

Clockwise from top left: plan of Clark's Field, showing the area to be developed as Eden Park estate; plan of plot 49, which became 4 Eden Park Crescent; cover of conveyancing document detailing the agreement between Border Engineering Contractors and the first purchaser of the house; picture of the house today (green garage door).

By 1958 Mawson had sold the land to Border Engineering Contractors for the building of Eden Park estate.

It was Tom Clark who leased the land from Mawson, and had the farm and butcher's shop at the top of Wood Street (north side). On his field the Botcherby Carnivals were held after WW2. All of this gave way to the new houses.

The new estate was popular and, by July 1960, James Malloy, a tar-macadam contractor of Merith Avenue, had bought site 49, which became 4 Eden Park Crescent. Mr and Mrs Banks, who had the Post Office at 1 Wood Street, were also early purchasers.

Eastern Way

Nothing had changed the face of Botcherby so drastically since the road-widening scheme on Victoria Road and Durranhill Road at the end of the 1920s, when the council estate was being built, as the construction of Eastern Way. It sliced through the eastern side of Botcherby, cutting Tilbury Road in half and making the old railway bridge and the old Durranhill Road to Harraby redundant.

It was constructed in the 1960s as part of a Ring Road scheme for the city, skimming the eastern side of Botcherby and Eden Park estate as it snaked its way to Harraby and London Road. The new Durranhill Road bridge opened on 31 January 1969. It was also the beginning of an enlarged Durranhill Industrial Estate, where new businesses sprang up and Border Television had its studio.

Left: construction of the new Durranhill Bridge, Eastern Way, in 1968. Jimmy Grieg is the workman vibrating the concrete, Brian Nelson watches in the dark pullover. Right: job done - Bill Boak's photo of traffic crossing Durranhill Bridge on Eastern Way in February 1969, with the old railway bridge to the left.

Riverside Housing comes to Botcherby

After taking over the stock of 7,200 council houses in Carlisle, Riverside, a Liverpool-based social housing charitable registered society, set up the Carlisle Housing Association (CHA) in 2002 with the promise of improving the housing stock and providing fair rents. By 1 April 2009, in a bid to cut costs, it decided to merge CHA with six others in the North-West, trading as Riverside Housing and saying that this would make it more efficient. Many concerns were expressed: that tenancies would be managed by bosses at Riverside's Liverpool HQ; that rental income might not be spent locally for the benefit of local tenants, but put into a central pot. Carlisle MP Eric Martlew said: *'You have to go back to what the tenants voted for – and that was Carlisle Housing Association.'* The Carlisle and Rural Tenants Federation collected 2,500 signatures in a petition against the merger which Mr Martlew presented to Housing Minister Margaret Beckett.

With Riverside giving legally-binding assurances that the 6,000 houses would still be managed from Carlisle; that there would be tenants' and council representatives on the Divisional Board; and that income from rents and property sales would 'primarily' be reinvested in Carlisle, the merger went ahead.

Riverside Housing refurbishes Botcherby

Riverside Housing developments. Above: Freshfield Court sheltered housing, flats and bungalows in Botcherby Avenue. Below: 16 one-bedroom flats were demolished in Borland Avenue to make way for this development which was completed in May 2014, comprising four three-bedroom houses, five two-bedroom houses and two two-bedroom bungalows.

By November 2009, the Botcherby Action Team at Riverside had produced a 56-page comprehensive report, *Botcherby Revitalisation Strategy 2009-2012* with the strapline *Moving Forward Together*. The previous 20 years had seen the quality of life in parts of the estate deteriorate and perceptions about living there had changed. This was in spite of attempts to generate change with schemes such as the Healthy Living Initiative, Botcherby Action Team and Police Community Support officers.

St Joseph's Court, Bramerton Orchard, Wood Street, St Andrew's Close

Above, left to right: the new houses built on Victoria Road and at St Joseph's Court, on the site of Feddon's Nurseries. Below, clockwise from the left: Bramerton Orchard; the newer houses at the bottom of Wood Street, including those in the close beside Casey's old farm ; two views of St Andrew's Close.

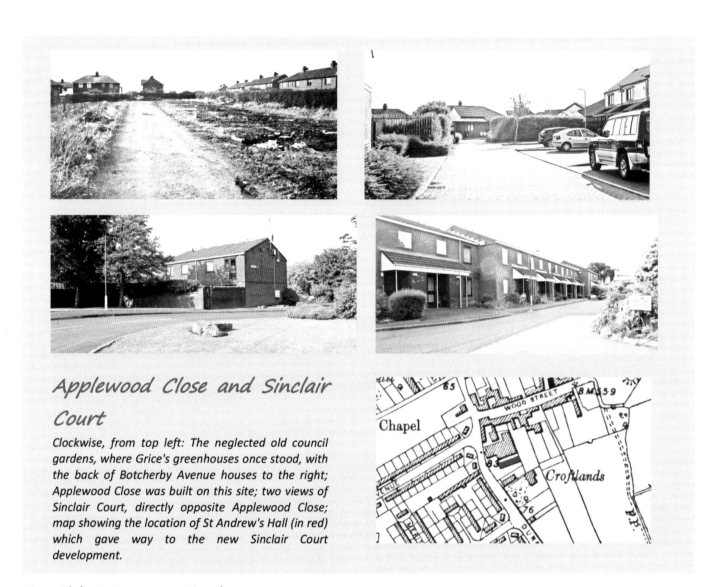

Applewood Close and Sinclair Court

Clockwise, from top left: The neglected old council gardens, where Grice's greenhouses once stood, with the back of Botcherby Avenue houses to the right; Applewood Close was built on this site; two views of Sinclair Court, directly opposite Applewood Close; map showing the location of St Andrew's Hall (in red) which gave way to the new Sinclair Court development.

Riverside's strategy set out its plan:

> 'High quality service can make a positive impact in an area. Good quality schooling and health services, pleasant parks & open spaces, affordable quality housing, safe streets and employment, training and learning opportunities improve the quality of life and opportunities for local people...

> 'We will ensure that our priorities contribute to the housing needs of those living in Botcherby, now and in the future. We will undertake a statistical review of all our housing assets by archetype and neighbourhood to test for sustainability and aspirational value. This will ensure that our housing stock in Botcherby is sustainable in the future and that we sustain balanced communities. Most importantly we will work together with our residents and stakeholders.'

The local stakeholders were representatives from local community groups, shops, businesses, school, the Fire Service and Citizens Advice Bureau. A consultation exercise threw up both negative and positive points, identifying where improvements could be made. A Revitalisation Open Day was held on 13 August 2009 where information was provided on projects in delivery, projects in development and ideas for the future - however, it was poorly attended and other methods of communication were planned.

Prior to the housing stock transfer in 2002, Carlisle City Council had invested heavily in the physical appearance and infrastructure around Botcherby between 1987 and 1995. Central heating had been installed, windows and doors replaced, new fencing erected, traffic-calming measures and street landscaping work implemented. Now it was time for a further upgrade.

It was all systems go!

Soon the estate was filled with builders' lorries and workmen's vans, as refurbishment went ahead. Roofs were re-tiled with new guttering and external plumbing installed; new coloured rendering was applied to external walls - the advantage being that no painting was required; new door canopies were fitted, together with new canopies on bay windows. There were boundary treatments, new fencing and garden improvements.

Where required, there was new heating, kitchens and bathrooms. Individual comments regarding the scheme included quotes such as *'Looks brilliant,'* *'Spot on'* and *'They look brand new.'*

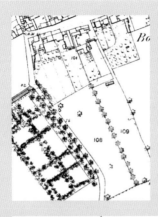

Broadoaks Grange, Broadoaks Court and Oakleigh Way

Above, clockwise from top left: broad oaks were a major feature of Botcherby for over 100 years, as this 1865 map clearly shows; a handful of oaks remained before the new property development got under way - Florida Stores is in the background, to the left; the oak stumps left after the clearance; Broadoaks Grange, leading to Broadoaks Court - the names are the only remaining link to the area's history; burning the felled oaks in front of Croftlands; the entrance to Broadoaks Grange. Below, clockwise from left to right: two more views of Broadoaks Grange; two views of Oakleigh Way, the other part of the development.

St Joseph's Gardens and Willow Park

Above, left to right: the end of Banks Lane before development, looking over to Melbourne Park with the cathedral on the horizon; two views of the relatively recent development, St Joseph's Gardens, which now marks the end of Banks Lane. Below, clockwise from the left: the rooftops of the Willow Park development are just visible as demolition continues around St Joseph's Home; map showing the grounds of Botcherby Home that were used for Willow Park highlighted in green; today's tranquil setting and a view of the development before the burned-out ruins of Botcherby Home were finally demolished.

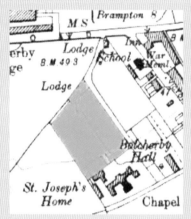

Freshfield Court stands at the bottom of Botcherby Avenue where flats and bungalows provide sheltered housing and the whole site is accessible by wheelchair. Built in 1985, it has been the subject of total refurbishment and development by Riverside and now provides a complex of 38 modernised self-contained properties with a communal lounge.

On a wet summer day in 2013, with bright umbrellas held high, Housing Minister Mark Prisk MP visited Botcherby to meet staff and residents. He presented certificates to Riverside star apprentices before going walkabout on the estate to see the improvements made. He then joined residents at Freshfield Court for coffee. It was 10 years since the transfer of stock and Botcherby was now the most improved neighbourhood in Riverside nationally, where £7.5m had been invested.

Possibly one of the most controversial things that Riverside Housing have done since they took over the Botcherby housing stock from Carlisle City Council in December 2002 was the razing to the ground of 16 one-bedroom flats at the bottom of Borland Avenue in August 2013. They said that this was part of the 'revitalisation plan' for the estate but, with the newly-introduced 'bedroom tax' on everyone's mind, it was not universally popular.

Walkmill Fields and Walkmill Crescent

Above, clockwise from top left: Walkmill Fields has had numerous names in its time - for many this view of it, from Warwick Road, will bring back memories of football matches played on Coop Fields well into twilight; the map from the early 20th century shows it as belonging to Captain Farrar; this view gives a good idea of the extensive area it covered and the last view shows work beginning on the entrance from Warwick Road, in preparation for the housing development. Below, clockwise from the left: map showing the the area historically designated as Walkmill Fields, stretching as far as Botcherby Mill; Walkmill Crescent today; the Premier Inn under construction and the finished hotel.

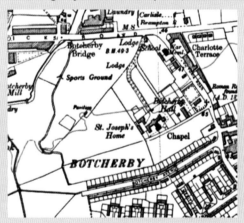

Today the headline-grabbing issue of the Borland Avenue flats is over - in spite of letters in the paper and petitions, with Councillor Robert Betton meeting MP John Stevenson, who raised the issue in Parliament. With Riverside sending a bulletin to all petitioners and councillors explaining how the planning decision was made in the belief that this was the best option for the area, the bulldozers went ahead. The new development

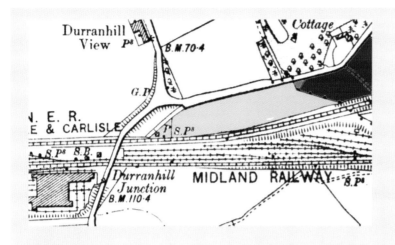

Scotby Gardens and Scotby Close

Left: 1901 map showing the area alongside the railway at Durranhill Junction used to develop Scotby Gardens and Scotby Close (marked in blue) - to the left of the plot is Durranhill Cottage, scene of the infamous murder. Below, clockwise from the left: Scotby Gardens with Eastern Way in the background; the view from Eastern Way; Scotby Close; a further view of Scotby Gardens, Scotby Close; the entrance to Scotby Gardens from Durranhill Road.

was complete in May 2014 and today the 11 units, comprising four three-bedroom houses, five two-bedroom houses and two two-bedroom bungalows and costing over £1m, look inviting.

However, some Botcherby stalwarts are still waiting for housing associations to be included in the Freedom of Information Act, which would enable closer scrutiny of their activities.

Other housing developments

Riverside are not the only developers of new housing at Botcherby. The years have seen many small developments appear on plots of land where other historic features and buildings once stood.

St Joseph's Court, for example, is a development on Victoria Road, on the site of Feddon's Nurseries, while **St Andrew's Close**, **Bramerton Orchard** and the **newer houses in Wood Street** stand on former orchards and farmland.

Pasture Walk and Alexandra Drive

Above, left to right: beginnings and endings - this used to be a cart track leading onto Durranhill Road with a magnificent horse chestnut tree on the left, and the tunnel under the railway at the other end, leading to Harraby - shown on the map in blue. Below, clockwise from the left: three views of the Pasture Walk development, and Alexandra Drive.

Applewood Close is run by Impact Housing, offering a mix of one-bedroom, single-person flats and disabled persons' bungalows - with 23 properties in all, built on the land where Dick Grice's greenhouses once stood on Durranhill Road.

Across the road, Two Castles Housing Association have three small developments: **Sinclair Court**, built on the land of the former Croft Nurseries, provides 19 one-bedroom flats for people over 55, while **Oakleigh Way** has a mixed tenure scheme, with 25 one-bedroom flats and a two-bedroom house. **Broadoaks Court** - where the oak trees once stood in the fields behind Croftlands - offers a mix of 20 flats and houses for general needs. **Willow Park**, off Banks Lane, has 40 bungalows for those over 55.

More recently Russell Armer Homes built 22 three- and four-bedroom homes and six two-bedroom apartments at **St Joseph's Gardens** in the former grounds of the Little Sisters of the Poor's Botcherby Home.

Other private developments are on **Kingfisher Park** (on Walkmill Fields), **Broadoaks Grange**, the site of **the former Army married quarters at Durranhill Camp, Scotby Gardens, Scotby Close, Pasture Walk** and **Alexandra Drive**.

Slightly further afield, on the site of the former Durranhill Convent, is **Waterton Court, Chapel Brow**, a conversion of the old buildings with modern additions. And where the convent residents used to have their vegetable gardens and recreational space, Persimmon Homes have built the **Barley Edge** development.

And just in case you thought there was no land left to develop around Botcherby, remember the old Co-op Dairy site at the top of Holywell Crescent - with outline planning permission for 66 new homes. Botcherby's development is far from over!

238

Durranhill Army Camp, Durranhill House and Chapel Brow

Above, clockwise from the left: map of Durranhill Army Camp, showing the old married quarters, bordering on Durranhill House; the landscaped new developments that were used to extend the old Army estate; two views of the refurbished properties that once housed Army families. Below, clockwise from the left: Durranhill House chapel which was converted into a four-bedroomed house; two views of Waterton Court, Chapel Brow, offering a range of apartments and semi-detached houses; the rest of the old convent was transformed into apartments.

Melbourne Park today

In the chapter on the building of Botcherby estate, the history of the origins of the Path across Melbourne Park was given. Since those early days in the 1930s a great deal has changed, not least the famous Path. Today

Barley Edge

Across the road from the Durranhill Convent/Chapel Brow development, stand 49 properties built by Persimmon Homes. This land was formerly used by the residents of the convent as a recreation area.

there are no wooden boards closing in on either side, but rather informal pathways that meander through what is now the upgraded Melbourne Park. Carlisle City Council proudly describe it on their website:

> 'Melbourne Park lies off Warwick Road, just east of the City Centre, flanking the River Petteril. The 28 hectare Park extends as far south as the merged Newcastle and the Carlisle-Settle Railway Lines at Durranhill.'

Instead of the solitary path from the bottom end of Botcherby Avenue across to Melbourne Road and on to Greystone Road, there are now many access points, as the path encompasses part of Walkmill Fields. On the eastern side is Botcherby with access points off Warwick Road, Walkmill Crescent, Ennerdale Avenue, Borland Avenue and Botcherby Avenue. To the west is St Aidan's, where access points are from Warwick Road, Riverside Way, Nook Street, Raven Street, Melbourne Road and Adelaide Street. The park may also be accessed, with care, along the informal pathways along the river Petteril from the south, off the London Road.

Now too there are facilities: the Petteril Valley Cycle Way runs north-south through the park with adjoining links from Botcherby Avenue and Adelaide Street. Children can be seen enjoying the play areas, one near Borland Avenue and one near Melbourne Road; there are five full-sized football pitches, and two junior football pitches with a changing pavilion, a floodlit multi-use games area/ball court and a BMX Bump Track. There are allotments for the gardeners and a Wildlife Conservation Area.

It's a far cry from the days when school dinners were served in prefabs beside Adelaide Street and local schools played football there. When boys fished for tiddlers in the beck. When the local bobby would warn boys riding bikes on the path, and sometimes they got fined. When summer holidays were spent paddling at the Bay.

The course of the river behind Raven Nook was changed after years of serious flooding and children could no longer play in the bay.

On 1 September 2014, and after more than 40 years, I took a walk along the path through the park, the rose-bay willow herbs were turning, with their white fluff blowing among the hawthorn berries and willow trees swayed in the wind. Only on one part of my walk did I feel a sense of place: at what remains of the beck where boys fished for tiddlers and played inside the large concrete culverts underneath the little bridge. That day there was no water in the beck, now full of wild flowers and grasses, and the steps to the concrete culvert, the scene of many fine games of hide and seek, were broken away.

But life goes on - and so does the campaigning spirit of the people of Botcherby. When the local council re-moved play equipment from Melbourne Park as part of its cost-cutting programme in 2014, a petition organised

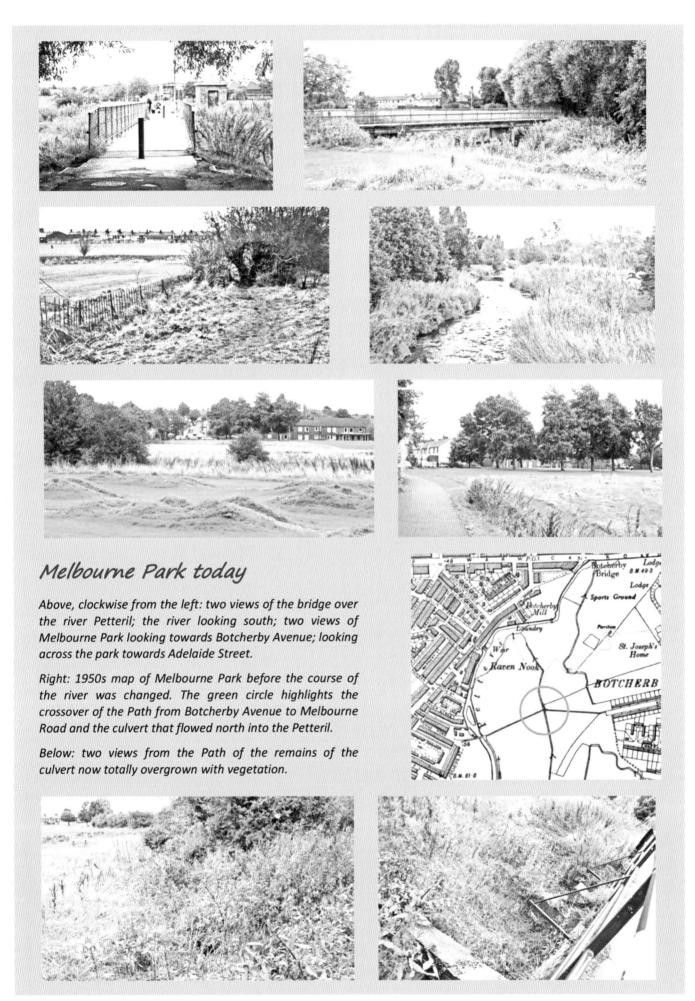

Melbourne Park today

Above, clockwise from the left: two views of the bridge over the river Petteril; the river looking south; two views of Melbourne Park looking towards Botcherby Avenue; looking across the park towards Adelaide Street.

Right: 1950s map of Melbourne Park before the course of the river was changed. The green circle highlights the crossover of the Path from Botcherby Avenue to Melbourne Road and the culvert that flowed north into the Petteril.

Below: two views from the Path of the remains of the culvert now totally overgrown with vegetation.

by Councillor Robert Betton and Jeff Bomford, a resident of Borland Avenue, gained so much support locally that, by July 2015, the council was heralding a £62,000 reinvestment of new equipment in the play area. Result!

The end of the Path

Left: Adelaide Street off to the left of Melbourne Road. Right: Melbourne Road, leading to Greystone Road.

Botcherby in 1996

By 1996, Botcherby had expanded beyond recognition from the housing estate of the 1950s. Gone were the wide open spaces of Three Fields and Broad Oaks, replaced by new housing and Eastern Way (CN - The Cumberland News).

A community that cares

Botcherby Community Centre has long been the hub for social activities in the village. Despite the loss of some of its stalwart supporters in recent years, and recurring damage by flooding, it remains at the heart of the community, ensuring that people always come first...

It is now over a hundred years since the premises at Botcherby Community Centre were opened as an all-ages, mixed school on 9 March 1900. Initially administered by the County Council, the 1912 boundary changes brought the building under the control of Carlisle City Council. When the building officially ceased to be used as a school on 21 January 1927 it was designated by the Education Committee for community use, although during WW2 it was still pressed into use for overflow classrooms. Since then it has had many uses over the years, catering for old and young alike - as well as those in-between.

The Evergreen Club

The women of Botcherby were not to be left out when the men formed a social club at the Magpie Inn, so they asked Carlisle City Council for permission to use one of the rooms in Botcherby School to hold meetings of their new club – the Evergreen Club. In 1946 permission was given by the council for the school to be used by the community for recreational purposes, and so by January 1951 the Evergreens were based there.

Kelvin Martin writing in the *Cumberland News* in 1993 describes the activities:

> *'In the early days such things as dressmaking classes and supper evenings were held and throughout the years the club held regular meetings on a Tuesday night. Members would attend to discuss things that had been happening in the area, and also pass on household tips and recipes – and enjoy exchanging any good gossip!*

> *'The club would run regular fêtes and other fundraising activities providing entertainment and support to the Botcherby community. They would open their centre to anyone in need and after the war they would entertain the wounded troops from the Fusehill Hospital.'*

Other names well-remembered are Carl Hodgson (an uncle of Jackie Stubbs) who was Chairman for many years, and Mrs Jeanie Thompson (née Hitchon and my great-aunt) who ran the choir and put on concerts.

The Evergreen Club celebrated its 43rd anniversary in January 1994 when Mrs Mabel Langhorne was President and still had a strong membership. In later years many of its activities were taken over by the Botcherby Residents' Action Group (BRAG).

When Botcherby rocked!

In 1960 the Youth Club was flourishing and the newly formed, Carlisle band The Ramrods started playing there. The initial line-up was Jimmy Henshaw on lead guitar, Mike Harrison on vocals and rhythm guitar and Alan Marshall on drums. They loved to play Johnny Burnette numbers and a favourite with the girls was *Red Sails in the Sunset*. From these early days until 1964, Jim Lothian was their roadie. Other members joined the group and in 1964 they became the VIPs and appeared on TV in *Thank Your Lucky Stars* with Adam Faith and Sandy Shaw. The group went on to acquire national and international fame – but it all began at Botcherby.

In 1966 the first Youth and Community Officer was appointed by Carlisle City Council and, on 19 June 1968, the premises became known as Botcherby Youth and Community Centre and were administered by the Further Education department until Local Government reorganisation in April 1974. By 1971 a Youth Extension had been built onto the premises and a Senior Administrator was appointed by the City. In 1981 the City Council changed the name to Botcherby Community Centre and by 1995 work started on an extended Youth Wing funded by Estate Action money which opened on 10 April 1996.

The Centre has provided many activities for all age groups over the years including line-dancing classes, parent and toddler group, playgroup, an after-school club, carpet bowls, dog-training classes, pensioners' clubs and a knitting and craft club. It has also run a range of courses throughout the year such as computer and WEA courses. It is truly at the heart of the community.

Something to BRAG about

The word community is everywhere these days. What does it really mean? At Botcherby it has long meant neighbourliness, looking out for other people, providing advice, help, skills, support for parents and fun for children.

With this in mind, in the summer of 2013 I went along to the Community Centre to a meeting of the BRAG and found there a lively group chaired by Elsie Baty and discussing all the relevant topics of the day. The Summer Show was about to happen, organised by the B.FRESH Youth Project and BRAG, where everyone could have a fun evening of singing and dancing and all for 50p.

Councillor Robert Betton was there to lend a hand with the organisation of the annual day trip to Lightwater Valley Theme Park in Yorkshire, where up to three busloads would spend an action-packed day.

The *Botcherby's Got Talent* show would happen later in the year, with a £200 prize going to some lucky child. The children are professionally coached and it has proved a popular event each year, where on average nine children enter for it. Elsie remarked, *'it keeps giving the opportunity to shine – it's not always about success – it's about trying to make it as good as we can – I think it's good.'*

The hub of the community for over a century

From its earliest days Botcherby School has been a centre for community activities, such as the celebrations of the coronations of Edward VII and George V.

The Evergreens and more... in the 40s, 50s and 60s

Above, clockwise from the left: an Evergreens group outside Botcherby School in 1949 - and some of the same group a year later; members of Botcherby Youth Club in the 1950s; the Carnival Queen cuts the cake at the Evergreen's dinner - with Mrs Parr, Mr Parr and Mrs Chadwick on her right and Annie Grice on her left.

Below, clockwise from the left: two photos of Botcherby Youth Club in the early 1950s; 'with all the frills upon it' - (mostly) ladies in their Easter bonnets; a very crumpled photo from the 1950s, including Douglas and Kenneth Porter, Pat and Michael Walsh, Irene Harrington, June Bell, Irene Skinner, Irene John, Mary Maddison and Pauline Wilson; waiting to serve at the pensioners' Christmas party; The Ramrods - on their way to success, they started off at Botcherby Community Centre.

As Elsie said, *'Everybody is working towards a better Botcherby.'*

Sadly since the day of that meeting we have lost Elsie's dynamic presence. Her death on 4 March 2014 left her family and the community stunned and saddened. Yvette Elsie Baty was born in Carlisle on 13 February 1932 and worked at Butlins and a hotel in London before returning to Carlisle to work at the Metal Box in Botcherby for 30 years, where she touched the lives of many. She married John Nathaniel Baty, known as Jacky, in 1956, and it is said that they were complete opposites: he was quiet and contemplative and she was outgoing and outspoken. He was to have the greatest influence on her life and his death in 1990 devastated Elsie.

An avid Labour Party supporter, she had a keen eye for injustice and wouldn't hesitate to help anyone in need. She had a sharp sense of humour but also a softer side. Her attitude to fairness was shown in her involvement

A miscellany of happy times at the community centre

Above clockwise from the left: Christmas 2001 celebrations - Mrs Proud reporting for duty; enjoying the dinner, dance and fancy dress - and the prizes awaiting the lucky winners. Below, clockwise from the left: students at University of Cumbria organised a party for local people at Botcherby Community Centre in 10 hours - tea dancing, bingo and an exhibition of WW2 memorabilia were on the menu; Councillor Michael Boaden presents a framed photograph to Vic Davis, in recognition of his work for Botcherby Community Centre, including more than 30 years as chairman; luncheon volunteers after the January 2005 flood; Community Centre reopens after flood damage repairs, October 2005; B-fresh youth cafe - part of Botcherby's healthy living initiative; Elsie Baty receives her Civic Award from Carlisle City Council for over 50 years' work with Botcherby Community Centre and other local groups, March 2010.

with the Carlisle& District Credit Union, which she said helped to stop people being ripped off. Elsie embraced life and was well travelled, taking trips to Hawaii, America and the Great Wall of China.

She worked selflessly for the Botcherby community for 50 years and this has been commemorated by 'Elsie's Garden' set at the base of the War Memorial in the grounds of the Community Centre. It was opened on 1 August 2014 and this is part of what Councillor Rob Burns said to the assembled guests on that day:

> 'In all my years as a community worker, I rarely met anyone with a passion for the place they live in like Elsie had. She was a unique, one-off character, with many of what, in most people, could have been a host of unlikeable contradictions, but in her, they made a personality full of effervescence, warmth and humanity.

> 'Although we had the (odd) disagreement, she was one of my favourite people and her enthusiasm, commitment, sheer bloody-mindedness, hard work and sense of fun, rubbed off on me and I rarely worked with a group who gave so much of themselves to other people without asking anything more in return than to be treated fairly and with respect than her and the others in that little band of comrades

who fought so hard to get Botcherby Community Centre up and running and then keep it going.

'Elsie was a "big" person in many different ways, but it was her big heart and her big hugs that I will miss the most and I know that if I'll miss them, then so will you.'

A lot to celebrate at the Community Centre!

Above, left to right: top - birthday celebrations; middle - Elsie and friends; Margaret and Marion tuck in; a day at the seaside, Silloth August 2012; bottom - Elsie and friend in party mood; Elsie and the two Marys; dinner at the centre. Below, left to right: Clara Queen and friends; Mary Jones and children; come on the blues!; bottom, left ot right; the Mayoress at the community centre; Elsie Baty with an armful of cans; Riverside's 10th anniversary award winners 2012 include Helen Fisher (fourth from the right) for all her hard work at the Community Centre.

Fun Day 2010

Above, clockwise from the left: head massage from a friend; are they from Botcherrby?; getting ready for the rush; the rush begins; jobs for the girls - and boys; balloons 50p plus confidential advice!
Below, clockwise from the left: more balloons for 50p plus face painting the Elsie and Marys' way; serving at the fun day; ready for anything, keeping things safe; the long and the short of it; I really can dance; three satisfied customers.

Vic Davies, her old friend and another Botcherby stalwart, died on the same day and Rob continued:

> *'I'd love to have been a fly on the wall at the Pearly Gates when those two were trying to persuade God to let them in!!... You remember that in the Bible, Jesus said, "In my Father's house, in heaven, there are many mansions." Well my guess is that Elsie will already have organised a survey of them to make sure that they all had decent double glazing and central heating and she'll have established a new Paradise Tenants and Residents' Group!'*

Elsie's view on life was that people should be loved – and that is her greatest achievement.

Mary Bridget Jones was another of the ladies who are the backbone of the Community Centre and one of Elsie's best friends. She too had given 50 years of service to the community. I had not seen her for very many years but, when I met her at the Community Centre, she welcomed me with open arms. On another lovely evening Theo and Joan Grice hosted a supper at their home on Eden Park where Elsie, Mary, Kathleen Dixon, Gil and I reminisced about 'the good old days'. Mary very kindly asked her nephew David Geddis if she could lend me the scrapbooks of his footballing days, which she did. Sadly, Mary died at the age of 82 on 30 April 2015. She was well known as one of the McCabe family who, along with her sister Margaret and brother Terry, lived in Borland Avenue, and she is remembered with joy and affection by the people of Botcherby.

A dream comes true, then suffers a setback

The Centre has never rested on its laurels - and in 2015 the long-awaited dream of having a gym was at last realised. The £135,000 project financed by Riverside Housing Association, Cumbria Waste Management, Cumbria County Council and Botcherby Community Association opened on 21 September.

On 10 September, Centre manager Helen Fisher explained to Roger Lytollis of the *News & Star*:

> *'It was put on hold when we had the recession... it's state of the art Techno-gym equipment, there's free weights and cardio equipment, including treadmills, rowing machines and cycling machines. The gym is accessible to everybody... we'll be employing a part-time instructor.'*

There is also a community cafe at the centre and free wi-fi.

Multiple Sclerosis is a debilitating neurological disease for which, at present, there is no cure and which affects people in many different ways. The MS Society's East Cumbria branch holds weekly meetings at the Community Centre and here members can socialise over a coffee and a chat as well as sharing experiences on new treatments. Debbie Berg is a neurological physiotherapist, working with patients who have conditions affecting their nerves. She says: *'I try to maintain fitness and independence, so people can function at their best.'* The sessions are split into two sections, the second half for wheelchair users, who concentrate on upper body strength. *'It's just a great social group,'* says Debbie. *'They offer each other a lot of support... I feel privileged to be able to help people make the best of life.'*

Making the best of life – a fine goal for any community centre – and at Botcherby they have it well and truly taped.

Except that no one is proof against natural disasters and the effects of Storm Desmond in December 2015 left the Community Centre swamped by three feet of floodwater. At the time of writing, it is hoped that it will re-open in early 2017.

Manager Helen Fisher talking to Roger Lytollis of the *News & Star* for the 10 March 2016 feature 'What's the Crack in Botcherby', explained that she and her colleagues are working from Petteril Bank Community Centre who kindly helped out with the accommodation. Many of the regular hobbies groups are also meeting there. Others are meeting at community centres and halls in Harraby, Currock, Denton Holme and Upperby - showing a true community spirit.

Helen said: *'We're hoping to be back towards the end of the summer. It's unsettling for everyone being outside Botcherby. But I can't stress enough how much we appreciate the Petteril Bank Community Centre putting a roof over our heads.'*

The new gym had only been open 11 weeks before the floods. Helen said, *'It already had 60 members. We just need to get everybody back.'*

Still reaching out to everyone

But life goes on and, by March 2016, the BRAG group's chairwoman Liz Jenkinson was being interviewed by Roger Lytollis for the *News & Star's* feature on 11 March, 'What's the Crack in Botcherby'. Well, the crack was that the BRAG group is still going strong but is looking for new blood. Liz said:

> *'We're trying to come up with new ideas. There are seven of us on the Committee. The youngest is about 40. Most are in their 60s and 70s. There's only us geriatrics! We're sort of stagnating. When we have an event we say to people "would you like to come and join us?" But people don't come forward... I understand... people have got work and families.'*

Nevertheless, these ladies are not deterred by hard times: although the December 2015 floods caused havoc. With the children's Christmas party having to be cancelled, they immediately began planning an Easter party for children up to 11 years old at Greystone Community Centre and making good use of the £200 donated by Riverside, with an Easter egg for every child.

The BRAG group reaches out to all members of the community and is considering whether information on events should be printed in Polish also, to assist Polish families in the area. St Cuthbert's School has benefitted from a gift of musical instruments and computers have been given to the Community Centre.

The last few years have been hard for the Community Centre but - as always - it is looking to the future, while building on the spirit of the past.

On the edge, but at the heart of the community

A Hundred Years of Service

Oh proud and noble building
You have served our community so well
If only you could speak
Your memories to tell

Botcherby was just a hamlet
As our local history will show
When they started building you
One hundred years ago

Your presence taken for granted
As we pass by on the bus
A century of sterling service
So thanks from all of us

Happy children in your playground
Local girls crowned carnival queen
Fancy dress side-shows and dances
So many happy times you have seen

A meeting place for pensioners
With memories evergreen
And two world wars have taken place
Since you came on the scene

Many functions sport and youth clubs
You have provided for us all
And when you have been needed
Have always answered the call

You have known many willing helpers
Their important part to play
Sadly some no longer with us
And those who still help you today

Now in the new millennium
And new challenges unfold
Long may you stand in Botcherby
For you are worth your weight in gold

Jack Stubbs, 2000

Above left - two views of the Community Centre; right - the late Elsie Baty, Mary McCabe and the late Mary Jones - stalwarts of the Community Centre for many years.

In memory of Elsie Baty

Elsie

Now she walks and talks with angels
No longer with friends down here,
A truly lovely lady
To her Botcherby was very dear.

Sadly on the streets of Botcherby,
She will not be seen again,
But Mrs Elsie Baty will live forever,
In the Botcherby memory lane.

Jack Stubbs

Acknowledgements

Many people have helped me in writing this book. I have been given wonderful memories, photographs and memorabilia and a great deal of kindness and support from all of them. In particular I must thank Jackie Stubbs for his great generosity in lending me the volumes of Botcherby history and photographs that he has compiled over the years, they have been a valuable resource. I must also thank him for his great patience with my never-ending questions!

I am also greatly indebted to:

John Barker and members of the Botcherby Forever Community Group: George Cornish, Sally Forster, Ron Maddison, Derek Nash, Alex Proudfoot, James Robinson, Kenny Simpson and Jackie Stubbs. The Group have given me wonderful support throughout the project, in doing research and finding contacts and photos. I could not have done it without you, my friends.

Helen Fisher, Marion Allinson and the staff at Botcherby Community Centre always made me welcome and I was introduced to members of the BRAG group and the Bingo afternoon players by the kindness of the late Elsie Baty.

The late Mary Jones for her enthusiastic support and the loan of her scrapbooks on the career of her nephew David Geddis.

David Geddis for permission to use items in the scrapbooks.

Mr Chris Wilkins, Michael Merrick, Mrs Pauline Moss and colleagues including Cath Cape and Dave Wilkinson at St Cuthbert's Catholic Community School, who gave me access to their archives, and Martin Daley, the former Chair of Governors, who gave his support.

Reverend Steve Donald of St Andrew's Church, who always made me welcome with information on the Church's history and developments.

Mandy Wright of Croftlands Trust, who gave me a tour of the house and gardens and provided a useful insight into the valuable work being done there.

Annamarie Desmond and her colleagues Deborah Earl and Tracy Edmondson at Riverside Housing Association, who gave me the detailed story of taking over the housing stock on the estate.

Denis Perriam, local historian, who generously gave me access to his personal resource files on Botcherby history, including Jim Atkinson's research into his Hamilton ancestors.

Ashley Kendall, local historian, for his generous help with photographs.

June M. Dunn, who gave me a copy of her fascinating Memoir of her mother *Lady Isobel*, recalling life in Botcherby in the 1930s.

Barbara Millican, who kept in touch from Australia, sending vivid memories about life in Botcherby and Durranhill Railway Cottage.

Sister Rosemary Clerkin, SHJM, who came up from Chigwell Convent to talk to the group about the history of Durranhill Convent and gave me historical documents and photographs.

Lynda Campbell, HR Manager, CROWN Bevcan, Botcherby.

Alison Sisson, Cumberland Newspapers.

Many other people welcomed me into their homes, met with me, or gave me written, telephone or email interviews. Many also looked out old photographs or gave me other contacts. Among these are:

Roger Atkinson, Colin Bardgett, Mrs Jacqueline Barton, Andy Beeforth of Cumbria Community Foundation, Dr Helen and the late Eric Bell, Felicity Blamires, Bill and Vida Boak, Brenda Burgess, John Burgess, Councillor Rob Burns, David Carter, Eileen Casey, Mrs Nellie Conley, Mark Conley, Brenda Cottam, Norman Crickett, Brian Davidson, Ann Ditchburn, Brian Dixon, Mrs Kathleen Dixon, Father John Dobson, Viv Dodd, Terry Doyle, Father Gerard Dunn, Mrs Mabel Duncan, Pat Farish, Reg Feddon, Eileen Ferguson, Mrs Joyce Fullerton, Mrs Margaret Goodland, Alison Graham, Theo and Joan Grice, Rachel Gwynne, John Hamilton, Mike Hamilton, Audrey Harker, Pete Hoban, John Hortop, Jacqueline

Huene in Canada, John Hughes, Mrs Jenny Hunter, Canon Jim Hyslop of Upperby Parish Church, Lesley Irving, Jonny Irving and Roger Lytollis - *News & Star*, Alison Jamieson, Chris Jardine, Mrs Mary McCabe, Councillor Niall McNulty, Mike Mapleton, Paul Marshall, Mrs Catherine Marshall, Glynis Milburn, Bill Mitchell, Kathleen and Alan Morland, Denise and Geoff Moses, John Myers, Rachel H. Nash, Tess Nash, Mr and Mrs James Ord, Albert Pollard, Susan Rigg, Miss Nancy Robinson, Arthur Sanderson, former Chairman of Cavaghan & Gray, Sam Shane, Greg Smith, the late Carmen Grice Smith, Stan Sullivan, Malcolm Sunderland, Connie Taylor, Irene Taylor, Ian and Rose Thompson, George N. Tweddle, Mrs Shirley Warren, Mike Wood.

I also wish to thank:

Stephen White and his colleagues at The Lanes Library, Carlisle.

Louise Smith and staff of Carlisle Archive Service.

Sarah Coombs, Highways Dept.

Chief Executive, Defra, Penrith.

Andy Brown, Environment Agency.

Post Office Users Consultative Committee.

Jim Henderson of the British Legion.

David Ramshaw of P3 Publications for his continuing help and support in publishing my book.

Gil Hitchon, my brother has been my editor and has done amazing work on the photographs and layout as well as providing sound editorial support reflecting his journalistic skills.

My sister-in-law Liz Hitchon has been a constant support, and contributed to the 'ghosties' section by making the pottery 'spooks'!

In particular, I would like to thank Hunter Davies and the Cumbria Community Foundation for awarding me a Bursary of £1000 towards production costs.

In addition I have received generous sponsorship from CROWN Bevcan, Botcherby and the Botcherby Forever Community Group, which is much appreciated.

◆◆◆

Photo credits

Many individuals and organisations contributed illustrations to this book. I particularly want to thank the following for permission to reproduce their images:

Eric Apperley - Cumbria County History Trust, Roger Atkinson, Jacqueline Barton, Felicity Blamires, Bill Boak, Botcherby Community Centre, Andy Brown, Carlisle Archive Centre, Carlisle Library, David Carter, Eileen Casey, Alan Cleaver - Creative Commons, Sr Rosemary Clerkin -SHJM, Commonwealth War Graves Commission, Mrs Nellie Conley, Peter Connon, George Cornish, Norman Crickett, Cumberland Newspapers, Ann Ditchburn, Brian Dixon, Mabel Duncan, Fr Gerard Dunn, English Heritage (RAF Photography), David Geddis, Mrs Margaret Goodland, Alison Graham, Theo Grice, John and Mike Hamilton, Audrey Harker, Gil Hitchon, Pete Hoban, Jacqueline Huene, John Hughes, Alison Jamieson, Chris Jardine, the late Mary Jones, Ashley Kendall, Mrs Bob Lowther, Ron Maddison, Glynis Milburn, Barbara Millican, Alan Morland, Denise and Geoff Moses, Derek Nash, Natural Environment Research Council (NERC) - British Geological Survey, Martin and Jean Norgate (Geography Department, University of Portsmouth), James and Jean Ord, Our Lady & St Joseph's Church, Denis Perriam, Alex Proudfoot, David Ramshaw, Susan Rigg, Riverside Housing Association, James Robinson, David Rogers - Creative Commons, St Cuthbert's Catholic Community School, Sam Shane, Greg Smith, Findlay Henderson Stirling, Jackie Stubbs, Tullie House Museum and Art Gallery Trust, Mike Wood.

Sources consulted

Apart from sources quoted directly in the text, I have also drawn on the following reference works for this book:

In the mists of time...

Kate Hirst, 'Scotby Road, Durranhill, Carlisle,' *PAST, The Newsletter of the Prehistoric Society*, No. 29, July 1998.

Richard Barkle, 'Botcherby Nurseries, Carlisle,' *PAST, The Newsletter of the Prehistoric Society*, No. 29, July 1998.

William Hutchinson, *The History and Antiquities of the City of Carlisle and its Vicinity,* Carlisle: F. Jollie, 1796.

Henry Summerson, *Medieval Carlisle*, Vols 1 and 2, Kendal: CWAAS, 1993.

Henry Summerson, *Edward 1st at Carlisle: King and Parliament in 1307*, Kendal: CWAAS, 2011.

John Bargh, *The King Edward 1 Monument – a History and Description,* Carlisle: P3 Publications, 2015.

Mike McCarthy, *Roman Carlisle and the Lands of the Solway,* Stroud: Tempus Publishing, 2002.

Isaac Tullie, *A Narrative of the Siege of Carlisle in 1644 and 1645,* Whitehaven: Michael Moon, 1988.

Mike McCarthy, *(Calendar State Papers, Domestic 16-14-5,552) WalkMill Fields and Botcherby,* 1996.

John Waugh and George Gill Mounsey, *Carlisle in 1745: Authentic Account of the Occupation of Carlisle in 1745 by Prince Charles Edward Stuart,* London: Longman, 1846.

The developing village

Denis Perriam, 'Was Wood Street named after William, an early entrepreneur of cotton spinning in Carlisle?' *Cumberland News*, 14 April 2006.

Derek Nash, *A Brief History of Bramerton Lodge*, Carlisle: private publication, June 2014.©

Irvine Hunt, *The Drover's Boy,* Sedbergh: Handstand Press, 2008.

Bob Lowther, *Watching Over Carlisle, 140 Years of City Police Force, 1827 – 1967*, Carlisle: P3 Publications, 2010.

H. R. Hallaway, *Margery Jackson 1722-1812, Life & Times of the Carlisle Miser,* Carlisle: Halstead Printers, 1991.

Gerald Findler, *Ghosts of the Lake Counties,* Clapham, N. Yorks: Dalesman Books, 1977.

Early industry and transport links

Warwick Bridge & District Local History Group, *The Toll Road 1828-1876: Turnpike from Carlisle to Brampton by way of Warwick Bridge,* local booklet.

Colin Smith, *A Guide to the Milestones, Mileposts and Toll Buildings of Cumbria,* Penrith: Brow Bottom Enterprises, 2011.

George S. Hearse, *Tramways of the City of Carlisle,* Corbridge: Hearse, 1962.

Denis Perriam, *Carlisle: an illustrated history,* Carlisle: Bookcase et al, 1992.

Peter Connon, *In the Shadow of the Eagle's Wing, A History of Aviation in the Cumbria, Dumfries and Galloway Region, 1825-1914.* Penrith: St Patrick's Press, December 1982.

Peter Connon, *Aeronautical History of the Cumbria, Dumfries and Galloway Region, Part 2: 1915-1930,* Penrith: St Patrick's Press, October 1984.

Peter W. Robinson, *Rail Centres: Carlisle No. 6,* Nottingham: Booklaw Publications, 2004.

Denis Perriam and David Ramshaw, *Carlisle Citadel Station-150 Years a Railway Centre,* Carlisle: P3 Publications, 1998.

The Great War hits hard

David Carter, *Carlisle in the Great War,* Barnsley: Pen & Sword Military, 2014.

Linda Hodgson & Sarah Lee, *The Stars of Night,* Carlisle: P3 Publications, 2014.

Colin Bardgett, *Better By Far a Cumberland Hussar: A History of the Westmorland and Cumberland Yeomanry 1819-1967,* Kirkby Stephen: Hayloft Publishing Ltd, 2001.

Douglas Sutherland, *The Yellow Earl, Almost an Emperor, not quite a Gentleman. The Life of Hugh Lowther, 5th Earl of Lonsdale,* Ludlow: Merlin Unwin Books Ltd, 2015.

The garden village

Jim Atkinson, 'The Hamilton's – A Roman Catholic Recusant family of Great Corby,' *Cumbria Family History*

Society Newsletter, May 2000.

Jim Atkinson, additional correspondence on Hamilton family research with Denis Perriam. 2001.

Thomas Arthur, *The Life of Billy Purvis (1784-1853),* Newcastle-on-Tyne: T Arthur, 1875. (Facsimile edition : pub. Newcastle-on-Tyne: Frank Graham, 1981.)

Sarah Jane Downing, *The English Pleasure Garden 1660 - 1860,* Oxford: Shire Publications Ltd, 2009.

Denis Perriam, 'The Dancing master who died from twirling his toes,' *Cumberland News*, 29 July 2005.

Joseph Hamilton, *A Treatise on the Hamiltonian System of Cultivating the Pine Apple,* London, 1844.

Fran Beauman, *The Pineapple-King of Fruits,* London: Chatto & Windus, 2005.

Jennifer Davies, *The Victorian Flower Garden,* London: BBC Books, 1991.

The Grice Family Register.

Joan Dunmore & Peter Ostle, 'A detailed history of Greenrow Academy,' Holme St Cuthbert's History Group, www.solwayplain.co.uk/greenrow/htm.

Lease of a Market Garden situate at Botcherby, S. G. Saul Esq. to Mr William Grice, 24 April 1900.

Lease of Dwellinghouse and Market Gardens situate at Botcherby near Carlisle, Mr Wannop to Mr William Grice, 1 February 1909.

Agreement for the letting of premises situate at Botcherby in the said City. The Mayor, Aldermen and Citizens of the City of Carlisle to Richard Grice, 8 March 1930.

George Stephenson, 'The Nurseryman's Tale,' *Cumbria Gardens Trust Occasional Papers*, Vol. 2, 2004.

Building the estate, growing a community

June M Dunn, *Lady Isobel - her life,* an unpublished memoir, 1999.©

Terence Ted Beckett, *The Cannibal mouse*, Carlisle: Terence Beckett, 2011.

Donald Scott and Alan Air, *Over the Garden Wall - Donald Scott's Carlisle Memories,* Carlisle: Alan Air, 1999.

Please Miss!

Consultation: a Proposal to federate St Margaret Mary Catholic Primary School and St Cuthbert's Catholic Community School, Governing Bodies of both schools, 14 March 2016.

A faithful community

Kevin A. Rafferty, *Portrait of a Parish (1798-1993) - to mark the Centenary of Our Lady & St Joseph's, Carlisle, 1893-1993*, Carlisle: Kevin A. Rafferty, May 1993.

Rosemary Clerkin, SHJM, *A Heart for Others,* Chigwell: Sisters of the Sacred Hearts of Jesus and Mary, 1983.

Sisters of the Sacred Hearts of Jesus and Mary, Chigwell: *Archives on Durranhill Convent,* unpublished.

Caroline Shepherd, *Little Sister of the Poor,* London: Incorporated Catholic Truth Society, 1984.

Richard Watson, *Upperby Parish History,* Carlisle: ca 1977.

The village inns

Olive Seabury, *The Carlisle State Management Scheme,* Carlisle: Bookcase, 2007.

John Hunt, *A City Under the Influence-the story of half a century of state pubs,* Carlisle: Lakescene Publications, 1971.

Steven Davidson, *Carlisle Breweries and Public Houses, 1894-1916,* Carlisle: P3 Publications, 2004.

Shops, street traders and industry

Kevin A. Rafferty, *The Story of Hudson, Scott and Sons: Metal Box, James Street, Carlisle,* Carlisle: Charles Thurnam and Sons Ltd, 1998.

Bob Tuck, *Robson's: The History of the Famous Name in Distribution,* Nynehead, Wellington, Somerset: Roundoak Publishing, 1990.

The Second World War

David Hay, *Carlisle at War - 1939-1945,* David Hay, 1989.

Ron Freethy, *Cumbria at War - 1939-1945,* Newbury: Countryside Books, 2009.

Sophie Jackson, *Churchill's Unexpected Guests, Prisoners of War in Britain in World War 11,* Stroud: The History Press, 2010.

Amber Minninges, 'Dancing to the Beat of Time: interview with Kathy Coupal,' Victoria, BC: *Lookout-Feature*, 12 December 2005.

Wing Commander Robert Oldaker, *Support in the Sky: In Caelo Sustineo, A History of No. 14 Maintenance Unit, Royal Air Force Carlisle*, 1996.

Floods and flood defences

David Ramshaw, *Carlisle Floods (January 8th 2005): a Photographic Record*, Carlisle: P3 Publications, 2005.
David Ramshaw, *The Carlisle Floods 2015 with recollections from 2005*, Carlisle: P3 Publications, 2005.
Sarah Watkins and Ian Whyte, *Floods in North West England: a history c. 1600 - 2008*, Lancaster: Centre for North-West Regional Studies, Lancaster University, 2009.
Floods special supplement, News & Star, 7 December 2015.
Carlisle Flood Investigation - draft report, Environment Agency and Cumbria County Council, May 2016.

Let's bring back the Carnival

Jackie Stubbs, *Botcherby: A Social History,* unpublished archive.©

The beautiful game

Kevin Beattie with Neal Manning, *The Beat*, Whitham, Essex: Skript Design & Publishing, 1998.
Rob Finch, *The Greatest Footballer England Never Had; The Kevin Beattie Story,* Beverley, North Humberside: Cult Figure Publishing, 2007.
Stephen Cameron, *Death in the North Channel – the Loss of the Princess Victoria, January 1953,* Newtownards, Co. Down: Colourpoint Books, 2002.
Keith A. Wild, *Carlisle United Fifty Seasons On - a factual and statistical history of Carlisle United AFC 1928 - 1984*, Cockermouth: K. A. Wild, 1984.
Paul Harrison, *Carlisle United: the Complete Record*, Derby: Breedon Books, 2008.
Simon Hughes, *The Secret Diary of a Liverpool Scout*, Liverpool: Trinity Mirror Sport Media, 2009.
Gordon L. Routledge, *McIlmoyle: the Legend of Brunton Park,* Longtown: Arthuret Publishers, 2004.

Whatever happened to Tom Clark's field?

All sources are quoted in the text.

A community that cares

All sources are quoted in the text.

Other resources consulted

In addition to the sources given above for specific chapters, I have used the following as general references:

June M Dunn, *Lady Isobel - her life,* an unpublished memoir, 1999.©
Jackie Stubbs, *Botcherby: A Social History,* unpublished archive.©
Mannix & Whellan, *History, Gazeteer and Directory of Cumberland, 1847,* Beckermet, Cumbria: Michael Moon, 1974.
Kelly's, *Post Office Directory of Westmoreland & Cumberland 1858,* Kendal: Titus Wilson & Son, reprinted 2009.
Morris, Harrison & Co., *Directory & Gazetteer of Cumberland 1861,* Whitehaven: re-published Michael Moon, 2000.
Minute Books, Carlisle City Council.
Carlisle Archive Centre.
Cumberland Newspapers archives.
Denis Perriam, files on Botcherby history.
Commonwealth War Graves Commission.
www.findmypast.co.uk.
Author's private collection.

You may also enjoy:

Sam Bough RSA-The Rivers in Bohemia. By Gil and Pat Hitchon.
The story of Carlisle's famous Victorian landscape and marine artist.

Chanel and the Tweedmaker: Weavers of Dreams. By Patricia M. Hitchon.
The 100-year history of Linton Tweeds in Carlisle.

Botcherby Heroes Remembered - 1914-1918. By James Robinson, Alex Proudfoot, Derek Nash.
The story of the 15 men commemorated on the Botcherby War Memorial.

Available from P3 Publications. http://www.p3publications.com